Everything in Common?

Everything in Common?

The Theology and Practice of the Sharing of Possessions in Community in the New Testament

FIONA J. R. GREGSON

Foreword by Steve Walton

◆PICKWICK *Publications* • Eugene, Oregon

EVERYTHING IN COMMON?
The Theology and Practice of the Sharing of Possessions in Community in the New Testament

Copyright © 2017 Fiona J. R. Gregson. All rights reserved. Except for brief quotations in critical publications or reviews, no part of this book may be reproduced in any manner without prior written permission from the publisher. Write: Permissions, Wipf and Stock Publishers, 199 W. 8th Ave., Suite 3, Eugene, OR 97401.

Pickwick Publications
An Imprint of Wipf and Stock Publishers
199 W. 8th Ave., Suite 3
Eugene, OR 97401

www.wipfandstock.com

PAPERBACK ISBN: 978-1-4982-8997-9
HARDCOVER ISBN: 978-1-4982-8999-3
EBOOK ISBN: 978-1-4982-8998-6

Cataloguing-in-Publication data:

Names: Gregson, Fiona J. R. | Walton, Steve (foreword)

Title: Everything in common? : the theology and practice of the sharing of possessions in community in the New Testament / Fiona J. R. Gregson; foreword by Steve Walton.

Description: Eugene, OR: Pickwick Publications, 2017 | **Includes bibliographical references and index.**

Identifiers: ISBN 978-1-4982-8997-9 (paperback) | ISBN 978-1-4982-8999-3 (hardcover) | ISBN 978-1-4982-8998-6 (ebook)

Subjects: LCSH: Wealth—Biblical teaching. | Sharing—Biblical teaching. | Bible. New Testament—Criticism, interpretation, etc.

Classification: BS2545.W37 G7 2017 (paperback) | BS2545.W37 (ebook)

Manufactured in the U.S.A.   11/06/17

Greek Bible text from: Novum Testamentum Graece, 27th revised edition, Edited by Barbara Aland and others, © 2001 Deutsche Bibelgesellschaft, Stuttgart.

The Scripture quotations from The New Revised Standard Version of the Bible, Anglicized Edition, copyright 1989, 1995 by the Division of Christian Education of the National Council of the Churches of Christ in the United States of America, and are used by permission. All rights reserved.

For those who have shared their lives with me
and taught me more of what it means to share my life with others.

Contents

Foreword by Steve Walton | ix
Preface | xi
Acknowledgments | xiii
Abbreviations | xv

1 Introduction | 1
2 The Common Purse: John's Gospel | 7
3 Holding in Common: Acts 2–6 | 42
4 Responding to Famine: Acts 11 | 79
5 Eating Together: 1 Corinthians 11 | 97
6 Giving and Generosity: 2 Corinthians 8 and 9 | 141
7 Limits on Sharing: 1 and 2 Thessalonians | 193
8 Sharing Possessions in Community in the NT: Christian Distinctives | 232

Bibliography | 243
Modern Authors Index | 259
Subject Index | 265
Ancient Documents Index | 269

Foreword

Dr. Fiona Gregson is a remarkable person and this is a remarkable book. It is at the same time thoughtful, provocative, and inspiring. In it, Dr. Gregson builds on two recent recoveries in New Testament Studies: the recovery of the significance of community as a key feature of early Christianity, and the recovery of practice as a vital feature of the lives of the early believers. These provide a firm foundation for her exploration of the nature of the networks both within and between the earliest Christian communities. "Within" because one key expression of community life was the local assembly of believers meeting in a particular place week by week for mutual encouragement, enrichment and, Dr. Gregson argues, material support. "Between" because the mutual care and support extended to believing communities in one place helping those in another place, including across the highly significant ethnic divisions of the ancient world.

Thus Dr. Gregson offers a fascinating, carefully researched study of the relationship of Christian practice in sharing material resources in these ways, and the thinking and theology which undergirded Christian sharing, in conversation with contemporary practice and thought in the Jewish and Greco-Roman worlds. She reads widely across the New Testament documents, including the shared purse of Jesus and his disciples (John), the sharing of possessions in Jerusalem among the earliest believers (the early chapters of Acts), the church-to-church response by the Antioch church to famine in Jerusalem (Acts 11), the shared meals in Corinth (1 Cor 11), gifts to the church in Jerusalem as part of Paul's collection (2 Cor 8–9), and the limits placed on sharing goods in Thessalonica (1 and 2 Thess). Along the way we learn much of the practice of sharing material goods among the rabbis and their disciples, in Essene and Pythagorean communities, through Jewish almsgiving practices, in Greco-Roman meal settings, in Roman and

Jewish responses to famine, among ancient associations, and in patron-client relationships.

The book you hold, then, covers great breadth—and it does so with great depth. Dr. Gregson's knowledge of the primary sources is excellent, and she has the happy knack of recognizing possible parallels and carefully assessing both similarities and differences. Out of this detailed work a clear picture emerges of early Christian distinctives in sharing possessions, a picture which places self-giving love, modelled on the cross, at the heart of this sharing, and which goes well beyond individual almsgiving because of the fact and the nature of the community formed by the cross.

The value of this book does not stop in the ancient world, although it offers much to support fresh thought and new appraisals of early Christian community life and material sharing. The book offers stimulation to Christians today to think and act in a cruciform way in poverty alleviation both within and without the Christian fellowship. It will inform those who bring international aid under a Christian banner to developing countries. It will provoke reflection on poverty and its elimination within individual developed countries, where phenomena such as food banks in the UK are all too common. It will enable careful and collegial thought and action among Christians engaged in helping refugees fleeing conflict or persecution in their homelands, and arriving in the West in great need.

This is, in sum, quite a book. We are in debt for the care and research which Dr. Gregson has put into it, having been provoked to this work through living in a number of countries in Africa and serving in parish ministry in materially deprived contexts in the UK.

Steve Walton
Professor in New Testament, St Mary's University,
Twickenham (London), UK

Preface

DURING MY LIFE I have lived and worked in four African countries and in the UK have worked predominantly in inner city parishes in areas of multiple deprivation. These experiences motivate my concern for Christian engagement with poverty and possessions and have raised questions about how we live as Christians in an increasingly globalized world, how we hold what we have in light of the relationship we have with other believers across the world, and the disparities in wealth and opportunity that are evident. This book is a reworking of my PhD thesis research, which grew out of questions I had about how Christians approach the sharing of possessions together. It examines a small number of these questions and focuses on the theology and practice of the sharing of possessions, including food, in community in the New Testament.

A significant proportion of the New Testament addresses questions around money, possessions, and sharing, and provides a range of examples of ways of sharing possessions. This book looks at six diverse examples of sharing possessions in the New Testament, from the Gospels, Acts, and the Pauline literature. It considers each example in its social context and then compares it to other examples of sharing in the surrounding cultures to find similarities and differences between the example and surrounding practice and thought. It then identifies across the comparisons ways in which Christians shared possessions that were consistently similar to or different from surrounding practice.

The book highlights a number of common characteristics across the New Testament examples of how Christians shared possessions. In the New Testament examples, sharing is practical and responsive; is based on communal identity; includes people from different backgrounds and various ways of contributing; is voluntary and yet includes assumptions; is both individual and communal; often responds to need; and includes eating together.

This book also identifies ways that Christians were consistently distinctive from the surrounding culture in how they shared possessions, including: subverting patronage expectations; having greater social diversity; having more flexibility in ways to participate; having a greater emphasis on the voluntary nature of contributing; each person being involved in giving; eating together more frequently; and having stronger intra-community relational bonds.

Acknowledgments

THIS BOOK IS AN adaptation of my PhD and as with any such endeavor there are a large number of people and organizations who have made it possible and to whom I would like to give thanks. First and foremost, I would like to thank Professor Steve Walton, who, from the start of our initial conversations about the possibility of researching under him, through the years of supervision, and since completion of the PhD, has provided encouragement, advice and enthusiasm, and has shared his wisdom, considerable experience, and practical advice.

I am grateful to the Women's Continuing Educational Trust, the Diocese of Birmingham and the Diocese of Bradford, who have all provided support towards the cost of undertaking my PhD research.

I would also like to give thanks for the support and prayers of the parishes (Aston and Nechells, Birmingham; St Philip Girlington, Bradford) that I have worked in, who have given me time to pursue my research alongside my parish commitments. My clergy colleagues in both places have provided cover. Colleagues, parishioners, and individuals within the Dioceses of Birmingham and Bradford have encouraged me and showed interest in the research.

I am grateful for the resources I have found, and fellowship I have experienced, at the various libraries across the UK who have provided resources and assistance at different stages of the project: Tyndale House Library, Cambridge; Leeds University Library; Birmingham University Library; Queens College, Birmingham; University Library, Cambridge; and the Bodleian Library, Oxford. I am also thankful for researchers from around the world who have been willing to share their studies and wisdom with me.

Adrian and Jill Chatfield have on numerous occasions shared their home with me, welcoming me with hospitality, which has enabled me to spend time at Tyndale House, Cambridge and to spend time out of the parish for a few days at a time to concentrate on the research. I am grateful for their encouragement and support. Particular thanks go to David Fletcher, Mike Gregson, Gill McIllwaine, and Joyce Robertson for proofreading various chapters along the way, and to Chris Robertson for providing IT advice. My family and friends have provided ongoing encouragement, support and prayers. Matthew, my husband, has continually encouraged me and enabled me to bring the research to publication. For all of these people and many more I give thanks to God and I pray that this research may be for his glory, and the edification of his body, the church.

Abbreviations

ABBREVIATIONS FOLLOW THE *SBL Handbook of Style* (1999) with the addition of the following abbreviations:

Aristides *Or.*	Publius Aelius Aristides, *Orations*
Comm.	Ambrosiaster, *Commentary on Paul's Epistles*
Comm. 2 Cor.	Theodoret of Cyrrhus, *Commentary on the Second Epistle to the Corinthians*
Diod. Sic.	Diodorus of Sicily
DNTB	*Dictionary of New Testament Background*, edited by Craig A. Evans and Stanley E. Porter, Leicester: IVP, 2000.
Ep.	Martial, *Epigrams.*
His.	Polybius, *The Histories.*
Hom. 10	Chrysostom, *A Sermon on Almsgiving*
IGRP	*Inscriptiones Graecae ad res Romanas Pertinentes*
LEP	Diogenes Laertius, *Lives of Eminent Philosophers*
Or. Hist.	Orosius, Paulus, *Seven Books of History against the Pagans: the Apology of Paulus Orosius.*
P. Lond.	*Greek Papyri in the British Museum.* VII, *The Zenon Archive*, ed. T. C. Skeat. 1974. Nos. 1930—2193.
P. Oxy.	*The Oxyrhychus Papyri*, London: Egypt Exploration Fund, 1898.
ps Diogenes *Ep.*	"The Epistles of Diogenes" from A. Malherbe, *The Cynic Epistles: a Study Edition.* Missoula: Scholars, 1977.

ps Soc *Ep.*	"The Epistles of Socrates and the Socratics" from A. Malherbe, *The Cynic Epistles: a Study Edition.* Missoula: Scholars, 1977.
TRENT	Traditions of the Rabbis from the Era of the New Testament
VP	Iamblichus *On the Pythagorean Life*

1

Introduction

POSSESSIONS, MONEY, RESOURCES, AND justice are themes that occur in the New Testament. Jim Wallis points out the centrality of wealth and poverty within scripture and notes that "some have even suggested [it] is the second most common topic found there, the first being idolatry."[1] He notes that one out of every sixteen verses in the NT; one out of every ten verses in the Synoptic gospels; and one out of every five verses in James addresses the theme.[2]

Use of and attitudes towards possessions and wealth are also important contemporary topics, particularly within a globalizing and changing world. Authors such as Witherington and Harries note critical contemporary questions around wealth and possessions. Witherington raises questions based on his study of passages about money and wealth about how institutions, nations, and individuals think about and use money in the context of the 2008 financial crisis.[3] In *Is there a Gospel for the Rich?* Harries argues that it is particularly pertinent to ask questions about how to live as a Christian in a capitalist society because of the end of communism, the rise of the Christian right, and the growth of an evangelical social ethic.[4]

---

1. Wallis, *Call*, 57.
2. Ibid., 58.
3. Witherington, *Money*, 116–21.
4. Harries, *Gospel*, 6–7.

Possessions, poverty, and riches in the NT have been addressed through the lens of contemporary questions;[5] through ethical studies;[6] as part of wider historical or topical studies;[7] and in NT studies.[8] Across these varied ways of approaching NT texts, questions have been asked on different levels: how should individual look and use their possessions; how should Christians approach economics and social welfare; and how should Christians relate to one another with their possessions and how they are held? It is this third question on which there has been less focus and on which this study concentrates. Within this area this study looks specifically at the theology and practice of the sharing of possessions in community in the NT.[9]

This study addresses a number of questions about the sharing of possessions in community in the NT. First, are there recognizable common themes in how Christians in the NT share possessions in community?

One of the challenges of asking questions about NT approaches to sharing possessions is the diversity of the witness within the New Testament, both in terms of different contexts, and in terms of the different things that particular texts espouse, which can sometimes seem to be mutually incompatible. Indeed Hengel and Johnson, alongside others conclude that there is no one doctrine or paradigm in the NT for sharing of possessions,[10] while Hoppe identifies communality across the diversity.[11] Johnson responds to the diversity by arguing that one approach to sharing possessions—almsgiving—is more practical and less prone to abuse.[12] This study considers a range of examples of sharing in community across NT genres in order to identify common themes across the diverse examples.

For each of the texts, the background to the theology and practice evidenced in the text is explored and possible causes or influences on the

---

5. See Sider, *Rich Christians*; Wallis, *Call*; Miranda, *Communism*; Schneider, *Materialism*; Anderson, *Kindness*.

6. See Burridge, *Imitating Jesus*; Hays, *Vision*; Meeks, *World*.

7. See Gonzalez, *Faith*; Grant, *Christianity*; Hengel, *Property*; Hoppe, *Poor*; Panikulam, *Koinōnia*; Saxby, *Pilgrims*.

8. See Blomberg, *Poverty*; Wheeler, *Wealth*; Witherington, *Money*; Bassler, *God and Mammon*; Johnson, *Sharing*.

9. For greater detail of how studies have analyzed NT approaches to wealth, poverty, and possession see Gregson, "Everything in Common?" 2–13.

10. Hengel, *Property*, 84; Johnson, *Sharing*, 9. Hays and Wheeler argue for the need to consider a range of texts to gain a NT perspective (Hays, *Vision*, 7; Wheeler, *Wealth*, 33).

11. Hoppe, *Poor*, 171–72.

12. Johnson, *Sharing*, 117–39.

INTRODUCTION

particular theology and practice expressed within the text are highlighted using exegetical and social-scientific approaches.

Second, is the Christian theology and practice of sharing possessions in the NT texts different from that seen in the surrounding cultures? The theology and practice evidenced and portrayed in each text is examined alongside examples within the surrounding culture of similar practice, to establish in what ways the practice and theology of the early church was similar to and different from its surroundings.

Third, was Christian theology and practice in the NT consistently distinctive from the surrounding culture? The comparisons are then compared with each other, which enables this study to show that there are common characteristics of how Christians shared across the NT examples. It also shows that there are ways in which Christian practice and theology within the NT is consistently different from its surrounding contexts, thus indicating a commonality in distinctives from the surrounding cultures.

In order to address the diversity of the NT, we consider a number of texts that show examples of sharing of possessions. The texts are chosen from across the Gospels, Acts, and Pauline Epistles in order to provide a range of examples of different kinds of sharing. The examples chosen allow us to consider a range of possibilities in terms of what is shared; the distance over which sharing happens; the geographical locations that sharing happens in; and the practice. We consider examples that show sharing within a community and those that show sharing between communities, however we do not consider the sharing shown in support for leaders within a community or from another community, thus we have not considered 1 Cor 9. We have limited ourselves to the Gospels, Acts, and the generally undisputed Pauline Epistles due to the space available in the book.[13] We have not examined the Gospel teaching on sharing, as it tends to be more general teaching rather than referring to a specific example of sharing in community.

In chapter 2 we consider the example within John's gospel of the common purse, an example of sharing between a relatively small number of itinerant people, with the money possibly coming from those outside the group. We reference the other gospels where they throw light on the practice of the historical Jesus and his disciples. In chapters 3 and 4 we look at two examples from Acts: in chapter 3, the selling, sharing, and holding in

---

13. Therefore, while 1 Tim 5 and Jas 2 provide possible examples of sharing within a community we do not consider them within this study: 1 Tim 5 because its authorship is disputed and Jas 2 because it is outside the group of texts being considered. In addition, James provides less evidence of the community/communities receiving the letter than the Corinthian and Thessalonian letters do and thus possible comparators would not be able to be identified with the same degree of confidence.

common of possessions within a community (Acts 2–6) and in chapter 4, the sharing of possessions with believers in a community in one location to those in another location (Acts 11). Chapters 5 to 7 consider three examples from the Pauline literature. Chapter 5 examines the sharing of food in one particular community (1 Cor 11). Chapter 6 explores the sharing of money with others who are at a distance geographically and culturally (2 Cor 8 and 9). Chapter 7 looks at the example of the ἄτακτοι in 1 and 2 Thessalonians and the limits or boundaries to sharing within a community which are expressed within the two letters.

Thus, our examples include texts from different authors and genres within the NT, which portray sharing of different types occurring within different contexts.

For each text, we ask a number of questions. We examine the background and context of the example and ask what kind of example of sharing is shown and whether it is positive or negative. For some texts there are different layers of examples. For example in John's gospel, there is the example that John presents to us and there is the example of what the historical Jesus and his disciples did. In such cases we identify and distinguish which layer we are working with.

We ask what motivates the sharing and whether there are particular theological reasons for the sharing. We look at whether need is the overarching motivational factor or whether there are other influences. The existing literature includes little about the way the corporate identity of believers impacted on the question of the sharing of possessions, therefore we ask how individual or corporate identity motivated the sharing and what the sharing says about identity.[14]

Various scholars identify the issue of sin and the "not yet" of Christian community and how it impacted approaches to possessions.[15] We therefore bear in mind the question of sin and the "not yet" as we examine each NT example.

As we consider examples of sharing between believers, we ask whether these examples indicate sharing with non-believers as well as with other believers.

Having examined the examples in the NT text in relation to the genre of the text and historical and literary background, we identify comparators for each NT example, which show similar situations and practice, and which are likely to be known by or familiar to the community in the NT example

---

14. Gregson, "Everything in Common?" 2–13.
15. Harries, *Gospel*; Lillie, *Studies*; Oddie, "Socialism."

(or where others use them as comparators at the time).¹⁶ The comparators are non-Christian in order to investigate the ways in which the early church's practice was similar to and different from surrounding practice and to identify distinctive elements of how Christians shared possessions.¹⁷

We compare the NT examples to the comparators and identify similarities and differences. For example in Acts 11, the church in Antioch responds to a situation of predicted famine in Judaea and we compare its response with examples of how famine was responded to in the Greco-Roman world.

Having examined the examples in each of the NT texts we compare them with one another and identify common characteristics. We consider whether there are reasons within their contexts for these similarities and differences. We then compare how they are similar to and distinct from the examples in the surrounding culture and whether there are any commonalities in distinctives or similarities from the surrounding culture.

Chapter 8 draws out the common characteristics across the NT examples as well as similarities and differences in how the early church shared possessions compared with the surrounding contexts.

This study provides an overview of the breadth of examples of the sharing of possessions in the NT and an analysis of the practice and theology shown by the examples. It identifies common characteristics across different kinds of sharing in the NT. While other studies draw comparisons between NT examples and the surrounding culture,¹⁸ this book provides a systematic study across different NT examples and their comparators. It is therefore able to identify consistent distinctives in how Christians shared possessions in relation to their surrounding cultures.

It provides a basis for exploring sharing possessions in contemporary Christian ethical studies, by providing an overview of the practice and theology of the NT with particular reference to Jesus and his disciples, the earliest Christians, and Paul. It also provides an analysis of how early Christian practice and theology related to the surrounding culture and whether it was

---

16. Thus, the Therapeutae are not used as a comparator in chapter 3 as they were a Diaspora community where the primary evidence is for their presence in Alexandria and the early church in Jerusalem is unlikely to have been familiar with them. In contrast we have included the Pythagoreans in chapter 3 because Josephus compares them to the Essenes (*Ant.* 15.371), although we conclude that it is not very likely that most of the early believers would have known of the Pythagoreans.

17. Thus, the Didache is not used as a comparator as it provides evidence of Christian practice. Further rationale for individual comparators is provided within each chapter (see pp. 21, 32–33, 35–37, 71–77, 93–96, 138–40, 181–91, 223–30).

18. For example: Capper, "Palestinanian Setting"; Winter, "Acts"; Ascough, "Community as Association."

influenced by it. The methodology used is a helpful contribution to ways of considering areas of divergence and difference in the NT.

2

The Common Purse
John's Gospel

THE PRACTICE AND THEOLOGY OF JESUS AND HIS DISCIPLES

THERE ARE A NUMBER of references in the gospels to Jesus and his disciples having a shared purse (12:6; 13:29)[1] and receiving money (Luke 8:3) from others towards their needs. This chapter considers the two references in the NT to the γλωσσόκομον (common purse), both in John. This example shows sharing between a small group of people for their own use and for the needs of the poor, which the early church may have looked back on. This chapter examines how these passages describe the practice of the common purse. It then considers other passages in the gospels that may hint at a common purse or collective approach to money/possessions, for example the hospitality of Martha, Mary, and Lazarus in Luke 10 and John 12, and the support of the women in Luke 8. Having considered the practice of Jesus and his disciples in the gospels and particularly in relation to the γλωσσόκομον, it considers possible parallels to the practice of Jesus and his disciples: rabbis and their disciples, the Essenes/Qumran, and Cynics.

---

1. Verse references in this chapter are to John's gospel unless otherwise stated.

This chapter examines both the historical practice of Jesus and his disciples, and also how John's early readers might have interpreted John's presentation of their practice. It demonstrates that while there are similarities between the practice of Jesus and his disciples and the surrounding cultures, particularly the Essenes/Qumran, there are differences from the surrounding cultures in the boundaries to the group and in the variety of ways of contributing.

Common Purse Passages

The word γλωσσόκομον, often translated "common purse," was originally the word for a container for carrying mouthpieces for flutes[2] and developed into a word for a case or a container before the first century CE.[3] Moulton and Milligan note that its origin suggests "small size and portability,"[4] although it is also used for larger containers (2 Chron 24:8,10 LXX; Josephus *Ant.* 6.11). However, in the occurrences in John, it does appear to refer to a portable container. It may be that γλωσσόκομον is used to allow for the fact that gifts were placed in the γλωσσόκομον, which might suggest a slightly larger or a different container than the usual purse.[5]

John 12:4–8

The first reference to the common purse is in John 12, where Mary has anointed Jesus at Bethany. Judas then questions her actions and suggests that the nard could have been sold and the proceeds given to poor. However, his motivation was not concern for the poor, but rather that κλέπτης ἦν καὶ τὸ γλωσσόκομον ἔχων τὰ βαλλόμενα ἐβάσταζεν (12:6). Beasley-Murray points out that "ἐβάσταζεν = 'used to take (away)'" and was used "to mean take away (surreptitiously) money."[6] The use of κλέπτης and the imperfect of βάσταζω suggest an ongoing situation of stealing rather than an innocent or one off removal of the money. Judas's comment about the poor suggests that there were instances where items were donated to the group of disciples and

---

2. MM, 128.
3. BDAG, xl, 202.
4. MM, 128.
5. In Luke's gospel the word βαλλάντιον is used to mean purse in Luke 10:4; 12:33; 22:35–36.
6. Beasley-Murray, *John*, 205.

then sold, with the money then being added to the common purse, and that money in the common purse could be used to give to the poor.

In response to Judas's comments, Jesus does not identify Judas as misusing the money, but does say that Mary is preparing him for the day of his burial and notes that the disciples will always have the poor with them, but will not always have him. Brown suggests that, in contemporary rabbinic thought, provision for burial was equated with mercy, which was valued more highly than almsgiving.[7] When *b. Sukkah* 49b reflects on Mic 6:8 it gives three reasons that kindness is better than charity or almsgiving, one of which is that kindness can be done to both the dead and the living, while charity can only be done to the living. However, as Calvin argues, while Jesus' reply is a reproof to Judas's hypocrisy, "we may learn from it the valuable lesson that alms for relieving the needs of the poor are sacrifices and of a sweet savour to God."[8] This would fit with the fact that Jesus speaks about the disciples always having the poor with them, but not always having the dead to prepare for burial.

John 13:28–29

The second occurrence of γλωσσόκομον is during the farewell discourse. It follows the prediction of betrayal and the question by the disciple Jesus loved about the identity of the betrayer. After giving Judas a piece of bread dipped in the dish, Jesus instructs him, Ὃ ποιεῖς ποίησον τάχιον (13:27). The disciples presume that because Judas has the common purse, he is being sent on an errand to buy something: either to provide for the feast or to give something to the poor.

While there is uncertainty about which day of the feast this refers to and therefore what kind of work was permissible,[9] it is certainly in the vicinity of Passover. Jeremias argues that it was usual for the poor to be supplied with food for Passover,[10] however, his sources do not necessarily support his point (*m. Pesaḥ.* 9.11 concerns Passover offerings that have been confused, *b. Giṭ.* 7b is about giving alms) and one that does (*m. Pesaḥ.* 10.1) may well be later.[11] Tobit does provide an example of giving to the poor at festivals (Tobit 1:6–8). Carson suggests that the fact it is night and that the disciples

---

7. Brown, *John*, 1:449. Jeremias, "Salbungsgeschichte," 77.
8. Calvin, *John*, 28.
9. Barrett, *John*, 448.
10. Jeremias, *Eucharistic*, 54.
11. Instone-Brewer, *Feasts*, 173–75.

assume that Judas is going to give to the poor, may point to it being Passover—otherwise "the next day would have done just as well."[12]

In contrast Calvin argues that this expectation indicates customary giving to the poor: "For the apostles would not have guessed that He was speaking about the poor unless it had been their custom to help the poor."[13] While the potential giving here seems to be in the context of Passover, Judas's comments about giving to the poor (12:5) and the fact that giving to the poor in Judaism was not limited to Passover (Josephus *Ant.* 15.299–316, 20.51–53; *m. Shek.* 5.6; *b. Giṭ.* 7b) supports Calvin's conclusion that it was the disciples' custom to give to the poor on other occasions.

There are contrasting views of the symbolism of the morsel of bread that Jesus gives to Judas. Keener highlights the two options: first that the bread is a sign of favor or secondly that the dipping is that related to the bitter herbs of the Passover meal and therefore implies a curse.[14] However, as it appears that the other disciples do not hear Jesus' words about giving the bread, or at least do not understand what he is saying about it (13:28–29), it is not possible to learn from their response which of the two options may be taking place.

The bread may have been given to Judas at the point in the Passover celebration where bitter herbs were shared. As each person would have shared some of the bitter herbs, it may have been less obvious that Jesus was singling Judas out. As each person would have partaken of the bitter herbs,[15] if Jesus handed the bread to Judas at this point, it would not necessarily follow that he was implying a curse and indeed could imply a sign of favor.[16]

Other John Passages

Apart from the two passages which refer to the γλωσσόκομον there are two other passages which may indicate some sort of common holding of money by Jesus and his disciples. In John 4:8 the disciples go to the city to buy food. This may be indicative of a common purse which the disciples used to supply their needs and Edwards comments that the provision of food for their

---

12. Carson, *John*, 475.
13. Ibid., 67.
14. Keener, *John*, 920.
15. *m. Pesaḥ.* 2.6 notes the herbs that can be eaten to fulfil the duty to eat bitter herbs, thus presuming that it was an obligation for each person to eat bitter herbs.
16. Brown, *John*, 2:578. Brown cites Ruth 2:14, where Boaz gives Ruth a morsel of bread to dip in the sour wine and honors her by inviting her to join with his workers in eating.

rabbi was typical behavior of rabbinic disciples.[17] While the text does not specify where the money came from or how it was held, it does indicate a communal purchasing of food, which would necessitate some arrangement for paying for it.

Prior to the feeding of the five thousand, there is a conversation between Jesus and Philip about the provision of food for the crowd (6:5). The implication in Jesus' question is that it will be a communal buying of the bread and this may suggest that there is some collective responsibility for money and purchasing, but as with the reference in John 4, this is not spelled out.

Summary of the Common Purse in John

What do these references indicate about the kind of practice that John portrays and the practice of Jesus and his disciples?

The γλωσσόκομον does not play a major role in the story or theology of John and it seems unlikely that John would have added this detail. Barrett does suggest the link with Judas may have been added by John to discredit Judas.[18] However, John presents Jesus as one who knows and therefore knows what Judas is up to with the γλωσσόκομον[19] and there are probably simpler ways for John to make additions that would discredit Judas, without creating the embarrassment of Jesus choosing an unfit treasurer. Keener therefore concludes, "By the criterion of embarrassment, it is likely that Judas's role as treasurer stems from genuine historical tradition; appointing someone who misadministrated funds could be scandalous, all the more if the one who made the appointment were now claimed to be omniscient."[20]

In addition, we have noted a couple of passages within John which, while they do not mention a common purse, would fit with the practice of a common purse. We will look at passages in the Synoptics which fit with the practice of having a common purse and provide possible further insight into the practice of Jesus and his disciples.

Therefore, since the γλωσσόκομον is not central to John's story and there seems no reason for it to be added in; since Judas's connection to the common purse does not fit with John's portrayal of Jesus and would be an embarrassment to the early church; and since there are other passages

---

17. Edwards, *Discovering*, 98. Edwards provides no evidence to support this assertion.
18. Barrett, *John*, 413.
19. See pp. 13–14.
20. Keener, *John*, 2:865.

which fit the practice, it seems likely that John's portrayal of the common purse and its association with Judas is historical.[21]

As we consider the different Johannine passages about the γλωσσόκομον, what can we conclude about the detail of the practice that John portrays? In general, scholars seem to have more conclusions than the evidence in John seems to sustain.

Various authors hazard a guess as to where the money in the common purse came from. Chrysostom (*Hom. Jo.* 72) and Capper see the money coming from supportive women.[22] Augustine (*Trac. Ev. Jo.* 40) sees the support as more generally from the "faithful,"[23] while Carson points to the money coming from "disciples who cherished Jesus' ministry, like the women mentioned in Luke 8:2,3."[24]

The reference in Luke 8 does suggest that there were women who contributed to the common purse. While the women are not mentioned specifically in John's gospel as contributing to the common purse, it is interesting to note that Mary's gift of nard (12:3) is a gift from a woman and a gift of considerable value. Additionally, Judas's expectation that it could have been sold and the money placed in the common purse would suggest that the money in the common purse included money from significant gifts from individuals, even if it was not limited to such money. However, there seems no reason to assume that rich women were the sole providers of finance, particularly if the boy in John 6 is an example to be emulated (6:9). For the example of the boy suggests that even those who are not particularly wealthy could and possibly should give to benefit the group and those whom the group was supporting.

Similarly, there are various suggestions about how the money in the common purse was used. Augustine sees the common purse being used to distribute "both to the needs of his people and to others in need" (*Tract. Ev. Jo.* 62.5). As we have noted earlier, Calvin also saw the money as being used to provide for the poor.[25] This might fit with a wider provision beyond the core disciples, which John 6 may suggest. The reference in John 13:29 to the assumption by the disciples that Judas might be buying something for the feast or giving something to the poor suggests that the common purse was used at the very least for buying items for shared events such as festivals and was used to contribute to those in need. The use of the money to contribute

---

21. Brown, *John*, 1:453.
22. Capper, "Holy Community," 113.
23. Sanders, *Historical*, 108.
24. Carson, *John*, 429.
25. See pp. 9–10.

to those in need is supported by the reference in John 12:5 to the possibility of selling the nard to give to the poor, and the contribution to the needs of the disciples seems to be supported by the references in John 4:8 and 6:5.

Howard-Brook looks at Jesus' words in John 12 and argues that in saying τοὺς πτωχοὺς γάρ πάντοτε ἔχετε μεθ᾽ ἑαυτῶν (12:8), Jesus espouses a view that "the poor . . . are to be an integral and permanent part of the discipleship community."[26] Howard-Brook contrasts Jesus' words about the poor being "with" them to the synagogue practice of collecting and then giving money or food and argues that Jesus is advocating a different approach to the poor, where they are part of the community. However, beyond the use of "with," Howard-Brook does not provide supporting evidence.

The Proximity of the Common Purse to Judas

So what does this description of the common purse suggest by way of an example to John's readers? In order to answer this question it is important to consider whether the connection of the γλωσσόκομον to Judas indicates that this is a negative example or whether, in spite of Judas's connection to it, it is a positive example.

On both occasions that the γλωσσόκομον is mentioned, Judas is mentioned as the keeper of the common purse, as the betrayer of Jesus, and, in John 12, as stealing from the common purse.

If we look more widely at how Judas is presented in John, we find that he is described as a "devil" (6:70–71), as being influenced by the devil (13:2), as someone into whom Satan enters (13:27), and as the one who guides the soldiers to the garden so that they can find Jesus (18:3–5).

In John, Jesus is portrayed as being the one who knows people (1:47–48; 2:24) and thus it would seem that within John's presentation, Jesus knows both that Judas is misusing his position, and is the one who will betray him. Lincoln therefore argues that the detail of Judas keeping the common purse is ahistorical and suggests that Judas would not have been "left in charge of the money-box if it was known that he was in fact stealing from it."[27] However, given John's portrayal of Jesus knowing people, it seems unlikely that John would have included Judas's role unless it had some historical base. Interestingly, as Haenchen notes "the tradition is not perturbed that Jesus appointed the least suitable man, a thief, to guard the cash box."[28]

---

26. Howard-Brook, *Becoming*, 272.
27. Lincoln, *John*, 338–39.
28. Haenchen, *John*, 1:84.

We might then ask the question why "the tradition is not perturbed"; why does Jesus allow Judas to continue keeping the common purse; and why does he offer Judas the piece of bread in a way that may appear to honor him.[29] Ambrose suggests it is so that Judas is not forced into betraying Jesus "because he was unhonored or in want" (*Off.* 1.16.64). This would suggest that part of what we see with Judas is a situation where grace is extended to someone who is known to be abusing their position within a group. When Augustine comments on this situation, he argues that by having "one ruined man among the twelve" Jesus was teaching that "we should tolerate the evil" and not divide Christ's body" (*Tract. Ev. Jo.* 50).

It is interesting to note that Judas is not the only disciple to fail Jesus. Peter also betrays Jesus (18:7, 25, 27). Jesus predicts his betrayal (13:38) and yet similarly continues to trust Peter as a disciple (21:15–22). With both Peter and Judas, Jesus knows about their faults and yet continues to trust and extend grace to them. This would suggest that while the common purse is always mentioned alongside Judas, this does not argue for a negative connotation to John's portrayal of the common purse. Rather, John's portrayal gives an example of continuing with communal holding and use of money for the followers of Jesus and for those in need, even when there is misuse of the system and ambiguities within it.

The argument that John is not negative about the common purse is supported by his wider presentation of his disciples and their responsibilities and identity as a group. When Jesus teaches about his disciples and followers, he uses corporate images—the vine (John 15) and the flock (John 10)—and corporate language (14:20; 16:32; 17:21). He gives responsibilities to his mother and the beloved disciple to look after one another. While there is an emphasis on individuals believing, for example, when people believe they have eternal life (3:15–16; John 20:31), which is relationship with God (17:3), eternal life is also spoken of in a more corporate and communal context, for example in the farewell discourse, which includes both the language about corporate identity and Jesus' prayer for his followers' unity (17:20–26).

Conclusions

John's portrayal of the γλωσσόκομον is not specific in its description of where the money comes from or how it was used. However, John does suggest that money in the γλωσσόκομον included money from the sale of gifts given to the group and that money in the γλωσσόκομον was used, at the very least, for

---

29. Lincoln, *John*, 379.

some common needs of the group and to give to the poor. Judas, who did not discharge his position honorably, kept the γλωσσόκομον. John portrays Jesus as being aware of this and yet allowing it to continue. John's wider portrayal of Jesus' followers suggests mutual responsibility and communal identity, which lends support to the communal holding and use of money being positive. However, John does not give a clear prescription for how this should be done, only that in whatever way sharing between followers of Jesus and provision for the poor occurs, it is likely to include those who are taking advantage of the system and misusing it, and that this is no reason not to do it.

Other Indications of the Practice of Jesus and his Disciples

There are a few other passages in the gospels, which add to the picture provided by the references to the γλωσσόκομον in John's gospel and may help us interpret the practice of Jesus and his disciples. These passages cohere with the evidence of the common purse in John's gospel and there is some evidence of their historicity. While space precludes the examination of the historicity of each text in detail, brief comments about historical evidence for the texts will be provided. After considering these passages, we look at possible parallels in the surrounding cultures.

The Call of the Disciples

In each of the Synoptic gospels, the calling of the disciples involves those who are called leaving things to follow Jesus (Matt 4:18–22; Mark 1:17–20; Luke 5:11, 28). This calling and leaving is generally seen as historical.[30] It is supported by multiple attestation and to an extent by double similarity as there were disciples in the Jewish context, and the presence of disciples who spent time with Jesus helps explain the growth of the early church.

This leaving and following is something that the disciples look back to: for example, Peter refers to leaving homes (Luke 18:28) or everything (Mark 10:28). In John's gospel, the leaving is less explicit and there is a greater emphasis on coming and seeing (1:39, 46; 4:29). However, the following is still there and there are situations where there is an implicit leaving. For example, two of John's disciples leave him and follow Jesus (1:37).

The idea of leaving and following is also found in Jesus' teaching. For example, when a young man comes and questions Jesus, Jesus instructs him

---

30. Hengel, *Leader*, 73–80; Sanders, *Historical*, 118–22.

to sell his possessions, give to the poor and then follow him (Mark 10:21). The parallel in Luke 18:22 has the same response to the ruler asking the question. The idea of selling and giving possessions is also part of the general teaching Jesus provides for the disciples, for example in Luke 12:33: Πωλήσατε τὰ ὑπάρχοντα ὑμῶν καὶ δότε ἐλεημοσύνην. The idea of leaving, particularly houses, is also present: Αἱ ἀλώπεκες φωλεοὺς ἔχουσιν καὶ τὰ πετεινὰ τοῦ οὐρανοῦ κατασκηνώσεις, ὁ δὲ υἱὸς τοῦ ἀνθρώπου οὐκ ἔχει ποῦ τὴν κεφαλὴν κλίνῃ (Matt 8:20).

The gospels also show Jesus and his disciples traveling together: over longer distances, for example through Samaria (John 4), and more locally, for example, across the lake (Luke 8:22–26).

The picture provided by both the Synoptics and John shows some of Jesus' disciples leaving behind homes, relatives, and ways of life to follow him. It is a picture that is supported by Jesus' response to individuals who ask him questions, his general teaching, and Jesus and his disciples traveling together. This leaving would have created a situation where the disciples were no longer connected to their usual support networks, and thus may have been the main impetus for some kind of common purse to provide for their needs. The picture in the Synoptics suggests that the disciples who traveled with Jesus left behind their property and possessions and therefore may well not have contributed to the γλωσσόκομον.

Non-itinerant Associates

As well as those disciples who are called by Jesus and follow him, we find a number of examples within the gospels of individuals who support Jesus and his disciples, provide hospitality to him, and in many ways take on board his teaching, but do not seem to travel around with him. Meier points out that these people do not feature in the twelve or the crowds or the wider group of disciples who follow Jesus, but are committed and supportive.[31] With some of the non-itinerant associates there are elements of embarrassment as Jesus and his disciples are recorded as associating with lepers and tax collectors.

In both John and Luke, we find Martha, Mary, and Lazarus. In Luke 10:38–42 Martha welcomes Jesus into their home and provides hospitality and Mary sits at his feet and listens to what he is saying. In John 11, they send a message to Jesus to let him know about Lazarus' illness: both have conversations with Jesus in the midst of their grief, and John notes Jesus'

---

31. Meier, *Jew*, 3:21. Sanders sees them as a wider group of sympathizers (Sanders, *Historical*, 125–26).

love for them (11:5). In John 12, Jesus visits and eats with them at their home in Bethany and Mary anoints him with nard, showing her devotion.

In Luke 19:1–10, Zacchaeus meets Jesus, hosts him, and decides both to give to the poor and pay back those he has defrauded. Again there is no reason to presume that Zacchaeus subsequently joins the group traveling with Jesus, but he does both host Jesus and give away money. In Matt 26:6, Simon the leper hosts Jesus.

Each of these people is presented as committed to Jesus, even devoted to him, supportive of him and the traveling group, but not traveling with them. Thus, while we do have a picture of a group of disciples who are called, leave [everything], and follow Jesus, we also have those with disciple-like qualities, who are not part of this group traveling with their common purse.

Capper suggests that two versions of discipleship exist in the gospels (and then continue in the early church)—an inner group who followed an ideal pattern of sharing goods in common and those who followed and gave generously, but did not fully share in the community of goods.[32] However, he does not fully examine the way some disciples leave property behind and then seemingly return to it, which we will consider later.

Luke 8 and the Women

One of the groups of people who fall somewhere between the group who leave possessions and travel with Jesus and the non-following associates, is the women listed in Luke 8. Jesus is described as traveling through cities and villages accompanied by the Twelve as well as by some women. The presence of the women "is firmly fixed in the tradition."[33] Thus, Sanders sees their presence as historically probable.[34]

Mary Magdalene, Joanna, Susanna, and others, are shown as traveling with Jesus, but still having access to their own resources.[35] Thus, they do not fit into the group who give up and leave things to follow Jesus. However, while they provide from their resources, they are presented, together with the Twelve, as traveling with Jesus.[36] This is the main passage in the gospels that points to a possible source of the money in the common purse. The sharing that is presented is one-way—the women provide the resources

---

32. Capper, "Types," 108.
33. Marshall, *Luke*, 315.
34. Sanders, *Historical*, 109.
35. Hengel notes although they are part of the group, the women do not have an obligation to leave their possessions (Hengel, *Leader*, 74).
36. Marshall, *Luke*, 317; Bauckham, *Gospel Women*, 112.

(Chrysostom *Hom. Jo.* 72)—and participative—the women are shown as traveling with the group for whom they are providing. The Twelve are not shown as contributing to this provision, which may well fit with the accounts of them leaving everything in order to follow.

The Sending Out of the Twelve and the Seventy-two

The other place in the gospels where a source of provision is shown is in the sending out of the Twelve and the subsequent sending out of the seventy-two.[37] While noting questions about the historicity of the actions of the disciples once sent out, Hengel argues that the sending out is historically probable.[38] The Synoptic accounts all presume the disciples will be provided for by those whom they visit. In Matt 10, Jesus sends out the Twelve, instructing them to take no money or bag, ἄξιος γὰρ ὁ ἐργάτης τῆς τροφῆς αὐτοῦ (Matt 10:10). In Mark, Jesus specifies that they should not take any bread (Mark 6:8). In Luke's account, Jesus precludes carrying both bread and bag (Luke 9:3). Similarly in Luke 10, when the seventy-two are sent out, Jesus specifies no purse or bag (Luke 10:4) and also indicates ἄξιος γὰρ ὁ ἐργάτης τοῦ μισθοῦ αὐτοῦ (Luke 10:7). In these examples, those who provide are those who are preached to, who welcome the disciples, and who are people of peace (Luke 10:5-8). However, the expectation seems to be the provision of food, drink, and accommodation, not the provision of money. In Matthew, there is a specific reference to giving without payment (Matt 10:8), and in Luke 10, reference to being provided with food and eating where they stay (Luke 10:7-8).[39]

Those who give and provide support in this instance are shown as being people of peace, but not necessarily those who know, follow or support Jesus. They are thus different from both the non-following associates and the women in Luke 8, who have an existing commitment to Jesus before they provide for him and his followers. However, the picture of the sending out of the Twelve and the seventy-two continues the picture of the following

---

37. Textual variation indicates either seventy or seventy-two with evidence evenly divided, however Kurt Aland notes that the widespread concept of seventy argues for seventy-two being normalized to seventy (Metzger and Aland in Metzger, *Commentary*, 126-27). As the decision between the two makes no difference to the argument, we shall refer to seventy-two.

38. Hengel, *Leader*, 73-80.

39. This practice of receiving food, but not money is one that continues in the Didache, where limits are placed on the length of time a prophet or apostle can stay, "And when an Apostle goes forth let him accept nothing but bread till he reach his night's lodging; but if he ask for money, he is a false prophet" (11:6).

disciples as those who have left things to follow Jesus, though presumably they must have still had some of the items Jesus instructs them to leave behind.

The Disciple Jesus Loved and Mary, and the Disciples after the Crucifixion

It is often at the point of testing or change, that the nature of relationships between people is seen. The crucifixion and resurrection narratives provide further evidence of the relationships between Jesus and his followers. Both have elements of embarrassment in them, for example Peter's betrayal and restitution (Matt 26:69–75; Luke 22:54–62; John 21:15–23). While the crucifixion itself is seen as historical, discerning the historicity of the elements of the texts we shall examine below is harder. However, they do cohere with the overall picture from John and the other passages we have considered. Even if not historical, they point to the importance of the relationships between the early followers and the perception that it was appropriate for these followers to share in various ways.

Jesus shows care for his mother and the disciple whom he loved and asks them to behave as family to one another (19:26–27). The disciple Jesus loved takes Jesus' mother into his home (19:27). In contrast to the early call stories in the Synoptics, he has a home, to which he can take her.

In Matt 28 and John 21, groups of disciples are still gathering together and traveling together. In Matt 28:16, after the crucifixion and the resurrection appearances, the eleven disciples travel together to Galilee. This suggests some level of continuity in terms of relationship and provision of support, although it may be that they used up the money that was in the common purse during this period.

John 21 provides a slightly different picture as we find a number of the disciples by the Sea of Tiberias fishing together. They may have had any number of motivating factors. They may have returned to a familiar task in the midst of their grief, turmoil, and confusion. They may have used up the common purse and no longer have found those who would contribute after Jesus' death. However, whatever the motivation, John 21 provides a picture of a group of disciples still being together. It is interestingly a group that includes some of the Twelve, as well as others such as Nathanael (21:2), who does not feature in any list of the Twelve. Also, while we have noted that in the Synoptics, the disciples leave their boats, yet now they have access to a boat, so they may have returned to that which they had left. These examples fit with the overall picture of a group traveling together and of disciples who left their property behind as opposed to selling it.

Summary (Other Indications of the Practice of Jesus and His Disciples)

The passages in the gospels that indicate the practice of Jesus and his disciples show a variety of ways that people followed and participated in the group that surrounded Jesus. There are those who are called and leave behind homes, ways of life, and family. There are those who travel with Jesus and the disciples and provide support out of their own resources and thus seem not to have left their resources behind. There are also those who do not travel with Jesus and the disciples, yet are committed, supportive, and provide hospitality.

There are hints at how Jesus and his disciples were provided for. The way in which non-following associates such as Martha, Mary, Zacchaeus, and Simon provided food as well as the provision from people of peace on specific mission trips, would have limited what the common purse would have been needed for. Luke 8:1–3 also suggests a possible source for money or gifts for the common purse.

Summary of the Practice of Jesus and His Disciples

Looking at the John passages about the γλωσσόκομον in the light of the other indications of the practice of Jesus and his disciples, we see that the γλωσσόκομον was one of a variety of ways that Jesus and his followers/supporters related to one another with their possessions, part of a network of relationships, and means of support. It appears that the γλωσσόκομον was specific to those followers who traveled with Jesus. The passages in the Synoptics with their emphasis on the disciples leaving everything, and the passages about Jesus and the disciples traveling may provide the motivation for the γλωσσόκομον, as they would have lost their existing means of support. They also suggest that these disciples, who have left everything, are less likely to have had things to contribute to the γλωσσόκομον.

However, it appears that there were also those who traveled with the group, who had not left everything and who contributed from their own resources to support the group. The women in Luke 8 may be contributing to the γλωσσόκομον. This is supported by Judas's words about the nard, where he indicates an expectation that Mary could have given the nard to be sold, which suggests that similar gifts had been received and sold in the past.

Thus, it seems possible that not only had some of those who were supported by γλωσσόκομον contributed to it, but also that there were others who received support, but had not contributed to it.

The money in the γλωσσόκομον seems to have been used for buying food (for the feast), providing for the poor and, if we assume that the women in Luke 8 contribute to it, for more general support. The money in the γλωσσόκομον seems to have been held in common and cared for by Judas. It was not, however, the only way that Jesus' supporters and followers held or used possessions, as there were those who retained at least some of their possessions and hosted Jesus and the disciples who traveled with him. Even for those who were part of the group who traveled with Jesus, it was not their only source of support, sharing or provision. While the γλωσσόκομον seems to have been provision specifically for those who traveled with Jesus, and while it is always presented alongside Judas's misuse of the funds, John's wider portrayal of Jesus' followers suggests mutual responsibility and communal identity which lends support to the communal holding and use of money as being a positive thing. John's account of Judas's role suggests that those who follow such an example of sharing may find that there will be those who abuse it. This is not however a reason to stop such sharing.

POSSIBLE PARALLELS

Rabbis and Their Disciples

There are a number of references in the gospels where individuals call Jesus ῥαββί (for example, Matt 26:25, 49; Mark 9:5, 11:21; John 1:39, 49). So in some sense, Jesus is seen in the gospels as a rabbi with disciples, alongside John and his disciples, and the Pharisees and their disciples (Mark 2:18). Therefore our first comparator for the practice of Jesus and his disciples is the practice of contemporaneous rabbis and their disciples. We consider what evidence exists for first-century rabbis and disciples and examine the evidence that hints at practice related to possessions and discipleship. We then look at the similarities and differences between what we know of first-century rabbis and their disciples and what we know of the practice of Jesus and his disciples.

Evidence about Rabbis and Their Disciples

Issues Surrounding the Evidence

While there are a number of sources of evidence about rabbis and their disciples including Josephus, the NT, Philo, Sirach, the Mishnah, and the Talmud, there are issues with using some of this evidence. First is the question of dating the material: much of the rabbinical material in the Mishnah and Talmud is codified well after the first century. Thus, the evidence may well refer to a considerably different post-70 CE context. As David Instone-Brewer points out, the status and situation of rabbis in the post-70 CE era was different from that in pre-70 CE Judaism.[40] Post-70 CE rabbis began to be ordained, there was a reduction in the diversity of Jewish groups and Judaism as a whole had to respond to the lack of a temple for liturgical worship. Therefore there was "an increasing emphasis on study and prayer."[41] Thus, after 70 CE there is a time of transition in terminology. For example, the term "scribe," which had referred to a learned man came to be used more generally, including referring to a copyist,[42] and "rabbi" which had been used honorifically became "reserved exclusively for scribes."[43]

However, it is possible to estimate the dating of some of the sayings within the rabbinic material by considering the rabbis named in conjunction with particular sayings. While this is not a guaranteed method, it at least gives some indication of dating. Similarly, sayings attributed to a later period may include earlier traditions or practices. Types of exegesis, logical precedence, particular temple references, and parallel sources may be used to estimate dates.[44]

Second is the issue of the location to which the evidence refers. Dunn points out that "with the Apocrypha several of the items come from the diaspora."[45] Thus, it might be questioned how relevant such information is to the situation of rabbis and their disciples in Palestine.

With these limitations in mind, we now turn to consider what may be found in this evidence.

---

40. Instone-Brewer, "Review," 282.
41. Ibid.
42. Daube, *Testament*, 211.
43. Jeremias, *Jerusalem*, 236.
44. Instone-Brewer, *Prayer*, 28–38.
45. Dunn, *Jesus*, 273.

Schools and Payment

There is evidence of paying fees[46] to study the Bible and Mishnah (*Num. Rab.* 14.2) and to schools (Sir 51.23; *b. Yom* 35b). Many of these references are later than the first half of the first century or are late texts referring to the first century.[47] Moore argues that the second century practice was "more universal and regular"[48] but that similar practices existed in the first century. If such practice did exist at the time of Jesus, it presents a very different picture of the relationship between teacher and disciple and of methods of learning.

How to Find Disciples/Become a Disciple

Meier argues that usually a disciple would seek out a master and not vice versa.[49] This is supported by Sirach 6.34-36: "Stand in the company of the elders. Who is wise? Attach yourself to such a one." While there are questions about accuracy and motivations, Josephus' account of his exploration of the sects and time with Bannus indicates that Josephus as the disciple was the one who chose to investigate and chose with whom he would spend time (*Life* 2.7-12). This taking of initiative also seems to happen with two of John's disciples when they follow Jesus to find out more about him (1:37).

The Relationship between Rabbi and Disciples

Once the relationship of rabbi and disciple was established, the disciple would spend time with the rabbi, learning through watching. There are several accounts of disciples learning from their rabbis by observation. Ben 'Azzai talks about following R. 'Akiba to the toilet and thus learning (*b. Ber.* 62a). R. Ḥiyya b. Abba speaks about watching R. Joḥanan eating and blessing the food (*b. Ber.* 38b) and Rab Hamnuna reports how he learned about the location of Tefillin by observation (*b. Ber* 24a). The second two instances involve rabbis in the third and early fourth century, the first example involves rabbis in the early second century. While there will have been changes in the post-70 CE era, we might expect that such observation for learning was built upon previous practice. This claim is supported by Sir

---

46. Philo refers to fees for learning (*Congr.* 127), but not to whether these are for rabbinic teachers.
47. Schürer, Vermes, Millar, and Black, *History*, 2:329.
48. Moore, *Judaism*, 1:321.
49. Meier, *Jew*, 3:53.

6:35, which indicates that the disciple should visit and wear out the doorstep of the intelligent person whom he wants to learn from.

The disciple also would be expected to honor and provide services to the rabbi. "R. Joshua b. Levi ruled: All manner of service that a slave must render to his master a student must render to his teacher, except that of taking off his shoe" (*b. Ket.* 96a). Similarly in *m. 'Abot* 6.3 the same rabbi teaches "those a person learns from should be honored." Both of these are from the early third century, but do fit with John the Baptist's words to Jesus: "after me comes one who is more powerful than I, whose sandals I am not worthy to carry" (Matt 2:11). This respect for the rabbi or teacher is also found in the Kerithoth tractate of the Mishnah:

> And so it is also with the study of the Law; if the son has been worthy [to sit] before the teacher, the teacher comes before the father in all places, because both a man and his father are bound to honor the teacher (*m. Ker.* 6.9).

The Example of Bannus and Josephus

One example of a disciple from the same period as Jesus and his disciples is Josephus' account of being a disciple of Bannus. Josephus writes of how he wanted "to gain personal experience of the several sects into which our nation is divided" (*Life* 2.9–10), which he sees as including the Pharisees, Sadducees, and Essenes. He reports that he tried out all three and then heard of Bannus, who lived in the wilderness and went to be his disciple for three years (*Life* 2.11). Josephus' account does not seem to hold together. Josephus' claim to have tested the various ways would have involved many years and yet Josephus reports that it all happened between the ages of 16 and 19, including the three years he spent with Bannus.[50] Josephus is also writing post 70 CE and in a situation of having Roman patronage, which probably colors his writing. However, there does not seem to be any particular reason for him to invent other information about his time with Bannus.

Josephus' account of his discipleship with Bannus shows him as choosing to associate with Bannus as opposed to Bannus calling him. It shows simplicity of lifestyle, depending on food and clothing that occurred naturally (*Life* 2.11).[51] It is also time limited and Josephus reports, "With him I

---

50. Ibid., 3:304.

51. This fits with simplicity and hardship noted in the later account in m. *'Abot* 6.4: "Thou shalt eat bread with salt *and thou shalt drink water by measure*, and on the ground shalt thou sleep and thou shalt live a life of trouble the while thou toilest in the Law."

lived for three years and, having accomplished my purpose, returned to the city" (*Life* 2.12). Josephus does not elucidate what this purpose was beyond exploring the various sects, but he does go on to conclude that he then began "to govern my life by the rules of the Pharisees" (*Life* 2.12).

Jesus, His Disciples, and the Pharisees/Rabbis—Similarities

There are two main areas of similarity between references to rabbis and their disciples, and Jesus and his disciples in terms of their relationships to one another and money: simplicity of life and precedence over family.

The Pharisees were contemporaneous with Jesus and his disciples and as we have noted earlier, at least some had disciples. The simplicity of life that Josephus ascribes to the Pharisees both in *Ant.* 18.12 as well as in his account of how he subjected himself to the various sects in *Life,* is similar to that found in the gospels. When Jesus sends out the Twelve and the Seventy-two, he tells them to take nothing with them in the way of provision.[52] When Jesus talks to prospective disciples, he warns them about the simplicity of lifestyle and hardship that they will encounter (Luke 9:57–62). It is however important to acknowledge the limits of our information about the Pharisees. Dunn points out the challenges of deciding which evidence to use and notes that some evidence has been preserved by Christians.[53] He concludes "As we have learned more about Second Temple Judaism, the more it has become apparent that we know less about the Pharisees than we previously took for granted."[54]

The precedence of the relationship between disciple and rabbi/teacher noted above is paralleled in Jesus' teaching.[55] For example, Jesus says, "Whoever loves father or mother more than me is not worthy of me; and whoever loves son or daughter more than me is not worthy of me" (Matt 10:37).

Jesus, His Disciples, and the Pharisees/Rabbis—Differences

However, despite these similarities and other similarities in teaching, there are considerable differences even in the limited evidence that we have.

The accounts we have of being disciples of a rabbi suggest that it was for a limited period, thus, Josephus can conclude after three years with

---

52. See pp. 11–13.
53. Dunn, *Jesus*, 256.
54. Ibid., 267.
55. See pp. 23–24.

Bannus that he had accomplished his purpose (*Life* 2.12) and can write of having "passed through the three courses" (*Life* 2.11) of the Pharisees, Sadducees, and Essenes. In contrast, Jesus calls his disciples to follow him without any obvious time limit. Manson considers Luke 14:26 and its parallel in Matt 10:37. Looking at the difference of μαθητής and ἄξιος, he argues that the Aramaic word behind them is more likely to be שוליא rather than אדימלת,[56] giving a picture of discipleship more akin to "apprenticeship to the work of the kingdom"[57] as opposed to completing specific learning of law. He argues, "Their work was not study but practice."[58]

The accounts also suggest that disciples found and chose the rabbi they wished to follow, as opposed to most of the accounts about Jesus, where he usually chooses and calls his disciples.

While we have shown evidence of disciples spending time with their rabbis and observing in detail the practice of the rabbis, the picture is one of the rabbis living in one place and the disciples traveling daily to see them. This contrasts with the picture of Jesus with at least some of his disciples traveling from place to place without a fixed abode. This fits with the contrast between Jesus' disciples who are called to leave their homes, families, and ways of life and follow and the rabbis' disciples who are exhorted to work as well as study the law (*m. 'Abot* 2.2; *b. Yom* 35b). We have noted the existence of non-following associates and it may be that there are more similarities between their situation and that of the rabbis and their disciples.

When we look at the relationship between rabbis, their disciples, and their possessions, the main evidence we have, albeit late, is of disciples paying for learning in some way. There is no record of shared possessions or money, or of them traveling together. While there is evidence that the honor due to teachers is above family, this is not specified in terms of support or provision and even if it were, it would not provide a parallel to the situation of Jesus and his disciples sharing out of a common purse. In fact, Hellerman concludes that the common purse "moves beyond anything we find operating among the early Israelites or Second Temple Judeans,"[59] with the exceptions of David and his followers in 1 Sam 21–30 and the community at Qumran.[60] It is to the community at Qumran and the Essenes that we now turn, to examine whether they provide a helpful parallel to the practice of Jesus and his disciples.

---

56. Manson, *Teaching*, 238.
57. Ibid., 240.
58. Ibid., 239.
59. Hellerman, *Church*, 71.
60. Ibid.

Essenes and Qumran

Evidence

The Dead Sea Scrolls (DSS) point to the community at Qumran practicing some degree of sharing of possessions. Josephus and Philo provide similar evidence about the Essenes. We will consider the evidence relating to the Qumran community and the secondary evidence relating to the Essenes and then consider the relationship between them.

THE RELATIONSHIP BETWEEN KHIRBET QUMRAN AND THE SCROLLS

While there are a number of proposed reconstructions of the site at Qumran including as a military site, a recreational villa, a commercial site, and a fortified manor, each proposal, except the one linking the site to the community who wrote the scrolls, has significant counter arguments. The walls of the site are not reinforced and the graves do not show signs of injuries incurred in battle, therefore it seems unlikely the site was a military one.[61] The quantities of fineware are small, there is a lack of commercial items and the site is not on a trade route, so it seems unlikely that it was a commercial site.[62] Catherine Murphy examines a number of theories and concludes that "The weight of the evidence, therefore points to the identification of the Qumran site as a sectarian community centre."[63]

In addition, evidence links the community to the scrolls found at and near the site. Some scroll caves are within the enclosure wall and the majority of scrolls were found in caves where "access to these caves required passage through or alongside the compound."[64] There is similar pottery in the caves and settlement,[65] including cylindrical jars.[66] The archaeological evidence points to the buildings and the scrolls having similar dates.[67] This would seem to indicate that the scrolls are from the community at Khirbet Qumran.

---

61. Murphy, *Wealth*, 350.
62. Ibid., 354.
63. Ibid., 358.
64. Ibid., 295.
65. Atkinson and Magness, "Josephus's Essenes," 324–25.
66. Murphy, *Wealth*, 295.
67. Beall, *Josephus*, 4.

There are also a number of physical indications that link the community at Khirbet Qumran with the scrolls. At the site, there are a large number of cisterns which could be baths for the ritual washings advocated by the scrolls.[68] Coins were "found in the community buildings but not in living quarters,"[69] and "the number of coins found suggest a simple lifestyle,"[70] which correlates with the sharing of money reported in the scrolls.

While various reconstructions of the Qumran site have been proposed, and while some scholars have raised questions of whether the scrolls are related to the community that inhabited the site, the scholarly consensus provides significant evidence supporting the proposal that the scrolls were written, or at least copied, by the community living at Qumran, which was a sectarian community. We will therefore assume such a link and will now turn to consider what the DSS say about the sharing of possessions.

Evidence of Sharing Possessions

The DSS point to two kinds of sharing of possessions. In 1QS we find a situation where the community eats together (1QS 6.1–4), and where entry to the community is staged. A man who wishes to join the community is first "examined by the Guardian at the head of the Congregation concerning his understanding and his deeds" (1QS 6.14). Then if he is accepted, there is a probationary year, where "he shall not touch the pure Meal of the Congregation," "nor shall he have any share of the property of the Congregation" (1QS 6.16–17). After this year, he is then examined again and if he is accepted "his property and earnings shall be handed over to the Bursar of the Congregation who shall register it to his account and shall not spend it for the Congregation" (1QS 6.19–20). During this second year, he is not able to partake in the drink of the Congregation and at the end of it is examined again and if he is accepted "his property shall be merged and he shall offer his counsel and judgement to the Community" (1QS 6.23–24). The Rule of the Community (1QS) also indicates a variety of punishments and penances for those who transgress the rule of the community, including those who fail to care for the property of the community. Those who cause loss to the property are expected to "restore it in full. And if he be unable to restore it, he shall do penance for sixty days" (1QS 7.6–8). If someone lies in a matter of property he shall do "penance with respect to one quarter of his food" (1QS 6.25). This raises the question of how an individual could

68. Broshi, "Essenes," 28.
69. Beall, *Josephus*, 4.
70. Murphy, *Wealth*, 316–17.

restore property, if each member of the community had handed over all his property to the community. Murphy suggests the possibility of restitution "may mean that they retained some of their own property or that their work could generate the income necessary to compensate for a loss."[71]

The *Damascus Document* provides a different picture. In it there are rules about keeping away from uncleanness and living in community (CD 7.1-5 and 6.15-20), where in order to be part of the congregation, the Guardian needs to approve the person's admittance. However, there is provision for those who are married (CD 7.6-9). The instructions for possessions are lighter:

> They shall place the earnings of at least two days out of every month into the hands of the Guardian and the Judges, and from it they shall give to the fatherless, and from it they shall succour the poor and the needy, the aged sick and the homeless, the captive taken by a foreign people, the virgin with no near kin, and the ma[id for] whom no man cares (CD 14.13-18).

While there are limits and common decisions on business transactions (CD 13.13-16), there does not seem to be the same kind of handing over of all possessions as in 1QS, although it would be possible for possessions to be handed over and then for a proportion of earnings to be handed over. As with 1QS, *Damascus Document* includes provision of punishment for those who transgress, including expulsion from the community (CD B2.2-5) and exclusion from the pure Meal (CD 9.20-25). This suggests that there is some kind of common meal within the community described by CD. However, it is not clear where this provision comes from and whether other possessions or earnings are handed into a common pot as in 1QS. While the two documents could be describing the community at Qumran, this appears less likely as CD has a number of references that only make sense in the case of a community that is in the vicinity of a town, for example the instructions on individuals doing business or interacting with those outside the community (CD 13.13-16) and the reference that "No man shall walk abroad to do business on the Sabbath. He shall not walk more than one thousand cubits beyond his town" (CD 10.20). This indicates that the writer is anticipating communities in different towns. CD 9.10-13 provides the procedure for "When anything is lost, and it is not known who has stolen it from the property of the camp in which it was stolen, its owner shall pronounce a curse." This indicates both communal property but also individual ownership at one and the same time. Thus, Murphy argues for a situation where property is both individual and communal. It has been handed over, however

---

71. Ibid., 158.

"there are still individual owners who may have their property stolen, it is the entire community that is deprived of the property's use."[72] This could fit together with Capper's suggestion that the instructions on giving two days of a month's salary are for those who had not become part of the community of goods in a town, but who supported the Essene community and contributed to their fund for giving to the poor.[73] This might make sense of the way that Josephus and Philo both point to a community of goods amongst the Essenes that is more comprehensive than that suggested by CD and more akin to that described in 1QS.

Murphy notes that 4Q348 documents a transaction and is predominately names, which could be "a significant witness to the practice of shared property."[74]

Josephus' description of the Essenes has similarities to both 1QS and CD. Josephus briefly mentions the Essenes in *Life* 2.10 and indicates that he spent time with them. However, as indicated earlier, Josephus' account leaves questions as to whether the three years allowed time for him to investigate all three sects and spend time with Bannus. In the *Jewish War*, Josephus provides a fuller description of the Essene way of life. He reports that they have community of goods and that new members hand over their property to the sect (*J.W.* 2.122). He also says, "They occupy no one city, but settle in large numbers in every town" (*J.W.* 2.124–5). Thus, when they travel from place to place they are able to stay with other Essenes and "all the resources of the community are put at their disposal, just as if they were their own; and they enter the houses of men whom they have never seen before as though they were the most intimate friends" (*J.W.* 2.124–5). While Josephus reports that the Essenes disdain marriage (*J.W.* 2.120), he indicates that there are some Essenes who allow wives (*J.W.* 2.160–61) and that the Essenes "adopt other men's children" (*J.W.* 2.120). When Josephus mentions the Essenes in *Antiquities*, he again speaks of how "they hold their possessions in common, and the wealthy man receives no more enjoyment from his property than the man who possesses nothing" (*Ant.* 18.20).

Like Josephus, Philo also writes of how there were many Essenes (over 4000) in various villages (*Good Person* 75; *Hypoth.* 11.1). Philo reports that they labor on the land and produce crafts, have a sense of equality and share possessions, including houses, wages, and meals (*Good Person* 85–86). In *Hypothetica* Philo reports how the wages once handed over are kept by the

---

72. Ibid., 49.
73. Capper, "Types," 114.
74. Murphy, *Wealth*, 397.

treasurer who is responsible for buying food "and anything else which human life requires" (*Hypoth.* 11.10).

The Relationship between the Qumran Community and the Essenes

Before we turn to considering the relationship between the Qumran community and Essenes, and Jesus and his disciples, we first need to consider the relationship between the Qumran community and the Essenes and whether we need to consider them as separate groups, or whether we can use the evidence of the DSS alongside the evidence from Josephus and Philo. For the most part there is consensus amongst scholars that the community living at Khirbet Qumran were Essenes.[75]

In addition to the evidence for a link between the community at Qumran and the Essenes, the following points provide further support. First, there is diversity within the DSS and within Josephus' description of the Essenes as well as between the different descriptions. Such diversity within Jewish groups was not unusual with both Hillel and Shammai belonging to the Pharisees.[76] Second, the communities may have developed their practice and theology over time.[77] The DSS were composed pre-31 BCE. Philo and Josephus are describing the first-century CE practice, which may be different.[78] Third, practice may have varied between Qumran and other communities. Schiffman suggests that Qumran was the only place where the third stage of entry into the community was possible.[79]

Fourth, the Qumran community also appears to have been part of a larger group, both by the number of scrolls copied as well as the way that the public rooms are larger, suggesting visitors to the site for festivals.[80] The presence of similar graves in Jerusalem adds to this evidence.[81]

Fifth, if the two groups are not related, then we have a situation where two similar communities existed, one of which left archaeological remains and scrolls, but no accounts or descriptions from outsiders and the other

---

75. Beall, *Josephus*, 124–29; Vanderkam, "People," 50. (Contra Baumgarten, "Who Cares?"). For further details of the arguments supporting this consensus see Gregson, "Everything in Common?" 253–58.
76. Broshi, "Essenes," 26.
77. Goodman, *Essenes*, 13.
78. Atkinson and Magness, "Josephus's Essenes," 340.
79. Schiffman, *Reclaiming*, 101.
80. Murphy, *Wealth*, 103.
81. Zias, "Cemeteries," 243.

was written about by outsiders, but left no other traces found as yet.[82] This seems unlikely. Therefore, given the similarities between the Essenes described by Philo, Josephus, and Pliny and the evidence about the community at Qumran in the DSS and the archaeological evidence, it seems probable that the community at Khirbet Qumran was part of a wider group, referred to by Philo, Josephus, and Pliny as Essenes. We will therefore use evidence from the DSS, Khirbet Qumran, Philo, and Josephus together when we look at comparing the Essenes to Jesus and his disciples and then to the early church.

Links and Relationship to Jesus and His Disciples

We have considered the evidence about the Essenes and Qumran. We now look at whether Jesus and his disciples would have known about or related to them. The knowledge that both Philo and Josephus display about the Essenes and their description of their numbers and the variety of towns or villages that they lived in, suggests that Jesus and his disciples would probably have come across the Essenes in their travels, or at least known about them.[83]

Capper goes further to posit a relationship between Jesus and his disciples and the Essenes. He argues that the beloved disciple in John was "not one of the twelve, . . . but a Jerusalem disciple,"[84] who hosts Jesus in Jerusalem in the lead up to Jesus' arrest.[85] Capper argues that the person hosting Jesus at such a key point would need to be someone known to him and that Jesus' instructions about following the man carrying water, suggest that Jesus was acquainted with the household.[86]

Capper then uses the location of the Upper Room and archaeological evidence about baths referred to in the Temple Scroll to argue that the Upper Room was located in the same quarter as the Essenes in Jerusalem.[87] Riesner similarly argues from archaeological and literary evidence that both the Upper Room and the Essene Quarter were in the SW quarter of Jerusalem.[88] Capper suggests that the reference to a man carrying water needed to be specific enough for the disciples to recognize the person to follow, but usual enough for those in the area so that it did not draw too much

82. Cross, "Early History," 68–69.
83. Capper, "Types," 113.
84. Capper, "Oldest Monks," 3.
85. Ibid., 14.
86. Ibid., 17.
87. Ibid., 21–26, 36–42.
88. Riesner, "Jesus," 202–14.

attention to them.[89] He thus argues that the household where Jesus ate with his disciples was one where there were no women and that this might well suggest it was an Essene household.[90]

Capper's argument rests on a number of conjectures which are difficult to prove or disprove: that the beloved disciple was not one of the twelve, that the beloved disciple lived in Jerusalem and hosted Jesus there before Jesus died, that Jesus was hosted by someone who lived at the Upper Room (as opposed to an arrangement having been made to use it), and that the man carrying the water was an Essene, to name but a few. Therefore while his conclusions may be correct, they do not seem to be compelling. However, his investigation of the location of the Upper Room, the *Bethso*, and the Essene quarter do suggest that it is likely that Jesus and his disciples were at the very least aware of the Essenes, if not acquainted with them, or in relationship with them. The times when Jesus appears to refer to or speak in contrast to some Essene teaching, for example about animals in pits on the Sabbath (CD 11.13–14; Matt 12:11),[91] may also support this.

Similarities

There are a number of similarities between what is described of the Qumran and Essene communities and what is known of the practice of Jesus and his disciples. First, there is the holding in common of at least some possessions and wages. Second, Philo points to money being held by a treasurer and in John's gospel, Judas is referred to as the person who kept the common purse. This treasurer is responsible for buying food and providing in other ways and in John's gospel, we find the assumption when Judas departs that he is going to get something for the feast or give something to the poor (13:29). Third, there are references to the Essenes/Qumran communities eating together and we find Jesus and his disciples eating together as well as being hosted by others (4:8; 12:2; 13:2). Fourth, CD refers to giving to those in need and each time the common purse is referred to we find reference to giving to the poor (12:5, 13:29). Fifth, there does appear to be some diversity in practice and way of life for those who are Essenes, particularly between those at Qumran and those in towns. This diversity in discipleship/membership is also seen with Jesus and his disciples: those who travel with him, those who support and travel with, and those who host. Sixth, there is an element of similarity between the way Essenes were able to travel and be

89. Capper, "Oldest Monks," 51–52.
90. Ibid., 52–53.
91. Charlesworth, "Dead Sea Scrolls," 20–21.

hosted by other Essenes and the way that Jesus and his disciples were hosted by non-following associates. This is part of a wider focus on community in both groups.

Differences

However, despite these similarities, there are a number of differences. First, there is a very different way of becoming a disciple or member of the community. Jesus generally calls individuals or in a few cases invites them to come and see, while with the Essenes/Qumran, there is a more structured and graduated entry with several stages of examination and teaching (1QS 3.13-15, 1QS 6.13-24).

Second, there is a difference in what happens to possessions on joining. In many instances when Jesus calls, his disciples leave their possessions or way of life behind, while with the Essenes and Qumran, they hand over their property to the group.

Third, while Josephus describes the welcome that Essenes receive when they travel, they are presented as static communities who happen to travel, while the practice of Jesus and his disciples with the common purse seems to be one where the common purse was for those who traveled with him.

Fourth, we see a difference in eating habits. With the Qumran and Essenes there are specific rules about with whom one may eat, about staged entry to eating and drinking, and about not eating with those outside (1QS 6.17, 20-1), while Jesus and his disciples eat with those others considered sinners or unrighteous (Matt 9:10).

Fifth, there is a difference in dealing with those who err. As noted earlier, John presents Jesus as one who knows and therefore presumably knows that Judas is misusing his position, and yet allows Judas to continue as one of the twelve and in that position. In contrast, there are strict penalties in the instruction in CD and 1QS. In CD if someone errs in a matter of property they are to be excluded from the pure meal (CD 9.20-4), while in 1QS we find that the person must restore the property and if he is unable to do so, he must do sixty days' penance (1QS 7.6-8).

Conclusions

What can we learn about the practice of Jesus and his disciples by comparing it with that of the Essenes? We have argued that Jesus and his disciples were aware of the Essenes, if not relating to Essenes. Therefore when Jesus and his disciples had the common purse, we may assume that they were aware of different ways of approaching sharing possessions. They may have picked up the similarities from the Essenes or they may have formed them themselves, but they presumably to some degree chose their differences. Some of the differences we see between the two groups are due to circumstance—the size, age, and development[92] of the two groups and also the traveling versus static nature of the groups.

However, other differences do not appear to be directly related to the group circumstances: the welcome to become disciples (either by call or invitation) without a staged entry process, an openness to the world beyond the community, evidenced by the way that Jesus and his disciples ate with others and the continued inclusion of Judas in spite of his misuse of the funds in the common purse. Thus, in comparison with the Essenes, Jesus and his disciples show an approach to community and sharing of possessions that is less organized, more open to people joining, less separate from those beyond the community and more inclusive of those who sin, without condoning it.[93]

Cynics

Evidence

Cynicism was a branch of Greek philosophy that started around the fourth century BCE and Diogenes Laertius catalogues past Cynics. It is difficult to ascertain the extent of their influence and location, but Hock and Crossan point to their presence in the first century CE.[94]

Cynics held to a simple life style, gave up money, often flouted norms, and sometimes had disciples. They were known for their shameless behavior and also their clothing, including a cloak, staff, and bare feet.[95] One Cynic reports of how a potential disciple "shared out his property among his family, slung on a satchel and a doubled worn cloak, and followed me" (ps. Diogenes *Ep.* 38.5). Epictetus reports "I am without a home, without a city, without property, without a slave; I sleep on the ground; I have neither wife nor children, no miserable governor's mansion, but only earth, and sky

---

92. Some of these differences may be related to different levels of organization, as Meier notes, "Jesus' movement shows a very low level of organization during his public ministry" compared to Qumran (Meier, *Jew*, 3:530).

93. There is no evidence in John's gospel that Jesus or the other disciples approved of Judas's behavior.

94. Hock, "Cynics," 1222; Crossan, *Historical Jesus*, 75–76.

95. Hock, "Cynics," 1223–24.

and one rough cloak. Yet what do I lack? Am I not free from pain and fear, am I not free?" (*Diatr.* 3.22.47) This renunciation of familial ties, particular clothing, and outspokenness were seen as characteristic of what it meant to be a Cynic. While Cynics themselves may have pointed to character and other parts of life, others identified Cynics by appearance: "But no, you say, what makes a Cynic is a contemptible wallet, a staff, and big jaws" (*Diatr.* 3.22.50). There are also examples of Cynics or other philosophers calling disciples to follow them, for example in the account of Xenophon becoming a pupil of Socrates: "'Then follow me,' said Socrates, 'and learn.' From that time onward he was a pupil of Socrates" (Diogenes Laertius, *LEP* 2.48).

When people became Cynics they also often gave away possessions and Laertius writes about Crates distributing his money "among his fellow-citizens" (*LEP* 4.87). This fits with the quote earlier from pseudo Diogenes about the disciple sharing out his property.

This giving away of possessions resulted in a simplicity of life and Cynics also spoke of the Cynic way as being hard, for example: "The love of money he declared to be mother-city of all evils" (Diogenes Laertius, *LEP* 2.50). Cynics also had an approach to all people as family and Epictetus reports, "the Cynic has made all mankind his children; the men among them he has as sons, the women as daughters; in that spirit he approaches them all and cares for them all" (*Diatr.* 3.22.81–82).

Links/Relationship to Jesus and His disciples

There is, however, the question of whether Cynics were in Palestine in the first century and whether Jesus and his disciples would have been aware of them and their practice or in any way related to them. There is significant discussion about the level of Hellenisation in the Galilee region with different scholars coming to significantly different conclusions.

Both 1 and 2 Maccabees point to Hellenistic influence in Jerusalem. In 1 Maccabees the author reports "they built a gymnasium in Jerusalem, according to Gentile custom" (1 Macc 1:14) and in 2 Maccabees Jason promises money to Antiochus if he gives permission for a gymnasium (2 Macc 4:9). Looking at ossuaries of the time, 39 percent of ossuaries in Jerusalem have only Greek inscriptions.[96] However, those who were able to afford ossuaries and inscriptions may have had a greater likelihood of also speaking Greek. Witherington concludes that there was widespread use of Greek, but

---

96. Fiensy, "Composition," 231.

this did not necessarily correlate to Hellenisation, and argues that Hellenisation principally affected the Jewish upper classes.[97]

The most obvious place to look for Hellenisation in Galilee is in Greek cities such as Sepphoris. The evidence for the degree of Hellenisation is mixed. Strange notes that Sepphoris was less antagonistic during the first Jewish revolt[98] and this may be indicative of the town being more hellenized than the surrounding villages. However, it could just indicate that there were richer people living there who had more to lose. Strange also notes buildings in Sepphoris that indicate a degree of Hellenisation,[99] for example the presence of a theatre.[100] However, Dunn points out that "the archaeological evidence for Sepphoris is as clear as for the rest of Galilee: no indications of large numbers of non-Jews and plenty of evidence of the same four indicators of Jewish religious identity (stone vessels, miqwaoth, absence of pork remains, burial in kochim shafted tombs with ossuaries)."[101] Similarly Strange notes the presence of ritual baths under houses in Sepphoris.[102] So it is unclear whether Cynics would have been present in first century Galilee. It should also be noted that Sepphoris is not mentioned in the gospels and we lack evidence that Jesus and his disciples spent time there. Witherington also points out that the parallels which Downing uses "almost without exception post-date the time of Jesus and in some cases even *post-date* the New Testament age."[103]

Similarities

The traditional dress of a Cynic with cloak, staff, and bare feet, without provision for the way and leaving home behind, shows some similarities, particularly to those disciples called and sent out by Jesus. There is the same sense of traveling simply (*LEP* 6.37) and relying on provision from others (ps. Diogenes *Ep.* 38.4, *LEP* 6.34). However, there are some differences as well. In Matthew, Jesus specifies that the disciples should not take a staff, nor a bag (Matt 10:10). This is the same in Luke 9:3 and while Luke 10 does not specify whether or not the seventy-two should carry a staff, it again points to the lack of a bag (Luke 10:4). By contrast our evidence about Cynics

97. Witherington, *Sage*, 121.
98. Strange, "Galilee," 393.
99. Ibid., 395.
100. Ibid., 396.
101. Dunn, *Jesus*, 299–300.
102. Strange, "Galilee," 396.
103. Witherington, *Sage*, 127, his italics.

includes both satchel and often staff (Epictetus, *Diatr.* 3.22.9–11; ps Diogenes *Ep.* 38.5). Downing argues that this is actually a point of similarity as he argues that both Cynic texts and the gospels vary in what they advocate taking when traveling.[104] However, while there is variance within both sets of texts, differences still exist between them.

There are similarities between Jesus' teaching in Matt 6 about concern about physical provision with some of the Cynic attitudes. Cynics also travel from place to place, which again is a feature of the gospel accounts of Jesus and his disciples (Mark 10:17, 32–46; 11:19, 27).

The accounts of Cynics selling their possessions on becoming Cynics parallel Jesus' call to disciples to sell their possessions and give to the poor. However, in many of the instances where Jesus calls prospective disciples to sell and give, they do not do so (Mark 10:17–22; Luke 18:18–25) and in the accounts of those who do follow Jesus, they leave home and property, but do not necessarily sell them. Also, when Cynics sell and give, they give to family and fellow citizens, not necessarily the poor.

Downing argues that the Cynics' vision of all people as family to all has a parallel in Jesus' words about his mother and brothers in Mark 3:31–35.[105] However, the words of Epictetus (*Diatr.* 3.22.81–82) give a picture of this relationship to all people, regardless of response, whereas Jesus' words in Mark 3:35 are concerning those who do the will of God.

Differences

Socrates' call of Xenophon (Diogenes Laertius *LEP* 2.48) shows some similarities to Jesus calling his disciples in the injunction to follow him, however it does not conform entirely either to the most common example in the Synoptics of how Jesus calls disciples from what they are doing to come and follow (Matt 4:18–22; Mark 1:17–20; Luke 5:1, 28), nor the examples in John where Jesus invites the disciples to come and see (1:39, 46; 4:29). While in John initiative on behalf of some of the disciples is shown, the testing questioning that Socrates uses, does not appear as part of Jesus' approach to calling disciples.

Witherington points out that while there were some similarities in terms of simple lifestyle between Jesus and his disciples and the Cynics, *"the motivation for the behavior is entirely different"*[106] and that while there are some similarities in dress, these could be similarities to most first century

---

104. Downing, *Cynics and Christian Origins*, 10–11.
105. Downing, *Christ*, 126.
106. Witherington, *Sage*, 124, his italics.

teachers.[107] Witherington further points out that Cynics aimed to improve human beings, while Jesus called his disciples to respond to the in-breaking of the kingdom.[108] Furthermore, while the Cynic are recorded as begging, there is no record of Jesus begging.[109]

There is one major difference in focus and relationships. In the Cynic literature while there are accounts of Cynics looking at all people as their family, there is substantial focus on αὐτάρκεια and no record of Cynics sharing possessions with one another or holding money in common. Downing notes that αὐτάρκεια is one of the words that those studying the Cynics focus on.[110] While Downing questions the reliability of focusing on catchphrases, he does not question the meaning behind them. This picture of Cynics valuing αὐτάρκεια is significantly different from the account of Jesus and his disciples. While there are references to contentment and not worrying (Matt 6:25–34), the Gospels also focus on the disciples' relationships with one another as a community, particularly in John's gospel, where we find a focus on relationship and interdependence rather than αὐτάρκεια.

Conclusions

There are a number of similarities between Cynics and Jesus and his disciples. However, the motivations for these similarities are sometimes rather different. At other times, it is not clear whether the similarities represent the closest parallel. Witherington points out that many of Jesus' sayings, which Downing parallels to Cynic teaching, have closer parallels in the Old Testament.[111] There are also questions about whether Cynics were present in Galilee during the time of Jesus to influence his practice and that of his disciples. Significantly, while Downing devotes substantial time to drawing parallels between Jesus and the Cynics, this mainly concerns teaching, and, in terms of practice, only covers their clothing and traveling. Furthermore, the passages concerning clothing and traveling also contain differences. If Cynics were present in Galilee during the beginning of the first century CE, it is interesting that Jesus' instructions to the Twelve and the Seventy-two

107. Ibid., 126.
108. Ibid., 130.
109. Ibid., 132.
110. Downing, *Christ*, 46–47.
111. Witherington, *Sage*, 129. Witherington does not give particular evidence about OT examples, but he does point out how the parallel of traveling widely is rather different in each case: Dio Chrysostom *Or.* 1.50 points to traveling widely and meeting all kinds of people, while the examples of the Roman Centurion and the Syro-Phonician woman are exceptions.

would show them as different from Cynics, which raises the question of whether Jesus was making sure that his disciples could not be mistaken for Cynics.

The fact that the parallels between the Cynics and Jesus and his disciples are often mixed with significant differences, of questionable dating, and that the Cynic examples do not show sharing of possessions, would suggest that the parallel does not add to our understanding of the common purse in John, except possibly in the sense that it emphasizes how the practice of Jesus and his disciples differed from the that of many of the groups around them.

CONCLUSION

The passages about the γλωσσόκομον in John's gospel, considered in the light of all four gospels, present a picture of holding possessions in common in a very particular context. The γλωσσόκομον appears to be predominantly for those who travel with Jesus, both those who have left home, livelihoods, and possessions to do so, and therefore may not have a means of support, and those who travel with the group and contribute to the γλωσσόκομον from their own resources. While there is not much information about the γλωσσόκομον, it appears to be used for buying food, giving to the poor, and wider needs.

The γλωσσόκομον is always mentioned alongside Judas, but it is not presented as a negative example. The γλωσσόκομον is not the only way that Jesus and his disciples related to one another with regard to possessions. We see the Twelve and the seventy-two receiving from and depending on those to whom they preach. We also find non-following associates who host Jesus and his disciples, but are not mentioned as either contributing to or receiving from the γλωσσόκομον.

When we consider the practice of Jesus and his disciples in comparison with that of rabbis and their disciples; the Qumran community and the Essenes; and Cynics, there are a few, primarily superficial, similarities. However, there are significant differences. There is no evidence of rabbis and their disciples, or Cynics holding possessions in common. While the Essenes and Qumran community do hold possession in common, the practice of Jesus and his disciples is different.

First, the NT texts we have considered present an example where there is considerable flexibility in how people participate in the sharing of possessions. Not only are there different groups with different practices, which can be seen in the Essene/Qumran comparator, but also there are different practices within the group that travels with Jesus. The Twelve have left things behind and seem not to be contributing to the γλωσσόκομον, while the women of Luke 8:1–3 retain their resources and contribute from them to the γλωσσόκομον.

Second, the giving to the γλωσσόκομον is more flexible. Contributing to the γλωσσόκομον does not seem to be governed by the same kind of rules seen in the DSS.

Third, Jesus and his disciples present an example of sharing, which is both more open to those outside the group, and also includes and extends grace towards those within the group who misuse their position. This is seen in the way Jesus and his disciples eat with those who are seen as outcasts and sinners, and in the way Judas is included in the Twelve and kept as treasurer. In contrast the Essenes and Qumran community have strict regulations about whom they eat with and punishments for those who misuse possessions or position.

3

Holding in Common

Acts 2–6

BACKGROUND QUESTIONS

Introduction

Luke's gospel is frequently seen as having a major focus on the poor[1] and on use of possessions.[2] While the author's second volume, Acts,[3] does not use the word πτωχός[4] and scholars such as Cassidy conclude that "Luke does not indicate such continuity with respect to concern for the poor,"[5] Acts does continue to focus on the use of possessions in providing both negative[6] and positive[7] examples of their use. Similarly Kim argues that while in Acts there

---

1. Johnson, *Luke*, 22. Contra Twelftree who sees the poor in Luke not as the disadvantaged, but as Israel as a whole (Twelftree, *People*, 184).

2. Johnson, *Jesus*, 97–98.

3. I am presuming that Luke and Acts have the same author and will refer to the author as Luke without making any claims about who "Luke" was.

4. Tannehill, "Ethics," 117.

5. Cassidy, *Society*, 24. Cassidy's point is that while the gospel of Luke focuses on the general poor, Acts considers the needy within the community as opposed to the poor in general.

6. For example, Judas's betrayal for money (1:18), Ananias and Sapphira (5:1–11) and Simon Magus (8:18–24). Biblical references in this chapter will be to Acts unless otherwise indicated.

7. For example, sharing so that none are in need within the community (4:34),

are, "no direct and clear exhortations towards the rich to give alms to the poor such as are often found in the Gospel,"[8] Acts includes examples of such behavior. Two of the main examples are the summary passages described in the early chapters of Acts, and the Antiochene collection for the church in Judaea. This chapters considers the sharing described in the summary passages in Acts 2 and Acts 4. The Antiochene collection will be considered in the next chapter.

The chapter begins by considering relevant historical questions about Acts, the intended readership, and purpose of Luke-Acts. It then considers the community described in the summary passages in Acts 2 and 4 and referred to in the examples and issues that arise in Acts 5 and 6. It examines the Jewish and Greek parallels to the language Luke uses and what this indicates about the community and the example Luke wants to portray. It looks at other passages in Acts that may illuminate the picture of the community in the early chapters of Acts, before examining the kind of practice and theology Luke may be trying to teach through the example of the early church presented in Acts 2–6. The chapter then examines how this example compares to the practice and theology of: Jewish almsgiving, the Qumran and Essene communities, and the Pythagorean community at Croton.

Historical Questions

The historical reliability of the description of the sharing of possessions in Acts 2 and 4 (and more widely of Acts and how it relates to the Pauline Epistles) has been questioned. Reta Halteman Finger provides a summary of the range of ways that the descriptions of the early church community in Acts 2 and 4 have been read, the historical questions that have been raised about it, and ways in which interpreters have read back their own values into the interpretation of the text.[9] Capper notes that the description of common property in Acts, "is almost universally read with suspicion and regarded as both idealized and barely historical."[10]

Within the historical criticisms there are helpful insights and useful questions. Moreland points out, "Histories, epics, biographies, and novels were written for many reasons, but it is quite clear that the goal of providing a historically reliable account (in the modern sense) was not an ancient

---

Barnabas (4:36–37), Dorcas (9:36), and Cornelius (10:1).

   8. Kim, *Stewardship*, 218.

   9. Finger, *Widows*, 12–46.

   10. Capper, "Jesus," 60.

objective."[11] Moreland reminds us that myths are part of social formation to reproduce values[12] and that Acts is written to form Christian identity in a context where there is "no unified Christian phenomenon in existence."[13] While Acts is written in the early days of the formation of Christian identity and has (self-confessed) formational and didactic roles, this does not necessarily mean that its account is not historical. As Bock points out, "The ancients understood history as the relating of deeds for edification,"[14] and "It is possible for ideology and historical data to be combined in a way that reflects an appropriate historical perspective."[15] This means we may look for the historical situation described by the account as well as for Luke's purpose in describing it.

Looking at the example of the sharing of possessions in the early chapters of Acts, Capper argues, using the works of Philo and Josephus as a comparison, that idealization in a text does not necessarily mean that it is ahistorical.[16] While analyzing such idealization will be helpful in understanding the practice and theology that Luke is trying to promote, its presence does not preclude the events being described having a historical basis. Indeed, as Bock points out, "where we can check Luke's work," it shows evidence "of being in touch with historical detail rather than being as creative with such detail as the epic classification suggests."[17] Luke's introduction to his gospel reminds us that he at the very least wants to portray himself as writing an accurate account.

In addition, the practice portrayed in the early chapter of Acts not only has parallels with surrounding communities,[18] but also has elements of continuity with the practice of Jesus and his disciples.[19]

Considering the emphases of Acts, Blomberg argues that Luke is concerned with the spread of the gospel to all people groups and thus his focus on the early church's sharing goes "against the grain of Luke's redactional emphases and therefore [is] particularly likely to be firmly rooted in the history of the early church."[20] While it could equally be argued that the focus

11. Moreland, "Jerusalem," 294.
12. Ibid., 297.
13. Ibid., 295.
14. Bock, *Acts*, 11.
15. Ibid., 5.
16. Capper, "Jesus," 77.
17. Bock, *Acts*, 3.
18. Capper, "Holy Community," 118.
19. See pp. 20–21, for example care for those in need.
20. Blomberg, *Poverty*, 160.

in the early chapters of Acts is a continuation both of the practice of Jesus and his disciples (seen in Luke 8) and of the focus in the gospel on the poor, Blomberg's comments remind us that such care is not the primary emphasis in Acts and thus may add historical weight to the account.

Purpose and Readership

Working out the motivations for writing Luke-Acts and for whom it was written, is not a simple matter and there is a whole range of theories.[21] Dunn notes a number of these, including justification of mission to the Gentiles,[22] showing the unity of the church,[23] and providing *"an apologetic strand in relation to the power of Rome."*[24] This apologetic could be for the church in general, or for Paul, imprisoned in Rome. However, while Luke-Acts does provide an account of, and justification for, mission to the Gentiles, and indicates the unity of the church, it seems unlikely that external political apologetics was the primary motivation for writing Luke-Acts. First, while Acts does on occasion present information that could be used in defense of Paul or Christianity, it includes a wider range of material, much of which would not necessarily be relevant to a defense argument and some of which might be challenging for an official in Rome to understand (Acts 5:1–11; 11:1–18; 15:36–41). Second, Luke's use of OT and LXX stylistic elements suggest an intended audience that was familiar with both.[25] Third, Pervo identifies Acts as "legitimating narrative" indicating that it is written to insiders to edify them,[26] and Haenchen argues that Luke adapts accounts to make them edifying.[27]

In addition Haenchen argues that Acts is written in light of the fact that the parousia had not come.[28] Bock adds the following as issues Luke addresses: explaining why Jews were generally unresponsive; "Jesus's role

---

21. Maddox, *Purpose*.
22. Dunn, *Acts*, xii. Also Haenchen, *Acts*, 94; Pervo, *Acts*, 22.
23. Dunn, *Acts*, xii.
24. Ibid., xiii (his italics). Witherington argues that the Acts 2 summary is crafted to convince Theophilus of the good character of the church (Witherington, *Acts*, 157). Haenchen also sees Luke addressing the political problems of Christianity beginning to be seen as separate from Judaism (Haenchen, *Acts*, 102).
25. Malina and Pilch, *Social-Science*, 7.
26. Pervo, *Acts*, 21.
27. Haenchen, *Acts*, 103–7.
28. Ibid., 95.

and function"; and the role of witnesses.²⁹ Peterson identifies an apologetic and evangelistic purpose to "help Christians in their engagement with unbelievers"³⁰ and Malina and Pilch argue that Acts is written to help believers make sense of their experiences.³¹ It seems likely that Luke includes several emphases. While we may not be able to narrow his audience down substantially, Kim's argument that Luke's references to rich and poor³² indicate that his community included a range of social backgrounds seems plausible.

While we may find it difficult to be precise about exactly where Luke is writing from and to whom he is writing, we can use hints from what Luke writes to help us understand the background of his initial readership. As we consider the sharing of possessions in the Jerusalem church in this chapter and the gift from the Antiochene church in the following chapter, we will be working with the text on three related levels—what happened in the early church, how Luke portrays what happened, and how Luke's readers may have read Luke's account.

THE EARLY COMMUNITY IN JERUSALEM

The Texts

Acts 2:42–47

The first summary of the life of the early church comes immediately after the Pentecost account and Peter's message. It provides a description of the activities of those who ἀποδεξάμενοι τὸν λόγον αὐτοῦ ἐβαπτίσθησαν (Acts 2:41). Hargreaves proposes dividing chapter 2 into three sections with the third section, verses 42–47, describing "how the early Christians *lived*" out their Pentecost experience.³³ Hume identifies a chiastic structure centered on Peter's speech,³⁴ where 2:1–4 parallels 2:41–47, which emphasizes the role of the Spirit in the actions of the community in 2:41–47. As we examine the summary passage, we need to bear in mind the description of the coming of the Holy Spirit and Peter's explanation of Jesus' resurrection and the promised Holy Spirit.

29. Bock, *Acts*, 6–7.
30. Peterson, *Acts*, 36–37.
31. Malina and Pilch, *Social-Science*, 10.
32. Kim, *Stewardship*, 46–50.
33. Hargreaves, *Guide*, 29.
34. Hume, *Early*, 91.

Luke describes these baptized people as ἦσαν δὲ προσκαρτεροῦντες (v. 42), which Bock argues "has the idea of persistence or persevering in something."[35] The four things they are devoted to are: τῇ διδαχῇ τῶν ἀποστόλων καὶ τῇ κοινωνίᾳ, τῇ κλάσει τοῦ ἄρτου καὶ ταῖς προσευχαῖς, which are then explained further in the rest of the summary passage. Barrett notes "It is not agreed whether in this verse Luke is describing the meetings of the Jerusalem Christians or their way of life in general."[36] Bauernfeind sees the fourfold description as liturgical and referring to stages in a worship service[37] and Jeremias sees the reference to ἡ κλάσις τοῦ ἄρτου indicating that it was "part of the church's cult."[38] It seems unlikely that κοινωνία refers to worship/cult activity because it is linked with the selling of property and sharing of proceeds in verse 45.[39] Looking at 2:43–47, verse 43 picks up the idea of the apostles' teaching. Verses 44 and 45 then seem to relate to the much-contested κοινωνία, with verses 46 and 47 then relating to the breaking of bread and prayers.

Κοινωνία has a range of meanings from generosity[40] to participation.[41] Κοινωνία could be "spending time together as in a social club," but it could also be sharing, including "the mutual obligations of partnership or association,"[42] and "the type of mutuality that takes place in marriage."[43] Therefore to understand what Luke is describing by κοινωνία, we need to examine more closely verses 44 and 45.

These two verses bring out very practical aspects of what Luke sees κοινωνία as including (selling possessions and distributing the proceeds) as well as aspects that may be more about the mindset of the group (they had all things in common). Therefore Dupont argues that, for Luke, κοινωνία involved material and spiritual sharing of possessions,[44] and Fitzmyer sees

---

35. Bock, *Acts*, 149.

36. Barrett, *Acts*, 162.

37. Bauernfeind, *Apostelgeschichte*, 54.

38. Jeremias, *Eucharistic*, 82–83.

39. Conzelmann, *Acts*, 23. Haenchen also argues that prayers are not just at the end of the service. In Acts 3:1, the believers pray at the temple and the summary points to the whole of life not just the service (Haenchen, *Acts*, 191).

40. Spencer argues that κοινωνία could include almsgiving and a common table (Spencer, *Journeying*, 49).

41. Dupont, *Salvation*, 85.

42. Malina and Pilch, *Social-Science*, 36.

43. Bock, *Acts*, 150. BDAG, 552–53; 3 Macc 4:6.

44. Dupont, *Salvation*, 87.

it as referring to the early church's "communal form of life."[45] Krodel also equates fellowship with unity and with the sharing of material goods.[46]

If κοινωνία includes both practical sharing and unity of the early believers, what did it look like in practice? The sharing described in verses 44 and 45 has sometimes been equated with an early form of communism, where all the believers sold all their possessions to contribute to a common fund, or where there is "some kind of joint ownership."[47] Indeed Klauck argues that verse 44 "scheint zunächst auf völlige Gütergemeinschaft und obligatorischen Besitzverzicht hinzudeuten"[48] (seems at first to point to complete community of goods and obligatory selling of possessions), particularly given that Peter is able to say in 3:6, Ἀργύριον καὶ χρυσίον οὐχ ὑπάρχει μοι. However, the summary suggests a somewhat different picture. First, selling possessions and distributing goods is described as an ongoing activity. Both ἐπίπρασκον and διεμέριζον are imperfect implying a continuous past activity and are qualified by the phrase καθότι ἄν τις χρείαν εἶχεν, suggesting that what Luke has in mind is "no once-for-all divestiture of property, . . . but periodic acts"[49] in response to need. This points to a situation where individuals "owned" their property and each "held his goods at the disposal of the others whenever the need arose."[50] While in 3:6 Peter claims to lack silver or gold, this may also be indicative of the general poverty of the early believers, whose company included those who had traveled with Jesus from Galilee and others who had come to Jerusalem for Passover and therefore were away from their sources of employment and support.

Alexander argues that "Luke is talking about disposable property rather than personal homes and possessions."[51] On the one hand, Luke uses a range of words for what is sold in the two summaries, but on the other hand, as we will see in more detail later, the examples of Barnabas and Ananias and Sapphira show the selling of property which does not seem to include the place where they were living at the time. Walton notes that the references point to properties other than those lived in being sold.[52] This does not necessarily mean that homes were considered in some way separate

---

45. Fitzmyer, *Acts*, 269.
46. Krodel, *Acts*, 92–93.
47. Marshall, *Acts*, 84.
48. Klauck, "Gütergemeinschaft," 69.
49. Blomberg, *Poverty*, 162.
50. Marshall, *Acts*, 84. Haenchen also argues that they did not sell everything, but rather responded to need (Haenchen, *Acts*, 192).
51. Alexander, *Acts People's Commentary*, 37.
52. Walton, "Primitive," 104.

from other possessions and not held in common. It may rather point to a different kind of holding in common. After all while some scholars question the summaries on the basis that that Mary still owns and lives in her house in 12:12,[53] the house is being used for the community and therefore could be argued to being held in some way in common.

Barrett argues that their eschatological beliefs may have prompted their sharing.[54] In a similar vein Haenchen argues that selling would not have been a long-term strategy.[55] However, in 2:45 and 4:34 "the reason given [for sharing] is not eschatological but social."[56] Also, while property is sold, it is not a total pooling, rather a holding in common, with selling happening as needed.

The summary goes on to describe the daily life of the early believers as they spent time together in the temple and in homes. Marshall points out they could just be using the outer courtyards of the temple or they could be participating in the sacrificial worship.[57] It seems likely that the time in the temple included attendance at the Jewish prayers as at the beginning of chapter 3 Peter and John go to the temple at the hour of prayer (3:1).[58] Both meeting in the temple and in homes seem to have included meals as well as praise and prayer. Wendel argues that in 2:46 both the participle clauses (τε . . . τε . . .) are dependent on the verbal phrase μετελάμβανον τροφῆς.[59] Therefore "Man kann nicht nur den zweiten Nebensatz syntaktisch unterordnen, den ersten dagegen als Hauptsatz übersetzen"[60] (It is not possible to subordinate the second clause while translating the first as a main clause). "Aus dieser Übersetzung folgt, daß die τροφή nicht nur hausweise beim Brotbrechen, sondern auch beim täglichen Templeaufenthalt eingenommen wurde"[61] (From this translation it follows that τροφή not only happened in the houses during the breaking of bread, but also during the daily temple meetings).

---

53. Krodel, *Acts*, 94. Johnson notes the summaries cannot be absolute because of the evidence of homes continuing to be owned (Johnson, *Sharing*, 21).

54. Barrett, *Acts*, 168.

55. Haenchen, *Acts*, 233.

56. Bock, *Acts*, 153.

57. Marshall, *Acts*, 85.

58. Schürer notes that while sacrifices were offered at dawn and dusk, in *Ant.* 14.65 Josephus refers to the evening sacrifice being at 3 p.m. (Schürer, Vermes, Millar, and Black, *History*, 2:300–301).

59. Wendel, *Gemeinde*, 183.

60. Ibid., 183.

61. Ibid., 184.

Whether this eating included an agape meal or early form of communion is disputed. However, as Newman and Nida point out the phrase τῇ κλάσει τοῦ ἄρτου in Acts 2:42 "occurs only here and in Luke 24:35,"[62] where it refers to Jesus being made known to Cleopas and his companion, and appears to point to this action being one they had seen before, which could include the breaking of bread at the Last Supper (Luke 22:19). Κλάω and ἄρτος are found together in Luke-Acts predominately in situations that seem to be eucharistic.[63] The possible exceptions are Luke 9:16 in the feeding of the five thousand, which nevertheless has eucharistic verbs (λαμβάνω, δίδωμι, εὐλογέω Luke 22:19) and Acts 27:35, which also has some of the verbs (λαμβάνω, εὐχαριστέω), though interestingly does not talk about Paul giving the bread. Thus, it is likely that the breaking of bread in 2:42 is some form of recollection of the Last Supper and even if the breaking of bread in 2:42 is not sacramental, Luke's choice of words would suggest that he sees the meal as evoking memories of Jesus. Acts 2:46 thus implies that though eating happened both in homes and in the temple, the more formal breaking of bread happened in homes.

Acts 4:32–35

Two chapters later, Luke again summarizes the life of the believers. Between the two summaries, there are examples of some aspects of the summary in chapter 2: praying in the temple (3:1) and at home (4:23–26), wonders and signs (3:7–8), more people believing (4:4), and the believers spending time together and having a common identity (4:23). Luke's summary at the end of chapter 4, which again follows the believers being filled with the Holy Spirit and speaking boldly (4:31) contains many similarities to the chapter 2 summary, leading Ehrhardt to argue that they are from the same report.[64] Both passages speak of unity, an approach to possessions that sees them in some sense as common, practical care being provided for those in need through sale of possessions and distribution, the apostles' teaching, and God's power being seen amongst them. However, there are interesting differences as well as similarities and some of the differences fit with the growth and development of the early Christian group.

Prayer at home and in the temple, and the shared meals, present in the first summary, are missing from the second summary. While it could be argued that the first summary leads into examples of prayer at home and

---

62. Newman and Nida, *Handbook*, 63.
63. Luke 9:16; 22:19; 24:30; Acts 2:46; 20:7, 11; 27:35.
64. Ehrhardt, *Acts*, 20.

in the temple and that Luke chooses to focus on the material sharing in the second summary to lead into the examples of Barnabas and Ananias and Sapphira,[65] this does not explain the absence of the common meals from the second summary. It is possible that the absence of meals from the second summary hints at the issues to come in chapter 6 with the waiting on tables.

In the second summary, instead of those who sell their possessions distributing to those in need, the proceeds are brought καὶ ἐτίθουν παρὰ τοὺς πόδας τῶν ἀποστόλων (4:35), who then distribute it to those in need. Johnson argues from both OT and NT examples that laying something at someone else's feet acknowledges "the power and authority of another over the self and what one has,"[66] and that the point of the second summary is to show the authority of the apostles.[67] However, as Johnson admits while in Josh 10:24, 1 Sam 25:24, Luke 8:35, and Luke 8:41 the authority (or power) of someone is recognized, it is people who fall at the feet of others, or sit at the feet of others.[68] The closest example Johnson provides to placing possessions at the feet of another is the woman who bathes Jesus' feet with her tears and anoints them with oil in Luke 7:37–39. Nevertheless Johnson argues that as possessions function symbolically in Acts, the laying of possessions at the feet of the apostles indicates submission of the person giving.[69] This is plausible, but the symbol could also function in other ways, for example, as a symbol of giving through the apostles to the wider community.

While apostles have authority in the summary, particularly in the combination of testimony and power,[70] the placing of proceeds at the feet of the apostles might rather be showing the transfer of authority over the possessions to the apostles (rather like the use of the sandal in Ruth 4:7). This move to the apostles distributing the proceeds also fits with a larger group in the process of setting up ways of organizing itself as it grew beyond a point where those selling would necessarily know who was in need. Placing the proceeds at the feet of the apostles additionally "transforms the reciprocal interaction, since by having the apostles distribute the goods, the original owner could not act as patron who would make others beholden as clients,"[71]

---

65. Bruce, *Acts*, 100.
66. Johnson, *Acts*, 87. Also Robinson and Wall, *Called*, 72.
67. Johnson, *Acts*, 91.
68. Johnson, *Function*, 202.
69. Ibid., 202.
70. Hume notes that Johnson reads the summary in the light of his experience of Western monasticism, but contextually the authority is due to the signs and wonders, and the proclamation in the face of opposition (Hume, *Early*, 135).
71. Malina and Pilch, *Social-Science*, 46.

because the goods are moved from the control of their former owners to that of the community.[72]

What is sold is also described differently and is more specifically χωρίων ἢ οἰκιῶν (4:34) rather than τὰ κτήματα καὶ τὰς ὑπάρξεις (2:45). This may be indicative of the ongoing need to support those from outside Jerusalem, which could have exhausted the smaller saleable items. Krodel argues that one of the issues (which he also uses to argue that the sharing is not an example of communism) is that the community does not have a means of production.[73] Luke may also tighten his description to fit with the examples he goes on to describe. The selling is again linked to preventing or relieving need.

This prevention and relief of need does not just appear: it follows from the presence of χάρις τε μεγάλη ἦν ἐπὶ πάντας αὐτούς (4:33), thus indicating that Luke sees their community as an outworking of the presence of God's grace.[74]

The summary starts with the group not claiming private ownership but rather ἦν αὐτοῖς πάντα κοινά (4:32), which is then elucidated in the description of the selling. Πωλοῦντες (4:34) is a present participle indicating an ongoing situation of selling.[75] Tannehill argues that verse 32 indicates "a fundamental renunciation of personal ownership, which would be implemented later as needs arose,"[76] while Klauck limits himself to arguing that "Besitzende nicht auf ihre Rechte pochten, sondern ihr Eigentum, etwa ihre Häuser, großzügig zur Verfügung stellten"[77] (Owners did not insist on their rights, rather they placed their belongings, for example their houses, at their disposal). Tannehill points out that Acts 4:32-35 picks up the same verbs (πωλέω, διαδίδωμι) that Jesus uses in Luke 18:22 with the rich ruler[78] where Jesus calls him to sell everything. However, in Acts, it is clear that not all property was sold as while they had possessions and property that was held in common (4:32), later chapters in Acts show they still had property that they were using (12:12). Furthermore, the phrase about selling indicates an ongoing as opposed to one-off selling (4:34).

---

72. Gaventa, *Acts*, 101.
73. Krodel, *Acts*, 117.
74. Robinson and Wall, *Called*, 77.
75. Zerwick and Grosvenor, *Grammatical*, 1:363.
76. Tannehill, "Ethics," 119.
77. Klauck, "Gütergemeinschaft," 69.
78. Tannehill, "Ethics," 119.

While Luke is not describing a situation where everything is sold,[79] his use of verbs which remind the reader of the rich ruler, suggests that he is communicating a significant shift in how individuals in the early church saw (and held) their own possessions and commending that shift to his readers. The specific description of what is sold, and the examples of selling at the end of chapter 4 and beginning of chapter 5 may limit those who could contribute in this way. This leads Kim to argue that it was less a common fund, rather "benevolent contributions of the wealthy towards the poor neighbors."[80] However, while only those who had fields or houses could contribute in this way, all could hold what they had, little or large, in common and consider it not just their personal possession. Additionally, what is sold is then placed at the apostles' feet and is thus transferred from being an individual's gift to being part of a wider way of holding possessions.

Luke's language in both summaries picks up Greek and biblical ideals. Οὐδὲ γὰρ ἐνδεής τις ἦν ἐν αὐτοῖς (4:34) picks up the language of Deut 15:4 (LXX): ὅτι οὐκ ἔσται ἐν σοὶ ἐνδεής. Καρδία and ψυχή of 4:32 can be seen in ὅλης τῆς καρδίας σου καὶ ἐξ ὅλης τῆς ψυχῆς σου καὶ ἐξ ὅλης τῆς δυνάμεώς σου (Deut 6:5) and the ψυχὴ μία in ὁ κατάλοιπος ισραηλ ψυχὴ μία (1 Chr 12:38). Bock notes a number of other places in the OT where the idea of unity of heart and soul appears (Deut 10:12, 11:13, Jer 32:39 [39:39 LXX]).[81] Dupont argues that Luke uses the reference to unity of heart and soul to indicate that "it is the spiritual unity existing among Christians which leads to their sharing material goods."[82]

However, similar language is also found in Greek thought and Gaventa notes the similarities with "other philosophical and religious groups that stressed the importance of friendship."[83] Friendship was often described as involving being a single soul and there were references to holding things in common. For example, Plutarch in his "Dialogue on Love" notes the phrase κοινὰ τὰ φίλων (*Mor.* 767E) is only valid where the souls of the people are joined. For Cicero, "the effect of friendship is to make, as it were, one soul out of many" (*Amic.* 25.92). Diogenes Laertius notes that Aristotle's reply, to the question of what a friend is, was μία ψυχὴ δύο σώμασιν ἐνοικοῦσα (A single soul dwelling in two bodies) (Diogenes Laertius *LEP* 5.19–20) and that Bion misuses the maxim Κοινὰ τὰ φίλων (friends share in common)

---

79. Fitzmyer, *Acts*, 314.
80. Kim, *Stewardship*, 252.
81. Bock, *Acts*, 213.
82. Dupont, *Salvation*, 96.
83. Gaventa, *Acts*, 81.

(Diogenes Laertius *LEP* 4.53).[84] Therefore, Luke's use of language would also "have reminded Luke's original readers of the notion of friendship which was prevalent at that time in the Greco-Roman world."[85]

However, these phrases operated as proverbs and as Mitchell points out they were used in different ways in different texts,[86] so how is Luke using them? Johnson asserts that the use of these phrases is analogous to their use in descriptions of a past Golden Age and that therefore Luke uses them to denote the ideal beginnings of the church.[87] However, Mitchell argues that Luke has a wider purpose in using these friendship proverbs and argues that he "used the friendship traditions to unify his community across social lines"[88] and to challenge "the reciprocity ethic."[89] We will examine friendship in Greco-Roman writings and then consider how Luke uses the friendship proverbs to draw on some aspects of the ideals of Greco-Roman friendship and yet paint a distinctive picture.

In descriptions of a Golden Age, for example in Plato's *Republic*, sharing is between members of a particular class, the Guardians, so that they can fulfil a role (*Resp.* 416D, 416E, 449C).[90] However, such sharing is not always seen as beneficial. In Aristotle's *Politics* there is an acknowledgement of the ideal of unity and communal holding, but Aristotle goes on to point out that people neglect commonly held property (1261b).

However, references to unity and sharing are not limited to descriptions of a Golden Age or politics. Having expounded some of the difficulties of sharing possessions and communal holding of possessions, Aristotle argues for an improvement in virtue so that those who are friends ἰδίας γὰρ ἕκαστος τὴν κτῆσιν ἔχων τὰ μὲν χρήσιμα ποιεῖ τοῖς φίλοις τοῖς δὲ χρῆται κοινοῖς (while owning their property privately put their own possessions at the service of their friends and make use of their friends' possessions as common property) (*Pol.* 1263a). Epicurus argues against holding property in common because common ownership implies a mistrust of friends (*LEP* 10.11).[91] Thus, Dupont argues that in Greco-Roman descriptions of sharing amongst or between friends: "There is no question in this case of

---

84. Aristotle also picks up this proverb in *Nic. Eth.* 9.2.
85. Dupont, *Salvation*, 97.
86. Mitchell, "Social," 256.
87. Johnson, *Sharing*, 120–21.
88. Mitchell, "Social," 258.
89. Ibid., 259.
90. Klauck, "Gütergemeinschaft," 49.
91. Dupont, *Salvation*, 90.

legal transfer of titles, for each individual remains owner of his possessions, but affection for his brothers impels each one to put what he has at their disposal."[92]

In *Nichomachean Ethics* Aristotle speaks of the way that friendship involves affection (1159a), approves of the proverb κοινὰ τὰ φίλων (1159b), and later agrees that friends have one soul (1163b). Thus, to assist a friend with money is to behave virtuously as a friend (1130a). However, this sharing between friends is based on equality between the people and equal shares (1131a). Aristotle does mention the existence of some unequal friendships, for example between husband and wife, and between parents and children (1158b), however he goes on to say that when inequality arises in friendship the people involved "no longer remain nor indeed expect to remain friends" (1158b–1159a). Thus, Hume argues that Greco-Roman friendships were normally between equals who could show reciprocity to one another and "The general rule in all kinds of friendship is that reciprocity is in some way expected or required."[93] Mitchell notes that in both horizontal and vertical (patron-client relationship) friendship "giving was done with an eye to receiving, whether it be for further material gain, honor, or prestige."[94]

When we look at Luke's summary passages and at the Greek ideas of friendship we do see some parallels. There is the sense of sharing at the beginning of time and the sharing at the beginning of the church. There is a holding in common of property, which seems to involve each person retaining their property, but holding it in common, ready to put it at the disposal of the others.

However, there are also differences. There is no mention of a return for the giving in the summaries, which fits with Luke 6:34–35a; 14:12–14; and Acts 20:35.[95] Dupont argues that Luke contrasts the unity of heart and mind with instances of "one's own." So Judas goes εἰς τὸν τόπον τὸν ἴδιον (1:25),[96] while the fishermen leave τὰ ἴδια (Luke 18:28). Mitchell notes that Acts 3, with the healing of the man, would normally be seen as a benefaction, yet Peter does not expect a return.[97] We have also noted the way that the placing of the proceeds of the sales at the apostles' feet circumvents the possibility of building individual patron-client relationships.

92. Ibid., 91.
93. Hume, *Early*, 52–53.
94. Mitchell, "Social," 264.
95. Ibid., 266–67.
96. While Mitchell argues that Judas also "buys a field of his own" (ibid., 268), this is not quite as specific in the Greek where simply ἐκτήσατο χωρίον (1:18).
97 Ibid., 271.

So Luke appears to be echoing the Greco-Roman idea of friendship involving holding property in common and sharing, while undermining the idea of reciprocity in friendship.[98] This is reinforced by the fact that while Luke does use friendship language, in these passages he does not call the members of the early church friends or brothers, but believers, which points to faith as the uniting factor and motivation.[99] The way that Luke picks up both OT language and ideals and Greco-Roman language and ideals[100] would also suggest that he is not simply lifting the Greco-Roman model and using it without modification.

Acts 4:36—5:11

As with the first summary, Luke follows the second summary with examples of what he has summarized: one positive and one negative. Luke uses this moment to introduce Barnabas, a Levite from Cyprus, who sells a field that belongs to him and then brings the money to the feet of the apostles. Barnabas is described as selling ἀγροῦ (4:37), not all his fields, or all his property, but a single one. It could have been the sum total of his fields, but is unlikely to be all he possessed as he presumably lived somewhere that was not a field. However, the fact that Barnabas has a field in the first place leads to questions. Luke reports that Barnabas was a Levite (3:36). Therefore according to OT law he should not have possessed any land (Num 18:20; Deut 10:9; 12:12; Josh 14:3–4). There are a number of ways to explain this situation. The field might have been part of the pastureland referred to in Josh 14:4. Alternatively the field could have been in Cyprus[101] or somewhere else outside Judaea, which seems plausible given that Barnabas is described as a native of Cyprus. Then the field would be outside the apportioning of the promised land referred to in the OT passages. A third possibility is that the field was in Judea and that Barnabas, like many other Levites[102] was not holding to this OT law on land as tightly as it he might have.

---

98. Indeed Mitchell argues that "Luke . . . uses friendship to equalize relationships in his own community" (ibid., 272).

99. Dupont, *Salvation*, 103.

100. Haenchen argues that "Luke has here completely fused his OT heritage, transmitted via LXX, with Greek material" (Haenchen, *Acts*, 231).

101. Malina and Pilch, *Social-Science*, 48; Alexander, *Acts People's Commentary*, 47; Krodel suggests in Cyprus or that the law was no longer in force (Krodel, *Acts*, 119), while Marshall argues the location of the field is unclear (Marshall, *Acts*, 110).

102. Josephus describes himself in *Life* 15 as being from a priestly family, yet in *Life* 76, he is seen possessing land and then receiving more land from Titus Caesar. See Bock, *Acts*, 216; Robinson and Wall, *Called*, 75; and Witherington, *Acts*, 209.

If it is this third option, then the selling of the field might be seen not just as an example of the summary passage, but also as Barnabas renewing the covenant and thus abiding by OT law being unable to own land.[103] This might then reduce its force as an example for Luke's readers if they did not see themselves as needing to abide by levitical norms, though it would build the image of the early church community living out the covenant. However, Luke passes no comment on the appropriateness or otherwise of Barnabas having a field in the first place and goes on to describe Ananias and Sapphira as a counter example. If Barnabas' example is primarily of a Levite returning to obedience to OT law, we might expect Ananias and Sapphira to provide a second example of levitical or priestly families selling their land, but there is no indication that Ananias and Sapphira are from a levitical or priestly background. Therefore it seems more likely that Barnabas is presented as a more generic positive example, even if the third option is the correct one and Barnabas is partly motivated by the OT law.

Several scholars, including Conzelmann, suggest that the reason that Luke only gives one positive example is that Barnabas was an exception and that Luke creates the summary by generalising from this example.[104] However, Finger raises a wider question of how we interpret Barnabas' giving. She observes that modern scholars may be using middle-class assumptions in approaching the text and comments that Barnabas is probably one of the few who owned land[105] and therefore was one of the few who was able to give in this way.

Luke does not just provide a positive example alongside the summary, but also a negative example: that of Ananias and Sapphira. Acts 5:1–11 is not an easy passage and Conzelmann concludes that "no historical kernel can be extracted."[106] While the passage is difficult to interpret, this does not necessarily mean that it wholly ahistorical, indeed Bock argues that "The very uniqueness of the story argues for its credibility."[107] The example of Ananias and Sapphira does not fit with an idealized picture of the early church, but rather shows that Luke is ready to consider problems in the early church.[108]

Ananias, with the consent of Sapphira, like Barnabas, sells a piece of property. Again, there is no mention of whether or not it is all his property,

---

103. Finger, *Widows*, 133.

104. Conzelmann, *Acts*, 36; Haenchen, *Acts*, 233; Dupont, *Salvation*, 93–94; Munck, *Acts*, 38–39.

105. Finger, *Widows*, 9, 133.

106. Conzelmann, *Acts*, 37.

107. Bock, *Acts*, 220. Also Jervell argues for a historical situation behind the narrative (Jervell, *Apostelgeschichte*, 199).

108. Bock, *Acts*, 150.

just that they sold a particular piece. However, unlike Barnabas, Ananias ἐνέγκας μέρος τι παρὰ τοὺς πόδας τῶν ἀποστόλων ἔθηκεν (5:2). What follows is a series of questions from Peter which are not straightforward to understand and where different scholars hypothesize different situations to explain Peter's words.

Peter's initial question picks up the words about Satan entering Judas (Luke 22:3) and accuses Ananias of lying to the Holy Spirit and νοσφίσασθαι ἀπὸ τῆς τιμῆς τοῦ χωρίου (5:3). Νοσφίσασθαι is often translated as "to keep back" (NRSV, NIV), but its use elsewhere suggests a stronger sense. Capper notes that the use of the verb in the NT, Apocrypha, and OT (LXX) points to stealing or pilfering, to taking what is not theirs to have (Titus 2:10; 2 Macc 4:32; Josh 7:1) and thus argues that "we are dealing with a matter of 'theft', i.e. that they had no right to retain any part of the proceeds of the sale of their property,"[109] a view also held by Lake and Cadbury, who conclude that "It is possible that the author of Acts regards the field of Ananias as thus vowed or dedicated before it was converted into money."[110] However, this is less clear since Peter goes on to ask οὐχὶ μένον σοὶ ἔμενεν καὶ πραθὲν ἐν τῇ σῇ ἐξουσίᾳ ὑπῆρχεν (5:4); this would indicate a situation where even when it was sold, the proceeds belonged to Ananias and Sapphira. So what actually constitutes the problem? Klauck highlights a tension in 5:2-3, about whether the issue is the withholding or the lying about the withholding.[111] It is possible that through the action of bringing the proceeds to the apostles' feet or through his words as he did so, Ananias presented what he was giving as the whole of the proceeds from the sale and thus that withholding from the amount constituted lying. Gaventa argues for an interpretation whereby the land and proceeds belong to Ananias and Sapphira, until they place it at the feet of the apostles, when the whole of the sale belongs to the group.[112]

The words of Peter also help us to interpret further the summary passage for while οὐδὲ εἷς τι τῶν ὑπαρχόντων αὐτῷ ἔλεγεν ἴδιον εἶναι ἀλλ' ἦν αὐτοῖς ἅπαντα κοινά (4:32), it is clear that it was still private property and it was the owner of the property who then took the choice to sell and bring the proceeds. Marshall concludes that "the things which each person possessed evidently continued to be his own property until it was found necessary to sell them for the common good."[113]

---

109. Capper, "Holy Community," 122.
110. Lake and Cadbury, Acts, 4:50.
111. Klauck, "Gütergemeinschaft," 70.
112. Gaventa, Acts, 102-3.
113. Marshall, Acts, 108.

Capper conceives of a situation similar to that in Qumran with a staged entry into community where property is handed over, but retained separately before being merged into the main amount. He discounts other options including: "dedication of the property in advance of sale,"[114] on the basis that it does not fit with Peter's assumption that the money is theirs after the sale; and a declaration of intent after the sale,[115] arguing that Peter would then have referred back to this declaration.

In Capper's model, the money would have continued to be Ananias and Sapphira's even once it had been handed over, which leads Capper to suggest that the Hebrew verb behind πραθέν may be מכר, which he argues has a wider meaning than sell and can include handing over. Peter would then be asking rhetorically "And after it was handed over, were not the proceeds at your disposal?" with Peter emphasizing "that Ananias was yielding his possession (i.e., control) of his property, but not his ownership of it, to the community."[116] However, there are various problems with this argument. First, this model presumes that this piece of property was all that they had, which is not clear from ἐπώλησεν κτῆμα (5:1). Second, the summaries both also suggest an ongoing selling and handing over in response to need, which would indicate that the proceeds were needed and used rather than being kept separate and that the situation was more fluid than that of a staged novitiate. Third, the early Acts accounts of entry into the Christian community do not generally show evidence of a staged entry; rather they show an immediate entry (2:37-39; 5:14; 8:36-39). The examples where there seems to be more of a process are Paul, where it takes time for other believers to accept him; and the inclusion of the Gentiles, where it takes time for the whole of the church community to accept the Gentile believers. However, neither of these equates to a staged novitiate.

Peter's accusation of lying suggests that either by their words (after the sale, possibly as they brought the proceeds) or by their actions, they had indicated that the amount of money they brought was the entire proceeds of the sale. The problem is then squaring the possibility, presumed by Peter's words, that they could have brought only a portion of the proceeds if they had been honest about it, with the summaries which describe a situation where no one claimed private ownership (4:32).[117]

---

114. Capper, "Holy Community," 118.

115. Ibid., 119.

116. Ibid., 125.

117. Harrill suggests that the judgment is in the context of the oath rituals often used in business/property transactions which included a self-curse for perjury (Harrill, "Judgment," 353).

It may be that there was an understanding that a sale might have more than one purpose: the person selling might have a particular need, which they would supply out of the sale, as well as contributing to the fund which would supply others in need. Money that was not handed over, but held openly by the individual who sold property, need not have been considered "their own": however, with Ananias and Sapphira, that which is withheld is hidden and therefore breaks the trust implicit in holding everything in common (even when it is not put in one pot). Alternatively it may be that the main practice of the group was of holding in common, but that different people became part of the group and participated in the group in different ways and at different speeds, with an understanding that honesty and transparency was paramount in their interactions with one another.

Acts 6:1–6

The other passage which points to some kind of shared possessions or community is Acts 6:1–6 where Luke recounts a complaint from the Hellenists that their widows are being neglected in the daily distribution of food (6:1).

This situation arises in the context of the growth of the church[118] and Krodel notes that the account is bounded by descriptions of growth (6:1, 7),[119] which leads Alexander to suggest that this increase in numbers leads to the church outgrowing "its original structures."[120] The situation also occurs in the context of persecution and Finger argues Luke uses the link between the end of chapter 5 and the beginning of chapter 6 to indicate that the issue arises at the same time as the persecution.[121]

The issue arises between the Hebrews and the Hellenists.[122] Bock and Bruce suggest that language is the main factor in distinguishing between the Hebrews and the Hellenists, with the Hellenists being those who used Greek[123] and who may have attended separate synagogues where Greek was used.[124] The Hellenists could be pilgrims who had come for Pentecost or

---

118. Jervell, *Apostelgeschichte*, 221.

119. Krodel, *Acts*, 131.

120. Alexander, *Acts People's Commentary*, 54.

121. Finger, *Widows*, 252.

122. Barrett notes that the term Hellenist is used by Luke in different ways (Barrett, *Acts*, 1:309).

123. Bock, *Acts*, 258; also Pao, "Waiters," 128; Jervell, *Apostelgeschichte*, 216; Fitzmyer, *Acts*, 346.

124. Bruce, *Acts*, 120.

who had come to die in the city,¹²⁵ but Fiensey argues they could also be Greek speaking Jews from the lower city.¹²⁶ Thus, the Hellenists could include relative newcomers (who came to Jerusalem for Pentecost and who had converted), newly settled (who had come to Jerusalem to die), and long term residents. However, despite the difference in language (and possibly synagogues), it seems likely that Hellenists and Hebrews did meet together in some form—if they were always separate why did the Hellenists complain? Also the summary accounts relate the believers all being together and it seems likely Barnabas was a Hellenist, given that he was from Cyprus.¹²⁷

In order to understand what went wrong and the solution, it may help to consider to what ἐν τῇ διακονίᾳ τῇ καθημερινῇ (6:1) refers. Bruce envisages money from the common fund being handing over by almoners.¹²⁸ Malina and Pilch highlight the NRSV translation of "distribution of food," but note that διακονία can have a more general meaning and suggest that the seven were some sort of supervising managers.¹²⁹ However, Capper argues that the help is given in the context of meal-fellowship¹³⁰ because Luke has already highlighted meal-fellowship in Acts 2:42, 46 and there is continued attestation in the NT of meal-fellowship (Acts 20:7–11, 1 Cor 11:17–34, Jude 12).¹³¹

The use of διακονεῖν τραπέζαις (6:2) also does not necessarily point one way or the other. Τράπεζα can be used of a table in the tabernacle, a table for a meal, figuratively for food, but also as a table that money-changers use.¹³² Pao notes that Luke uses τράπεζα for both a banker's counter (Luke 19:23) and a dining table (Luke 16:21; 22:21).¹³³ Διακονία similarly can include service as part of "preparations for a meal," the office of prophets and apostles, and aid support or distribution.¹³⁴ Pao notes Luke uses διακονία alongside τράπεζα in his account of the Lord's Supper (Luke 22:21–30).¹³⁵ He argues

---

125. Haenchen, *Acts*, 266.
126. Fiensy, "Composition," 235.
127. Finger, *Widows*, 161.
128. Bruce, *Acts*, 120–21.
129. Malina and Pilch, *Social-Science*, 55.
130. Capper, "Reciprocity," 4.
131. Ibid., 3–14.
132. BDAG, 1013.
133. Pao, "Waiters," 135.
134. BDAG, 230.
135. Pao, "Waiters," 135.

that as the words are rarely used together elsewhere, Luke is indicating serving at a meal. In addition, 2:45 and 4:35 use different words for distribution.[136]

Finger argues that the reference to serving at tables points back to the communal meals of Acts 2, which included everyone.[137] Finger notes that it is important for us to remember that in first century Palestine most are poor, not a minority, therefore the question is less about whether a few people are receiving alms, but rather whether everyone is being included in the provision.[138] It does seem likely that there could be large numbers who could be dependent on such provision. Not only were many poor in Palestine, but there would also be those who had come from Galilee with the group of disciples and were away from their homes and livelihoods, as well as those who had come to Jerusalem for Pentecost, converted and may have stayed on for some time. In addition as persecution arose, it may have led to believers being denied other provision or finding it difficult to get daily work. For larger numbers in need, buying and cooking together would be more economical. Wendel's analysis of 2:46,[139] shows the early church ate together both in the temple courts and in homes and gives a picture where distribution could have happened in and through shared meals in the temple courts.[140] Therefore it seems likely that the provision being described in Acts 6 occurred in the context of meal-fellowship.

In this situation of distribution for daily provision of meals, who is being overlooked and how? As Capper points out the fact that people are being overlooked and are in need does not contradict the presence of sharing as, if proceeds of sales were placed at the feet of the apostles, it would have been in the hands of a few, rather than accessible to all.[141]

This seems to have led to some people being overlooked as distributions were made, specifically the Hellenistic widows.[142] Finger notes that, in first-century Palestine, widows could be vulnerable. If they had living sons, they would probably be cared for by them and they could keep part of their dowry, but this would have kept them for only about a year after their

---

136. Ibid., 135–36.

137. Finger, *Widows*, 257.

138. Ibid., 255–56.

139. See pp. 46–50.

140. Wendel goes on to suggest that the eating together in the temple could have been open to more than the believers and sees evangelism taking place in the context of the sharing of meals (Wendel, *Gemeinde*, 219–20).

141. Capper, "Palestianian Setting," 350.

142. Jervell notes that wives were generally younger than their husbands as background to the presence of widows (Jervell, *Apostelgeschichte*, 216).

husband's death.[143] Finger notes the options of remarriage and prostitution as forms of survival and argues that this latter option would not have been open to Christian women. Additionally prostitutes who had left their former life to follow Jesus, would have found it difficult to remarry.[144] Spencer argues that Hellenist widows were more vulnerable than other widows as they were "isolated from wider kinship support networks in their Diaspora homelands."[145] While this would have been true for Diaspora Hellenists, it would not have been the case for Jerusalem Hellenists. Haenchen argues the Hellenists and Hebrews may have been seen as distinct by outsiders so that one was persecuted and the other not,[146] however in Acts 5:18 it is the apostles who are arrested, who are presumably Hebrews rather than Hellenists.

Finger suggests an entirely different interpretation of the overlooking of the widows. She argues that the situation in Acts 6 arises in the context of daily meals,[147] where most of the tasks of preparing and clearing up are seen as primarily female,[148] that the early church may have had a particular role for widows within this,[149] and that the women may have been competing for various roles and honors involved with serving, or that those who served the women at the end may have refused to serve the Hellenist widows.[150] This provides another angle to consider the picture from. Acts 6 does arise in the context of daily meals. However, there does not seem to be clear evidence or a way to prove that the overlooking is of positions rather than provision. Finger's proposal presumes that everyone eats together and then certain women are missed out in the honors. However, this raises the question of why it becomes a particular issue at this time and the solution in Acts 6 suggests that the group of believers may not generally be meeting all together, for προσκαλεσάμενοι δὲ οἱ δώδεκα τὸ πλῆθος τῶν μαθητῶν (6:2), rather than simply addressing the issue when they are together in the temple courts, which if the situation in 2:46 were continuing is what might be expected. It is possible that a change in context of meals and provision is taking place that has precipitated the overlooking of the widows.

We suggest a third possibility that could encompass the overlooking of the widows either in being served or in roles in the serving. Acts 2:46

---

143. Finger, *Widows*, 211.
144. Ibid., 211–13.
145. Spencer, *Journeying*, 76.
146. Haenchen, *Acts*, 266.
147. Finger, *Widows*, 257.
148. Ibid., 262.
149. Ibid., 213, 260.
150. Ibid., 264.

suggests that the early church had meals in two ways: in homes and in the temple courts. The persecution and growth described in the subsequent chapters, and particularly noted in 5:40—6:1 may have made it difficult to meet together in the temple court to eat. The early church community would then have needed to find other ways of managing meals and food distribution. With people from different locations around the city and different language backgrounds, it may have been easy to overlook particular people either as recipients or for roles in the distribution of food. In this third possibility, those appointed need to have a connection to the Hellenists, to be able to oversee the process of food distribution (or who gets to distribute the food), and probably to have some form of leadership role as the persecution may have made it difficult for the whole church to gather together for teaching and prayer as well as sharing meals.

Whether the widows were being overlooked in the roles given or in the food shared, or both, a problem arises in the process. The early church responds by προσκαλεσάμενοι δὲ οἱ δώδεκα τὸ πλῆθος τῶν μαθητῶν, which as Finger points out indicates the significance of this daily provision in their sight.[151] Seven men are then appointed to deal with the issue. Those who are appointed have Greek names.[152] Their exact remit is not clear as when we come across them later in Acts, they are preaching, evangelising, and being martyred (Acts 7; 8:5, 26–40), which leads several scholars to point to the main point of the story being to introduce the seven as leaders for the Hellenist community.[153] However, as Barrett points out "it would be bad writing first of all to make up a job for them and then represent them as neglecting it for another."[154] Therefore overseeing the provision is part of their remit.

Spencer sees the appointment of the seven as "resisting Jesus' comprehensive ministerial program."[155] However, the text points to the whole group knowing what is happening and communication between them. They come to a decision together. That decision is for provision, rather than against provision and does not suggest that it was a lower standard of provision that was afforded to the Hellenist widows. The summaries in Acts 2 and 4 do not indicate that everyone sells everything, but rather that individuals do not hold their possessions as their own and therefore are ready to sell and give when there is a need (Acts 2:45; 4:34–35). Therefore provision for

---

151. Ibid., 267.

152. Ibid., 272.

153. Haenchen, *Acts*, 265; Capper, "Palestianian Setting," 354—includes care as part of the leadership remit.

154. Barrett, *Acts*, 306.

155. Spencer, *Journeying*, 66.

widows, irrespective of whether it is through shared meals or money is not necessarily a step back from this position, but potentially an outworking of it. The introduction to the issue indicates that it takes place in the context of change, both increasing numbers of believers and persecution, which would have made it harder for all the believers to meet together and eat together as regularly as they did in the initial stages. This growth would also have meant there was a natural need for more leaders and therefore when the seven were appointed to oversee the provision, their remit may well have grown. The criteria for choosing the seven (6:3) are ones that could also be used to choose those to be involved in teaching and mission.

Other Key Acts Passages

While there are a number of passages in the early chapters of Acts that relate to the use of possessions among believers, this picture does not continue through Acts. However, there are a number of passages which touch upon issues to do with money, possessions, and giving, primarily through their descriptions of individuals. In Acts 8:18–23 Simon offers money in exchange for the power of praying for people to be given the Holy Spirit. Peter's response (8:20) makes it clear that God's gift cannot be bought with money. In 9:36 Dorcas, also known as Tabitha, is described as πλήρης ἔργων ἀγαθῶν καὶ ἐλεημοσυνῶν ὧν ἐποίει.

In Acts 10:1 Cornelius is described as ποιῶν ἐλεημοσύνας πολλὰς τῷ λαῷ. It is notable that his devoutness and prayer are mentioned alongside his acts of mercy and almsgiving. In Philippi, Lydia's response to believing and being baptized is to extend hospitality to Paul and Timothy (16:15).

In Paul's speech to the Ephesian elders and at the very end of Acts there are hints of how Paul lived. Acts 20:33–35 indicates Paul worked to support himself and others. Paul then uses Jesus' words to exhort the elders to follow his example in supporting the weak: Μακάριόν ἐστιν μᾶλλον διδόναι ἢ λαμβάνειν (20:35).

At the end of Acts, Luke describes Paul under house arrest in Rome where Ἐνέμεινεν δὲ διετίαν ὅλην ἐν ἰδίῳ μισθώματι, καὶ ἀπεδέχετο πάντας τοὺς εἰσπορευομένους πρὸς αὐτόν (28:30). There are a couple of ways of translating this phrase. Bock points out that μισθώματι is a NT hapax and may suggest "earning," but that Ἐνέμεινεν can suggest the locale giving two options: either Paul lived "at his own expense" or in his "own rented quarters."[156] In the first instance Paul is the one responsible for financing his stay, while in the second, he is in his own quarters and Bock suggests

---

156. Bock, *Acts*, 757.

that the Philippian contribution may have helped pay for it. Paul welcomed those who came to him, whether this was simply to discuss with them, or a wider hospitality is unclear, but it seems plausible that Paul's welcome may have included hospitality or some sharing of food as some of his visitors spent the whole day with him (28:23).

As well as the examples of individuals who show mercy, give alms, and work to support themselves and others, there is 11:19–30 with the account of the gift from Antioch and Paul's description in 24:17 of how ἐλεημοσύνας ποιήσων εἰς τὸ ἔθνος μου παρεγενόμην, which Bock sees as referring to the collection.[157] In chapter 4 we will look in greater detail at the gift from the church in Antioch to the believers in Judaea and then in chapter 6 at the collection.

The Example of the Early Church

So given these different passages and examples, what example of theology and practice does the early church give and how does Luke intend his readers to interpret his account?

Various issues have led to questions about the historical basis of Luke's description of the early community's sharing and whether it is, or whether Luke intends it to be, an example for his readers to follow. First, the tensions and discontinuities between the early and later chapters of Acts,[158] and the idealization present in the summary passages[159] have led some scholars to question the historicity of the descriptions.[160] However, the presence of idealization does not mean a description is ahistorical, for example Philo and Josephus idealize their descriptions of the Essenes.[161] Similarly, Kim argues the presence of internal evidence in the named positive and negative examples, and external evidence in the Qumran and Essene communities suggest that the description has a historical basis.[162]

Even if there is a historical basis to the account, we should not necessarily assume that Luke intends it to be an example for his readers. Several scholars argue that sharing happened in the early church, but led to impoverishment and the need for others beyond Jerusalem to support the early church. Bruce suggests that funds running out and the famine led to

---

157. Ibid., 693.
158. Capper, "Reciprocity," 5.
159. Capper, "Palestianian Setting," 325.
160. Conzelmann, *Acts*, 24.
161. Capper, "Jesus," 77.
162. Kim, *Stewardship*, 229–31; also Capper, "Palestianian Setting," 335–36.

dependency in the Jerusalem church,[163] while Dupont suggests such giving may be behind "the impoverishment of the whole community"[164] and Conzelmann asserts "Luke does not present this way of life as a norm for the organization of the church in his own time."[165]

However, the difficulties and need in the Jerusalem church may arise out of the specific social and political context in Jerusalem.[166] Haenchen notes the presence of "famine and continued unrest"[167] and Theissen comments on the inequalities in distribution of goods and overpopulation.[168] It is possible that those in particular need might move to Jerusalem "to beg from those who came to the Temple."[169] In addition the presence of those from outside the area in the church, and persecution may have made it more difficult for the early church. These factors mean that the church in Jerusalem could easily be in need without the sharing in Acts 2 and 4 being the cause of that need. Indeed, Finger argues that the survival of the community in Jerusalem "may very well be attributed to their community of goods."[170] Therefore it seems unlikely that Luke intends the summary passages to be a negative example for his readers.

We have already noted that history in the ancient world was often recounted to edify the reader.[171] The presence of idealized motifs may imply that Luke intends his readers to aspire to emulate the examples presented. Hume argues that Luke crafts his summaries is "to present his readers with an idealized model of life in their own congregations,"[172] which should include sharing possessions.[173] However, the summary passages providing an example to Luke's readers need not mean that Luke presumes that they will reproduce the situation. Kim argues that in Luke's gospel the disciples

---

163. Bruce, *Acts*, 101.

164. Dupont, *Salvation*, 94.

165. Conzelmann, *Acts*, 24.

166. Some issues are questioned, for example Sanders argues that Roman taxes were set with the local situation in mind and therefore would have taken into account the temple taxes and tithes (Sanders, *Judaism*, 162, 167).

167. Haenchen, *Acts*, 235.

168. Theissen, *Followers*, 40–42.

169. Walton, "Primitive," 109.

170. Finger, *Widows*, 140.

171. Pervo, *Acts*, 21.

172. Hume, *Early*, 12. Hume is here referring to an unpublished PhD thesis: William Andy Chambers "An Evaluation of Characteristic Activity in a Model Church as set Forth by the Summary Narratives of Acts," 227–30. Also Wendel, *Gemeinde*, 281–83.

173. Hume, *Early*, 147.

are seen as models to follow,[174] but that Luke was encouraging almsgiving rather than community of goods.[175] Kim's conclusion is based on the variety of examples presented in both the gospel and Acts. If we are to take the variety of material seriously, what kind of example is Luke giving us through the summary passages? Both Capper and Kim argue for two kinds of discipleship.

Capper argues that what we see in Jesus' followers in the gospels and in Acts are forms of virtuoso religion, with a similar framework to that seen in the Essene and Qumran communities.[176] In this model, there are two standards for those who are followers of Jesus.[177] Those who are in the traveling group[178] are required to give up everything as they learn about using spiritual power[179] and take on a calling involving teaching and authority.[180] This was partly to give moral legitimacy,[181] so that they could speak incisively into the lives of others. Those "not called to wield spiritual authority"[182] had private property, but practiced hospitality and generosity.[183] These two forms of discipleship could explain the situation with Ananias and Sapphira.[184] Capper argues that in placing the proceeds at the feet of the apostles, Ananias and Sapphira are signifying their desire to become members of the virtuoso group. Capper hypothesizes that as the early church grows, the gospel spreads to new groups who are "not incorporated into the central property-sharing group,"[185] but that the sharing seen in the early summaries continues with the presence of peripatetic missionaries who renounce possessions and who were supported by others.[186]

While we agree that the expansion of the church brought changes to the way that possessions were shared, Capper's model of virtuoso religion relies on Barnabas, Ananias, and Sapphira bringing all that they have to the common fund and, as we have commented earlier, this is not necessarily the

---

174. Kim, *Stewardship*, 93.
175. Ibid., 231.
176. Capper, "Jesus," 72.
177. Ibid., 63.
178. Ibid., 64.
179. Ibid., 68.
180. Ibid., 71.
181. Ibid., 73.
182. Ibid.
183. Ibid.
184. Ibid., 78.
185. Ibid.
186. Ibid., 76, 79.

case. Also the model in the gospels[187] is that those who become part of the traveling group leave what they have, as opposed to necessarily putting it into the common pot. The models presented in the gospels and Acts seem more varied than simply a virtuoso and a non-virtuoso group: people give and contribute in different ways, not simply in two ways. For example, there are women who travel with and contribute to the common purse while others leave their possessions to follow.[188]

Kim also suggests that we see two kinds of disciple: itinerant and sedentary.[189] Kim argues that Luke has a particular interest in the sedentary disciple.[190] In such sedentary discipleship, and for Luke in general, the emphasis is not on renunciation, but on the right use of wealth.[191] Kim argues that Luke's repeated use of the master-servant relationships[192] and stewards[193] provide a motif for sedentary disciples (and particularly for the rich within Luke's community[194]) to use in how they approach possessions.[195] Kim argues that the fund in Acts 2 and 4 is used to support widows, and church leaders who had left their jobs. While it is likely that the fund was used to support these two groups, it is not clear that it is only these two groups. In both 2:45 and 4:35, those who receive are described much more generally as those in need. Also giving, or at least holding in common does not seem to be specifically limited to the rich. Kim's suggestion of the stewardship motif is helpful in how we understand what Luke is communicating through his gospel and Acts. However, in the summaries, relying solely on this motif or interpretative matrix would ignore many of the elements within the text. It is to examining the details of the example presented in the early chapters of Acts that we now turn.

First, the example provided is not static, but one where the changing situation leads to changing practice. In 2:45, it is those who sell their possessions who distribute to those in need, while once the community is larger, the proceeds of sales are brought to the feet of the apostles and the proceeds then appear to be distributed from a central point (4:35). Then when the

---

187. See pp. 15–16.
188. See pp. 17–18.
189. Kim, *Stewardship*, 100, 102.
190. Ibid., 109.
191. Ibid.
192. Ibid., 128.
193. Ibid., 130.
194. Ibid., 109.
195. Ibid., 130.

group grows further and issues arise in the daily distribution, men are appointed to new positions for the task (6:3).

Second, it is an example that occurs in very particular circumstances, in a society where there was already the example of the Essenes, in Jerusalem where there would have been higher numbers of those in need, and shortly after the crucifixion and resurrection, when there would have been Galilean followers of Jesus who were away from their livelihoods and support structures.

Third, the sharing in the summary passages is linked to the presence of God's grace and the Holy Spirit. Both summaries follow the believers being filled with the Holy Spirit (2:1–4; 4:31) and the second summary describes the grace among them (4:33). This leads Klauck to comment, "Lukas versteht die Gütergemeinschaft als sichtbares Werk des Geistes, der in der Gemeinde wirkt"[196] ("Luke understands the community of goods as a visible work of the Spirit who works in the community").

Fourth, this work of the Spirit leads to spiritual unity, where the believers are together and of one mind and heart, viewing their possessions in common and not claiming private ownership. Dupont argues that there is a virtuous circle whereby:

> Union of hearts and souls is a prior condition among Christians which impels them to pool their possessions. Yet sharing their goods also facilitates the full development of growing union of souls. Thus union of souls is at once the cause and the effect of an attitude by reason of which each individual considers his goods as belonging to all.[197]

Thus, fifth, the community sees their possessions as at the disposal of one another, or held together with others, and therefore are ready to respond to need, by selling possessions or property and distributing it (2:45).

Sixth, the community sees the care of those in need and eating together as key. One of the four key things they devote themselves to in 2:42 is sharing food as they break bread. We then see how there is daily distribution of food in Acts 6:1–6 and the way that it is such an important issue when some members are being overlooked, that the apostles call the whole community together.

Seventh, the sharing of possessions in this way is voluntary, but there are also assumptions about it. Peter can ask questions which make it clear that Ananias and Sapphira had a choice about what they did with their property (5:4), but there was an assumption that they had given the whole

---

196. Klauck, "Gütergemeinschaft," 74.
197. Dupont, *Salvation*, 101.

of the proceeds to the group in the way they gave. Capper argues that, in giving in this way, Ananias and Sapphira are joining the common purse,[198] but from the summaries it would appear possible for people to be part of the common purse without necessarily selling land and giving it into the fund; for not claiming private ownership precedes the selling of specific pieces of land, which is ongoing and occurs when need arises.

Eighth, the processes the community develops cut against patronage, for by bringing the proceeds to the apostles' feet, those who sell are no longer in a position to make individuals who receive beholden to them as patrons. Similarly in Acts 6 the community may be choosing to increase the diversity of those in leadership.

Parallels in the Surrounding Culture

Jewish Almsgiving Practice

In Acts 4:34, Luke picks up the language of Deut 15:4 and indicates that the early church enjoys God's blessing[199] and fulfils the OT law of caring for those in need. Deut 15:7–11 goes on to point to giving alms and lending. Jeremias argues that some of the early church practices were modelled on the Jewish practice of תמחוי and קופה.[200] In this next section, we consider what evidence we have for first century Jewish practice with regard to tithing and almsgiving and how this compares to the example we have found in the Acts summaries.

Tithing and almsgiving were key parts of Jewish life. Part of the tithe went to those in need.[201] The third tithe was every third year and was given to the poor (Deut 14:27–29, Josephus *Ant.* 4.240).

This concern for those in need can be seen in Tobit where he recounts many acts of charity (1:16), notably to give food and clothing and to care for burial (1:17; 2:2–3, 4; 4:16). Tobit also provides several exhortations to give alms (4:7–11; 12:8–9; 14:8–9).

The Mishnah shows this concern continued in the post-70 CE era, for example *b. Giṭṭin* 7b: "Mar Zuṭra said: Even a poor man who himself subsists on charity should give charity."

There is also evidence of more organized forms of almsgiving to the poor, for example the Chamber of Secrets where individuals could

---

198. Capper, "Holy Community," 120.
199. Johnson, *Function*, 200.
200. Jeremias, *Jerusalem*, 131.
201. Sanders, *Judaism*, 147–48.

contribute and money was giving out of it for the "poor of good family" (*m. Shek.* 5.6). In *m. Peah* 8.7 there is reference to תמחוי and קופה, which Jeremias argued influenced early Christian practice.[202] The תמחוי involved more regular provision, with the stipulation that "If a man has food enough for two meals he may not take aught from the [Paupers'] Dish." The קופה seems to have involved a more weekly provision as if the person has "enough for fourteen meals he may not take aught from the [Poor]-Fund" (*m. Pe'ah* 8:7). This fund was "collected by two and distributed by three" (*m. Pe'ah* 8:7). Schürer suggests that the תמחוי was available to any poor person on a daily basis and that קופה was distributed weekly to those who were known and regularly in need.[203]

However, Seccombe argues that there is no evidence that this distribution occurred before the destruction of the Second Temple.[204] For example, *m. Pesaḥ* 10.1 stipulates that those who are poor should be provided with what they need for Passover and that it should be not less than "four cups of wine to drink, even if it is from the [Paupers'] Dish." Jeremias argues that "it can only refer to the time when the Passover was still celebrated in Jerusalem."[205] However, Seccombe argues that this is not necessarily the case as the "Minhah Service" did not "cease at the destruction of the Temple"[206] and that *m. Pesaḥ*. 10.1 gives instructions about practice as opposed to describing "what once happened in the Temple."[207] Instone-Brewer argues that while the initial phrase of *m. Pesaḥ*. 10.1 may predate 70 CE, the mention of the four cups "suggests that the end of this tradition is post-70 because the fourth cup probably did not become institutionalized till after 70 CE."[208] However, Instone-Brewer suggests that giving to those in need at Passover may have happened on a more *ad hoc* basis prior to 70 CE.[209]

As well as arguing against the evidence that Jeremias presents, Seccombe also points to the example of a woman who is found "picking barley grains in the dung of Arab cattle" (*b. Ket.* 66*b*). He argues that this is unlikely to have happened if there was organized poor relief.[210] While Seccombe presumes that the Chamber of Secrets did happen, he argues that

---

202. Jeremias, *Jerusalem*, 131.
203. Schürer, Vermes, Millar, and Black, *History*, 2:437.
204. Seccombe, "Charity."
205. Jeremias, *Jerusalem*, 133.
206. Seccombe, "Charity," 141.
207. Ibid.
208. Instone-Brewer, *Feasts*, 175.
209. Ibid., 175.
210. Seccombe, "Charity," 142.

the description of those who receive "looks suspiciously selective."[211] While Seccombe's arguments do indicate that the practice of תמחוי and קופה is unlikely to have been fully developed and functional during NT times, they do not disprove the existence of embryonic forms similar to the idea of the תמחוי and קופה. Thus, in comparing the practice of the early church to contemporary Jewish practice, we will allow for an embryonic form of the תמחוי and קופה to be developing in NT times.

So how does Jewish almsgiving compare with Luke's portrayal of the early church in the summary passages? Both Jewish practice and the summaries have a strong concern for those in need.

There is also some similarity between the διακονεῖν τραπέζαις in Acts 6:3 and the תמחוי in that both involve daily provision.

However, there are also differences. First, the descriptions of almsgivings tend to focus on the needs of the poor in the Jewish practice as opposed to the spiritual unity that we find in the summary passages. Second, as Capper points out, if the early church was following the Jewish model, we might expect to find weekly as opposed to daily provision.[212] Third, while Tobit sends his son to bring someone to eat with him (Tobit 2:2–3), there is not the same focus on eating together in the Jewish almsgiving as there is in the first summary passage.

Qumran and the Essenes

Capper suggests that the practice of the early church was analogous to and influenced by the Qumran and Essene communities.[213] We have argued that Jesus and his disciples would probably have come across Essenes in their travels or at least known about them.[214] The same arguments (Josephus and Philo's knowledge and description of their spread[215] and their presence on the south-west hill of Jerusalem in the same quarter as some of the early church[216]) hold for the early church. It is probable that the early church would have been aware of their presence and practice.[217] Capper goes on to suggest that many of the early Christian converts were Essenes[218] and

---

211. Ibid., 141.
212. Capper, "Palestianian Setting," 351.
213. Ibid., 356; Capper, "Holy Community," 120–21.
214. See pp. 32–33.
215. Josephus: *Ant.* 18.20–21, *J.W.* 2.12–15; Philo: *Hypoth.* 11.1, *Good Person* 75.
216. Capper, "Palestianian Setting," 334.
217. Riesner, "Jesus," 202–15.
218. Capper, "Holy Community," 120.

"may have brought into the Jerusalem Church the language and procedures of Essene property-sharing."[219] As noted in chapter 2,[220] this is difficult to prove or disprove, however Klauck's conclusion seems likely: "Daß die Urgemeinde die essenisch-qumranischen Formen der Gütergemeinschaft kannte, halte ich für höchstwahrscheinlich"[221] ("I consider it most likely that the early community knew the Essene/Qumran version of community of goods").

When we look at the Essene/Qumran communities alongside early church practice, we can identify some similarities, but there are also differences. The comparison is complicated by the diversity of practice in the evidence we have about the Essenes. There are more straightforward parallels with the descriptions in some of the secondary evidence about the Essenes in towns and villages. Both communities involve contributions into a fund, which is then used for provision (*Hypoth.* 10.10) and both involve eating together[222] (*Hypoth.* 10.10-11), as well as caring for those in need (*Hypoth.* 11.13). Capper also argues that there are parallels between the two forms of Essenism and early church community. He equates the community in Acts 2 and 4 with the community described in 1QS and then the Hellenist community with that described in CD. However, as we have seen in our examination of the text, the distinctions between the community in Acts 2 and 4 and the Hellenist community of Acts 6 are not so clear-cut.

The sharing in both the Essene community and the early church community involves collections and provision; however there are some differences in how that collection and provision is made and the motivation of the two communities is also different. Hargreaves argues that the sharing amongst the Essenes is by rule rather than individual choice,[223] and Fitzmyer that it is more structured.[224] While there were expectations in the way the early community shared, Luke does not include rules and regulations for how possessions are handed over. However, the sharing does appear to be more than simply individual choice. Individuals appear to choose when to sell (and to retain the right of disposal of their property), but the expectation of holding in common precedes the selling of property.

The selling and giving in the early church community is ongoing in response to need, whereas that amongst the Essenes is either total (but staged)

---

219. Capper, "Reciprocity," 2.
220. See pp. 32–33.
221. Klauck, "Gütergemeinschaft," 78.
222. Kim, *Stewardship*, 251.
223. Hargreaves, *Guide*, 31.
224. Fitzmyer, *Acts*, 270.

or daily through wages. This means that for the early church community, not everyone may have contributed to the common fund even though they held everything in common. Kim goes as far as to limit the common fund to "benevolent contributions of the wealthy towards the poor neighbors"[225] though this does not take full account of the idea of holding in common. In contrast, in the Qumran community everything was handed over to be controlled centrally and in the Essene communities in towns, everyone contributed a certain amount on a regular basis. While the early church community had a greater sense of spiritual unity and identity and arguably a sense that all they had belonged to the others within the group, this did not mean that each person necessarily contributed into the fund in the same way. Capper suggests that daily contributions may have occurred in the early church, but that as they would have been less noticeable Luke may not have heard of them.[226]

Additionally, for the community at Qumran at least, the purpose of the sharing seems quite different. Kim argues that the sharing at Qumran was "a means of maintaining such an isolated and self-supporting community, but as it was practised in the Jerusalem community one aspect of it was a means of helping the poor in the community in relieving them of their hunger."[227]

While there are similarities, particularly with the Essenes who lived in towns, there are differences. Luke focuses more on the unity and identity of the early believers and their practice of sharing, in comparison with the focus in the DSS literature on the need for holiness and the rules and regulations which dictate the practice of the Essenes.

Pythagoras and the Community at Croton

Josephus makes the comparison between the Essenes and the Pythagorean community (*Ant.* 15.371) and Grant compares the sharing of possessions in the Pythagorean community with that of the early church in Acts.[228] This section will consider the evidence about the community at Magna Croton, whether or not the early church is likely to have known about it, and what similarities and differences the two communities have. The two main sources of information about the Pythagorean community are Porphyry's (234–c.305 CE) *Life of Pythagoras* and Iamblichus's *On the Pythagorean Life*. However, Gillian Clark points out that Iamblichus writes in the context of

225. Kim, *Stewardship*, 252.
226. Capper, "Palestianian Setting," 352.
227. Kim, *Stewardship*, 251.
228. Grant, *Christianity*, 100.

"the pagan-Christian debate of the third and fourth centuries"[229] and that it is difficult to tell how far back what he is describing goes and whether he is influenced by Christian practice or by Pythagoreans.[230] Porphyry writes of Pythagoras that "His friends he loved exceedingly, being the first to declare that the goods of friends are common, and that a friend was another self" (*Vit. Pyth.* 33). The Pythagoreans "held all property in common" (*Vit. Pyth.* 20; *VP* 6.30). They had a staged entry to the community where potential was tested (*VP* 17.71), and then they were ignored for three years before being silent for five years (*VP* 17.72). "During this time each one's property was held in common, entrusted to particular students who were called 'civil servants' and who managed the finances and made the rules" (*VP* 17.72). At the end of the five years they either entered the inner circle or were sent away with double their initial property (*VP* 17.72–73).

There are a number of similarities in the descriptions of the Pythagorean community and the early church. Both are described as having their property in common and entrusting the property to particular people. There are also some interesting similarities that are not directly related to their sharing of possessions. Pythagoras is described as being perceived as godlike (*VP* 5.20) and he drew many to hear him (*Vit. Pyth.* 19). The community were expected to be "trustworthy without oaths" (*VP* 9.47).

However, there are also differences. The entry to the Pythagorean community is staged, with a possible exit route, which, while it involves the community forming a grave for the person leaving, also involves the person leaving with double what they came with. This is quite different from the community in Acts where there is no evidence of a staged entry, nor of an easy route to leave the community. Pythagoras drew the rich (*Vit. Pyth.* 19) and the community was one focused around philosophical learning (*Vit. Pyth.* 18–19). Some allowance is made for those who just come to study and do not become part of the perpetual community (*VP* 18.81) and the distinction is also made between Learners who were younger men with time to learn and Hearers, who were older with less time to learn and therefore were given instruction without the reasoning behind it (*VP* 18.88). While the Acts community was focused around the apostles' teaching, they were not primarily a philosophical community, but rather a worshipping and praying one.

While Pythagoras' teaching included instruction that one should not "renounce a friendship because of misfortune" (*VP* 22.102), he also argued, "It is upbringing which distinguishes humans from beasts, Greeks

---

229. Clark, *Iamblichus*, x.
230. Ibid., xviii.

from foreigners, free men from household slaves, and philosophers from ordinary people" (*VP* 8.44). In contrast the Acts community shows richer and poorer together: there are those who have lands or houses they can sell (4:34) and there are those who are in need and receive (2:46). There is little about the Pythagoreans eating together, apart from an instruction that "not more than ten people ate together" (*VP* 21.98), while eating together was a key part of the early believers' practice (2:42, 46). There is also no evidence that the Pythagoreans were particularly concerned for the poor or for those in need.

While Josephus does compare the Essenes to the Pythagoreans (*Ant.* 15.371), Josephus is likely to have traveled and read more widely than some early believers. Our other sources on the Pythagoreans are third and fourth century texts and it does not seem very likely that most of the early believers would have known much about Pythagoras or the Pythagoreans.

While there are a couple of similarities, there are significant differences; it is also unclear that the early church would have known about the Pythagorean community, and, even if they did, that they would have been an influence on the thought or practice of the early believers.

CONCLUSION

The early chapters of Acts describe a community in a particular situation that shares possessions. It is a community in the early days of development, where rapid growth and increasing persecution change the context in which the community lives and operates, which leads to changing practice. The sharing is linked to God's grace, and the presence of the Holy Spirit which leads to unity amongst the community. All they have is held in common, yet not held communally. While private property in name continues, possessions are both seen as common, but also sold and used as needs arise within the community. Sharing is voluntary, for each person's possessions are in their control, but with assumptions, as the community operated on the basis that possessions were common. The process by which possessions were sold and distributed, with the proceeds being laid at the apostles' feet, may have worked against individuals promoting patron-client relationships within the community.

Luke echoes both OT and Greco-Roman language and ideas in his description of the community, and there are some parallels with quite a wide range of communities and practices including Jewish almsgiving, the Essenes/Qumran, and the Pythagoreans. Both the Acts example and Jewish almsgiving show concern for the poor and those in need, and include provision of food. The Essene/Qumran example shows similarities in sharing possessions, concern for the poor, and eating together. The Pythagorean community shows similarities in property being held in common and entrusted to particular people. However, there are also significant distinctives.

First, the community in the early chapters of Acts is drawn from a variety of backgrounds rather than one social class (in comparison with the Greek friendship ideals and the Pythagoreans). In addition there is no indication of reciprocity being expected for the giving which takes place, which is the case in Greek friendship ideals. Luke does not use the word φίλος but instead talks of πιστευσάντες/πιστεύοντες, indicating that the community is not based on the members being friends (or of the same status or background), but rather it is based in their belief in and following of Jesus.

Second, the example of sharing is one where eating together is seen as important. This is evidenced in the way those in need are provided for through daily communal meals rather than the weekly provision seen in the קופה.

Third, there is a greater emphasis on God's grace and the presence of the Holy Spirit—on the unity of the community and their practice of sharing, rather than the rules and regulations of how to share seen in the Essene/Qumran comparator.

Fourthly, the example is one where the sharing/giving is more of an ongoing process of selling in response to need, as opposed to all possessions being sold and pooled. There is also more flexibility in how the believers contribute to the fund in Acts 2 and 4 compared to either the Essenes/Qumran or the Pythagoreans.

The early church brought together those with some wealth and those in need and was based around their shared belief in Jesus, in his death and resurrection and the presence of the Holy Spirit uniting them.

4

Responding to Famine

Acts 11

INTRODUCTION

IN ADDITION TO THE examples of sharing in the summary passages in the early chapters of Acts, Acts also provides a key example of giving to those in need in the Antiochene collection for the church in Judea. This example is one of giving at a distance—between two communities where there was an existing relationship between the communities. This chapter will examine Acts 11:27–30 and Acts 12:25—the response of the Antiochene church following the predication of famine. It will briefly consider historical issues surrounding the passage including its relationship to Acts 15, Gal 2, and Paul's gift. The example is then compared with Greco-Roman responses to famine situations, particularly the practice of appointing an affluent *curator annonae*.

THE TEXTS

Acts 11:27–30

Acts 11:27–30 follows the beginning of the move of the gospel to the Gentiles. This move is seen both in the account of Cornelius in Caesarea in Acts 10 and 11:1–18, and the account of the men of Cyprus and Cyrene in Antioch in 11:19–21, where the contrast with the previous verse where "they spoke to no one except Jews" suggests the author intends to indicate that they were Gentiles and not simply Greek speaking Jews. In 11:19–26, following the persecution after Stephen's death, the believers are scattered and a number come to Antioch and proclaim the Lord Jesus and "a great number" become believers. The church in Jerusalem, on hearing the news, sends Barnabas to Antioch. He rejoices in God's grace and fetches Saul to come and teach in Antioch with him. It is into this context that the prophets come down from Jerusalem to Antioch.

The account begins with prophets coming down from Jerusalem to Antioch. One of the group of prophets, Agabus, then prophesies the coming of a famine: λιμὸν μεγάλην μέλλειν ἔσεσθαι ἐφ' ὅλην τὴν οἰκουμένην (11:28). The prophecy refers to ὅλην τὴν οἰκουμένην which would seem to indicate the whole world, or at least the whole inhabited world, however as Winter points out a wide range of vocabulary is used to indicate famine or food shortage and it is not easy to tell from the different words the severity or extent of the food shortage.[1]

While Luke uses οἰκουμένην, which Johnson argues is generally used to denote the inhabited world, Johnson asserts that Luke's other uses of οἰκουμένην, which occur in Luke 2:1 and Luke 4:5, both indicate less than the whole world.[2] This is certainly the case in Luke 2:1, where the reference is presumably the extent of the Roman Empire at the time; in Luke 4:5, while practically difficult to conceive, it would seem to intend to point to the whole world.

An inscription of 163 CE speaks of a famine which κόσμον ἐπέσχε[θ]ε πάντα ("spread over all the world"),[3] which suggests a widespread if not worldwide famine. However, while the inscription talks about the severity of the famine, its σαρκοβόρος (flesh eating) nature and how βούβρωστις κατὰ γαῖαν (ravenous appetite across the earth), the cattle are saved by being moved elsewhere which would suggest that while the famine might have spread over an area, it was not universal.[4] Also, Winter notes that thus far no other evidence for famine in 163 CE has been found,[5] which thus gives an example of using words that might suggest a widespread famine for one affecting a region.

---

1. Winter, "Acts," 62.
2. Johnson, *Acts*, 205.
3. Winter, "Acts," 66.
4. Le Bas and Waddington, *Inscriptions*, n. 1192; Winter, "Acts," 66.
5. Winter, "Acts," 66–67.

In addition, Winter notes the possibility of using "worldwide" with a sense of poetic exaggeration.[6] Gapp hypothesizes that when a population experienced famines they "sometimes imagined that other countries experienced the same distress, although they had definite knowledge only of local conditions."[7]

Thus, while ὅλην τὴν οἰκουμένην could point to the whole world, or at least the whole known world, it could also be used of a region, and allowing for poetic exaggeration to a smaller area.

Similarly, λιμός can have a range of meanings and may refer to a severe famine, or to the existence of hunger or shortage in an area, and these may have a range of causes. In his study on famine, Garnsey distinguishes between *famine*, where there is an increase in starvation and mortality, and *food crises*, where there is hunger bordering on starvation and food prices are affected.[8] He argues that "famines were rare, but that subsistence crises falling short of famine were common."[9] However, he also notes that "it cannot be assumed that *fames* or *limos* are always employed in the narrow sense of famine as opposed to hunger."[10]

Grain shortages, and thus food crises or famine, could arise from a number of different causes: crop failure, the need for transportation to cities where the surrounding area could not produce enough grain, and difficulties in transportation—particularly by sea, and the need to supply Rome.[11]

Rome as the capital city, with political importance, took priority in terms of grain distribution and had a permanent administration to coordinate the distribution of grain.[12] Thus, if Rome was short of grain, we can presume a widespread shortage in the Empire, or key disruption to transportation to Rome. Within the Empire, Egypt was one of the main grain producing areas and a shortage there led to shortages elsewhere. Witherington adds that shortage of grain or famine always affects the poor disproportionately as there is rarely a complete absence of food, rather the shortage of food pushes the price up,[13] thus famine within an area affects some people and not others.

---

6. Ibid., 67; also Lake and Cadbury, *Acts*, 4:131.
7. Gapp, "Famine," 263.
8. Garnsey, *Famine*, 6, 24.
9. Ibid., 6.
10. Ibid., 19.
11. Winter, "Acts," 61.
12. Ibid., 72.
13. Witherington, *Acts*, 372.

The use of οἰκουμένην and λιμόν could refer to widespread food shortages and increased prices, caused by poor harvests in particular areas.

We now turn to the evidence of famines or grain shortages in Judea and more widely in the Roman Empire and we do not find a shortage of references. Josephus reports how at the time of the visit of Helena,[14] the mother of Izates, to Jerusalem, λιμοῦ γάρ αὐτῶν τήν πόλιν κατά τὸν καιρὸν ἐκεῖνον πιεζοῦντος καὶ πολλῶν ὑπ' ἐνδείας ἀναλωμάτων φθειρομένων (for at that time the city was hard pressed by famine and many were perishing from want of money to purchase what they needed)(*Ant.* 20.51). Earlier Josephus refers to a severe famine, possibly the same one under Claudius. He comments on the lack of wheat and its price (*Ant.* 3.320-21). Orosius refers to the same famine and places it during the fourth year of Claudius's reign and notes that it affected the whole of Syria (*Hist.* 7.6). Therefore Krodel argues that "Judea suffered hard times and food shortages during AD 46 to 48,"[15] but asserts that there was no worldwide famine. Conzelman and Gaventa support this conclusion, while Haenchen argues for local famines, but no worldwide famine.[16]

However, there are references to famines during the reign of Claudius which affect other areas in the empire. Tacitus reports a shortage of corn resulting in famine in Rome, noting that "the capital had provisions for fifteen days, no more" (*Ann.* 12.43) and that due to the food shortage Claudius was hounded in the Forum (*Ann.* 12.43; also Suetonius *Clau.* 18.2). Given the priority of transporting grain to Rome, this would suggest a shortage elsewhere as well.

There is also evidence of crop failure and food shortages in Egypt. Pliny records about the Nile: "If it has not risen more than 18 feet, there is certain to be a famine, and likewise if it has exceeded 24 feet; for it retires more slowly in proportion as it has risen in greater flood, and prevents the sowing of seed" (*Nat.* 18.168). He also records, "The largest rise up to date was one of 27 feet in the principate of Claudius" (*Nat.* 5.58), which points to a famine in Egypt during the time of Claudius. P. Mich. 594 records high numbers of people owing poll, pig and dike tax in the village of Philadelphia in 45/46 CE, an increase in 46/47 and then a slight decrease in 47/48, which would suggest reduced crops or crop failure in 45-47.[17] Witherington comments "in terms of its effects one could well talk about an Empire-wide

---

14. Josephus sets this visit after the time of Herod Agrippa's death (*Ant.* 20.1) and notes that Helena and Izates convert to Judaism (*Ant.* 20.17, 38).

15. Krodel, *Acts*, 209.

16. Conzelmann, *Acts*, 90; Gaventa, *Acts*, 180; Haenchen, *Acts*, 62; Fitzmyer, *Acts*, 482; Jervell, *Apostelgeschichte*, 327.

17. Browne, *Papyri*, 64-67.

famine if there was a severe one in Egypt."[18] It may be that the crop failures in Egypt led to the recorded food crises in both Judea and Rome.

In order to consider whether this is the case we need to look at the dates of the recorded crises in Judea and Rome, while bearing in mind that prices could rise prior to a bad harvest, if it was predicted and grain was hoarded to try and gain higher prices.[19] The evidence for Egypt shows issues particularly in 45–47 CE. When we look at Josephus' evidence, Helena's visit occurs during the procuratorship of Tiberius Alexander, which suggests either 46 or 47 CE.[20] Gapp argues that as Helena purchased grain from Egypt, the food supply in Egypt was improving as the situation in Judea worsened.[21] The situation in Rome seems to have occurred later still. However, there are discrepancies in the evidence as to the exact year.[22] Tacitus indicates it was the beginning of Claudius' eleventh year (*Ann.* 12.43), Orosius reports two famines: one in Syria in the fourth year of Claudius' reign and another in Rome in the tenth year of his reign (*Hist.* 7.6), which would place the most difficult period in 44 or 50–51 CE, which could either indicate two separate times of need or inaccuracies in one of the accounts. Eusebius simply notes that a famine took place in the time of Claudius (*Hist. eccl.* 2.8–12).

These references indicate widespread food shortages across the Empire, during the reign of Claudius, particularly in the late 40s and early 50s CE. Hemer argues that famine "was not a matter of widespread harvest failure and sudden crisis so much as an accumulation of local failures and difficulties which progressively priced the available supplies out of the reach of the poor before the rich were affected."[23] While there may not be evidence for a definite worldwide famine during a particular year, the evidence does suggest food crises across a wide area of the known world over a relatively short period of time, which could have been considered as a widespread famine.

This suggests that despite the questions about the accuracy of the prophecy and its fulfilment, the account in Acts 11 correlates with wider historical evidence about widespread food shortages. However, Acts 12 reports that around the time of Barnabas and Saul being sent to Jerusalem, King Herod persecuted members of the church and arrested Peter (12:1–3). Subsequently Herod died (12:23). This creates some issues for dating as

18. Witherington, *Acts*, 373.
19. Gapp, "Famine," 260.
20. Ibid., 260.
21. Ibid., 262.
22. Dupont, *Études*, 163.
23. Hemer, *Acts*, 165.

Herod died in 44 CE and most of our evidence of famine in Judea is later than this. Luke may have misplaced the timing of the visit to Jerusalem (the question of correlating the Acts and Galatians accounts will be addressed later) and the visit of Saul and Barnabas may actually have taken place during the 45–47 CE famine in Jerusalem. Alternatively there may have been two separate famines, one referred to by Luke and one by Josephus. However, this seems less likely as there does not seem to be much other evidence of an earlier famine.

In addition, while Luke does place his account of Herod's death between the prophecy and Saul and Barnabas' return, he introduces the section on the church in Jerusalem and Herod's death with the words: Κατ' ἐκεῖνον δὲ τὸν καιρόν (12:1) and is not specific about which time he is referring back to: the time of the days when the prophets visited Antioch (11:27), the time of men from Cyprus and Cyrene preaching about Jesus in Antioch (11:20) or at some point in between the two. It may be that 11:19–30 and 12:1–24 parallel one another during a period of over a year (for once Saul comes to Antioch, he teaches for ἐνιαυτὸν ὅλον [11:26]), the one chapter recording events in Antioch, the other events in Jerusalem, which could place the visit by Saul and Barnabas to Jerusalem after the death of Herod, potentially near the beginning of the famine in 45 CE.

The Response to the Prophecy of Famine

While there are still some questions about dates, there is evidence of widespread famine in the region in the late 40s, which could correlate with Agabus' prediction of λιμὸν μεγάλην μέλλειν ἔσεσθαι ἐφ' ὅλην τὴν οἰκουμένην (11:28). As Pervo points out, this raises the question of why the believers in Antioch responded to the prediction of a widespread famine by collecting and sending relief to Judea, as opposed to any of the other areas affected,[24] and instead of providing for themselves. Additionally, Dunn asks why the Jerusalem church would be seen as needing help,[25] and Haenchen queries why the church in Antioch would want to help the church in Jerusalem as he hypothesizes a break between the remaining church in Jerusalem and the "Hellenistic fugitives,"[26] with the church in Antioch being independent.[27] However, as Walton points out, there is a lack of evidence for the Hellenists

---

24. Pervo, *Acts*, 296.
25. Dunn, *Acts*, 157.
26. Haenchen, *Acts*, 377.
27. Ibid., 379.

and Hebrews having distinct theologies.[28] One could equally expect the Diaspora Jews to be more conservative[29] (given that they had chosen to travel and settle in Jerusalem) instead of expecting them to be more liberal about the temple. In addition, Luke uses Ἑλληνιστής in a number of ways: for believers (6:1), for those who are probably Jews but not believers (9:29) and for those as we have seen earlier who are not Jews (11:20),[30] therefore it is unclear whether there is such a significant rift between the Hebrews and the Hellenists. In 6:1, the believers in Jerusalem address the issue of the Hellenist widows being overlooked together. Therefore there does not seem sufficient evidence for a Jerusalem-Antioch (Hebrew-Hellenist) split which would preclude the Antiochenes seeking to help those in Jerusalem.[31]

There are also several reasons why the Antiochenes may have focussed on the brothers in Judea as the recipients of the relief fund. First, there was an existing link to Judea and to Jerusalem in particular. It was some of those who had fled from Judea, who had evangelized Antioch. As Calvin notes the brothers in Jerusalem were the "brothers from whom they had received the Gospel."[32] So Jerusalem was their founding or mother church,[33] and the "Antiochian community . . . owed its very existence to refugees from Jerusalem."[34] Johnson and Conzelmann both note the importance for Luke of showing that there is continuity with Jerusalem and Jerusalem's centrality in the growth of the gospel.[35] However, the text goes beyond simply showing continuity or centrality, it shows ongoing relationship: a relationship that starts with the men of Cyprus and Cyrene (11:20), and continues with the sending of Barnabas (11:22) and the coming of the prophets (11:27).

---

28. Walton, "Minority," 305.

29. Ibid., 207.

30. Ibid., 202.

31. Even if there were a split and the Antiochene church then chose to give to the Judean church, it could indicate the importance the Antiochene church placed on the relationship between the communities. However, Luke's account suggests an existing and ongoing relationship between the two church communities.

32. Calvin, Acts, 196.

33. Barrett, Acts 1:558.

34. Krodel, Acts, 210.

35. Johnson, Acts, 207; Conzelmann, Acts, xlii-xliii. For Luke, Jerusalem is where his gospel starts (Luke 1:5-25), it is where Jesus journeys to (Luke 9:51; 17:22), and it is where the gospel ends (Luke 24:50-53). Jerusalem is also where Acts begins (Acts 1-7) and where the council takes place to decide about Gentiles who believe the good news (Acts 15:1-21). It is from Jerusalem that Barnabas is sent out to investigate the reports about the church at Antioch (Acts 11:22) and where Paul returns and begins being tried (Acts 21:1—23:22).

It is these prophets, including Agabus, who have come from Jerusalem, and who therefore are in an ideal situation to report the situation of the believers there and in Judea (as they would presumably have traveled through part of Judea whether they traveled wholly by land or for some of the way by sea). In addition, the believers in Jerusalem and Judea would not have been wholly unknown to the Christians in Antioch, for those who had initially scattered following the persecution and Barnabas would presumably have known some of them personally, and shared something of their experience in the community in Jerusalem.

Thus, some of the Antiochenes would have had personal relationships with the believers in Judea and through the ongoing relationships and the arrival of the prophets would have had up to date insight into the economic situation and tensions in Jerusalem. Therefore they would have been aware of issues that potentially made the community in Jerusalem more vulnerable to food shortages. Cassidy notes the possibility of the practice of the common purse in Acts 2 and 4 depleting resources and creating need, but notes that Luke does not indicate this.[36] However, many of Jesus' first disciples were Galilean, and therefore, when they were in Jerusalem they would have been away from their main occupation and thus may have found it more difficult to earn. This would also apply to any of those who had traveled to Jerusalem at Pentecost, became believers and stayed in Jerusalem. Both of these possibilities could have added to the vulnerability of the believers in Jerusalem.

Beyond issues within the church, Calvin notes a wider issue that "Judea was impoverished by war and other disasters."[37] Thus, while Fiensy argues that the make up of the Jerusalem church was economically diverse reflecting the economic diversity of the city,[38] such wider issues in Jerusalem and Judea would have affected the Jerusalem church. These issues include: the large number of people who returned from the Diaspora to Jerusalem in their old age,[39] the confiscation of land by Herod the Great,[40] the increase in the number of large land holdings,[41] the greed of the high priestly families,[42]

---

36. Cassidy, *Society*, 29.
37. Calvin, *Acts*, 196.
38. Fiensy, "Composition," 226.
39. Johnson, "Manual," 133.
40. Theissen, *Reality*, 89–90.
41. Guijarro, "Family," 43–46.
42. Hengel, *Property*, 23. It should be noted that Hengel is reporting post-70 rabbis commenting on the pre-70 era and that they may have a particular take on the situation.

and high taxes and tithes.[43] In addition Jeremias notes that 47/48 CE was a Sabbath year,[44] which would have exacerbated any difficulties from the previous years, if it were observed. As the Antiochene believers had an ongoing relationship with the Jerusalem church, it is likely they would have known that the Sabbath year was approaching and would create further food storages. Gapp also argues that Jerusalem would have been more severely affected than Antioch, because the expense of transporting grain to Jerusalem would be greater than transporting it to Antioch, which was a commercial center.[45]

Thus, both because of their relationship with believers in Jerusalem and Judea, and because of their knowledge of the challenges in Jerusalem and Palestine, it would seem a natural response for the Antiochene church to send relief to the believers in Judea.

There is a certain degree of ambiguity about how the relief is collected and decided about. While in 11:29 it is clear that amounts are dependent on ability,[46] καθὼς εὐπορεῖτο, and that there is an element of individual decision, ἕκαστος αὐτῶν, it is interesting to note that ὥρισαν is in the plural, not in the singular to match ἕκαστος.[47] This indicates that there are individual contributions to the collection, but that it is seen as a corporate venture. As Haenchen observes, the length of the collecting is not noted.[48] While the placement of the description of the collection would seem to indicate an immediate response to the prophecy, it could have taken place at the time of the prophecy or later on as they saw the prophecy being fulfilled.[49]

The relief fund is then sent to the brothers living in Judea. It is sent to the elders via Barnabas and Saul. Marshall notes that this is the first mention of the elders in Jerusalem and suggests that the seven referred to in 6:1–6 may have become known as elders,[50] while Blomberg suggests that the elders may have replaced the twelve and the deacons.[51] In any case the account points to the fund being handed over to leaders of some kind in

---

43. Guijarro, "Family," 44–45.
44. Jeremias, "Sabbathjahr," 99.
45. Gapp, "Famine," 260.
46. With similarities to the giving according to ability espoused by Paul in 2 Cor 8:3.
47. Moulton et al. note that ἕκαστος occurs more often in the NT with the correct singular verb (twenty-five times) than with a plural verb (eleven times) (Moulton et al., *Grammar*, 3:312).
48. Haenchen, *Acts*, 375.
49. Conzelmann, *Acts*, 91.
50. Marshall, *Acts*, 204.
51. Blomberg, *Poverty*, 171.

Judea, as opposed to being distributed by Barnabas and Saul, and thus control of the money is handed over to the local leaders.

Historical Questions—Acts 11, Acts 15, Galatians 2, and the Pauline Collection

While we considered the general historicity of Acts in the previous chapter, there are specific questions about the historicity of Acts 11; how Acts 11, Acts 15, and Paul's account in Gal 2 of his visits to Jerusalem relate to one another; and the relationship between the Acts 11 collection and the collection mentioned in 2 Cor 8 and 9 and Rom 16.

Johnson presumes that the Pauline collection and Acts 11 are referring to the same collection and that Luke is historically inaccurate,[52] while Bruce argues that the famine relief is not the same as the final visit with the collection (Rom 15:25).[53] The situation in Jerusalem and Palestine which created an increased need and the fact that there seem to be so many famines referred to under Claudius, suggests that there could well be a need for more than one trip with provisions or funds for the believers in Jerusalem/Judea, and Jeremias suggests that Paul's experience of the 47/48 Sabbath year might have led to his desire to collect for "eine ansehnliche Gabe" (a sizeable gift) to take to Jerusalem in the light of the 54/55 Sabbath year.[54] So there seems to be no good reason why there would not have been more than one collection.

The main issue with regard to the relationship between Acts 11, Acts 15, and Gal 2 is that Paul claims, and indeed declares before God (Gal 1:9), that he has only been once to Jerusalem after his conversion (Gal 1:18 and presumably correlating to Acts 9:26–29), before his visit of Gal 2 where he discusses the issues about preaching the gospel to Gentiles and whether they need to be circumcised. If the Gal 2 visit relates to the council of Acts 15, it would not seem to allow for Paul visiting Jerusalem in Acts 11. There are three main options:

- Acts 11, Acts 15, and Gal 2 all refer to one visit and Luke has reported the visit twice possibly through having two sources.[55]

---

52. Johnson, *Acts*, 208.
53. Bruce, *Acts*, 275.
54. Jeremias, "Sabbathjahr," 102–3.
55. Ibid., 102; Barrett, *Acts*, 1:560.

- Acts 15 is the same as the Gal 2 visit.[56] The arguments for this view include: Gal 2:2 pointing to a later place in Paul's ministry than Acts 11; Gal 2:9 indicating that it is after the death of James (brother of John); and Acts 11 not fitting Paul's desire to remember the poor.[57] However, as Longenecker points out there are various problems with identifying Acts 15 and Gal 2. While similar people are involved in both visits there are differences in the role of Paul, the motivation for the visit, and the nature of the meeting.[58] In Gal 2:1–10, Paul has a central role (Gal 2:2, 7, 9), goes up to Jerusalem in response to a revelation (Gal 2:2), and the meeting takes place in private (Gal 2:2), while in Acts 15, Peter, Barnabas, and James also have key roles (Acts 15:2, 7, 13), Paul is one of a group sent to Jerusalem (Acts 15:2) and the meeting seems to be more public (Acts 15:4–5, 12). In addition, if the Acts 15 did correlate to the Gal 2 visit, why does Paul not mention the result of the council meeting in the letter "which decision would have served as the *coup de grace* to the conflict at Galatia"?[59]

- Acts 11 is the same as the Gal 2 visit. The arguments for this view include: the challenging issue of Gentile converts and circumcision probably requiring more than one discussion (therefore Gal 2 can relate to Acts 11, with Acts 15 being a further discussion of the topic)[60] and Gal 2:10 pointing to the fact Paul was already in the process of helping the poor and wished to continue.[61]

The number of famines under Claudius and the specific needs in Jerusalem suggest the likelihood of more than one visit with aid. The Acts 15 visit, while it has superficial similarities to the Gal 2 visit, has a number of differences. Therefore the third option while holding problems, for example, why the account in Acts 11 makes no reference to the meeting and discussion about the circumcision of Gentile converts, does seem most likely. By Acts 11:27, Paul has already been teaching in Antioch for "an entire year" (11:26), even before the arrival of the prophets. We then need to allow time

---

56. Dibelius argues that Acts 11 does not refer to the conference and may be in the wrong place chronologically (Dibelius, *Studies*, 93).

57. Hengel presumes James brother of John would have been mentioned immediately before him if he were still alive at this point (Hengel, *Acts*, 111–12). However, if chapter 12 parallels chapter 11, the argument about James, John's brother, would not necessarily hold, as Acts 12:2 could have taken place before Acts 11:27–30.

58. Longenecker, *Galatians*, lxxvii–lxxviii.

59. Ibid., lxxix.

60. Marshall, *Acts*, 205.

61. Ibid., 205; Witherington, *Acts*, 275.

for the collection to take place and for the journey to Jerusalem. Paul could thus legitimately talk about his concern that he "had not run in vain" (Gal 2:2). Paul's comment in Gal 2:10 about remembering the poor could easily refer to what he was currently doing as well as his further desire to do so, and Marshall's point about difficult subjects being repeatedly discussed seems sensible. Luke would not necessarily have catalogued each time it was discussed, nor every part of each meeting or journey that Paul made. Hemer's work on possible dates for the crucifixion, Paul's conversion, and the Gal 2 visit to Jerusalem shows that equating Acts 11 with Gal 2 is possible if the visit is made around 46–47 CE,[62] which would then fit with Paul and Barnabas arriving in the midst of the famine in Jerusalem.

Whichever of the three main options one goes for, Luke has still chosen to write the story where the Christians in Antioch respond to the need presented by Agabus and send a collection to the brothers in Judea. Therefore, whether or not it is historically accurate, Luke still wants his readers to learn from the narrative. However, we would argue that Luke is not simply amalgamating sources to produce a particular impression, or to make a particular point, but rather reporting a situation which is historically plausible and thus the story is not only also an example in history, but also an example that Luke thinks is important to record.

Acts 12:25

The conclusion of the 11:27–30 account in 12:25 also raises textual problems. These center on the preposition with Jerusalem, which is one of εἰς, ἀπο or ἐξ. The most difficult reading, and also the strongest by nature of its difficulty, which is supported by "the earliest and best witnesses"[63] is εἰς.[64] According to 11:27–30, Barnabas and Saul are already in Jerusalem and therefore it does not make sense for them to return there and by 13:2 Barnabas and Saul are back in Antioch ready to be sent out again. Additionally, Witherington points out that returning to Jerusalem, bringing with them John Mark, does not make sense either, as 12.12 places John Mark's home in Jerusalem.[65] Various solutions have been suggested: Pervo emends the text to "to Antioch from Jerusalem";[66] Haenchen and Johnson keep εἰς

---

62. Hemer, *Acts*, 264.
63. Metzger, *Commentary*, 351.
64. Supported by ℵ, B, 𝔐.
65. Witherington, *Acts*, 374. After all, 12:12 places John Mark's home in Jerusalem.
66. Pervo, *Acts*, 316.

Ἰερουσαλήμ, but attach it to the participial phrase as its object[67] (i.e., "when they had fulfilled their relief mission in Jerusalem"[68]). This latter solution fits the flow of the narrative, otherwise Barnabas and Saul twice journey to Jerusalem without Luke noting their returns and 12:25 fits a return journey to Antioch better than another journey to Jerusalem. It also makes sense of the addition of John Mark to their group in 12:25. This interpretation has Luke placing Paul and Barnabas in Jerusalem during the persecution,[69] adding to the sense of solidarity expressed by the sending of the gift.

THE EXAMPLE OF THE COLLECTION FOR JUDEA

In 11:27–30 and 12:25 we are presented with the example of believers in Antioch responding to predicted need, each according to their means. The response is both corporate and individual: each of them, according to what they have, contributes and yet they decide. They send the collection via Barnabas and Saul, the two people who the preceding verses of the chapter tell us have been teaching the believers for an entire year (11:26). It thus appears that the sending of the collection was considered an important task (for Barnabas and Saul would not be able to continue their teaching while they traveled) and one which was given to those the Antioch church could trust. The relief fund is sent to the elders, which suggests a handing over of it for them to distribute.[70]

The account in Acts shows a sharing of possessions based on the need that is highlighted in Agabus' prophecy. It is a sharing of possessions that comes out of existing relationships and in a context where the church in Antioch has already received from the church in Judea/Jerusalem and so there is an element of reciprocity in the relationship, even if it is not like for like: the church in Antioch has received the gospel from some who were scattered from Jerusalem following the persecution and believers in Judea now receive from the church in Antioch. In addition some of the believers in Antioch originated from the church in Jerusalem and would probably still have family and friends living there.

It is a sharing of possessions that seems to cross the Jew/Gentile boundaries and shows continuity with the birthplace of the new movement and demonstrates "the unity of Gentile and Jewish Messianists."[71] For, as we

67. Johnson, *Acts*, 216.
68. Haenchen, *Acts*, 381.
69. Jervell, *Apostelgeschichte*, 337.
70. Thomas, "Church," 151.
71. Talbert, *Acts*, 116.

saw in 11:19–20, Luke makes a distinction between the proclaiming of the Lord Jesus in Antioch, and other places where "they spoke to no one except Jews" (11:19). Thus, there is within the text innovation in terms of those to whom the word is proclaimed and we would expect the church in Antioch to include those who came from Jewish backgrounds and those who came from Gentile backgrounds. The believers who result from this innovation show their relationship with the "mother" church by this collection for the need that exists or at least is known to be about to exist. While Acts shows the diversity of the church in Jerusalem with its account in chapter 6 of the need of the Hellenistic widows, there is not the same distinction or contrast with that mention to indicate that the Jerusalem Hellenists[72] were not Hellenistic Jews and we may assume that the majority of the church in Jerusalem came from a Jewish background.

This sharing between Jewish and Gentile believers is not limited to possessions. The effect of the placement of 12:25 is to locate Saul and Barnabas in Jerusalem during at least some of the persecution that is reported in chapter 12, even if, in reality, chapters 11 and 12 are concurrent and it is hard to tell how much of the time they are in Jerusalem or Judea. While Barnabas and Saul both come from Jewish background, they are representatives of the more mixed Jewish-Gentile church in Antioch and thus this church shares "not only in the material want of the Jerusalem congregation, but also in its danger."[73]

It is interesting that the believers in Antioch are called μαθητῶν in verse 29, when they decide to send relief to the ἀδελφοῖς in Judea. This suggests the sharing of possessions in this way was part of learning to follow/being discipled to Jesus, which would fit with the words of Jesus which are quoted by Paul in 20:35, "It is more blessed to give than to receive."[74] The use of ἀδελφοῖς also points to the relationship between the Antiochene and Judean believers.

It is a sharing of possessions that acknowledges the "not yet" nature of both the world and the Christian community. First, it is a response to a need

72. While Luke uses Ἑλληνιστής in a variety of ways (11:20), in general Ἑλληνιστής refers to "a Greek-speaking Israelite in contrast to one speaking a Semitic language" (BDAG, 319). Therefore, in Acts 6:1 we would expect the Hellenists to be Jews, as Luke gives no indication otherwise and the context of the Pentecost festival.

73. Haenchen, *Acts*, 376.

74. Bruce argues that given that the first book Luke wrote is about what Jesus began to do, Acts is what he "continued to do after his ascension" (Bruce, *Acts*, 21). If this is the case and connecting it with Acts 20:35 and Tannehill's argument of the way that in Acts stories are used to demonstrate the teaching from Luke, we might build an argument that in this pericopae ὁ πιστεύσας ἐπέστρεψεν ἐπὶ τὸν κύριον (11:21) are continuing the work of Jesus as they follow and learn as disciples, by contributing to the collection.

brought about by a famine, showing the continued existence of need within the world. Second, it is a very carefully sent gift, which minimizes the risk of misappropriation. In Acts 11:30 the gift is sent from the Antiochenes by the hands of those who have positions of responsibility within their community, Barnabas and Saul, and to those who have positions of responsibility with the community of the brothers living in Judea, the elders. Entrusting the gift to the leaders in Jerusalem may reduce the chances of Barnabas and Saul being seen as patrons and the possibility of them undermining the existing structure of the community. As Calvin writes about these verses he concludes that they "teach us we must not only be sincere and trustworthy but also wise and orderly in our choice and in all the administration."[75]

RESPONSES TO FAMINE AND FOOD SHORTAGE IN THE GRECO-ROMAN WORLD

Having considered the example of the collection for Judea in Acts 11, we now consider contemporaneous responses to famine and food shortage and how these compare with the example in Acts 11.

Food crises were an ongoing issue and Garnsey reports that Samians and Athenians debated grain supply each year.[76] Thus, strategies were developed both in Rome, but also in other cities to respond to times of need. Food supply in Rome was particularly important politically. For example Dionysius of Halicarnassus writes about Spurius Maelius who in the context of famine in Rome (c. 438–435 BCE) "conceived it to be the best time for aiming at tyranny and turned to currying favor with the multitude" (*Ant. rom.* 12.1.1; also Livy 4.13). He used money from his own funds to distribute corn "among the citizens, measuring out a peck for two denarii instead of for twelve denarii, and upon all those whom he perceived to be utterly helpless and unable to defray the cost of even their daily subsistence bestowing it without payment" (*Ant. rom.* 12.1.2–3). Tacitus points to the way that Claudius was "surrounded by a wildly clamorous mob" (*Ann.* 12.43) during a period of corn shortage and it is not surprising that Suetonius relates that Claudius "resorted to every possible means to bring grain to Rome, even in the winter season" (*Clau.* 18.2). Suetonius notes that he did this by underwriting losses from storms and offering privileges to those who built merchant ships (*Clau.* 18.2–19). Tacitus reports that Tiberius made a maximum price for grain by "compensating merchants at the rate of 2 sesterces per modius" (*Ann.* 2.87).

75. Calvin, *Acts*, 197.
76. Garnsey, *Famine*, 16.

Outside Rome, Garnsey notes that "there was little regulation of the food supply by local governments" and that "it was left very much to members of the elite acting in a private capacity to protect ordinary citizens against a breakdown of the food supply system."[77] However, he argues that this provision "was so regular as to be an institutionalized feature of society"[78] where members of the elite, on their own or with others took on the role of responsibility for grain supply.[79] This mix of private and public fits with Hands' assessment that city states were mainly financed on a "voluntary" basis where important individuals were expected to give for buying corn, or for rebuilding and might expect some form of reward,[80] for example being given titles in response for subsidising the market.[81] Hands also notes that when food prices went up, it could become more difficult to find someone to take on the responsibility of subsidising the market and "a single individual, or group of individuals acting together, might agree to hold several offices in the same year, or to hold the same annual office consecutively year after year."[82] For example, in Oenoanda, an inscription notes that the town clerk took on the responsibility of the corn dole again and in a particularly difficult time ἐπιδεδωκότα δὲ καὶ ἀργυρικὴ(ν) διάδοσιν καθ' ἕκαστον τῶν πολειτῶν ἀνὰ δηνάρια δέκα (he also gave a distribution in money to each of the citizens—ten denarii).[83] The same inscription reports his concern for honor.[84] Winter notes that under this practice of appointing a benefactor as *curator annonae*, the person would then enable the sale of grain below the going rate.[85] While one incentive for such a role was that honor could be gained, it was also "in the interests of the rich in a city to assist not merely from love of honor, but out of self-interest, knowing the alternative would be rioting and plundering of their goods and stores."[86]

A similar pattern of rich patron or benefactor is seen in Josephus' account of the visit of Helena to Jerusalem. It does not appear that she came in response to the famine. Josephus reports that γίνεται δὲ αὐτῆς ἡ ἄφιξις πάνυ

---

77. Ibid., 43.
78. Ibid., 15.
79. Ibid., 15.
80. Hands, *Charities*, 42–43.
81. Ibid., 53.
82. Ibid., 54.
83. *IGRP* III 493.
84. In his documents section, Hands catalogues a number of other inscriptions that record situations where benefactors are appointed with a range of dates, for example: 2 (330–325 BCE), 7 (c. 150 BCE), 9 (c. 100 BCE) (Hands, *Charities*).
85. Winter, "Acts," 72–74.
86. Ibid., 74.

συμφέρουσα τοῖς Ἱεροσολυμίταις (Her arrival was very advantageous for the people of Jerusalem)(*Ant.* 20.51) as she then used the money she was carrying to send her attendant to buy grain from Egypt and figs from Cyprus, which she distributed to those in need. When her son Izates learnt of the famine, he then sent πολλὰ χρήματα τοῖς πρώτοις τῶν Ἱεροσολυμιτῶν (a great sum of money to [the] leaders of the Jerusalemites)(*Ant.* 20.53), which may be in order to place them in a position of being able to do what was seen as their duty and provide for the needs of the city in return for honor.

The example in the surrounding culture in times of food shortage was therefore for rich individuals or groups of richer people to contribute to a fund to subsidize the price of grain, or to distribute money. Such subsidies could be rewarded with honor, including titles and citations on inscriptions.

When we compare the example of the Antiochene church with the evidence we have of how Greco-Roman society generally responded to food shortages, we find not only a major difference, but also a potential similarity. If the Antiochene church had lifted its pattern from the surrounding world, we would expect the richer members of the community to contribute to a fund, or, if they were rich enough, to do it by themselves. However, Winter notes, in the example of Acts 11 "[t]he role of benefactor was assigned not only to the Christian of substance but to all members of the community who could work."[87] It is not clear how Winter concludes that it is only those Christians who work who contribute as the text actually says τῶν δὲ μαθητῶν καθὼς εὐπορεῖτό τις ὥρισαν ἕκαστος αὐτῶν εἰς διακονίαν πέμψαι (11:29), which seems to have a greater sense of "*according to his* (financial) *ability*"[88] rather than "according to whether they have a job," although the two may in many cases be related. However, the first allows for a wider contribution of all according to what they have, irrespective of whether they have a job. Thus, in Acts 11, there is an expectation of a much wider group contributing, as opposed to a contribution from a limited number of richer people. While it is not clear whether there were richer people among the Antiochene believers, we can expect some social differentiation and it is still the case that Acts 11 presents a wider ownership of contributions than the Greco-Roman examples.

There is also a difference in relationships. In the Greco-Roman examples, the giving seems to be based more on wealth and position in society. In contrast, the Antiochene example is based in more direct and personal relationships between the two communities. The example of Helena and Izates may have characteristics of both, for while they do not seem to have

---

87. Ibid., 75–76.
88. BDAG, 410.

a direct and personal relationship with the people to whom they give, they may be motivated by their relationship to the Jewish community in Jerusalem through conversion as well as by their positions in society.

When we consider Izates' actions in sending the money to the prominent citizens of Jerusalem, we find a similarity to the action of the church in Antioch, which sends money to the elders. This is not necessarily a conclusive parallel, as it is a singular example, because much of the evidence about benefactors has the person or people taking on the role in their existing sphere of influence, rather than sending it to another location. It is however interesting that for Izates, a convert to Judaism, the obvious people to send his gift to were the prominent people in Jerusalem, rather than his mother, whom Josephus has not recorded as having left Jerusalem, and who had been responsible for the initial distribution.

CONCLUSION

In Acts 11:27–30 and 12:25, Luke presents an example of the sharing of possessions which is based on and confirms committed relationships. It is from believers to other believers, but beyond that is between two groups of believers who have existing relationships: the gospel is first proclaimed in Antioch by those who have fled from Jerusalem, Barnabas is sent from Jerusalem to Antioch, and later the prophets come down from Jerusalem to Antioch (11:19, 20, 22, 27). It is an example where individuals contribute according to their ability, but it is also an example which shows corporate responsibility for the sharing. For each of them contribute and they decide together to contribute. The example is presented as something that is key to being disciples of Jesus. It is an example that evidences practical and careful stewardship. The gift is sent carefully with those who are seen as responsible, to those who are seen as responsible. It is a sharing of possessions in response to need. The response to a perceived need in a time of famine is also distinctive when compared with the way that Greco-Roman society usually responded in that the Antiochene church spread the responsibility amongst all its members according to their ability, rather than restricting the giving to a few richer members, and based the giving in their relationship rather than in their riches or position in society. The response has a similarity to the giving of Izates who sends money to the prominent people in Jerusalem.

5

Eating Together

1 Corinthians 11

INTRODUCTION

So far this book has considered instances where sharing is mainly financial: the common purse in John; the selling of property and houses to provide for those in need in Acts; and the collection in Antioch to send to the believers in Judaea. However, in the first two of these examples, food is also shared. The gospels recount many stories of Jesus and his followers sharing food (Matt 14:13–21; 15:29–39; Mark 2:13–17; Luke 10:38–42, 24:30–32; John 13:1–5, 21:7–14). In Acts 2:46 the believers eat together,[1] while in Acts 6 the choosing of the Seven arises out of disagreements in the daily distribution of food, which we argued included eating together.[2] While 1 Cor 11 does not include financial sharing, it is an example where sharing food appears to have led to problems, and where Paul writes to the Corinthians to address some of the issues they are facing. While Paul's criticism suggests a lack of sharing, his catechesis to the Corinthians indicates that he wanted them to be sharing food with one another

---

1. See pp. 46–50.
2. See pp. 60–65.

and this is why we are examining 11:17–34[3] as part of this study looking at sharing possessions.

This chapter considers what is happening in the church in Corinth and what Paul thinks should be happening in the church in Corinth. It examines the ways in which the practice, and Paul's instructions, look similar to and different from the practice in the surrounding culture.

In order to explore what may be happening, we start by looking at the different forms that shared meals could take and the different situations they could take place in in the Greco-Roman context and some of the elements that are similar across the situations. Having highlighted the common aspects of meal sharing, we also look at the patronage system that was widespread in the Greco-Roman era and specifically ways in which this might interact with meal sharing.

We then consider the background of Corinth and of the Corinthian correspondence, before examining the text of 11:17–34 in detail, and other relevant passages, to assess what may be going on in Corinth, or at least what Paul thinks may be going on in Corinth, from the reports he has heard. We examine Paul's response to the situation he perceives: his criticism, catechesis, and solution. As well as the primary evidence considered in the background to meals and patronage, we will look in greater depth at the evidence of the meals of the society of Diana and Antinous at Lanuvium (136 CE), and the Iobacchoi (dated 164/165 CE, though providing evidence of formation in the early second century), which both give detailed instructions about groups eating together. The Iobacchoi provide evidence from Rome and the Society of Diana and Antinous from Athens. Both cities had influenced Corinth society. While they are later than 1 Corinthians, there is evidence of other societies dining together in the first century BCE (*IG* V, 1 209) and in the first century CE (*IG* X, 2.1 259). These earlier inscriptions provide evidence that such societies existed, but less evidence about the detail of the arrangements. Therefore informed by the evidence of earlier groups meeting, we will use the more detailed evidence from the Society of Diana and Antinous and the Iobacchoi in conjunction with the more general evidence of meal sharing for comparison with the pattern of sharing food that Paul is advocating in Corinth.

GRECO-ROMAN BACKGROUND

First we consider the different situations and forms that shared meals could take in the Greco-Roman context, the common aspects of meal sharing,

---

3. Biblical references in this chapter will be to 1 Corinthians unless otherwise stated.

and the ways that patronage might interact with meal sharing. This will help us understand what may be taking place in Corinth and the ways in which Paul's instructions look similar to and different from the practice in the surrounding culture.

Meals in the Greco-Roman World

In his comprehensive *religionsgeschichtliche* study of the Lord's Supper in 1 Corinthians, Klauck provides comparisons between the Lord's Supper and various Jewish and Greco-Roman meals[4] and concludes that while there exist parallels, "keiner aber is mit dem Herrenmahl völlig dekkungsgleich"[5] (none is fully comparably with the Lord's Supper). Klauck's study aims to understand the multilayered influences on the Lord's Supper[6] by the time of 1 Corinthians; however our aim in this chapter is to consider what happened at the church in Corinth, what the pattern of meals in the surrounding Corinthian culture may have been, what Paul is advocating in 1 Corinthians, and how the three relate. We turn therefore to consider the background of Greco-Roman meals in Corinth, so that we can then identify similarities and differences when we look at 1 Corinthians. Smith points out that when people met for a purpose, be it religious or social, in the Greco-Roman world, they would have a meal.[7] While there were differences between the meals in specific situations, "the evidence suggests that meals took similar forms and shared similar meaning and interpretations across a broad range of the ancient world."[8]

Different Meal Contexts

There were various groups which had meals together. There were clubs, which included Greek clubs, Roman *collegia*, and voluntary associations (VA);[9] philosophical groups; and mystery cults. Within Roman cities only three types of *collegia* were allowed: professional *collegia* for a recognized trade, religious *collegia* (to worship a foreign god, which could be a front for an unrecognized trade), and burial *collegia* which catered for burial for

---

4. Klauck, *Herrenmahl*, 365–68.
5. Ibid., 368.
6. Ibid., 370.
7. Smith, *Symposium*, 2.
8. Ibid., 2.
9. For further details about VAs see pp. 227–29.

the poor.[10] Professional *collegia* would have a patron deity and thus worship would still be involved. Christians and Jews were often seen as clubs/VAs.

Meals took place in different contexts including funeral/memorial meals, sacrificial meals, and public meals. Funerary meals took place on the day of the funeral or at the end of a period of mourning (Homer, *Od.* 3.309–311).[11] Memorial meals took place on the anniversary of the deceased's birthday (Diogenes Laertius, *LEP* 10.18) and allowed for continued fellowship with the dead.[12] In some cases they presumed that the dead could enjoy the pleasures of living.[13] While the Lord's Supper looked back to Jesus' death, it was not yearly and remembered his death rather than taking place on his birthday.

Sacrificial meals included an animal being killed and often its entrails being inspected.[14] The participants would then usually eat the animal. If there was no accompanying meal, it was usual to specify that they were θυσίαι ἄδαιτοί (meal-less sacrifices).[15] The gods could be "thought to be present as guest or host in the meals held in their honor."[16] Such meals could take place at a temple. In Acrocorinth there is evidence of up to 40 dining rooms at the temple.[17] Stambaugh notes that the Senate met at temples "so that the gods could be consulted through augury."[18] However, as Klauck points out there is no evidence of a sacrifice taking place within the Lord's Supper.[19]

Meals could also be very public occasions, for example the public banquets[20] which could be bestowed by emperors or governors.

Jewish Meals

As we have already seen there were also Jewish meals of various kinds, from the yearly Passover celebrations, to the meals of the Essenes, and meals at

---

10. Stambaugh and Balch, *Social World*, 125.
11. Smith, *Symposium*, 42.
12. Jamir, "Exclusion," 62.
13. Smith, *Symposium*, 41–42.
14. Stambaugh, "Functions," 577.
15. Smith, *Symposium*, 69.
16. Jamir, "Exclusion," 63.
17. Coutsoumpos, *Paul*, 21.
18. Stambaugh, "Functions," 580.
19. Klauck, *Herrenmahl*, 366.
20. Pervo, "PANTA KOINA," 184.

Qumran.[21] There were also Pharisaic meals and meals of the *ḥaverim* where purity laws were very important.[22] The story of *Joseph and Aseneth* is sometimes used for comparison to the Lord's Supper. Both meals involved "the blessing of bread and partaking of bread and wine as a sacred meal."[23] Joseph and Aseneth refers to the bread and cup: "And may she drink the cup of thy blessing" (8.11), however the bread and cup are also referred to in conjunction with oil "the blessed unction of incorruption" (8.5). While there are some similarities, these are merely in the eating of bread and drinking of wine, which are not unusual for a meal, and there are differences, both in the presence of oil and the setting of the account. In addition, it does not seem likely that those at Corinth would have known this story.

There is some evidence for the presence of Jewish Christians in the Corinthian church. However, there is little evidence of Essene/Pharasaic meals in Asia Minor and the Lord's Supper is celebrated more often than Passover. It therefore seems unlikely that regular Jewish meals are the most appropriate place to look for influence for the patterns of behavior in Corinth that Paul criticizes, although Paul's catechesis is likely to be influenced by his Jewish background.

Meals: Form and Structure

While meals could take place in a number of contexts: homes, temples, *scola* of associations/*collegia* and for a variety of occasions, there are aspects which may be seen across many of the meals. We now turn to look at the form or structure of these meals. In some instances the evidence comes from accounts or rules for special clubs, in other instances, the descriptions are from literary stories.[24]

By the time of 1 Corinthians the Greek δεῖπνον and the Roman *cena* had moved from being main meals at lunchtime to being evening meals. In a Greek δεῖπνον, thirty-six or more people could be accommodated,[25] while

---

21. See pp. 28–31.
22. Smith, *Symposium*, 151–52.
23. Coutsoumpos, *Paul*, 28.
24. While Meggitt helpfully highlights the elite nature of most literary sources (Meggitt, *Paul*, 12–13; Meggitt, "Sources," 242–43), Longenecker provides evidence that the Corinthian church was more socially varied than Meggitt allows for (Longenecker, *Remembering*, 226–48) and argues that "Meggitt's own advocacy of binary dichotomization is in full accord with the rhetorical construction of the elite" (Longenecker, *Remembering*, 42).
25. Jamir, "Exclusion," 18.

a Roman dining room could only hold multiples of three,[26] which would normally be six, nine, or twelve people dining together.[27] While Greek meals generally only included men, Roman meals included men and women.[28]

A larger group of guests in a Roman villa-style house would be split between rooms, with the more important guests on the couches in the *triclinium* and others accommodated in the *atrium*, standing or on chairs. "This arrangement immediately divided those who attended into first- and second-class members. Not only was it more prestigious to have a place in the dining room, but it was a lot more comfortable."[29]

For some meals the host provided the food: for *eranos* meals, those attending contributed in some way rather like a "potluck" meal.[30] This could involve people bringing their own food.[31] Plutarch (*Quaest. conv.* 646C) refers to bringing food in baskets and Homer to individual portions (*Od.* 1.226–7). There were also occasions where money was brought as a contribution.[32] However, there was also criticism of individual portions (*Od.* 1.226–7) and Xenophon recounts Socrates giving orders for sharing (*Mem.* 3.14.1).

Coutsoumpos notes that Roman meals traditionally had three parts: the *gustatio* or *promulsis* where the appetite was whetted with *mulsum*, the *ferucla* or courses where the main dishes were eaten[33] and the *mensae secundae* where nuts, fruit, and cake were served with the *convivium*, drinking party, which normally involved entertainment.[34] There was a similar split in the Greek tradition where the drinking happened after the main eating of the δεῖπνον in the συμπόσιον. Smith notes that by Roman times, a Greek δεῖπνον also included appetizers.[35]

Usually as guests arrived water would be brought for them to wash before eating (*Od.* 7.170–179) and through the meal they would be served by slaves.[36] Plutarch notes the importance of dedicating dishes (*Quaest.*

---

26. Smith, *Symposium*, 26.

27. Jamir, "Exclusion," 18.

28. d'Arms, "*Convivium*," 312.

29. Mitchell, "Amen," 258.

30. Jamir, "Exclusion," 13, 15.

31. Lampe, "Party," 4.

32. Coutsoumpos, *Paul*, 46. Also possibly seen in Martial *Ep.* 60.

33. Bach points out that main courses usually involved the staple (*sitos*), accompaniment (*opson*), and drink (*poton*) (Bach and Glancy, "Morning," 452–53).

34. Coutsoumpos, *Paul*, 45; Smith, *Symposium*, 27.

35. Smith, *Symposium*, 27.

36. Ibid., 28.

conv. 7.4.703), although it not clear whether Plutarch is talking about the dedication of the pot or what it contains. As the meal moved into the *convivium* or συμπόσιον stage, the transition would be marked by libations (*Od.* 3.330–347, 7.135–140, 7.162–167; Plato *Symp.* 176A), which would involve "a chant to the god" even when the meal was "a symposium of a secular nature."[37] This second stage of the meal could also include newly arrived guests (Plato *Symp.* 175 C–D).[38]

In some smaller cult meals there could be a range of people involved where "the individuals contributed according to their abilities: the wealthier members made dedications and undertook necessary reconstruction" while "the poorer members contributed the minimum fees to the group's treasury, and performed such duties as they could."[39] However, this did not necessarily mean that each had an equal standing at a meal, as we will see later when we examine the Society of Diana and Antinous. Indeed in many instances meals "were used to create and maintain social divisions in status."[40]

There is some discussion about the extent to which meals were religious or secular in nature. For example, Coutsoumpos argues that even in temple settings not all meals at temple were sacramental,[41] and Smith notes meals could take place in temples for they could be meals on social or familial occasions like marriage and birthdays.[42] However, earlier, Smith himself argues that meals "have an integrative function in ancient society in which they combine the sacred and the secular into one ritual event."[43] The distinction between sacred and social seems to be anachronistic.

As well as having religious elements, "Meals in Greco-Roman society were a central focus of social intercourse."[44] This can been seen in the evidence for meals in a variety of contexts from the ways that temples included

37. Jamir, "Exclusion," 90.
38. Coutsoumpos, *Paul*, 47; Smith, *Symposium*, 31.
39. Stambaugh, "Functions," 599.
40. Smith, *Symposium*, 68.
41. Coutsoumpos, *Paul*, 22. Coutsoumpos seems to have a relatively narrow definition of sacramental in this instance, using it to refer to meals where a sacrifice had taken place with a religious ceremony or which related to initiation and thus sees meals to celebrate coming of age as non-sacramental.
42. Smith, *Symposium*, 76. In contrast, invitations to meals in honor of Lord Serapis indicate they could take place "in private homes as well as temples" (Coutsoumpos, *Paul*, 35).
43. Smith, *Symposium*, 6.
44. Cheung, *Food*, 35.

dining rooms, to the invitations to dinners at temples and in homes, and the way that synagogues had meal facilities.[45]

Status and Stratification at Meals

Meals gave the opportunity for gaining or showing status[46] due to the stratification that was obvious in many meals. Saturnalia was the one occasion where there was an opportunity for equality. At the feast of Saturnalia, the rich were meant to entertain the poor (Lucian *Sat.* 15) and people were to sit freely and be served the same food and drink (*Sat.* 17). However, Lucian still indicates that some form of return should be made, whether garlands of flowers or grains or frankincense (*Sat.* 16). It was an occasion where "slaves were permitted to take the place of their master, including at the banquets"[47] and where the poor could be invited in and treated well.[48]

However, Saturnalia was not the normal approach to how people from different backgrounds ate together. Those from different backgrounds would usually be given different places to sit and different food and drink.[49] Juvenal notes that when a supper invite is a repayment for a client they can expect the lowest place on the lowest couch (*Sat.* 5.12–18). Those of lower rank still would not recline but sit.[50] Invitations might also be rejected due to status concerns.[51]

Juvenal satirizes the contrasts in the food for people of different rank served up at meals: the "huge lobster" compared to the "shrimp" (Sat. 5.80–85), "fruits such as grew in the never-failing Autumn of the Phaeacians" compared to "a rotten apple" (*Sat.* 5.150–55). Not only could the type and quality of the food vary but also the size of the portions.[52]

The etiquette of meals was one of Greco-Roman writers' concerns and some advocated equality.[53] Plutarch addresses the question of whether a host should assign his guests places or leave them to choose themselves.

---

45. Blue, "House Church," 221–24. For the importance of meals to the Jewish communities see also Jamir, "Exclusion," 23–60.

46. Witherington, *Conflict*, 244.

47. Jamir, "Exclusion," 84.

48. Witherington, *Conflict*, 241–42.

49. Stambaugh and Balch, *Social World*, 114.

50. Smith, *Symposium*, 10–11.

51. Jamir, "Exclusion," 70.

52. Smith, *Symposium*, 92. Martial indicates that sometimes the differentiation was masked (*Ep.* 4.85).

53. Jamir, "Exclusion," 84.

He gives the example of his brother Timon allowing free seating, but then when a late-arriving rich foreign guest comes, he refuses to enter as "he saw no place left worthy of him" (*Quaest. Conv.* 8.615). Their father then argues against free seating, urging the need for organization and for the honor due to each person to be observed (*Quaest. Conv.* 8.615–616B).

Pliny argues against the disparity in quality and quantity of food served at meals, asserting that he provides the same food for all at his dinners (*Ep.* 2.6). However, as Crossan and Reed point out, his solution is not that he raises the standard of the food he serves, but rather that all get served the more basic food.[54] Plutarch argues that when everything is shared, meals are better for fellowship and that not sharing sows enmity (*Quaest. conv.* 643E). However, he notes some of the challenges of this approach, for example, people grabbing from the shared dishes as quickly as possible, which causes conflict, providing an argument for equal portions. Plutarch notes that while this might be seen as destroying companionship, it is not the case if there is equality in the portions (*Quaest. conv.* 643E–644D), but that it causes issues where people have different food requirements (*Quaest. conv.* 643C).

However, while there is evidence of equality at meals being a topic for discussion, it seems unlikely that meals generally involved free seating and equal food and portions. The arguments put forward by the writers suggest that equality of portions and free seating was something that was being tried out on occasion, rather than the norm. Plutarch's description of the variety of Timon's guests is also telling: they are varied because they include "foreigners as well as citizens, friends as well as kinsmen, and, in a word, all sorts of people" (*Quaest. conv.* 615D). While this indicates some variety, there is no evidence that they represented a particularly wide range of social backgrounds in terms of wealth or influence. Blue argues that "It was uncommon for different classes to eat together."[55]

While equality was on the agenda for some, there is ample evidence of differentiation in meals. In *collegia*, there was different treatment for officers, even though *collegia* were likely to be more socially homogeneous than the Corinthian congregation.[56] Plutarch, for all his arguments for equality, only goes so far: while he argues to leave portions of food from the dinner for the slaves that they may share with them, it is a sharing that involves them eating it afterwards rather than partaking in the meal at the same time

---

54. Crossan and Reed, *Search*, 339.
55. Blue, "House Church," 239.
56. Coutsoumpos, *Paul*, 88.

(*Quaest. conv.* 703D–E).[57] Smith argues that writers such as Martial and Pliny "can be seen as reflecting aspects of common meal etiquette even as they argue against prevailing customs."[58] Pliny argues that there are dangers of equality (*Ep.* 9.5) and Lucian recounts Alcidamas complaining about sitting rather than reclining (*Symp.* 13). Therefore, rather than encouraging equality, meals more often reinforced status and hierarchy, and in some cases created it.[59]

Patronage[60]

Another way that people from different backgrounds would meet together, and eat together, is through the patronage system, which Horsley argues is a likely background for some of the relational issues in Corinth.[61] Patronage was one of the main organization structures in the Graeco-Roman world. Indeed Crossan and Reed argue that patronage was the main ordering in the Roman world,[62] and Braund that personal patronage was pervasive.[63] Patronage involved hierarchy and a web of relationships where favors were exchanged between patrons and clients.[64] Patronage relations were key for gaining resources and prestige, therefore having powerful patrons and bestowing benefaction were both seen as important.[65] "[S]uch relations might also be one of the important channels through which scarce resources, such as powerful positions in the imperial government or local government were distributed."[66] Plunder and charity were often distributed according to

---

57. Pervo notes that in general both in terms of meals and charity, those who were poorer received less and that "when the poor did receive anything like equality, it would be upon a religious occasion." (Pervo, "PANTA KOINA," 186).

58. Smith, *Symposium*, 45; Martial *Ep* 3.60.

59. Jamir, "Exclusion," 103, 73–75.

60. For further details about patronage, see pp. 185–91.

61. Horsley, *Paul*, 125.

62. Crossan and Reed, *Search*, 297; also Wallace-Hadrill, "Patronage," 72.

63. Braund, "Function and Dysfunction," 137. There is some disagreement about the involvement of the very poor within patronage relationships. For example, Cloud argues they were excluded because they had no vote (Cloud, "Relationship," 210), but this presumes that the vote was key and also does not acknowledge the patronage relationships seen in the hierarchy of VAs (McRae, "Eating," 166, 171).

64. Garnsey and Saller, *Empire*, 148.

65. Garland, *1 Corinthians*, 5.

66. Chow, *Patronage and Power*, 64.

wealth and position and therefore if you wanted access, you needed to be or to know someone with either wealth or position.[67]

These patronage relations also worked on a household level and Meeks points out that a household was not simply members with common kinship, but would include "slaves, former slaves who were now clients, [and] hired labourers"[68] who might well live clustered around the patron's house.[69] The head of the household, the *paterfamilias* had a key position.[70] Freedmen would still owe allegiance to their former owner and they would often take the owner's *praenomenon* and *nomen* and could not harm their patron or bring a case against them.[71] A patron or head of a household could also have literary or philosophical clients as well as freedmen clients.[72]

A household was in effect a small pyramid connected into a much bigger pyramid of patronage relationships where the emperor was the patron of the whole empire.[73] As Corinth was a Roman colony, the emperor would be seen as Corinth's patron and we can see this in the titles ascribed to the emperor in Corinth and the presence of imperial cult.[74] Chow also argues that because Corinth was a Roman colony and patronage was important in empire, we can expect to see its importance in Corinth.[75] Government officials operated as clients to the emperor and patrons to others.[76] They could bestow "citizenship, offices and honors from Rome."[77] In Corinth, we see a number of inscriptions (*Corinth* 8,3: 159–63) which honor Claudius Dinnipis for his patronage in his role as a *curator annonae*, a role which he undertook three times.[78]

While patron-client relationships were widespread, Saller points out that *cliens* is not necessarily used to refer to clients because it could be seen

---

67. Horrell, *Ethos*, 70.

68. Meeks, *Christians*, 30.

69. Crossan and Reed, *Search*, 309.

70. Horrell, *Ethos*, 68.

71. Chow, *Patronage and Power*, 70. Stambaugh and Balch, *Social World*, 115. Wallace-Hadrill points out that this was different from many patron-client relationships because the relationship had a position in law (Wallace-Hadrill, "Patronage," 76).

72. Chow, *Patronage and Power*, 72.

73. Mitchell, "Amen," 252; Chow, *Patronage and Power*, 41; Garnsey and Saller, *Empire*, 150. Suetonius provides evidence of emperors providing meals (*Vesp.* 19 and *Dom.* 7).

74. Chow, *Patronage and Power*, 43–44.

75. Ibid., 40.

76. Ibid., 52–57; Saller, *Personal Patronage*, 30–31.

77. Garnsey and Saller, *Empire*, 151.

78. Horsley, *Paul*, 116.

as being demeaning.[79] *Patronus* was more regularly used, although it was used more of "the mediators who supported the careers of young senators and equestrians."[80] The presence or absence of the word would not necessarily indicate the presence or absence of a patronage relationship.[81]

Amicitia could include "exchange relationships between men of equal, as well as unequal, social status."[82] Where their statuses were unequal, this was a patronage relationship, where their statuses were more equal, this might involve a relationship, where there was a responsibility to help the clients of the other[83] who would then be obligated to the new patron as well, or be friends with friends of friends. For example, Cicero mentions a persistent invitation to dinner from the friend of a friend (*Fam.* 7.9.3).[84] Saller notes that patronage language was used for a range of relationships and notes the overlap between *amicitia* and *clientela*.[85] Patronage thus took place at different levels of society.[86]

Within a patronage relationship a client might gain food (*sportulae*),[87] finance, and opportunities, while the patron gained dignity, status, and praise.[88] Occasionally the client might be invited to dinner, although they would receive poorer food and there would be a hierarchy in the seating arrangements.[89] Clients would also be expected to visit their patron in the morning to perform the morning *salutatio*, one way to give honor. Depending on the status of the client or protégé they would have been received in different ways at the morning *salutatio*. Peers would have been received in private, lesser *amici* in the atrium in groups, and *clientes* en mass, in some cases outside.[90] Clients might also accompany a patron on his business or applaud him in court.[91]

---

79. Saller, *Personal Patronage*, 9; Garnsey and Saller, *Empire*, 153.

80. Garnsey and Saller, *Empire*, 153. Garnsey and Saller argue that this form of patronage may be seen as an example of superior/inferior friendship (Garnsey and Saller, *Empire*, 152).

81. Saller, *Personal Patronage*, 11.

82. Ibid., 15.

83. Ibid., 25; Pliny *Ep.* 2.13.2.

84. Chow provides more information about the kinds of bonds in patronage relationships (Chow, *Patronage and Power*, 35–36).

85. Saller, "Patronage and Friendship," 57, 61.

86. Wallace-Hadrill, "Patronage," 77.

87. Garnsey and Saller, *Empire*, 151.

88. Chow, *Patronage and Power*, 73.

89. Ibid., 74. For further details, pp. 104–6.

90. Saller, *Personal Patronage*, 11.

91. Garnsey and Saller, *Empire*, 151. Crossan and Reed argue that Paul's refusal to

CORINTH AND THE CORINTHIAN CHURCH

We have considered the wider meal practice and patronage background of the early church in Corinth and we now turn to look at the city itself and the evidence we have for the situations and issues in the early church there. Examining the background and make up of the church in Corinth, together with the wider issues the church was facing will help us assess what may be happening when they meet together to celebrate the Lord's Supper.

In 146 BCE Corinth was levelled to the ground by Roman soldiers.[92] It was refounded as a Roman colony in 44 BCE[93] and in 27 BCE become the seat of the governor of Achaia, before becoming a senatorial province in 44 CE.[94] The Roman colony was settled by a range of people, some former soldiers, some Greek, some Jewish and was "Rome's most important colony in the East in this era."[95] It was also somewhere that freedman had more possibilities for advancement than elsewhere.[96]

The city was situated on an isthmus, in a key position for East-West and North-South trade.[97] As an important center for trade and with settlers from different backgrounds and places, Corinth included people from diverse social and religious backgrounds (Pausanias *Descr.* 2.6).[98] There is evidence of Greek religions and philosophy, mystery cults, different shrines, as well as the Jewish presence we have already mentioned.[99] It seems likely that some of these shrines were established by non-citizen residents who wanted to create "some sense of ethnic identity by establishing local cults of their native gods."[100] There are more Latin than Greek inscriptions for this period[101] and the coins are generally Latin as well.[102] This evidence indicates

---

accept support at Corinth is because of the level of patronage in Corinth and because Paul wished to avoid being seen either as patron or client to those within the congregation with the expectations that that would bring (Crossan and Reed, *Search*, 332–6) and the ways that it might limit "gospel ministry" (Walton, "Paul," 232).

92. Barrett, *First Corinthians*, 1–2; Thiselton, *Shorter*, 5.
93. Barrett, *First Corinthians*, 2; Thiselton, *Shorter*, 5.
94. Conzelmann, *Corinthians*, 12.
95. Winter, *Paul*, 21.
96. Clarke, *Leadership*, 21.
97. Barrett, *First Corinthians*, 1.
98. Murphy-O'Connor, *Paul's Corinth* (1st edition), 23.
99. Jamir, "Exclusion," 111; Philo *Legat.* 281–82 (Murphy-O'Connor, *Paul's Corinth* (1st edition), 78).
100. Meeks, *Christians*, 13.
101. Thiselton, *Shorter*, 19–20.
102. Winter, *Paul*, 11.

that the city was thoroughly Roman. We see further evidence for this in the layout of dining rooms in temples and *triclinia* and *atria* in villas in Corinth.[103]

Our knowledge of the Corinthian church comes mainly from the two extant letters to the Corinthian church and from the account in Acts 18:1–18[104] and is therefore limited to Paul's side of the correspondence and relationship.[105] The Delphi fragment indicates that Gallio was proconsul in either 50–51 CE or 51–52 CE.[106] Therefore using Acts 18:12, it is likely that Paul was in Corinth 49–51 or 50–52 CE.[107] First Corinthians is Paul's response to a letter from the Corinthian church (7:1), which Horrell suggests may have been brought by Stephanas, Fortunatus, and Achaicus (16:17),[108] and the report from Chloe's people (1:11). Paul addresses issues that have been raised by the congregation and that have come to light from those who have journeyed to see him. These issues range from leadership and wisdom, to sexual immorality and gifts of the Spirit.

In Acts and 1 Corinthians we see evidence of a church where there are people from different backgrounds and walks of life. We find mention of Priscilla and Aquila (Acts 18:2), who were artisans, accommodated Paul, and hosted the congregation. They also had the means to travel.[109] Chloe's people may have been slaves or other members of her household (1:11) and Chow points out that Fortunatus and Achaicus' names may have a servile

---

103. Ibid., 8; Witherington, *Conflict*, 195.

104. There is significant discussion about the unity of each of the Corinthian letters and the relationship between Paul's visits and letters. Crossan and Reed construct a series of five letters (of which 1 Corinthians is one, 2 Corinthians is the amalgamation of two letters and there are two lost letters) and three visits (Crossan and Reed, *Search*, 332–33). Conzelmann addresses the question of whether 1 Corinthians is one letter and argues that while there are transitions of thought and different degrees of knowledge about circumstances that "the existing breaks can be explained from the circumstances of its composition" (Conzelmann, *Corinthians*, 3–4) and Thiselton notes that we have an early, nearly complete Greek manuscript and that there is not agreement about where the letter would be partitioned (Thiselton, *Epistle*, 36–37). We will follow Conzelmann and Thiselton's position as we consider 1 Corinthians.

105. Chow, *Patronage and Power*, 84.

106. Barrett, *New Testament Background*, 48–49.

107. Conzelmann, *Corinthians*, 12. Horrell suggests that the visit is earlier and that the edict of Claudius expelling Jews from Rome is earlier, with Acts 18 presenting a conflation of two visits (Horrell, *Ethos*, 73–74). However, this would still place one of the visits during the time that Gallio was proconsul.

108. Horrell, *Ethos*, 91; also Grosheide, *Corinthians*, 14.

109. Horrell, *Ethos*, 99. Crossan and Reed suggest that Priscilla and Aquila rent property as they move around (Crossan and Reed, *Search*, 329), although they could have a base in one place, which they owned, and rented in other places.

origin and may indicate that they were freedmen or dependants of Stephanus (16:17).[110] Erastus is mentioned in Rom 16:23 as οἰκονόμος, which Crossan and Reed note is "a notch below the office of aedilis."[111] Gaius hosted Paul and the whole church (Rom 16:23, 1 Cor 1:14), Phoebe, διάκονος at Cenchreae was προστάτις of many (Rom 16:2). Phoebe also travels which again suggests riches.[112] The litigation in 1 Cor 6 would also have required wealth.[113] So we see evidence of some more affluent and influential people among the congregation. However, we can also find evidence of less affluent members.

When Paul addresses the Corinthians he reminds them ὅτι οὐ πολλοὶ σοφοὶ κατὰ σάρκα, οὐ πολλοὶ δυνατοί, οὐ πολλοὶ εὐγενεῖς (1:26). We find slaves (7:21), as well as those who are not slaves (7:22), addressed in 1 Cor 7. In 11:21 there are ὃς [μὲν] πεινᾷ. Thus, while "most of the people named by Paul probably belonged to the upper class,"[114] the church as a whole was made up of people from a range of social backgrounds.[115]

However, Meggitt argues that most people in Corinth would have had "brutal and frugal lives characterized by struggle and impoverishment."[116] He then argues that the references in 1:26 and 4:10 do not necessarily point to the presence of more affluent members of the church or to those from the ruling classes. In 4:10 Meggitt argues that Paul "is making reference to the Corinthians' sense of spiritual (rather than social) self-importance."[117] However, as Thiselton points out, Meggitt himself acknowledges evidence is limited,[118] and Holmberg argues that Meggitt dismisses evidence that points to socio-economic diversity.[119] Thiselton notes that while Meggitt makes important points, for example the way the "*plebs urbana* lived

---

110. Chow, *Patronage and Power*, 90–91.

111. Crossan and Reed, *Search*, 330.

112. Horrell, *Ethos*, 96.

113. Ibid., 95. Also Clarke, *Leadership*, 59–68.

114. Jamir, "Exclusion," 117.

115. Ibid., 114. There are various arguments about the make up of the early church as a whole. Chow summarizes the history of the arguments about the make up of the early church and the Corinthian Church specifically (Chow, *Patronage and Power*, 11–27). Meeks points out the new consensus that there was more social diversity in the early Christian church and notes that sixty-five people are mentioned by name in the letters of Paul or his disciples with another thirteen names in Acts, which show a diversity of backgrounds (Meeks, *Christians*, 52, 55–56).

116. Meggitt, *Paul*, 73.

117. Ibid., 106.

118. Thiselton, *Epistle*, 25; Meggitt, "Sources," 252.

119. Holmberg, "Methods," 263.

on the breadline,"[120] this does not preclude differences in social standing within, nor the presence of some more affluent Christians in the Corinthian church.[121] As Horrell points out, Meggitt's hypothesis is too binary.[122] While there may not have been elites who were part of the Corinthian congregation, there could have been better off members.[123] Longenecker's careful analysis of named individuals in the Corinthian congregation shows a variety of economic backgrounds though not members of the top elite.[124]

As well as the diversity of economic background, there is also evidence of other aspects of social diversity and social tensions.[125] When Paul arrives in Corinth, he preaches at the synagogue (Acts 18:5) and Crispus, the synagogue leader, and his household believe (Acts 18:8). Priscilla and Aquila are also Jews (Acts 18:2). Horrell suggests that Apollos and Cephas' visits may have increased the number of Jewish converts.[126] Paul also spends time at the house of Titius Justus, σεβομένος τὸν θεόν. Thiselton notes that Paul refers to those who are prominent in Roman, Greek, and Jewish society.[127] However, Paul is also able to write to the Corinthians that they were idolators before coming to faith in Jesus (12:2).

In addition to the evidence of a mix of Jews, godfearers, and pagans, there is also evidence of different factions with different leaders. Paul refers to different people aligning themselves with different leaders (1:12; 3:4) and to quarrels and disputes (3:3). As Chow points out, "The problem does not appear to be between Apollos and Paul,"[128] as Paul sees Apollos as a fellow-worker (3:9) and is in communication with Apollos (16:12). Chow suggests that individuals may have identified with different missionaries[129] sometimes linked to whoever baptized them (1:16).

Particular leaders may have been favored by particular groups as a result of their "philosopher" credentials which could have included their rhetorical skill and whether they accepted financial help. Paul's account of

---

120. Thiselton, *Epistle*, 183.
121. Ibid., 26.
122. Horrell, "Space," 358.
123. Ibid., 357.
124. Longenecker, *Remembering*, 220–52.
125. Horrell, *Ethos*, 101.
126. Ibid., 92.
127. Thiselton, *Epistle*, 28. Meeks argues that Paul's letters show "no visible connection or even contact between them and the synagogues" (Meeks, *Christians*, 168).
128. Chow, *Patronage and Power*, 103.
129. Ibid., 94.

his own preaching as lacking rhetorical skill, itself uses rhetoric[130] and it may be that some of the Corinthians sought and valued the rhetorical ability of the leader they identified with.[131]

Philosophers had four ways that they might be supported: charging fees, having a rich patron, begging, and working.[132] Some patrons may have felt that Paul was dishonoring them by refusing help, particularly if other leaders accepted help. Both Chow and Smith argue that if householders allowed a congregation to meet in their home, they may have seen themselves as patron to the church.[133] Barrett notes Paul's lack of reference to a president of the shared meal or a treasurer (16:2) and argues that the Corinthian church in this period "had no clearly marked form or structure."[134] This may be the case and the lack of a leadership structure could exacerbate the potential for different people to be competing for power.

We have seen a number of aspects of diversity within the Corinthian congregation: economic, religious, and factions possibly linked to patronage. All three may have influenced the different opinions on eating εἰδωλόθυτον that Paul addresses in his letter. The different groups may have had different experiences of eating meat offered to idols and therefore associated it with different events. People of different social standing would have had different levels of engagement in wider society and thus different opportunities to be involved in wider society.

Chow points out that those who were patrons would probably have had responsibilities and ties with those who were pagans.[135] Coutsoumpos notes that some may have had "social or business responsibilities"[136] that meant they would be invited to dinners or to shrines and suggests it is those who are richer who are continuing to eat meat offered to idols.[137] Similarly Theissen argues that the rich would have needed to maintain social contacts to keep business.[138] In contrast the poor may not have eaten meat often,[139] possibly only at cultic meals.[140] This might have placed those who were

---

130. Thiselton, *Epistle*, 43.
131. Chow, *Patronage and Power*, 104–5.
132. Ibid., 109.
133. Ibid., 110; Smith, *Symposium*, 177.
134. Barrett, *First Corinthians*, 24.
135. Chow, *Patronage and Power*, 114.
136. Coutsoumpos, *Paul*, 93.
137. Ibid., 93.
138. Theissen, *Setting*, 130–31.
139. Coutsoumpos, *Paul*, 93.
140. Theissen, *Setting*, 125–27.

poorer in the position of associating eating meat with cultic meals. However, Meggitt cites the presence of *popinae* or *ganeae* (cookshops), which were popular and accessed by poorer people and sold stews that included meat.[141] Therefore Meggitt argues that meat was "a familiar enough part of everyday life of the 'non-elite' that 'numinous' qualities could not have been ascribed to it."[142] While Meggitt has shown the likelihood of the non-elite eating meat in particular contexts, nevertheless it is still possible that particular groups would have been more likely to eat certain types of meat in religious contexts.[143]

Other suggestions for some of the issues that factions gathered round are: Gnosticism, over-realized eschatology, and tensions over the Apostolic Decree of Acts 15.[144] Schmithals argues that the background to many of the issues was Gnosticism,[145] however Winter argues that while there may have been some incipient Gnostic thought, full-blown Gnosticism is not evident.[146] Such incipient Gnosticism might be seen in the valuing of knowledge (8:1), the argument that all things were lawful (10:23) and areas where "The world is rejected in a theoretical way in order to profit from it in a practical."[147] Thiselton points out the evidence in 1 Corinthians does not make Gnosticism a necessary cause.[148] It may be that over-realized eschatology is partly what Paul is addressing in 1 Cor 4[149] as he argues that leadership is less "have it all" (4:8) and more "commit it all" (4:10–13). It is also possible that some Corinthians may have focused more on their past experience of transformation, so their resurrection focus was no longer in the future.[150] Through 1 Corinthians Paul emphasizes that the Corinthians

---

141. Meggitt, "Meat," 138.

142. Ibid., 140.

143. Witherington argues that the rich may have used dining rooms at the temple for other occasions and that the poor would generally have associated meat with religious occasions (Witherington, *Conflict*, 188, 190).

144. Jamir suggests range of possibilities based on the issues addressed in the letter "A freedom party (5.2); ascetics (chap. 7), pneumatics (chap. 12) and sceptics (15.12–19)." (Jamir, "Exclusion," 132).

145. Schmithals, *Gnosticism*, 218–58.

146. Winter, *Paul*, 25.

147. Theissen, *Setting*, 136.

148. Thiselton, "Eschatology," 525.

149. Thiselton, *Epistle*, 345, 357.

150. Thiselton, "Eschatology," 524. In contrast, Tomlin suggests an Epicurean background for the issues around the resurrection, food, and sex (Tomlin, "Christians," 57–65). He also argues that the Eucharist could have been seen as a funerary meal (ibid., 66). However, as argued in pp. 99–100 this seems unlikely.

have "not yet arrived" and the need for ongoing effort and commitment, as well as the interim nature of the Lord's Supper.[151]

It is not clear how the debates over eating meat offered to idols relate to the Apostolic decree of Acts 15. Paul does not mention the decree in his discussion of the issue. Coutsoumpos suggests that the debate is "connected to outside attempts to introduce the Apostolic Decree into the Corinthian Church."[152] Similarly Winter suggests that Paul may have had an "unguarded emphasis" on freedom and then after the Jerusalem council[153] his initial letter (referred to in 5:9) was an attempt to introduce the apostolic decree. Barrett thus posits that 1 Corinthians is Paul's attempt to mediate between the decree and the freedom the Corinthians think they have.[154]

We have seen how "the Christian congregation in Corinth encompassed various groups and classes, many cultures, ethnic and social identities and thus various interests, customs, assumptions and stratification."[155] We now turn to considering 11:17–34: what is happening during the Lord's Supper in Corinth, and Paul's response.

FIRST CORINTHIANS 11:17-34

What is Happening in the Corinthian Church?

In the second half of 1 Cor 11 Paul addresses what is happening when the church meets to celebrate the Lord's Supper. Paul has heard reports from the church (11:18)[156] and writes to correct their practice and remind them of them of what they are celebrating.

The issue concerns how the Corinthians eat the Lord's Supper when they gather together. In eating together as they met, early Christians were doing something that most groups in the ancient world would have done as they met together.[157] Horrell suggests that the Corinthians probably would have met weekly,[158] which would fit with the reference to the first day of

---

151. Thiselton, "Eschatology," 519, 522.
152. Coutsoumpos, *Paul*, 90.
153. Winter, *Paul*, 26.
154. Barrett, *First Corinthians*, 7.
155. Jamir, "Exclusion," 118.
156. Possibly from Chloe's people if περὶ δέ does introduce issues raised in the Corinthian's letter (Horrell, *Ethos*, 90; Hurd, *The Origins of 1 Corinthians*, 63; Thiselton, *Epistle*, 35), but note Mitchell, "Concerning," 229–56.
157. Smith, *Symposium*, 174, 279. See pp. 99–101.
158. Horrell, *Ethos*, 80.

every week in 16:2. How they met would have been important, therefore Paul would have addressed "proper procedure and protocol at the table"[159] and would have established it "during his mission to Corinth."[160]

The Corinthians gather together (συνέρχομαι).[161] Meeks argues that Paul's use of κατ' οἶκον (16:19) suggests that "individual household-based groups"[162] may have met which then came together as a larger group, ἐν ἐκκλησίᾳ (11.18), ἐπὶ τὸ αὐτό (11:20), and ἡ ἐκκλησία ὅλη ἐπὶ τὸ αὐτό (14:23). It should be noted that 16:19 refers to a household community not in Corinth, but rather where Paul is as he writes. However, the references to households within the Corinthian church—τὸν Στεφανᾶ οἶκον (1:16) and τῶν Χλόης (1:11)—do support a model where individual worshipping households may then have gathered together. Crossan and Reed suggest that such gatherings of households or assemblies would have taken place in one of the bigger houses.[163] It is possible that different households constituted different factions within the Corinthian church.[164]

As these different households come together, Meeks identifies four aspects to the celebration: common meal, imitation of Jesus' last meal, commemorating his death on their behalf, and eschatological expectation.[165] However, all is not well as the Corinthians gather, in fact, Paul can go as far as saying: Τοῦτο δὲ παραγγέλλων οὐκ ἐπαινῶ (11:17). The issue is serious because the "congregation of brothers precisely in their gathering for worship, presents a shameless picture of social cleavage."[166] It is possible that those who were better off were treating the meeting as a private party and that "the social stratification of the congregation was overemphasized and exacerbated."[167] As Crossan and Reed point out important people in the congregation could be "very good for help, support, and protection, but also very bad for unity, equality, and commonality."[168]

In the process of the Corinthians eating together ὃς μὲν πεινᾷ, ὃς δὲ μεθύει (11:21) and τοὺς μὴ ἔχοντας (11:22) are shamed by the way the

159. Blue, "House Church," 225.

160. Horrell, *Ethos*, 87.

161. Blue notes that συνέρχομαι is used five times in 1 Cor 11:17–34 and has only three other occurrences in Paul, all in 1 Corinthians (Blue, "House Church," 225).

162. Meeks, *Christians*, 75.

163. Crossan and Reed, *Search*, 340.

164. See pp. 220–21 and Adams, *Places*, for other ways Christians may have met together.

165. Meeks, *Christians*, 158.

166. Bornkamm, *Christian Experience*, 126.

167. Witherington, *Conflict*, 241.

168. Crossan and Reed, *Search*, 338.

Corinthians are sharing (or not sharing).[169] As Meeks points out this implies that there is a proper meal taking place.[170] This is supported by the way the tradition Paul conveys speaks of μετὰ τὸ δειπνῆσαι (11:25). One of the key words for understanding what is going on is προλαμβάνω (11:21), which then has implications for interpreting ἐκδέχομαι in verse 33.[171] There are three main ways of interpreting προλαμβάνω: a temporal meaning, a temporal and spatial meaning, and an intensive meaning: devouring.

Witherington argues that προλαμβάνω has a temporal force: the rich eat earlier and the poor then arrive at the meal at the συμπόσιον stage.[172] Surburg also argues for a temporal meaning, but sees the situation as involving "a multifaceted and interrelated complex of issues that included where people ate, what they ate, how much they ate, and *when they ate*."[173]

Theissen asserts a temporal and spatial meaning. He argues that before the words of institution food is private and that some people are starting earlier.[174] Jamir argues that some people are going ahead, but that there is a lack of sharing even when there is concurrent eating.[175] It may be as Johnson suggests, that people were in different parts of the villa, giving spatial as well as temporal divisions.[176]

The third option is to see the προ as strengthening the verb and therefore Winter suggests "devour."[177] Winter goes on to argue that its use with "the aorist articular infinitive is meant to convey the idea in 11:21, that it was during the meal that each took or devoured his own dinner."[178] Surburg argues that προ does not tend to be used for strengthening in verbal contexts[179] and that the example from Asclepius that Winter uses (*SIG* §1170,

---

169. There are various options of who the τοὺς μὴ ἔχοντας are and why they were vulnerable including the famine (Blue, "House Church," 233–8) and patronage relations (Jamir, "Exclusion," 130). It seems unlikely we will ever fully know. Meggitt argues the "have nots" do not have the bread and wine as he does not see it as an economic reference, partly as he argues it is used elsewhere with an object (Meggitt, *Paul*, 118–20). However, there could be an implied object.

170. Meeks, *Christians*, 158. Also Schrage, *Brief*, 3:12.

171. Garland summarizes the key scholars who support each of the options (Garland, *1 Corinthians*, 540).

172. Witherington, *Conflict*, 195.

173. Surburg, "Situation," 17.

174. Theissen, *Setting*, 151.

175. Jamir, "Exclusion," 136.

176. Johnson, *1 Corinthians*, 202–3.

177. Winter, *Paul*, 148.

178. Ibid., 149.

179. Surburg, "Situation," 29.

11.7,9,16) could also have a temporal meaning.[180] Most of the evidence is for a temporal meaning and "devour" seems less persuasive, however the presence of the "ἐν τῷ + infinitive" form suggests a contemporaneous time,[181] so that the taking of what is seen as τὸ ἴδιον δεῖπνον happens during the collective eating. This suggests a nuanced meaning, which could allude to time, but also to "taking before" during the meal. This could happen if the food available was offered to some people or to those in particular rooms first, leaving others to pick at whatever remained.

There are various ways this distinction between people and meal could be happening. There are three main ways that meals could be provided: those coming could bring food, those hosting could provide food, or those coming could bring money to contribute to the expense of the meal.[182] If those hosting were providing the food, they may have treated the meal like any other meal which they hosted and distinguished between guests by where they sat them and what they gave them to eat. If a patron/householder was providing the food, it may not have seemed unusual for him to make social distinctions in the quality and quantity of the food provided.[183] Even if several richer believers provided the bulk of the food, they may not have seen the discrepancies in quantity as an issue, rather they may have seen themselves as providing for the poor.[184]

If the context was people bringing food or money for a shared meal, the background of Greek meals was one where more food, at least for officials was the norm.[185] This could mean that both the size and quality of the food could still be at issue here. Crossan and Reed argue "early Christians brought whatever they had and shared it among one another,"[186] not just at Corinth, but also more widely, for example in Thessalonica. Both Bruce and Schottroff[187] agree that the context and form of the meal was a bring and share meal, but that actually they brought and did not share, so that "the poor were not only unsatisfied but embarrassed and humiliated."[188] While Smith argues against bring and share on the basis that even the poorest

---

180. Ibid., 25. Winter, *Paul*, 145.
181. Wallace, *Greek*, 595.
182. Chow highlights the first two possibilities (Chow, *Patronage and Power*, 111).
183. Meeks, *Christians* 68, 159.
184. Horrell, *Ethos*, 103.
185. Theissen, *Setting*, 153.
186. Crossan and Reed, *Search*, 339.
187. Schottroff, "Holiness," 53.
188. Bruce, *Corinthians*, 110. Also Barrett, *First Corinthians*, 263.

would be able to bring enough bread to feed themselves,[189] this does not seem conclusive as the disparity in food could still be considerable.

Another potential issue in a bring and share situation would be the possibility of Jewish and Gentile Christians eating together,[190] where what each group were happy to eat might be different. If one group were a minority or less well off, they could end up being able to partake of less of the food.

Winter notes that one would expect sharing within a family, but the Corinthians have their own private meal,[191] suggesting that they have not understood the familial nature of the bonds between them as Christians.

If the church met in a villa-type house such as the Anaploga villa,[192] there would not have been room for the whole church in the dining room,[193] so they may have followed the norm where important guests were in the dining room and others elsewhere.[194] Smith notes that 14:30 shows participants sitting rather than reclining and this might fit with a situation where there were more people than could easily fit to recline.[195] It is unclear whether all would have met for this section of proceedings in the atrium, or whether everyone would have crowded into the triclinium.

However, more recent research has questioned whether the Corinthians would necessarily have met in a villa-style house.[196] Horrell argues that the Anaploga villa was adapted and the excavated set-up is later than often assumed.[197] Gehring suggests an alternative meeting place would have been a workshop style taberna, such as that where Prisca and Aquila are likely to have lived and worked.[198] Adams suggests the church may have rented space, for example dining rooms,[199] although Fotopoulos argues that as the church was not yet established they would not have been able to rent space.[200]

---

189. Smith, "Problem," 533.
190. Barrett, *First Corinthians*, 261.
191. Winter, *Paul*, 158.
192. Murphy-O'Connor, *Paul's Corinth* (3rd edition), 178–85.
193. Crossan and Reed note that houses excavated at Corinth include one with a *triclinium* for nine and an *atrium* which would have accommodated two to three dozen (Crossan and Reed, *Search*, 315).
194. Witherington, *Conflict*, 241; Thiselton, *Shorter*, 182.
195. Smith, *Symposium*, 178.
196. Adams, *Places*; see also pp. 220–21.
197. Horrell, "Space," 353–54.
198. Gehring, *Church*, 134–35.
199. Adams, *Places*, 166–71.
200. Fotopoulos, "Dining," 152.

Horrell points to the lack of firm evidence of where early Christians may have met and particularly the lack of evidence about poorer housing.[201]

However, even if the Corinthians were not meeting in a villa-style house, there could still have been issues with socio-economic distinctions. Walter notes that meals were an opportunity to show and compete for honor and status[202] and McRae points to the hierarchy in evidence during VA meals.[203]

As the Corinthians met and ate together, they shared together the bread and the cup. There is some discussion about how the meal, the bread, and the cup fit together. One group of scholars argues that after the blessing, the bread is shared, then the meal eaten, after which the cup is shared (Bread, Meal, Cup—BMC);[204] the other group argues that both the bread and the cup come after or towards the end of the meal (Meal, Bread, Cup—MBC).[205]

The MBC option potentially explains why the Corinthians were unconcerned about the discrimination in the provision of food if "they so completely regarded this [the bread and cup] as the main thing that the preceding meal became a thing which one could shape according to his own likes and for his own enjoyment."[206] However, the BMC option seems a more likely order as it fits with the tradition that Paul cites and he does not indicate that the order of eating is an issue for the Corinthians (11:25). This order also fits with the Greco Roman meal pattern of bread to begin and wine to transition to the συμπόσιον. Yet it is possible that people arrived over time and this could have led to a situation that did not fully fit in either BMC or MBC[207] and which had some fluidity, for example if it was bring and share, how many people needed to be there for them to bless the bread and start?

In whatever precise order the elements of the meal occurred, Paul criticizes how the Corinthians eat together.[208] For Paul, even if the issues are

---

201. Horrell, "Space," 359–60. He suggests that they may have met in a building such as the East Theater Street Complex (361–68).

202. Walters, "Paul," 356.

203. McRae, "Eating," 171.

204. Surburg, "Situation," 19. Also Käsemann, "Guests," 63.

205. Coutsoumpos, *Paul*, 109 (Coutsoumpos argues for a main meal before the blessing and then sacramental meal between bread and cup); Jamir, "Exclusion," 134; Bornkamm, *Christian Experience*, 128; Conzelmann, *Corinthians*, 195, 199.

206. Bornkamm, *Christian Experience*, 128. Also Jamir, "Exclusion," 151.

207. Schrage, *Brief*, 3:14–15. Schrage provides two further possible orders.

208. See pp. 122–24.

in the meal prior to the bread and wine, he sees a problem as he "considers the whole of the fellowship meal as the 'Lord's Supper.'"[209]

Other Background Issues

As well as the Greco-Roman context, which we have considered, there are other questions about what is going on as the Corinthians meet to share the Lord's Supper together.

Idol Meat

First, do the questions about εἰδωλόθυτον influence what is happening at the Lord's Supper? One of the issues of conflict and discussion at Corinth involves idol meat, whether meat that has been offered to idols, then sold later in the market, or idol meat consumed at temples during a ceremony. We look briefly at the passages which relate to idol meat in later in this chapter.[210] If, as seems likely, some Corinthians saw no issues with eating meat which had been offered to idols and others did see an issue, and if the meal at the Lord's Supper was of a bring and share variety, the questions about idol meat may have directly impacted the Lord's Supper. Some believers, who had no issue with idol meat, may have brought it to share at the Lord's Supper. If others could not, on account of their consciences, eat the meat, they may then have gone hungry, particularly if those who had no issue with the meat were those who were more affluent and in a position to provide a greater proportion of the food for the meal.

Why now?

Second, why does the Lord's Supper become an issue at this point for the Corinthian church? Given that Paul was the person who had preached at Corinth and then spent some time there, presumably teaching (Acts 18:18), why did issues arise around the sharing of the Lord's Supper: had Paul not addressed the issue? If he had taught about how to share the Lord's Supper, why were there issues for the Corinthian Church now? Blue asserts that Paul would have addressed the issue, but argues that the context may have changed with the presence of food shortages.[211] Crossan and Reed point to

---

209. Jamir, "Exclusion," 134.
210. See pp. 132–35.
211. Blue, "House Church," 232, 237–38.

a clash between "Paul's radical horizontal Christian equality ... with Roman society's normal vertical hierarchy."[212] Winter suggests that the issue may not have arisen while Paul was there, or may have now arisen in a new way.[213] The church would have continued to be surrounded by, and probably, in other contexts, participated in other ways of eating together. The draw to behave "at this dinner in the same way as other Corinthians did at theirs"[214] may have been strong, particularly as the church grew and new believers joined. In 11:17–34 Paul is reminding the Corinthians of what he has already taught them.

Paul's Response

Having considered what may be happening as the Corinthians meet together, we now turn to consider Paul's response to them and as we do "we shall learn something of what Paul expected or wanted the community to be like, and of his reactions to the reality."[215] As Paul responds to what he has heard of what is happening at the Lord's Supper, he criticizes what is happening, provides catechesis about the nature of the Lord's Supper, and gives instructions for how the Corinthians should act as they come together and share food.

Criticism

Paul criticizes the divisions that are apparent as they share food together, the way individual meals, as opposed to the Lord's Supper, are eaten, and the way that some within the group go without and are humiliated. Paul has already referred to the divisions among the Corinthians in 1:10–12, although whether these divisions are the same divisions as those Paul now refers to in 11:18 is a matter of dispute. Grosheide argues that the divisions in chapter 11 are not the same as those indicated in chapter 1. He argues that those in chapter 1 are around particular leaders and theology (1:12), while those in chapter 11 are based in the social differences within the community.[216] Theissen agrees and suggests that even if the group "supports itself through mutual generosity, those who are able to contribute the most come to achieve

---

212. Crossan and Reed, *Search*, 296.
213. Winter, *Paul*, 4.
214. Ibid., 142.
215. Horrell, *Ethos*, 125.
216. Grosheide, *Corinthians*, 265.

a certain position of superiority—even if that does not correspond to the group's self-understanding."[217]

Jamir suggests a wider set of divisions, based on the diversity of social and religious backgrounds of the believers.[218] We have already noted the possibility of different beliefs about idol food contributing to division and some going hungry during the shared meal. A similar argument could be made if there were Jewish believers as part of the Corinthian church. If they were unable to eat much of what other believers brought to share, they may have gone hungry.[219] Smith argues that when one considers the congregations at Antioch, Corinth, and Rome, all evidence divisions at table and "in all three cases, these divisions can be seen to be related to Jewish dietary laws."[220]

Whether the divisions are between rich and poor, Jew and Gentile, those with a believing patron and those without a believing patron, allegiance to different leaders, or based on different theological approaches to topics, Paul is clear that there are divisions among the Corinthians. Blue highlights three comparisons which may indicate both the kind of divisions and the effect of the divisions: between their homes (11:22) and the house church (11:18), between the Lord's Supper (11:20) and their own meals (11:21), and between those who have and those who have not (11:22). "[B]ehaviour which may be acceptable in the house (οἶκος/οἰκία, vv. 22, 34) is not appropriate for the 'church' (ἐκκλησία) when gathered in the house."[221]

Behavior that saw the meal as for themselves rather than a shared meal, the Lord's Supper, was not appropriate. Wealthy Christians could have seen the meal as their own,[222] particularly if they were bringing larger contributions of the food, or food other than bread and wine.[223] However, it may not have been how they viewed the meal, but rather what they did during it,

---

217. Theissen, *Setting*, 162.

218. Jamir, "Exclusion," 112.

219. The Sardian decree, recorded by Josephus (*Ant.* 14.259–61) indicates that "kosher" meat was available in market places and Winter argues the presence of Jews and synagogue in Corinth mean that it is likely that such stalls were present in the Corinthian market (Winter, *Paul*, 295). However, Winter also notes the increase in opposition and the possibility the removal of such markets may have been part of the outworking of such opposition (299). Even if "kosher" meat were still available in the Corinthian market, it may not have been seen as a key issue for those believers who did not come from a Jewish background.

220. Smith, *Symposium*, 180.

221. Blue, "House Church," 227.

222. Coutsoumpos, *Paul*, 77.

223. Theissen, *Setting*, 153.

that leads Paul to say that they were eating their own meals. Coutsoumpos,[224] Garland,[225] and Witherington[226] argue that the way that the believers ate, created and exacerbated divisions, which meant that "Their behavior was totally in contradiction with the nature and purpose of the meal."[227] If those who were wealthier used the meal to honor one group more than another, it could not be the Lord's Supper.[228] "Es gibt aber keine wahre *communio* am Tisch des Herren ohne *communio* mit dessen anderen Tischgenossen"[229] (There is no true communion at the Lord's table without communion with the other people eating at the table). Their meal could hardly be the Lord's Supper when their actions showed contempt of God and those who God "has called into his church"—the "not many wise, not many mighty, not many nobly born."[230] As Witherington points out "The Lord's Supper was meant as a sacrament of both horizontal and vertical communion."[231]

Pervo argues that the distinction between ἴδιον and κυριακόν (11:20–21) is also one between personal and shared food[232] and Schottroff similarly argues that the issues is that the better off "have treated common property . . . as if it were private property . . . at a time when it was already common property, consecrated to God."[233]

Eating their own meals as opposed to the Lord's Supper, led to divisions between the haves and the have nots,[234] with the have nots being humiliated,[235] social division being exacerbated[236] and their fellowship in Christ ignored.[237] "Paul's accusation is that the meal that was supposed to be a sign of their integration and unity has become a flashpoint highlighting their inequality and alienation."[238]

---

224. Coutsoumpos, *Paul*, 112.
225. Garland, *1 Corinthians*, 533, 536.
226. Witherington, *Conflict*, 241.
227. Jamir, "Exclusion," 165.
228. Thiselton, *Shorter*, 182; Mitchell, "Amen," 260.
229. Schrage, *Brief*, 3:23.
230. Barrett, *First Corinthians*, 262
231. Witherington, *Conflict*, 243.
232. Pervo, "PANTA KOINA," 169.
233. Schottroff, "Holiness," 54.
234. Blue, "House Church," 226.
235. Witherington, *Conflict*, 249.
236. Theissen, *Setting*, 160.
237. Bruce, *Corinthians*, 115.
238. Garland, *1 Corinthians*, 536.

Catechesis

However, Paul does not simply criticize the Corinthians for their behavior as they gather and eat together, he also teaches them, passing on tradition, indicated by his use of παρέλαβον and παρέδωκα (11:23) (*qibbel* and *masar*).[239]

Paul indicates that the Corinthians already know this tradition—he has already passed it on to them (11:23). Bornkamm and Coutsoumpos argue that the Corinthians have not forgotten the tradition.[240] After all they are still observing what they see as the Lord's Supper, even if Paul does not think that it is the Lord's Supper (11:20). Therefore, they have not forgotten or stopped the tradition, rather they have been mis-practicing it.[241]

As we have seen, Paul presumes the Corinthians have an awareness of the tradition, Schottroff goes further to argue that Paul presumes the Corinthians are familiar with the blessings and prayers at a Jewish meal: that his restating of the tradition only includes those parts of the prayer that are pertinent to the situation.[242] Paul has previously presumed a knowledge of Jewish practice (5:7) and his presentation of the tradition has parallels to the way the president explains parts of the meal in the Haggadah,[243] which may suggest that he assumes a similar level of awareness here, but we lack evidence from the text to confirm this suggestion. Paul is not specific about the thanksgiving prayer that is to be used. It may be that he anticipates that the Corinthians will have a knowledge of Jewish thanksgiving prayers, but it may also be that different hearers would imagine different benedictions depending on their backgrounds.[244]

Paul reminds the Corinthians of Jesus' actions at the meal and encourages them to imitate Jesus' self-giving (11:26),[245] remembering the meal, Jesus' death, and the effect of his death. "What the saying of the words over the bread and wine represents is the idea that with the sharing of the bread and the wine one is sharing in the result brought about by that death."[246] Therefore "Die Korinther müssen sich bewußt werden daß sie „Gäste des Gekreuzigten" sind"[247] (The Corinthians must become aware that they are

---

239. Barrett, *First Corinthians*, 265; Schrage, *Brief*, 3:29.
240. Bornkamm, *Christian Experience*, 127; Coutsoumpos, *Paul*, 124.
241. Coutsoumpos, *Paul*, 124.
242. Schottroff, "Holiness," 52.
243 Thiselton, *Epistle*, 874.
244. Smith, *Symposium*, 190.
245. Longenecker, *Remembering*, 154.
246. Smith, *Symposium*, 190.
247. Klauck, *Herrenmahl*, 372.

"Guests of the Crucified One"). Jamir notes that Jesus had brought people together around meals, and that Paul wants the Corinthian's meal to show community[248] and unity with the Lord and each other.[249] This emphasis on unity with God and one another as a result of Jesus' death could also be indicated in the slight change in order of words concerning the bread. In 1 Cor 11:24, Jesus says: Τοῦτό μού ἐστιν τὸ σῶμα, while in the gospels Jesus says: Τοῦτό ἐστιν τὸ σῶμά μου (Luke 22:19; Matt 26:26; Mark 14:22). The location of the μού in 11.24 focuses more attention on the "my,"[250] which could point to Jesus' body and death and its effect, and also to Jesus' body the church and its unity. The tradition of the Lord's Supper was founded on Jesus' words as he pointed to his own death and to its sacrifice as "an act of divine deliverance by which sins were forgiven and a new covenant set up between God and men, who being reconciled to God, were now united among themselves."[251]

However, Paul does not simply reiterate the tradition, he also explains it and warns about possible judgment that as they eat they could be ἔνοχος, liable or chargeable for Jesus' death.[252] This idea of eating judgment picks up the idea of eating as a covenant sign.[253] Paul is clear that in the sharing of the bread and wine τὸν θάνατον τοῦ κυρίου καταγγέλλετε, ἄχρι οὗ ἔλθῃ (11:26).[254] This proclamation is one that happens in the eating and drinking as well as in the words.[255] When they do not proclaim Jesus' death, whether by contradicting "the purpose of Christ's self-offering" or "the Spirit in which it was made,"[256] as Paul thinks is currently happening,[257] "they are on par with those who were responsible for the death of Christ."[258] However,

---

248. Jamir, "Exclusion," 156.

249. Ibid., 175.

250. Winter, *Paul*, 154.

251. Barrett, *First Corinthians*, 272.

252. "The syntax therefore *implies not a sacrilege against the elements of the Lord's Supper* but answerability or being held accountable for the sin against Christ of claiming identification with him while using the celebration of the meal *as an occasion for social enjoyment or status enhancement without regard to sharing in what the Lord's Supper proclaims*" (Thiselton, *Epistle*, 890, his italics). Ramelli argues that the sickness in the judgment is spiritual rather than physical (Ramelli, "Weakness," 146–59).

253. Ciampa and Rosner, *Corinthians*, 555.

254. For Barrett this includes all Christians sharing "the benefits secured for them through the blood of Christ." (Barrett, *First Corinthians*, 232).

255. Ibid., 270; Thiselton, *Epistle*, 870.

256. Barrett, *First Corinthians*, 273.

257. Garland, *1 Corinthians*, 549.

258. Jamir, "Exclusion," 168.

this judgment is a judgment that is remedial and educative (11:32),[259] for as Bornkamm points out it "redeems them from the world and excludes them from the final damnation."[260]

The Way Forward

Having reminded the Corinthians of the nature of the meal they are sharing, what they are remembering and proclaiming, and the danger of judgment if they do not proclaim Jesus' death, Paul then provides a way forward, so that they may appropriately share the Lord's Supper and not their own suppers. Paul's solution has three main elements: discerning the body, waiting, and examining. We look at each of these in turn before considering Paul's comments about eating at home, and how they relate to possible love-patriarchalism (the argument that Paul keeps some of the patriarchal forms from society while tempering them with the belief of equality in Christ and agape-love).

In 11:29 Paul warns against μὴ διακρίνων τὸ σῶμα and therefore we see the implicit expectation that the Corinthians should discern the body. However, to which body is Paul referring? We have already noted the link between Jesus' death and the unity with God and one another for believers, which is seen again in 12:13 as Paul talks about the believers as one body and in 12:27 as Paul points to the believers as σῶμα Χριστοῦ.

However, there are other possibilities to consider. The σῶμα the believers are meant to discern could be about discerning the food eaten remembering Jesus' death from ordinary food, the Lord's body in the bread, and the way the elements represent Christ's death.[261] Barrett argues against the body referring to the church because there is also mention of the cup in 11:27.[262] While Paul does refer to the cup, the discerning Paul asks them to do is of the body of Christ, not the cup. We have seen above that Paul in other places in the letter uses body to describe the believers, particularly their unity and equality. Thus, "body" indicating "the church" would fit with Paul's concern with how the believers treat one another. (11:22). Discerning the body would then involve the Corinthians having a responsibility

---

259. Barrett, *First Corinthians*, 276.

260. Bornkamm, *Christian Experience*, 50.

261. Barrett, *First Corinthians*, 274; Garland, *1 Corinthians*, 552. Each gives three options which overlap.

262. Barrett, *First Corinthians*, 273.

towards one another[263] and evaluating "their relationships to others in the church when they observe the Lord's Supper."[264]

The identification of the body to be discerned with the church does not preclude other meanings. Jamir highlights what he sees as "rhetorical word play"[265] in Paul's use of σῶμα: "the σῶμα that has come into existence because of the σῶμα that was broken in sacrifice on their behalf."[266] Thus, σῶμα is multivalent.[267] Indeed Johnson sees the reference as including the "Lord's own physical body, not as mystically present in the bread but in the saving significance of his death and the consequent social behavior of all who are identified with him."[268]

Having indicated that the Corinthians should be discerning the body, Paul also instructs them that when they meet together ἀλλήλους ἐκδέχεσθε (11.33). Ἐκδέχομαι can have various meanings including "wait,"[269] "expect,"[270] "receive,"[271] "undertake,"[272] and "welcome."[273] Winter asserts that the verb is used in 16:11 to indicate "expecting" and that in 1:7 it is used with the prefix ἀπό to indicate waiting. He therefore argues that we would expect this second form in chapter 11 if it were indicating waiting.[274] However, 16:11 could include a waiting meaning, and it seems likely this is the case here. This does not preclude an element of welcome or receiving of one another.[275]

As Barrett points out it is important to note that it is for one another that they are waiting,[276] not a particular person. The onus is on all of them to wait for everyone else. Paul does not give instructions to particular leaders or officers.

---

263. Bornkamm, *Christian Experience*, 149.

264. Chow, *Patronage and Power*, 183. Indeed Barrett seems to follow Bornkamm in suggesting "a 'fellowship' use." (Barrett, *First Corinthians*, 275).

265. Jamir, "Exclusion," 198. Also Mitchell, *Rhetoric*, 157.

266. Jamir, "Exclusion," 197.

267. Bach and Glancy, "Morning," 457.

268. Johnson, *1 Corinthians*, 210. Also Thiselton, *Shorter*, 187–88.

269. BDAG, 300; MM, 192.

270. BDAG, 300.

271. MM, 192.

272. Ibid.

273. Thiselton points out that it is used in Rom 15:7 for welcome (Thiselton, *Shorter*, 189). Also Surburg, "Situation," 36–37.

274. Winter, *Paul*, 151.

275. 3 Macc 5:26 (LXX); ibid., 151.

276. Barrett, *First Corinthians*, 276.

Surburg argues that just waiting does not deal with the problem,[277] but that including the idea of receiving or welcoming would "end the various ways the 'haves' have shamed the 'have-nots'—whether by the where, what, how much of the meal ... or the *when*."[278] However, there is one way in which the waiting could deal with the issue. If the issue at hand is a "pot luck" meal before the Lord's Supper to which only some are invited, only some come, or where the food is not fully shared, then waiting and starting any eating with the invocation with the bread could provide a solution.[279]

Whether ἐκδέχομαι solely indicates waiting in a context where some of the Corinthians had been holding a limited or discriminatory meal before the Lord's Supper, or whether Paul uses the verb in the wider of sense of receiving and welcoming,[280] the overall intention is the same. Paul is expressing his concern that the Corinthians should be eating together and equally, without particular people getting favored in the distribution of food or drink. It is not surprising that Paul has to reiterate this, as for the Corinthian church this would be a pattern at odds with the patronage system of the world that they lived in.[281]

As well as discerning, and waiting/welcoming, Paul also urges the Corinthians δοκιμαζέτω δὲ ἄνθρωπος ἑαυτόν (11:28). This is in order that they may not be judged (11:29)[282] and involves them making sure that they are not eating or drinking in a manner that is ἀναξίως (11:27). Ἀναξίως covers behavior which is "in contrast with the character or nature of something."[283] Ciampa and Rosner argue that this indicates eating in a way that demeans or dishonors a brother or sister,[284] because the brother or sister is holy.[285] Paul does not here go as far as arguing from the holiness of the believers, but Paul does include criticizing the Corinthians for humiliating members of the church (11:22) and indicate that the right approach of believers is to honor one another (12:23), because they are all part of one body, Christ's (12:12, 27).

---

277. Surburg, "Situation," 37.
278. Ibid., 37.
279. Crossan and Reed, *Search*, 340; Coutsoumpos, *Paul*, 50.
280. Blue, "House Church," 231.
281. Mitchell, "Amen," 232.
282. Barrett, *First Corinthians*, 276.
283. Jamir, "Exclusion," 164.
284. Ciampa and Rosner, *Corinthians*, 554.
285. Ibid., 51.

This examining of self has often been seen to be an examination of "moral worthiness,"[286] but as Jamir argues Paul's focus here is not on introspection with regard to "moral worthiness," but rather "an introspection of one's attitude and motive at the Supper, and then one's action towards fellow members in the community,"[287] so that they conform "to the gospel message that they proclaim through partaking in the Supper."[288] Their examination is to be of the way they approach the meal and one another in the light of Christ's sacrifice for all.[289]

Paul's next comments in verse 34 seem to potentially undermine his focus on sharing and equality between believers. Conzelmann argues that Paul's instruction εἴ τις πεινᾷ, ἐν οἴκῳ ἐσθιέτω (11:34) separates satisfying hunger from the sacrament.[290] Others see Paul as criticizing those whose sole motive is their hunger—i.e., if they are only coming because they are hungry, they should rather eat at home,[291] or if they "are so hungry that they cannot wait"[292] or if they are only coming because of the food,[293] then they should rather eat at home, so that when they come together hunger is not the issue.[294]

Bach and Glancy and Theissen suggest food may not be being shared because it is not part of the words of institution and Paul is thus limiting what is eaten when they gather.[295] Grosheide sees the situation as one where both a love feast and the Lord's Supper are taking place. The love feast is optional and the way that the Corinthians are celebrating it is then spoiling the Lord's Supper and thus he argues that they should eat at home.[296]

However, Paul's account of the Last Supper points to its background as a Jewish meal, and has elements that suggest a Passover background.[297] Schottroff argues that while many modern scholars and the church tend to separate the meal from the sharing of the bread and wine, in Jewish tradi-

---

286. Jamir, "Exclusion," 194.

287. Ibid., 193.

288. Ibid., 194.

289. Garland, *1 Corinthians*, 551. Also Thiselton, *Epistle*, 880, 893.

290. Conzelmann, *Corinthians*, 195.

291. Bornkamm, *Christian Experience*, 129; Grosheide, *Corinthians*, 277; Bruce, *Corinthians*, 116.

292. Barrett, *First Corinthians*, 277.

293. Garland, *1 Corinthians*, 555.

294. Ciampa and Rosner, *Corinthians*, 559.

295. Bach and Glancy, "Morning," 456; Theissen, *Setting*, 155.

296. Grosheide, *Corinthians*, 268.

297. Paul's use of Paschal Lamb, the use of wine, and the fact that the meal was in the evening (11:23) (Marshall, *Supper*, 59–64).

tion "the blessing over bread embraced all the foodstuffs that were on the table."²⁹⁸ This would suggest a situation where Paul would be able to argue that what was brought should be shared. Similarly within the tradition which Paul passes on to the Corinthians, it is clear that there is a supper and Paul in verse 33 still envisages them eating together: συνερχόμενοι εἰς τὸ φαγεῖν ἀλλήλους ἐκδέχεσθε.

Other scholars argue that Paul is providing a halfway house, an option that allows those who are strong/rich to continue their own lifestyle privately.²⁹⁹ Thus, Pervo argues that Paul does not try to persuade the strong/rich to give up their lifestyles "so much as not to flaunt them."³⁰⁰ If the rich want to eat "on their own terms," they should do it in their own homes or those of friends.³⁰¹ Thus, Pervo and Theissen both see Paul arguing that the rich can eat what they want, but only at home, something Theissen sees as being a response of "love-patriarchalism."³⁰² In doing this, Smith argues, Paul is no different from other Greco-Roman moralists and gives the example of Plutarch *Quaest. conv.* 616C.³⁰³

However, this argument does not fit very well with Paul's assertion that they are one body (12:12) and his concern elsewhere in the letter for how they behave outside of the times that they gather together (5:1; 6:1). Therefore it may be that Paul is not necessarily presenting an option for them to use, but rather further criticism of how they have been observing the Lord's Supper. If hunger was the excuse³⁰⁴ some of the congregation were giving either for going ahead with the meal, or for eating more of the meal, Paul's comment then potentially highlights the way they are using it as an excuse by showing them an obvious alternative approach. He is then not intending them to eat at home rather to recognize their excuse and therefore eat and share together.³⁰⁵

Similarly Paul could be using irony. Margaret Sim observes Paul's frequent use of irony to address the issues that have arisen among them and argues that irony should be considered if a phrase seems to be contradicting what we know of Paul's views.³⁰⁶ If those who were wealthier thought they

---

298. Schottroff, "Holiness," 56.
299. Mitchell, *Rhetoric*, 264.
300. Pervo, "PANTA KOINA," 165.
301. Ciampa and Rosner, *Corinthians*, 546.
302. Theissen, *Setting*, 139; Pervo, "PANTA KOINA," 166.
303. Smith, *Symposium*, 193.
304. Schottroff, "Holiness," 53; Jamir, "Exclusion," 202.
305. Jamir, "Exclusion," 202–3
306. Sim, "Irony."

were feeding the needy, Paul's comment could be ironically highlighting the fact that they think they are feeding the needy, but they are using their own hunger as an excuse for the inequality and should know that those who are really hungry cannot eat at home in the same way.

We have considered 11:17–34, the issues within the Corinthian church as they celebrated the Lord's Supper: when they were meant to be sharing, some were going hungry; what was meant to be unifying divided. We have noted a number of possible divisions and causes. Paul criticizes the divisions, individualism, and lack of fellowship. He provides catechesis based on the Last Supper tradition, and the need for the Corinthians' actions to be consonant with Jesus' self-giving and with their new-found identity. He then provides instruction for the way forward: they are to discern the body and wait for/receive one another. We see in Paul's response to the Corinthians his expectation that they should share food with one another. Before we compare Paul's expectations of how the Corinthians should share food with meal practice in the surrounding culture, we will consider other texts in 1 Corinthians which may add to the picture.

OTHER TEXTS

We now turn to other texts in 1 Corinthians which may help us interpret what is happening in Corinth as they share food together and what Paul is advocating in 1 Cor 11:17–34.

In chapters 8 and 10, Paul addresses issues around eating food sacrificed to idols. Paul presents a nuanced argument, which agrees that it is possible to eat food sacrificed to idols without harm (8:8), but that such food should not be eaten if it will affect others with a weak conscience (8:10). However, Paul is much firmer around the possibility of sharing in a sacrifice to demons (10:21), possibly in the instance of eating at a ceremony at a temple, in comparison to eating meat offered to idols at someone's house (10:27) or eating at a temple but not part of a sacrifice (8:10).[307] His argument is that such sharing in a sacrifice implies partnership (10:20) and that Christians cannot have partnership with both Christ and demons (10:21).

There is obviously disagreement among the Corinthians about what is appropriate with respect to eating food offered to idols and discussion about the extent to which meat, whether in the temple, or in the market

---

307. Newton assesses the evidence for temple dining rooms and notes the possibility at Asklepios of the dining rooms accommodating those who had not been involved in sacrifices (Newton, *Deity*, 91–98).

would have been sacrificed to idols.[308] Part of the issue may be related to the Corinthians' understanding of the reality or otherwise of idols.[309] Newton also questions whether Paul and the Corinthians saw εἴδωλον differently.[310] Who the weak are in Paul's discussion is less clear. Theissen argues that "the socially weak of 1:26-27 are identical with those who are weak in the face of consecrated meat."[311] His argument is two pronged. The poor would have had fewer opportunities to eat meat and therefore may have identified it more strongly with idol worship,[312] as public sacrifices may have been the only time they got to eat meat.[313] However, *popinae* and *ganeae* would have provided opportunities for the poor to eat meat.[314] While the rich would have had more opportunities and more varied opportunities to eat meat,[315] they may also have had more need to frequent temples which "incorporated banking, markets, museums, libraries, landmarks, and meeting places."[316] The wealthy may have been more dependent on participating in such meals in order to maintain their status and connections. These may have included marriages, funerals, and civic religious ceremonies, such as those surrounding the Isthmian Games or the imperial cult.[317] Such meals were opportunities to connect with the powerful and gain influence.[318] Theissen suggests that Paul does not argue that all cultic meals should be avoided, but rather that "All that is prohibited is disturbing a weak person by doing so."[319]

However, Theissen's view does not fully take into account Paul's argument about association in 1 Cor 10:14-22. In chapter 10 Paul draws upon the experience of the Israelites in the wilderness and argues that they experienced judgment even though they had been baptized into the cloud and the sea (10:2, 5). Paul warns the Corinthians that neither baptism nor the Lord's

---

308. Smith notes the issues around diet are not unique to Corinth (Smith, *Symposium*, 177). See Rom 14 and Acts 15:1-21.

309. Newton, *Deity*, 134. For example, they may have had different views of Roman imperial images (160-73) and whether the Roman cult involved worship or honoring (211). Similarly, was all of the food sacrificial or only the portions dedicated to the gods (195)?

310. Ibid., 278-82.

311. Theissen, *Setting*, 125.

312. Ibid., 128. Also Witherington, *Conflict*, 190.

313. Theissen, *Setting*, 128.

314. See pp. 108-15.

315. Theissen, *Setting*, 125-28.

316. Newton, *Deity*, 299.

317. Chow, *Patronage and Power*, 146-50.

318. Ibid., 151, 156.

319. Theissen, *Setting*, 139.

Supper gives them a *carte blanche* to do whatever they will. Specifically Paul tells them that sharing the cup of the Lord is incompatible with sharing the cup of demons (10:21). Sharing the Lord's Supper involves sharing with other believers, but also participation in Christ,[320] and sharing in his death.[321]

Paul argues that partaking of the Lord's Supper is "no guarantee against falling into sin."[322] It unites the person to Christ and therefore idolatry is treachery.[323] Being united to Christ, unites them with one another.[324] Therefore they should not be eating food offered to idols within worship contexts (10:14), but also they should be concerned about the welfare and conscience of their brothers and sisters with whom they have been united (8:12). In contexts where they are with unbelievers they should be concerned with the conscience of the unbeliever (10:28) and presumably the witness that their eating, or not eating provides. Meeks helpfully suggests that the distinction between when it is permissible to eat food offered to idols and when it is not, is dependent on the symbolism involved. When the meat has a symbolic connection to the idol, for example, when it is in the temple at a ceremony, when the belief of the weak makes it symbolic, or when the cultic link is named, then there is an issue with consuming it.[325]

Paul also addresses the issue of the man living with his father's wife, which points to the Corinthians regularly eating with one another (5:11). Again it is possible that patronage may be involved. If the man is a rich patron,[326] this might explain why the church is ready to accept the man, for he would be able to contribute to the wellbeing of the church and association with him may have brought advantages to the church. Paul's recommendation is that the Corinthians should not even eat with this man (5:11). Chow suggests that having their own court may have benefitted the weak[327] and may also have allowed for a freed man to address issues with a former patron. This would place believers on a more even standing as they related to one another.

We see from these passages further evidence of issues around food and of the Corinthians eating together, both direct evidence of eating together

---

320. Ciampa and Rosner, *Corinthians*, 553.

321. Bornkamm therefore sees a difference between the references to body in verses 16 and 17 with the first referring to Jesus' death and the second to the believers as the body (Bornkamm, *Christian Experience*, 144).

322. Barrett, *First Corinthians*, 234.

323. Ibid.

324. Ibid.

325. Meeks, *Christians*, 160.

326. Chow, *Patronage and Power*, 130.

327. Ibid., 182.

and also indirect (the issues around idol meat presume a level of knowledge about one another's eating habits and may indicate occasions of eating together).

THE EXAMPLE OF SHARING IN 1 CORINTHIANS 11

We have considered the situation at the Lord's Supper in the Corinthian church, Paul's response of criticism, catechesis, and presentation of a way forward, and other passages that add to our understanding of the relationships within the Corinthians church regarding food and patronage. We are now ready to summarize Paul's teaching about the Lord's Supper in the context of his wider teaching in 1 Corinthians.

Central to Paul's teaching to the Corinthians about the Lord's Supper is the way that as the Corinthians eat together they have communion and participation in Jesus Christ (10:16–17, 21). This participation and communion in Jesus is rooted in his death and in his self-giving (11:23–26). As the Passover lamb (5:7) Jesus brings them into communion with each other and the meal is a covenantal meal (11:27–29), where the covenant is based on Jesus' death (15:3) and brings communion with God and one another. Paul's concern is that the Corinthian's behavior should be in character, rather than ἀναξίως (v.27), with the reality of the covenant meal they are eating and with the pattern of Jesus' self-giving that establishes the covenant.

In Jesus they are one body (10:17; 11:29; 12:12–14, 17, 27) and therefore should not be divided (1:10–12; 11:18), whatever their background, wherever they sit during the meal, whatever is happening. In fact Paul identifies divisions that involve quarrelling and jealously with a lack of maturity (3:1–4; 12:21–26).

Paul argues for unity and for some sense of equality. He is clear that the church is made from people from different backgrounds and that there should not be social divisions within the congregation. He argues, for example, that leaders are not superior (3:5–9). He presents a model of eating together that is at odds with the cultural norm, as it involves both a wider variety of people eating together, and speaks against inequality and food becoming a measure of hierarchy or divisiveness within the community (11:21).

He emphasizes that the Corinthians are each chosen by God and should therefore boast in God rather than in themselves (1:27–31) and each one of them has a part to play (12:4–7).

This unity and equality should lead to caring for one another. This is seen in sharing, so that one is not hungry and one drunk (11:21), so the meal is not ἴδιον, but rather κυριακόν, so that individuals are not humiliated (11:22), but rather honored (12:23). This expected care and concern for one another is also seen in Paul's addressing of the wider food issues (chapters 8 and 10), in particular where he argues that individuals should not be a cause of stumbling to others within the community (8:9–13). Their concern should be the wellbeing of others. It is seen in Paul's example through his ministry where he lays down his rights (9:19–23), which gives the Corinthians an example of what it might look like to follow the example of Jesus' self-giving. Likewise the Corinthians are to use their gifts to benefit each other (14:1–5, 26).[328] Paul's chapter on love (13) reiterates his desire that they should care for one another.

Paul's instruction to the Corinthians is based in his theology of what the meal is that they are sharing and who they are. They are people who are sharing in a covenantal meal, who are one body, called to proclaim the Lord's death (11:26) in their actions and their words. Therefore they are to share with one another and care for one another.

SPECIFIC EXAMPLES OF MEALS IN THE GRECO-ROMAN WORLD

Having considered the evidence of what is happening in Corinth and Paul's response to the Corinthians, we now turn to look at specific examples of eating meals in the Greco-Roman world to ascertain in what ways Paul's exhortation about how the Corinthians should eat together is similar to and different from contemporary meal practice. We have already examined some of the forms of meals and issues around patronage; this section will look at two examples of meals, which we will then use together with the more general evidence about shared meals as a comparator to what Paul is advocating.

First, we consider the evidence of by-laws of the Society of Diana and Antinous in Lanuvium, Italy. Here we discover that members pay to join, "an initiation fee of 100 sesterces and an amphora of good wine" and then "monthly dues of 5 asses" (*CIL* 14.2112). The society looked after the funeral and burial of its members and there are instructions about when a person becomes ineligible through not paying their dues, what is due to a person to pay for their funeral, what should be disbursed at their funeral and how

---

328. While Paul does number the gifts with the potential for gifts being seen in some kind of hierarchy, his primary concern in terms of assessing gifts seems to be about them being used for the common good and about gifts being assessed in the way they build up.

arrangements work if someone dies away from town. The society had four "Masters of the dinners" who "shall be required to provide an amphora of good wine each, and for as many members as the society has a bread costing 2 asses, sardines to the number of four, a setting, and warm water with service." It appears that this responsibility rotated, although it is unclear whether it rotated round the whole of the membership list. However, it is clear that when the group met to eat, food was provided by only some of the members, those appointed at that time "Masters of the dinners."

The *quinquennalis*, the secretary, and the messengers were exempt from being "Masters of dinner," but each received a larger share of what was provided at the dinners, in the case of the *quinquennalis* twice as much and in the cases of the secretary and the messenger one and a half times as much. In addition the *quinquennalis* also had particular responsibilities for rituals on festive days and it was considered an honored position.[329]

There are also instructions about when business may be brought up and strictures against moving around or causing a disturbance. Smith argues that these rules "suggest that a value was placed on one's assigned position at the meeting."[330]

Second, in the Society of the Iobacchoi, there are regular monthly meeting and particular yearly festivals (*IG* II2 1368, lines 42–44), as well as other meetings that are more business-focused to deal with offenders (84–90). There is a concern for good order, for example there are penalties for occupying someone else's couch (73–83).[331] Members pay an initial entrance fee (32–41) and a wine fee (46–47). When they meet for banquets, meat is distributed with preference to people in particular positions (118–26). There are references to couches and to penalties for occupying someone else's couch.[332] For those in particular positions of responsibility there is a greater financial commitment, for example the treasurer is responsible for buying lamp oil (151–5), but there are also particular benefits such as the distribution mentioned or the waiving of fees (157–9).

So as we look at the initial material we considered as background material and these two specific examples of meals in the Greco-Roman world, we see a pattern of eating together, in which where one sat was important, those who were considered more important received more and better quality food and better places to sit. There is also evidence of particular people being given the responsibility of providing the food.

329. Smith, *Symposium*, 99–100.
330. Ibid., 101.
331. Ibid., 120.
332. Ibid., 123.

COMPARISON

We now turn to compare Paul's teaching of what the Lord's Supper should look like with what we see of the pattern of shared meals in the Greco-Roman world.

There is no specific meal type that provides a good comparator. For example, Paul stresses the factual basis of the Lord's Supper; he locates its origin in recent real time history rather than the mythical backgrounds of the mystery religions.[333] When meals were held to honor a person, they occurred on the birth date of the individual; while the Lord's Supper commemorates the death of Jesus,[334] and occurs more frequently than once a year. While there are similarities between memorial meals and the Lord's Supper, for example the links to death and remembering, Bornkamm notes that in Hellenistic memorial meals the main focus is not worship.[335] In the Lord's Supper, there is a focus on worship, particularly if chapters 12–14 are seen as addressing the rest of the mealtime activities.

Therefore, it seems unlikely that one type or form of meal will provide the best comparison to the Lord's Supper and we will be comparing what Paul is advocating to the general characteristics of Greco-Roman meals rather than a specific meal or type of meal, drawing on the evidence from earlier in this chapter[336] as well as the evidence from Lanuvium and the Iobacchoi.

There are three areas where we see similarities. First, order: Paul is concerned with good order as he writes.[337] This can be seen in his concern about the divisions (11:18) and the way that some people are going ahead with their meals (11:21). It can also be seen later in his discussions about how they should conduct things during the rest of their meeting together, particularly his instructions about how they should share in building each other up (14:26–33). This concern with good order can also be seen in the regulations that govern the Society of Diana and Antinous (*CIL* 14.2112 line 24) and the Iobacchoi (*IG* II2 1368 line 65).[338]

Second, Paul is concerned with the Corinthians being a community or society. He is concerned about the divisions he sees among them (11:18) and about the way that some of them are humiliated as they meet together

---

333. Witherington, *Conflict*, 250.
334. Coutsoumpos, *Paul*, 132.
335. Bornkamm, *Christian Experience*, 140.
336. See pp. 99–106.
337. Coutsoumpos, *Paul*, 134.
338. Smith, *Symposium*, 206.

(11:22). In contrast he refers to them as the church of God (11:22), as brothers (11:33), and instructs them that they should discern the body (11:29). We see a concern for the formation of the society in the instructions for how one becomes a member of the society at Lanuvium: the entry fee, the ongoing fees, and the instructions about when one forfeits one's benefits from the society (*CIL* 14.2112).

Third, there is some similarity between Paul's discussion about all sharing together and waiting for one another so that some should not be shamed with Pliny's teaching about equality (*Ep.* 2.6) and wider discussions about equality at meals (Plutarch *Quaest. conv.* 8.615–616B, 643E–644D).

However, there are also differences. First, as Meeks points out, Paul does not write in the pattern of clubs where there are leaders with lots of titles.[339] Paul does not instruct particular officials about what they should do as they meet together, rather he instructs the congregation as a whole (11:33).[340] In contrast the societies generally specify particular people with responsibilities to conduct sacrifices, or provide the food (e.g., the Masters of the dinners at Lanuvium *CIL* 14.2112).

Second, the evidence from the early church is that they met in homes rather than in temples. As Stambaugh notes "Over and over the early Christians wrote that they had no temples except the community of the faithful, the ecclesia which was the assembly of members."[341] This contrasts with many of the societies that appear to have had a hall or temple (temple room) that they would have regularly met in (*IGRP* I 1151). Stambaugh also suggests that the early church may have met at grave precincts, because they were less conspicuous there.[342]

Third, the evidence within 1 Corinthians and Acts points to a congregation that was more socially diverse than many of the other groups who would have met together. While there are discussions about equality in provision of food (Plato *Symp.* 3.175B where there is an instruction to serve indiscriminately) and giving diners the choice about where they eat (Plutarch *Quaest. conv.* 8.625), Plato and Plutarch both appear to be writing for more socially homogeneous groups. They also make it clear that equality in that context is novel.

Fourth, Paul has a concern for a common meal, particularly that those who have nothing should be included, which we do not see in the general Greco-Roman meal patterns.

---

339. Meeks, *Christians*, 134.
340. Smith, *Symposium*, 213; Barrett, *First Corinthians*, 24.
341. Stambaugh, "Functions," 602.
342. Ibid., 604.

CONCLUSION

Meals in first-century Corinth were important culturally, as meals are today. This chapter has looked at 1 Cor 11:17–34 as an example of sharing food within a group. Paul criticizes the Corinthian church for how they share the Lord's Supper and much of what he criticizes shows similarities to some wider aspects of Greco-Roman meals. Having criticized their practice, Paul provides catechesis, reminding them of the tradition they have already received. He then provides a way forward, which involves discerning the body, waiting/welcoming, and self-examination. Paul grounds his instruction in the Lord's Supper being a covenantal meal, which brings believers as one body, united, into the reality of Jesus' death, which they are to then proclaim by their actions (including those to one another during the meal) and their words.

Paul's presentation of what he hopes the Corinthians will do shows some similarities with meals of *collegia*/VAs: the concern for good order and concern for society membership (though with significant differences of what that means). His concern for equality also has some similarities to discussions about equality in meals in Plutarch and Pliny.

However, there are also differences. First, there is evidence of greater social diversity in those eating together at Corinth than would be usual in most Greco-Roman shared meal settings.

Second, Paul criticizes the situation where some have more or better food than others and thus advocates a situation where all are provided for equally. This sense of equality and community may also be seen in the way that Paul makes no reference to leaders having a role within the Lord's Supper and his addressing the exhortation to the whole group.

Third, the Corinthians are eating together more frequently than societies or clubs would. This may partly explain why the Lord's Supper took place in homes rather than temples or halls.

Fourth, the practice Paul advocates focuses on relationships and unity between the Corinthians which is a result of their relationship with Christ. Their relationships with one another, and therefore their actions towards one another as they meet together and share the Lord's Supper (and also in general), should reflect the relationship they have been brought into with God-in-Christ.

6

Giving and Generosity
2 Corinthians 8 and 9

INTRODUCTION

EARLIER IN CHAPTER 4 we considered an example of sharing over a distance in the Antiochene collection for the believers in Judaea. We now turn to another example of sharing over a distance: the collection described in 2 Cor 8 and 9, where Paul encourages the Corinthians to reawaken their commitment to contributing to the collection for those in need in Jerusalem.

This chapter will focus on the collection from the evidence in 2 Cor 8 and 9, looking at the practice that Paul advocates and the theology that underpins his exhortation, and how these compare to other examples of sharing and giving. We first place 2 Corinthians in the context of Paul's relationship with the Corinthians, before briefly considering how chapter 8 and 9 relate to each other and the rest of the extant letter. We then consider the text of 2 Cor 8 and 9 including the arguments Paul provides for the Corinthians' involvement in the collection, the practical arrangements he puts in place for the collection, and the role of generosity in the Christian life. We look at other texts that have been seen as referring to the collection: 1 Cor 16:1–4; Acts 11:27–30, 21:17–26; Gal 2:10; and Rom 15:25–32. We consider whether they are specific to the collection and the ways in which they may illuminate our understanding of Paul's instructions in 2 Cor 8 and

9. The passages that refer to the collection raise questions about Paul's aim in the collection and we consider for whom Paul intended the collection, why it was specifically for Jerusalem, and whether Paul hoped that it would have an eschatological aspect.

Having considered the relevant scriptural passages we summarize the example of sharing that is presented in Paul's exhortation in 2 Cor 8 and 9. We will briefly compare the example of the collection with the "at a distance" example, Acts 11:19–30, and its comparators, that we considered in chapter 4: the practice of *curator annonae* and the account of Helena and Izates. We then compare the example with other contemporary forms of sharing: the Temple Tax (from the Jewish Diaspora to Jerusalem); and patronage, benefaction, and benefit exchange (while not necessarily an "over a distance" example, there are linguistic connections). We then summarize our findings of the theology and practice that Paul advocates in 2 Cor 8 and 9 and the similarities to and differences from the surrounding cultural practices.

THE CORINTHIAN CONTEXT

Paul's Relationship with the Corinthians

Between 1 and 2 Corinthians there appears to have been a deterioration in the relationship between Paul and the Corinthians.[1] First Corinthians refers to a previous letter (1 Cor 5:9) and indicates a previous visit (presumably that of Acts 18:1–21). After he wrote 1 Corinthians Paul made a brief visit to the Corinthians and then wrote a sorrowful letter (2:1; 7:8–9; 12:14; 13:1–3).[2] Traditionally commentators often identified this letter as 1 Corinthians,[3] but it does not have the tone or content that would fit with Paul's descriptions in 2:2–4 and 7:8–9. Others have identified it with 2 Cor 10–13, but this section does not mention the issues around the offender (2:5–11) and so is unlikely to be the sorrowful letter, which is probably lost.[4]

In between the writing of 1 Corinthians and 2 Corinthians issues seem to have arisen between Paul and the Corinthians around the acceptance

---

1. It is generally agreed that 2 Corinthians (whether as an integrity or in parts) follows 1 Corinthians. Barnett, *Second Corinthians*, 9–15; Barrett, *Second Corinthians*, 5–10; Furnish, *Corinthians*, 27–29, 41–48; Harris, *Second Corinthians*, 58–59, 64–67.

2. Unless otherwise specified biblical references in this chapter will be to 2 Corinthians.

3. Matera, *Corinthians*, 19. Chrysostom *Hom. 2 Cor.* 15:2–3 NPNF12; Calvin, *Second Corinthians*, 98–99.

4. Matera, *Corinthians*, 19.

of money[5] (12:11-18) and the presence of those whom Paul designates as superapostles (11:5). Matera also suggests that further divisions and immorality may have arisen within the Corinthian community.[6] It thus seems possible that interest in the collection may have waned during this time[7] and that the Corinthians stopped their weekly setting aside for the collection (1 Cor 16:2).[8]

Paul has also sent Titus to Corinth during this period, and Titus' report encouraged Paul (7:5-16). Therefore as Paul writes 2 Corinthians he has some positive news, but also an awareness of ongoing and increased issues which he needs to address including his change of travel plans (1:12—2:4); why he faces hardship (4:1—5:10); why he has refused their money (12:11-18); and what apostolic ministry involves (5:11-21).[9]

Form(ation) of 2 Corinthians

There are significant differences of opinion about the formation of 2 Corinthians and whether it was written as one letter or whether it is made of multiple letters or letter fragments. Betz provides a history of the various theories.[10] These include proposals that 2 Corinthians is two letters (1-9 and 10-13)[11] or three letters (1-8, 9, 10-13).[12] Theories of partition generally argue that there are differences in tone, for example in chapters 10-13,[13] and topic. For example Georgi argues that 2:14—7:4 or at least 6:14—7:1 is likely to be a later insertion.[14]

Chapters 8 and 9 raise further questions. They are sometimes seen as separate from one another, whether as two different letters or as parts of two different letters,[15] for a number of reasons: περὶ μέν (9:1) is seen as introducing a new topic; the reference in 9:2 does not necessarily fit with using

---

5. Ibid., 250.
6. Ibid., 15.
7. Bruce, *Corinthians*, 220; Calvin, *Second Corinthians*, 111-12.
8. Hughes, *Second Corinthians*, 304; Harris, *Second Corinthians*, 583-84; Furnish suggests the collection may not have been taken up (Furnish, *Corinthians*, 419).
9. Matera, *Corinthians*, 7.
10. Betz, *Corinthians*, 3-34.
11. Furnish, *Corinthians*, 41-47; Hanson sees 9:11-14 as implying an ending, Hanson, *Second Corinthians*, 74; Downs, *Offering*, 49-50.
12. Thrall, *Corinthians*, 2:503.
13. Lambrecht, *Second Corinthians*, 8.
14. Georgi, *Remembering*, 76.
15. Nickle, *Collection*, 17.

the Macedonians as an example in 8:1–5; Paul gives different reasons for sending the brothers in 8:20 and 9:3–5; the reference in 9:2 to the recipients as Achaians rather than Corinthians; and the fact that 8:15 could imply that the collection in Macedonia is finished.[16] In addition, the repetition about the brothers in 8 and 9 and the reference to Achaia (9:2) might indicate that the chapters were to two different groups,[17] with Betz arguing that Paul had a different relationship with the Corinthians to the Achaians.[18] Georgi argues that 9:1 only makes sense if chapter 9 is not linked to chapter 8 and that we would expect Titus to be mentioned in the introduction in chapter 1 if 2 Corinthians were a unity.[19]

Betz and Stirewalt see chapters 8 and 9 as copies of letters giving authority. Betz highlights the presence of σπουδή and its cognates (8:7, 8, 16, 17, 22) as indicating administrative letters[20] and argues that they are similar in form to letters of appointment,[21] while Stirewalt argues that they are letters of authority.[22]

However, despite the various arguments for partition, it is by no means clear that the evidence precludes the extant letter being written as one letter. As Lambrecht and Plummer point out there is no textual evidence showing partition[23] or "that 2 Corinthians ever existed without viii. or without ix.."[24] Indeed Tasker points out that we cannot find evidence of partition in early Christian writers.[25]

Therefore a number of scholars argue for the unity of 2 Corinthians. Hughes argues for the unity of the letter[26] on the basis that it is around the one theme of "strength in weakness."[27] Keener concludes that "it is easier . . . to account for the letter's current unity if it were written as such."[28] While there are changes in topic and tone, these can be accounted for: Paul may have received new information during the time he was writing the letter and

---

16. Furnish, *Corinthians*, 429–31.
17. Lambrecht, *Second Corinthians*, 8.
18. Betz, *Corinthians*, 49.
19. Georgi, *Remembering*, 77.
20. Betz, *Corinthians*, 58.
21. Ibid., 133.
22. Stirewalt, *Paul*, 78.
23. Lambrecht, *Second Corinthians*, 9.
24. Plummer, *Second Corinthians*, 252.
25. Tasker, *Corinthians*, 24.
26. Hughes, *Second Corinthians*, xxiv–xxvi.
27. Ibid., xxx.
28. Keener, *Corinthians*, 201.

it is not unusual to have interruptions[29] or subject changes[30] within Paul's letters. In addition there are links between different sections of the letter that are often seen as separate. For example, chapter 8 links to chapter 7. In 7:13–15 Paul builds confidence in Titus and his concern for them, before introducing his task in chapter 8.[31] Similarly Paul refers to the earnestness of the Corinthians in 7:11–12 before praising the Macedonians in 8:1–5.[32] Harris point out the existence of conceptual and verbal links between chapters 7 and 8[33] and therefore argues that 7:4–16 is the launch for the appeal.[34]

While there are arguments for the partition of chapters 8 and 9, there is also evidence of unity. Indeed O'Mahony shows that rhetorical analysis can equally point to the unity of chapters 8 and 9.[35] Harris identifies an *inclusio* involving a number of words and phrases (ἡ χάρις τοῦ θεοῦ, δοκιμή, περισσεύω, ἁπλότης, διακονία) between 8:1–5 and 9:12–15.[36] While 9:1 has often been used as an argument for the separation of the chapters, Bruce argues that the presence of the γάρ indicates that the subject has already been referred to[37] and Harris notes that there is "no evidence in extant Greek literature that the phrase περὶ μὲν γάρ ever has an introductory function."[38] Additionally 9:3 needs chapter 8 to understand who the brothers are.[39] Furnish notes that 9:1–5 can be seen as an extension of 8:16–24[40] and Lambert argues that Paul uses Achaia in 9:2 to balance his use of Macedonia.[41]

Therefore because of the lack of textual evidence of partition and the presence of links in language, structure and theme, we will work on the basis of the unity of 2 Corinthians.

---

29. 1 Cor 9:1–27; Matera, *Corinthians*, 31.

30. Best, *Second Corinthians*, 75.

31. Barnett, *Second Corinthians*, 387.

32. Furnish, *Corinthians*, 408.

33. Harris, *Second Corinthians*, 558. E.g., σπουδ- root (7:11–12; 8:7, 16–17).

34. Ibid., 557.

35. O'Mahony, *Persuasion*, 79 (words used, *inclusio*), 96–102, 140 (rhetorical structure).

36. Harris, *Second Corinthians*, 647; also McCant, *Corinthians*, 77.

37. Bruce, *Corinthians*, 225.

38. Harris, *Second Corinthians*, 617. Thrall acknowledges this, but suggests the γάρ may be redactional (Thrall, *Corinthians*, 2:564).

39. Harris, *Second Corinthians*, 617–18.

40. Furnish, *Corinthians*, 432.

41. Lambrecht, *Second Corinthians*, 150.

SECOND CORINTHIANS 8 AND 9: PAUL'S EXHORTATION ABOUT THE COLLECTION

By the time Paul writes 1 Corinthians, the Corinthians are already aware of the collection. It is possible that Paul might have referred to it in his letter prior to 1 Corinthians (referred to in 1 Cor 5:9)[42] or that they may have heard about it from the Galatian churches.[43] In 1 Cor 16:3 Paul has already indicated that the collection will be sent to Jerusalem and therefore does not need to specify this again in 2 Corinthians.[44]

The Example of the Macedonians

Paul's exhortation to the Corinthians is dominated by grace[45] and starts somewhat indirectly with the example of the Macedonians' generosity in giving. Matera points out that Paul may well use this indirect approach because of the continuing fragility of his relationship with the Corinthians and his uncertainty about how they may respond.[46]

While Paul lauds the example of the Macedonians, he also emphasizes that their generosity is based in the grace that God has given them (8:1)[47] and the way that grace is rooted in Jesus' actions.[48] His concern is to communicate the grace they have received to the Corinthians (8:1). The giving of the Macedonians is voluntary.[49] It is the Macedonians who ask Paul (8:3–4) for the privilege of participating.[50]

The Macedonians' giving is not just voluntary, it is also generous. Ἁπλότης is difficult to translate. In the NT it occurs only here, 2 Cor 9:11, 13 and Rom 12:8; and there is a possible breadth of meanings.[51] BDAG notes "simplicity, sincerity, uprightness, frankness" "esp. of personal integrity

---

42. Harris, *Second Corinthians*, 555.
43. Ibid., 556.
44. Best, *Second Corinthians*, 75.
45. Watson, *Second Corinthians*, 58; Barclay, "Because," 1.
46. Matera, *Corinthians*, 185.
47. McCant, *Corinthians*, 79.
48. Barclay, "Because," 1–2, 17.
49. Furnish, *Corinthians*, 400.
50. Barnett, *Second Corinthians*, 390; Tasker, *Corinthians*, 112.
51. Betz provides the following breath of meaning "the term is used to describe the Macedonians as people of 'simplicity, sincerity, uprightness, frankness,' as well as 'generosity and liberality'" (Betz, *Corinthians*, 44).

expressed in word and action."⁵² While BDAG notes the suggestion of "*generosity, liberality*" for NT occurrences, BDAG thinks the first meaning is sufficient.⁵³ Thrall notes a possible instance in Josephus (*Ant.* 8.332) where ἁπλότης could be used with generosity as its meaning,⁵⁴ although it could also be interpreted there as "sincerity." Thrall notes that "To give unconditionally is to give generously with sincere, single-minded concern for the recipients"⁵⁵ and this may be the idea behind Paul's use of ἁπλότης as he speaks of the Macedonians' generosity. In a similar vein, Griffith suggests it indicates "the integrity of the heart rather than the quantity of the gift."⁵⁶ A dual meaning seems probable as it is unclear in 8:2 what a wealth of sincerity or integrity would involve. The Macedonians' generosity to the collection is not the only example of their generosity. Paul's letter to the Philippians records that they had been generous to him in the past also (Phil 1:5; 4:15–16).⁵⁷

The Macedonians' giving was also characterized by being first to the Lord (8:5). There is some discussion whether this is a question of priority in importance⁵⁸ or in importance and time.⁵⁹ However, in both cases the priority of giving themselves to the Lord is key. As Chrysostom notes "Everything else flowed from that" (*Hom. 2 Cor.* 16.3). It is also important to note that they gave "themselves" first to the Lord: "The ἑαυτούς is in an emphatic position, and this suggests that the contrast implicit in the πρῶτον has ἑαυτούς as one of its terms,"⁶⁰ therefore their generosity was not simply a question of giving just money.⁶¹ Indeed their giving of themselves may be seen as giving themselves in service to the Lord, through the Lord to Paul,⁶² and through the Lord to the collection.⁶³

The Macedonian example of giving is one that involves generosity in the midst of poverty and challenge. Barnett notes that it is likely that Achaia

52. BDAG, 104.
53. Ibid.
54. Thrall, *Corinthians*, 2:524.
55. Ibid.
56. Griffith, "Abounding," 226. Griffith also suggests that it may refer to human grace.
57. Harris, *Second Corinthians*, 563.
58. Betz, *Corinthians*, 48; Plummer, *Second Corinthians*, 236.
59. Harris, *Second Corinthians*, 568.
60. Thrall, *Corinthians*, 526.
61. Barnett, *Second Corinthians*, 400.
62. Betz, *Corinthians*, 48; Plummer, *Second Corinthians*, 236; Tasker, *Corinthians*, 112.
63. Harris, *Second Corinthians*, 568; Barnett, *Second Corinthians*, 399.

was probably richer than Macedonia.⁶⁴ Livy 45.30c reports the separation of the region and mining restrictions and this could have led to economic difficulties.⁶⁵ This is in around 167 BCE and the situation may have changed. Even if the legacy of these actions is no longer current, persecution is likely to have impoverished the Macedonian Christians.⁶⁶ Acts (16:11—17:15),⁶⁷ 1 Thessalonians (1:6, 2:14; 3:3–5) and Philippians (1:29–30)⁶⁸ all report the persecution of believers in the Macedonian region. Their poverty is described as severe "down to depth"⁶⁹(κατὰ βάθους—8:2) and it is possible that "the Macedonians who knew firsthand the pain of poverty through persecution felt a deep fraternal affinity with the persecuted Jewish believers in Judea."⁷⁰ It is the Macedonians' poverty that overflows into generosity (8:3).⁷¹ Their generosity is not limited by their own needs as they give beyond their ability.⁷²

Paul's Instructions to the Corinthians

Having communicated the example of the Macedonians Paul turns to instructing the Corinthians about participating in the collection.⁷³ Harris notes that Paul may not be aiming to embarrass the Corinthians, but that his words could have had that impact: Paul implores "them to finish their collection (vv. 7, 11); the Macedonians had implored him to let them begin theirs (v. 4)!"⁷⁴ Paul's instructions are focused around the example of Jesus and χαρίς. Paul crafts his words carefully to encourage the Corinthians to participate, but also to prompt their contribution to be freely given.

Paul reminds the Corinthians of the gifts they abound in (8:7) and therefore encourages them to καὶ ἐν ταύτῃ τῇ χάριτι περισσεύητε (8:7).

64. Barnett, *Second Corinthians*, 393.
65. Ibid., 219; Plummer, *Second Corinthians*, 233.
66. Thrall, *Corinthians*, 2:523.
67. Ibid., 2:522.
68. Best, *Second Corinthians*, 77.
69. Barrett, *Second Corinthians*, 219.
70. Ibid., 393. Briones argues that one of the characteristics of the Philippian κοινωνία with Paul and God is their sharing in suffering with Paul, which is why Paul allows them to financially support him (Briones, *Policy*, 116–17, 129)
71. Furnish, *Corinthians*, 400.
72. Hughes, *Second Corinthians*, 290.
73. Downs notes that rivalry was often used in benefaction contexts but that it is different here as there is a focus on love and zeal, and giving does not lead to receiving honor (Downs, *Offering*, 131–32).
74. Harris, *Second Corinthians*, 569.

There are textual variations in 8:7. Furnish argues for τῇ ἐξ ἡμῶν ἐν ὑμῖν ἀγάπῃ.[75] This is the more difficult reading, as it would make the Corinthians responsible for Paul's love to them. It also has support from some of the earliest witnesses.[76] Harris proposes that Paul is referring to the Corinthians' love engendered by Paul's love.[77] Whichever of the variants is Paul's original intention, the movement of the love reminds the Corinthians of Christian models of giving love in the lead up to the exhortation that they might participate in a model of passing on grace.

Paul wants the Corinthians' giving to be voluntary.[78] He is not commanding them (8:8). As Matera points out his language is very careful, to avoid insisting that they contribute.[79] Just as the Macedonians voluntarily contributed, Paul wants the Corinthians to contribute voluntarily.[80] Furnish and Héring see Paul as giving the Corinthians advice/counsel[81] and Héring suggests that this is all that is needed because they are already willing (8:10–11).[82]

Paul reminds the Corinthians that he is not urging them to do anything that they have not already expressed a desire to do (8:10). He points out that their desire to be involved precedes that of the Macedonians (9:2).[83] He now urges them to complete what they desired and willed to do (8:11).[84] McCant argues that by using ἐπιτελέω, Paul "evokes the image of a benefactor who fulfills an obligation."[85] Danker points out that ἐπιτελέω is used on inscriptions describing a benefactor completing something,[86] and Downs notes it could be used of the "performance of sacred rites."[87]

Central to Paul's exhortation for the Corinthians to contribute is the example of Jesus,[88] who gives up voluntarily (8:9).[89] Jesus is the "supreme

75. Furnish, *Corinthians*, 403.
76. For example 𝔓46, B.
77. Harris, *Second Corinthians*, 574.
78. Plummer, *Second Corinthians*, 240.
79. Matera, *Corinthians*, 189.
80. Barnett, *Second Corinthians*, 394.
81. Furnish, *Corinthians*, 409; Héring, *Second Corinthians*, 60.
82. Héring, *Second Corinthians*, 60.
83. Barrett, *Second Corinthians*, 225.
84. Martin, *Corinthians*, 260.
85. McCant, *Corinthians*, 82.
86. Danker, *Benefactor*, 362.
87. Downs, *Offering*, 135.
88. Barrett, *Second Corinthians*, 224.
89. Ibid., 408.

model"⁹⁰ and while Paul is careful not to command the Corinthians, the example of Jesus may be seen as commanding them,[91] or at least as being such a strong example that Paul has no need to command them.[92] Barclay goes further to see Jesus' actions not just as an example, but as "a divine momentum in which believers are caught up, and by which they are empowered to be, in turn, richly self-sharing with others."[93]

Paul is clear that Jesus is an example of grace and giving, however there is some discussion about what Paul is indicating that Jesus gave up and took on in this process. Georgi and Barnett see Paul as referring to Jesus giving up his heavenly state.[94] Tanner argues that Jesus gains the believer's poverty/need, so that the believer may gain God's riches.[95] However, while Tasker and Harris see Jesus as giving up riches in the incarnation, others see it more in terms of giving up communion with the Father and his willingness to give up in this way bringing spiritual benefits and salvation to the Corinthians.[96] Spencer draws together a whole range of possible areas of poverty that Jesus takes on: being part of a poor family, becoming human, obedience, "living for the poor," "being rejected by humans," and "by dying on behalf of human sin."[97]

Barclay identifies an alternative to this range of possible meanings of riches and poverty. He points out that if Paul is referring to Jesus giving up his heavenly pre-existent state,[98] there is a need for a shift from the metaphorical in language use to the literal[99] when it is then applied to the Corinthians. Barclay notes that Paul talks about the Macedonians' wealth in terms of their generosity (8:2, 13) and in 8:7 exhorts the Corinthians καὶ ἐν ταύτῃ τῇ χάριτι περισσεύητε, that is they are to abound or be wealthy in the grace of generosity.[100] He concludes that

---

90. Harris, *Second Corinthians*, 578.

91. Hughes, *Second Corinthians*, 302.

92. Plummer, *Second Corinthians*, 240; Matera, *Corinthians*, 191; Best, *Second Corinthians*, 81.

93. Barclay, "Manna," 421.

94. Georgi, *Remembering*, 83; Barnett, *Second Corinthians*, 408.

95. Tanner, *Economy*, 79.

96. Harris, *Second Corinthians*, 578–79; Tasker, *Corinthians*, 115; Lambrecht, *Second Corinthians*, 143.

97. Spencer, *Corinthians*, 136–37.

98. Barclay, "Because," 5.

99. Ibid., 9.

100. Ibid., 14.

in 2 Cor 8–9 there seems to be a consistent effort to give the abundance and wealth metaphors a paradoxical twist, so that both Christ and the Corinthians may be said to be "wealthy" not in their possessions but in their generosity; metaphorical "wealth," in other words, is gained precisely when literal wealth is passed on or shared.[101]

Paul does challenge the Corinthians' picture of what it means to be rich in his description of the Macedonians (8:2). Nevertheless, while Barclay's analysis that Paul is including within wealth the idea of generosity/giving away is persuasive, this does not necessarily preclude Paul intending a multireferent meaning in what Jesus gives up in becoming poor, and in what it means to be rich/wealthy.

"The Macedonians gave when they were desperately poor; Christ gave when he was incalculably rich. In their present economic circumstances the Corinthians fitted somewhere between these two extremes."[102] The Macedonians gave παρὰ δύναμιν (8:4). Jesus δι' ὑμᾶς ἐπτώχευσεν (8:9), yet Paul holds back from urging the Corinthians to give in the same way.[103] Rather he specifies that they should give according to what they have but not necessarily beyond that (8:12).[104] Furnish suggests that Paul may be addressing a situation where the Corinthians have stopped the collection because they were concerned that what they would collect would be too little for them to send.[105]

Paul goes on to reassure the Corinthians that the aim is not for them to become hard up, but rather equality and that their current provision will supply the need of those in Jerusalem (8:13–14). In addition to our arguments in chapter 3[106] about the particular needs of the Jerusalem congregation, Strachan also notes that the presence of pilgrims would have raised demand and prices and therefore increased the plight of the Jerusalem believers.[107] While Jesus and the Macedonians gave beyond equality, Paul's encouragement for the Corinthians is that they should give to effect equality (8:13).[108] The aim is not that they become poor or suffer economic

---

101. Ibid., 17.
102. Harris, *Second Corinthians*, 581.
103. Georgi, *Remembering*, 83.
104. Hughes, *Second Corinthians*, 305; Matera, *Corinthians*, 192.
105. Furnish, *Corinthians*, 419.
106. See pp. 66–71.
107. Strachan, *Second Corinthians*, 131–32.
108. Spencer, *Corinthians*, 141.

hardship,[109] but rather that there is equality[110] and relief from want.[111] Ambrosiaster comments that while Paul does not want them to cause hardship to themselves "a person ought not to keep more than he needs for himself" (*Comm.* CSEL 81.260).

However, while Paul is clear that the aim is ἰσότης (8:13), it is important to remember that equality in the Greco-Roman world is not identical to today's ideas of equality. The only other place that Paul uses the word is in Col 4:1 where he talks about what is fair for slaves.[112] In Greco-Roman thought equality between people of different social and economic backgrounds did not necessarily mean equal shares, but could mean shares in proportion to their relative advantage (Aristotle, *Eth. nic.* 5.5.8–10). BDAG defines ἰσότης as being a "state of matters being held in proper balance, *equality*," a "state of being fair, *fairness*."[113] Philo notes that equality has several forms (*Heir* 144) and speaks of equality being proportional, giving the example of requiring payment from a citizen that is "proportionate to the valuation of his estate" (*Heir* 145). Georgi wonders whether Paul had a similar background to Philo in terms of Greco-Roman thought when he came to think about the word,[114] although he acknowledges that Paul uses both Hellenistic wisdom and Apocalyptic concepts.[115] There is probably insufficient evidence in Paul's two uses of the word to conclude exactly which backgrounds Paul was particularly influenced by and it is probably more helpful to consider the context in 2 Corinthians in which Paul uses the word to understand what Paul has in mind by its use.

We have already noted that Paul does not desire that the Corinthians are hard pressed, but instead contrasts that with equality. He goes on to define this equality in terms of reciprocity based on responding at times of need (8:14)[116] and also gives the example of the manna in 8:15 (quoting Exod 16:18).

There is some discussion about the kind of reciprocity Paul has in mind and whether Paul foresees the Jerusalem believers being in a position to provide material help to the Corinthian believers. Barnett argues the reciprocal help could be "spiritual fellowship and unity" and then if

---

109. Harris, *Second Corinthians*, 589.
110. Best, *Second Corinthians*, 79.
111. Hughes, *Second Corinthians*, 306.
112. Furnish, *Corinthians*, 407; Georgi, *Remembering*, 84.
113. BDAG, 481.
114. Georgi, *Remembering*, 86.
115. Ibid., 91.
116. Lambrecht, *Second Corinthians*, 138.

circumstances allowed material.[117] Martin sees the help in an eschatological context suggesting that "Israel's future will enrich them in due time by accelerating the close of the age."[118] However, as Matera points out, there is no reference to spiritual help or aid and therefore the aid envisaged is probably economic.[119] Thrall argues that in the context of changing economic situations "The theoretical prospect of future aid from Jerusalem to Corinthian might well seem realistic,"[120] noting that Paul did not know about the Jewish War at this point.[121]

While some have looked to Paul's words in Rom 15:27 to argue that the reciprocity here is one which swaps material for spiritual blessings,[122] in 2 Corinthians Paul does not indicate that he has spiritual blessings in mind.[123] Indeed, while Rom 15:27 envisages the Gentiles in some sense repaying the blessing they have already received, in 8:14 Paul foresees a situation where the Jerusalem believers in the future will supply what the Corinthians need, using the same words to indicate abundance and need (περίσσευμα, ὑστέρημα) for both the Corinthians and the Jerusalem believers.

Paul's second way of defining equality is the quote he uses from Exod 16:18, bringing to mind God's provision for the Israelites in the wilderness through daily manna (8:15). Philo uses the same verse and story when he writes on equality.[124] Philo indicates that the equality was characterized by each person having sufficient manna (*Heir* 191). Hughes argues that the manna was collected and then distributed,[125] but there does not seem to be evidence of redistribution of the manna. A more helpful approach may be found in Lim and Best, who both note that hoarding manna brings no benefit.[126] This idea of sharing rather than hoarding would link with Paul's desire that none should go short.[127] However, there is a contrast between the Israelites in the wilderness and what Paul hopes for the Corinthians:

---

117. Barnett, *Second Corinthians*, 414.

118. Martin, *Corinthians*, 269.

119. Matera, *Corinthians*, 193. Also Hughes, *Second Corinthians*, 308; Plummer, *Second Corinthians*, 245.

120. Thrall, *Corinthians*, 2:542.

121. Ibid., 2:542.

122. See pp. 173–75.

123. Matera, *Corinthians*, 193.

124. Betz, *Corinthians*, 69.

125. Hughes, *Second Corinthians*, 307.

126. Best, *Second Corinthians*, 80; Lim, "Generosity," 28.

127. Witherington, *Conflict*, 421.

The equality that the people of God of old experienced in the wilderness was the result of a divine miracle and was enforced and inescapable. The equality to be experienced by the new people of God, on the other hand, would be the result of human initiative and would be voluntary and so not automatic.[128]

Barclay argues that, in contrast to other Jewish writers of the time (Josephus, Philo, Wisdom of Solomon), "Paul alone connects the gathering of the manna with a human mechanism of (re)distribution."[129] He argues that Paul blends the Exod 16 story with Jesus' model of self-giving.[130] Similarly Han notes that Paul "identifies the Corinthians with the Israelites, but, implicitly, also with their Lord by urging them to do the very thing that was done miraculously by the God of Israel."[131]

Titus and the Brothers

Paul then introduces Titus and the two brothers, whom he is sending to help with the collection. Titus comes to the Corinthians freely (8:17)[132] and is already known to the Corinthians through previous visits and therefore trusted.[133] Accompanying him are two brothers who are not named (8:18, 22). There is considerable discussion about who these two brothers are and why they are unnamed. Despite the amount of discussion on the range of possibilities of individuals and places, it is unlikely that we will be able to discern who these two brothers are; however it is probable that, given that they are appointed by churches to accompany the collection, they are from one of the church communities involved in the collection.[134]

Between them Titus and the brothers have considerable authority: personal (Paul's commission), ecclesiastical (chosen by the churches), and Christological (δόξα Χριστοῦ 8:23).[135] In addition to indicating authority from Christ, δόξα Χριστοῦ also brings to mind benefaction links.[136] Harrison suggests that by using "δόξα Χριστοῦ (2 Cor 9:23), Paul implicitly confronts the Corinthians with a choice between the 'glory' of two houses

---

128. Harris, *Second Corinthians*, 594.
129. Barclay, "Manna," 419.
130. Ibid., 421–26.
131. Han, "Swimming," 122.
132. Spencer, *Corinthians*, 143.
133. Kreitzer, *Corinthians*, 89.
134. Harris, *Second Corinthians*, 602–3.
135. Ibid., 595–96; O'Mahony, *Persuasion*, 155.
136. Harrison, "Brothers," 182.

and their dependents."[137] It would also seem logical that the phrase indicates that the brothers promoted the glory of Christ.[138]

Titus and the two brothers are equipped and commissioned and have a number of possible roles. First, is the role that Paul is clearest about—that of securing probity (8:21–22). Second Corinthians 2:17, 7:2, and 12:14–18 suggest that Paul is defending himself against some accusation, though whether it is of financial misappropriation,[139] peddling God's word,[140] or a more general Corinthian suspicion about Paul's relationship with them and with finance[141] is less clear. However, Paul desires that the collection is not misused, nor seen to be misused (8:20–21; Chrysostom, *Hom. 2 Cor.* 18.1).

Second, Titus and the brothers may be seen as making the collection more secure from outside attack as Paul takes it to Jerusalem.[142] Watson points out that these first two reasons fit the "conventions surrounding the movement of money in the first century."[143]

Third, Georgi suggests that the reference to the first brother's service in the gospel indicates that he is a skilled teacher, who could then explain the full meaning of the letter.[144]

Fourth, Betz and McCant suggest that the group's role is organizational: the Corinthians are willing (8:10–12), but not so good at organizing the collection, and so Titus and the two brothers are to oversee the organization of the collection (9:5).[145] The two brothers are appointed by the churches and Paul,[146] but Thrall also argues they were "the legal and political *persona* of the churches they represented"[147] and Betz argues that Titus had a similar role of representing Paul[148] with the letter functioning as a letter of authority.[149] However, O'Mahony points out that the language Paul uses is not necessarily administrative.[150] There does not seem to be sufficient evidence

---

137. Ibid., 185.
138. Thrall, *Corinthians*, 2:555.
139. Best, *Second Corinthians*, 83; Downs, *Offering*, 139.
140. Hanson, *Second Corinthians*, 68.
141. Barnett, *Second Corinthians*, 417.
142. Harris, *Second Corinthians*, 600; Matera, *Corinthians*, 197.
143. Watson, "Collection," 168. Contra Becker who asserts that "fiscal oversight is a Western democratic notion" (Becker, Χάρις, 122).
144. Georgi, *Remembering*, 74.
145. Betz, *Corinthians*, 93; McCant, *Corinthians*, 91.
146. Barnett, *Second Corinthians*, 421.
147. Thrall, *Corinthians*, 2:556.
148. Betz, *Corinthians*, 71, 78–79.
149. See pp. 195–98.
150. O'Mahony, *Persuasion*, 172–74.

within the text to point to chapters 8 and 9 being of a specific administrative form and while Paul does commend the two brothers who are coming with Titus, this does not seem to be the sole purpose of these chapters, but rather part of his broader argument to encourage the Corinthian participation in the collection.

At the end of his endorsement of the role of Titus and the two brothers, Paul emphasizes that his desire is that their contribution to the collection should be ὡς εὐλογίαν καὶ μὴ ὡς πλεονεξίαν (9:5). Thrall suggests that there are three different possible meaning for πλεονεξία here: grudgingly given, which fits the sentence but seems "to distort the natural meaning"; that if Paul compels "the Corinthians to give, he will seem to be exacting the money in a greedy spirit" (which would give a different subject for εὐλογία and πλεονεξία); or the third option, which Thrall proposes, of the word referring back to Exod 16:18 and those who "have too much."[151] "The Corinthian contribution to the collection is not to be an expression of any such 'desire to have more' than their fellow Christians of the mother church."[152] While there are issues with the second option, the first meaning could be combined with the third with πλεονεξία indicating "*a gift that is grudgingly granted by avarice.*"[153]

Why Give?

Paul then turns to give a basis for generous giving. Strachan sees this final section as Paul presenting the "moral interest" reasons that the Corinthians should give.[154] However, Paul's argument seems wider, including the idea of God as provider (9:8, 14–15) and that the Corinthians should not fear need if they give.[155] "Above all he speaks of God, who is the creative source of their generosity and who is also continually giving in abundance."[156] One example of this reference to God's generosity is the way that Paul uses the same word of sowing generously as Prov 22:8 LXX (which Paul goes on to quote) does of God's blessing.[157]

One of the images that Paul uses to communicate this point is that of farming—of seeds and harvest. It is God who will provide both the seed

---

151. Thrall, *Corinthians*, 2:571–73.
152. Ibid., 2:573.
153. BDAG, 824.
154. Strachan, *Second Corinthians*, 137.
155. Tasker, *Corinthians*, 125.
156. Lambrecht, *Second Corinthians*, 151.
157. Wright, *Corinthians*, 102.

GIVING AND GENEROSITY

and the generosity[158] and therefore giving results in God's honor.[159] Betz notes that the language here is not necessarily Christian.[160] Yet while Paul uses words and images that would fit with Jewish thought and with Greco-Roman thought, he bases his argument about generosity and giving, not only around the general generosity of God, but also around God's generosity seen in the gospel of Jesus (8:9) and he sees the Corinthian contribution as being part of their confession of τὸ εὐαγγέλιον τοῦ Χριστοῦ (9:13).

Paul continues to emphasize that giving should be voluntary, not forced; not a burden, but joyful (9:7).[161] As we have already seen there is a tension between: the strength of the examples that Paul uses, particularly that of Jesus (8:9); the way that Paul has previously told them that all things come from God (1 Cor 4:7); and the fact that Paul continues to place the onus on the Corinthians to make the decision to give in their own heart (9:7).[162] The decision to give should not be compelled (9:7), but the giving should be done generously (9:6)[163] and cheerfully (9:7). In 9:7 Paul picks up Prov 22:8a LXX. Han notes there are verbal correspondences and matches between this section and Prov 22:8-9 with "the same idea of sowing and reaping imagery and cheerful giving" being "followed by the promise of abundance or nourishment."[164] Paul makes a small change to Prov 22:8a and uses ἀγαπᾷ instead of εὐλογεῖ. Betz argues he may be quoting from memory, but also that he may have consciously made the change to fit with his argument.[165] Han helpfully suggests this may be to focus on the "attitude of the giver. The giver's interest should not be in God's blessing as a result of the giving, but in reflecting God's manner of giving by having a cheerful and generous attitude."[166]

Paul does not just encourage the Corinthians to decide to give or give them examples of generous giving, he also asserts that God is able to provide for them to give and that giving brings its own rewards (9:8, 11). As Tasker points out:

> Generous giving for those who have little to give seems very hazardous; but the risk tends to be forgotten when the greatness

158. Matera, *Corinthians*, 2078.
159. Martin, *Corinthians*, 293.
160. Betz, *Corinthians*, 99–100.
161. Lambrecht, *Second Corinthians*, 177.
162. McCant, *Corinthians*, 93.
163. Hughes, *Second Corinthians*, 328–30.
164. Han, "Swimming," 128.
165. Betz, *Corinthians*, 107–8.
166. Han, "Swimming," 129.

of God's power is kept steadily in mind. All our resources, great or small, come ultimately from God; and God is able, Paul insists, to increase those resources. Where the generous spirit exists God will provide the means by which it can be expressed.[167]

Paul started chapter 8 by reminding the Corinthians of God's giving nature (8:1). Indeed Barnett argues that the fact that δεδομένην is a passive perfect points to God continuing to give.[168] Here in 9:6–15, Paul continues to remind the Corinthians that God gives and will provide for them that they may also give. As Furnish points out, because it is God who provides, consequent giving gives glory to God.[169]

Paul uses the classically Stoic word αὐτάρκεια (9.8), which means "'self-sufficiency' in the sense of 'independence,' then gener. 'sufficiency'" and could internally refer to "*contentment*."[170] As Keener points out, it is not just used by Stoics (Prov 30:8 LXX, Ps Sol 5:16).[171] Paul also uses the word in a sense that is different from the usual Stoic sense.[172] "The Stoic's sufficiency is from himself, whereas Paul's sufficiency is the gift of God, the result of his grace (χάρις),"[173] which Georgi sees as "the simplicity of an open, trusting, and faithful heart."[174] McCant observes that in Phil 4:11 Paul transforms the word's meaning[175] using it with the sense of contentment.[176] Here Paul seems to view "*autarkeia* as a sufficiency of material wealth, supplied by God, which believers can disperse to those in need."[177] Thus, the idea of freedom is retained, but it is a freedom to give and to bless.[178] Also, as Plummer points out, the idea of not being bound to possessions/contentment creates the possibility to give.[179]

Whether God's blessing includes not just the means, but also the desire, as Harris asserts is not clear.[180] However, it is possible and the πρῶτον

---

167. Tasker, *Corinthians*, 126.
168. Barnett, *Second Corinthians*, 391.
169. Furnish, *Corinthians*, 446.
170. BDAG, 152.
171. Keener, *Corinthians*, 213.
172. Barrett, *Second Corinthians*, 237.
173. Ibid., 237; also Martin, *Corinthians*, 290; Harris, *Second Corinthians*, 638.
174. Georgi, *Remembering*, 160.
175. McCant, *Corinthians*, 95.
176. Also 1 Tim 6:6.
177. Matera, *Corinthians*, 206.
178. Watson, *Second Corinthians*, 99; Witherington, *Conflict*, 427.
179. Plummer, *Second Corinthians*, 260.
180. Harris, *Second Corinthians*, 638.

τῷ κυρίῳ καὶ ἡμῖν διὰ θελήματος θεοῦ (8:5) may cohere with this idea.[181] Becker sees δύναμις in 8:3 "as an allusion to the Χάρις of God at work in the Macedonians."[182] Other factors that may add weight to this possible reading include the way that Paul references both his own action and God's action in 1 Cor 15:10,[183] and the way Paul indicates that knowing Jesus/encountering the divine leads to transformation.[184] Elsewhere Paul does indicate that God provides both motive and means (Phil 2:13) and thus we concur with Thrall who suggests it is likely here,[185] as well as noting with Griffith that Paul still sees a role for believers being willing and the need for them to have the right attitude to God.[186]

Paul then quotes from Ps 111:9 LXX. While Barrett suggests other scriptural allusions,[187] Han points out that 9:9 is a verbatim quote of LXX Ps 111:9 but "τοῦ αἰῶνος is missing."[188] In the Psalm, the subject of the verse is the righteous person, however in 2 Cor 9 the subject is less clear as in verses 8 and 10 the subject is God. The subject of 9:9 could be God,[189] the person,[190] or a combination.[191] Furnish argues for a combination of the person's acts and God.[192] However, the person's acts do not seem a straightforward subject for the first half of the verse grammatically. While verse 8 does have God as the subject, it speaks about God's provision so that the Corinthians may abound in every good work, which could point to God's righteousness being seen in the person's righteousness. This would fit with Han's argument that the close link between the person and God in Ps 111 and Paul's quoting of the Psalm suggest that "God is providing for the poor through the Corinthians. Even when the Corinthians help the poor, it is in fact God who is helping them through his people."[193]

---

181. Becker, Χάρις, 145.
182. Ibid., 81.
183. Griffith, "Abounding," 169.
184. Rabens, Spirit, 180, 182, 242.
185. Thrall, Corinthians, 578.
186. Griffith, "Abounding," 205, 214, 252.
187. Barrett, Second Corinthians, 238.
188. Han, "Swimming," 32.
189. Murphy-O'Connor, Theology; Witherington, Conflict, 427.
190. Matera, Corinthians, 206; Lambrecht, Second Corinthians, 147; Hughes, Second Corinthians, 332; Harris, Second Corinthians, 640.
191. Georgi, Remembering, 99.
192. Furnish, Corinthians, 448–49.
193. Han, "Swimming," 136.

The focus in all three verses seems to be on God providing, so that the Corinthians can in turn give. The fact that the subject of verse 9 could be ambiguous in some ways only highlights Paul's point that God gives so that the Corinthians may also give.[194]

Having reassured the Corinthians that they can confidently give because God will provide all that they need in order to give (and indeed go on giving) (9:8, 10–11),[195] Paul turns to focus on what the result of the collection will be. Paul has already pointed out that the result should be the alleviation of need (8:14) and he now repeats that (9:12) and adds that the Corinthians' participation in the collection will involve God being thanked and glorified and the Corinthians being enriched and prayed for.

However, as in Philippians (1:3; 4:10–20),[196] thanks will not be given to the Corinthians, but rather to God (9:11–12).[197] Paul affirms God "as the sole object of thanksgiving"[198] because God is ultimately the benefactor and provider in the relationship.[199] It is not altogether clear who is doing the thanking: in verse 11 it happens δι' ἡμῶν and then in verse 12 the collection results in many thanksgivings as well as the supply of the needs, so it may be that those whose needs are supplied are the ones who abound in thanksgiving to God. Griffith notes that the genitive absolute in verse 13 suggests a change of subject from the previous verse which would suggest that the subject of verse 13 is the Corinthians and that of verse 12 is the Jerusalemites.[200] Matera acknowledges both possibilities but argues that it is the Corinthians who glorify God, as otherwise the change of subject would be rather abrupt.[201] The phrase διὰ τῆς δοκιμῆς τῆς διακονίας ταύτης which is dependent on δοξάζοντες fits more naturally with the Corinthians as the subject. This also fits with the possibility that Paul sees the collection itself as worship and Witherington argues that for Paul, "Generous giving to the saints is not merely a civic obligation but also an act of worship and thanksgiving to God."[202]

---

194. Barnett, *Second Corinthians*, 436, 439; Betz sees God providing to the Corinthians "both the material means and the inner disposition to become cheerful givers" (Betz, *Corinthians*, 110).

195. Han sees a phrasal link with Isa 55:10 LXX and argues that Paul uses the link to emphasize the certainties of God's provision (Han, "Swimming," 137, 140).

196. Peterman, *Paul*, 9.

197. Georgi, *Remembering*, 102.

198. Downs, *Offering*, 143.

199. Harris, *Second Corinthians*, 646.

200. Griffith, "Abounding," 235.

201. Matera, *Corinthians*, 210.

202. Witherington, *Conflict*, 428. "In the normal and healthy Christian life,

In addition to God being thanked and glorified (probably by the recipients as well as by the Corinthians by their very act of giving), Paul also asserts that the Corinthians will be enriched and prayed for by those who receive the collection and therefore who have affection for them (9:14).[203]

In 2 Cor 8 and 9 Paul does not name Jerusalem as the destination of the collection.[204] Harris sees the reference in 9:12 to οἱ ἅγιοι as an abbreviation of the οἱ πτωχόι τῶν ἁγίων τῶν ἐν Ἰερουσαλήμ (Rom 15:26)[205] that functioned almost as a title for those believers in Jerusalem. However, as we shall see later, it is not clear that οἱ ἅγιοι was used in this way.[206] The Corinthians probably would have seen the recipients as the Jerusalem believers because Paul had already specified in 1 Cor 16:1 that the collection was going to be taken to Jerusalem. We will examine Paul's aims for the collection in more detail and how he perceives it influencing the relationship between Jewish and Gentile believers after we have considered other NT texts that deal with the collection. For now we note that Georgi argues that the submission in 9:13 is to God and therefore shows the Jerusalemites the equality of the Corinthians' faith[207] and thus encourages unity between Jewish and Gentile believers.[208]

In 8:14 Paul envisages a return to supply the Corinthians' need and in 9:11 he talks about them being enriched in every way. This raises the question of what the Corinthians would receive and how they would be enriched. Augustine saw the material giving resulting in the spiritual blessing of eternal life (*Ep*. 268) and Chrysostom saw the benefit in the actual giving (*Hom*. 10.4). Theodoret of Cyrrhus saw the benefit the Corinthians received as being the prayers of the poor (*Comm. 2 Cor.* 336). However, in 8:14, Paul's phraseology does not preclude material benefits and thus Best argues that the enrichment is not necessarily just spiritual.[209] Indeed particularly in 9:8 and 10 where Paul is emphasizing God's provision for generosity and giving, he seems to suggest that God will continue to supply in order that they may continue to give/sow.

---

everything proceeds from God's generosity, and everything returns to God in thanksgiving" (Wright, *Corinthians*, 103). "The final goal of all giving is God's honor" (Martin, *Corinthians*, 293).

203. Barrett, *Second Corinthians*, 447; Thrall, *Corinthians*, 541.
204. Furnish, *Corinthians*, 402.
205. Harris, *Second Corinthians*, 567.
206. See pp. 175–76.
207. Georgi, *Remembering*, 105, 117.
208. Ibid., 109.
209. Best, *Second Corinthians*, 85.

Having talked about the enrichment and prayers that would be the result of the collection, Paul comes back to God's grace and gift and finishes with a concluding exclamation of praise to God (9:15). While 9:15 follows 9:14 which recounts God's grace resulting in the Corinthians' contribution to the collection, the whole passage points to God's generosity, with various scholars seeing the gift as Jesus.[210] Chrysostom (*Hom. 2 Cor.* 20.2)[211] argues that it is the gift of Jesus or the gift that Jesus bestows, which Matera takes forward arguing that the gift in mind is salvation.[212] It is not necessary to distinguish between Jesus and salvation as the gift, as both fit within the context of Paul having focused on God's grace and on Jesus' generosity in salvation. However, as Matera points out this exclamation of praise "emphasizes the relationship of the collection to God's overall work of redemption."[213]

Grace, Service, Fellowship, and Blessing: Paul's Use of Theologically Significant Words

This relationship of the collection (and more generally of generosity) to God's grace, Jesus, and salvation are also seen in the way that Paul uses theologically significant words throughout chapters 8 and 9. We turn therefore to examine some of the theological words that Paul uses within his argument and what we may discover from them.

Central to Paul's argument is χάρις and words consistent with it.[214] Paul uses the word with a range of meanings throughout the letter[215] and indeed starts and ends 2 Corinthians with χάρις.[216] He uses it ten times in chapters 8 and 9 and Harris identifies six meanings in the two chapters: God's grace (8:1; 9:8, 14); privilege or favor (8:4); act of grace (8:6); grace of giving (8:7); offering (8:19); and thanks (8:16; 9:15).[217] Hughes identifies four: God's grace (8:1); favor from the apostle (8:4); gift (8:6); and thanksgiving (8:16).[218]

---

210. Barnett, *Second Corinthians*, 448; Hughes, *Second Corinthians*, 342; Strachan, *Second Corinthians*, 145.

211. Bray, *Corinthians*, 282.

212. Matera, *Corinthians*, 210.

213. Ibid., 210.

214. Barnett, *Second Corinthians*, 389.

215. Furnish, *Corinthians*, 399.

216. Matera, *Corinthians*, 186.

217. Harris, *Second Corinthians*, 559–60.

218. Hughes, *Second Corinthians*, 294. NB also the range of meanings in BDAG, 1079–81.

Griffith argues that Paul uses χάρις to emphasize the voluntary nature rather than the obligation of the gift.[219]

As O'Mahony notes it may be particularly apt that Paul speaks to the Corinthians "using the language of χάρις to a community where χαρίσματα were so highly esteemed and played so much a part in the community's identity."[220] Indeed Barclay argues that "the term χάρις is not idly chosen, but freighted with theological, and specifically Christological connotations."[221] It is τὴν χάριν τοῦ κυρίου ἡμῶν Ἰησοῦ Χριστοῦ (8:9) which is seen in Christ's self-giving in incarnation and salvation and it is χάρις (9:15) which is given to God in response to the gift of Jesus. However, it is also χάρις that prompts the giving of the Macedonians (8:1), χάρις for the Macedonians to participate (8:4) and χάρις for the Corinthians to give (8:6,7). Harris thus sees Paul as presenting a circle of grace: "God gives his 'grace' to his people (8:1, 9:14), who then give a 'gift of grace' (8:7), which prompts the giving of 'thanks' (εὐ-χαρισ-τία, 9:11b–13) to God."[222] Contributing to the collection is thus placed within God's grace, generosity, and salvation.

Paul also uses the word λειτουργία (9:12), which could be used in a number of contexts: public service of citizens, pagan religious service, and Jewish religious contexts, "in our lit. almost always used w. some sort of relig. connotation."[223] "In Athenian democracy this word was used to denote a public service undertaken by private citizens at their own expense."[224] Such public service could include supporting events, such as drama; institutions; or other public activity, for example, training gymnasts.[225] It was also used in both Jewish (Num 8:22; Exod 37:19; Josephus *J.W.* 1.26) and pagan worship (*Diod. Sic.* 1.21.7) for cultic service.[226] Downs and Hanson both argue that Paul has deliberately chosen the word because of its religious and cultic associations.[227] Indeed Downs argues that Paul has used the language "to frame the Jerusalem fund as a religious offering."[228]

---

219. Griffith, "Abounding," 11.
220. O'Mahony, *Persuasion*, 150.
221. Barclay, "Because," 1.
222. Harris, *Second Corinthians*, 650. See also Becker, Χάρις, 144.
223. BDAG, 591.
224. Watson, *Second Corinthians*, 100.
225. Furnish, *Corinthians*, 443; Strachan, *Second Corinthians*, 144.
226. Hanson, *Second Corinthians*, 72–73, Strachan, *Second Corinthians*, 144.
227. Downs, *Offering*, 120, 123, 130; Hanson, *Second Corinthians*, 72–73. Contra Betz, *Corinthians*, 117.
228. Downs, *Offering*, 130.

Paul uses λειτουργία in conjunction with διακονία: ἡ διακονία τῆς λειτουργίας ταύτης (9:12), and this may help us clarify whether Paul does have a theological/religious background in mind. Like χάρις, διακονία is used repeatedly by Paul through the letter with a range of meanings,[229] for example: in 3:3, to describe the way the Corinthians have been served by Paul with the gospel; in 3:7 and 9 to contrast the ministries of the old and new covenants; in 4:1 and 5:18 to describe the ministry received from God; in 5:18 of the ministry of reconciliation; and in 6:3 and 11:8 to refer to Paul's ministry. Yet here, in chapters 8 and 9, Paul uses the word to describe administering the gift (8:19–20) and the gift itself (9:12–13). In 9:13 as we have seen the ministry is linked to glorifying God and Paul thus links the διακονία of the gospel to the διακονία of the gift and its administration to glorifying God. Therefore when he uses λειτουργία Paul probably does have a religious/theological background in mind.

Two other words Paul uses that have theological emphasis are κοινωνία and εὐλογία. Κοινωνία is used in 8:4 and 9:13 in the context of the Corinthians participating in and sharing in the collection.[230] Paul's use of κοινωνία also brings to mind the descriptions of the early church in Acts and the role κοινωνία has in those descriptions.[231] It is possible that Paul has in mind some of what he has seen and heard of the Jerusalem community as he uses the word. However, more pertinently Paul uses κοινωνία in Philippians. Briones has analyzed Paul's description of his κοινωνία with the Philippians and argues that it is a three-way partnership that includes God and involves sharing in suffering and in gift.[232] He then compares the Philippians to the Corinthians and argues that the Corinthians "acted as if gifts ended with them rather than handing them onto others"[233] so that part of what Paul is doing in 1 and 2 Corinthians is to encourage the Corinthians to see themselves in this three way κοινωνία.[234] Thus, by using κοινωνία Paul reminds the Corinthians of their fellowship and partnership with other believers and with God and thus their call to participate in the collection.

---

229. Keener, *Corinthians*, 203.
230. Martin, *Corinthians*, 254.
231. See pp. 46–50.
232. Briones, *Policy*, 116–29. Phil 4:14–15.
233. Ibid., 150.
234. Briones argues that in 1 Corinthians Paul presents God as the source of χάρις, Paul as a mediator of χάρις and the Corinthians as unworthy recipients (Ibid., 153–7). Ogereau argues that Paul's use of κοινωνία together with ἰσότης points to him not simply advocating charity but to him reforming "structural inequalities" (Ogereau, "Collection," 377).

Paul also refers to the gift as εὐλογία (9:5, 6), a word that can be used to mean "*praise,*" "*false eloquence, flattery*" (Rom 16:18), "act or benefit of blessing, *blessing*" (Rom 15:29; Gal 3:14; 1 Cor 10:16; Josh 15:19 LXX) or "generous gift, *bounty*."[235] Thus, while Paul seems to use εὐλογία in 2 Cor 9:5b as gift and in 2 Cor 9:6 as bounty, Paul's use of εὐλογία would probably remind the Corinthians of God's blessing (indeed BDAG suggests the use in 2 Cor 9:5a could be either blessing or gift),[236] and points to the collection as being a theological act.

Furnish argues that these theological words imply that Paul is showing unity between Jewish believers and Gentile believers as part of the outcome of the collection.[237] Matera similarly sees the fact that Paul does not mention money in chapters 8 and 9 as indicating that the collection is not simply about economic assistance.[238] More generally these theological words indicate the way Paul sees the collection as key, both as part of the Corinthians' faith, but also as imaging God's character and actions.

Questions about Paul's Argument

Before we look at other NT texts that may shed light on the collection, we consider two questions about Paul's argument to the Corinthians, which will help us understand more of Paul's theological basis for the collection.

First, in using the example of the Macedonians is Paul manipulating the Corinthians? For in 8:1–5 he uses the example of the Macedonians' giving to exhort the Corinthians to participate in the collection, yet he then reveals in 9:2 that he has been boasting to the Macedonians about the Corinthians. "Paul holds up the Macedonians to the Corinthians and the Corinthians to the Macedonians as examples to imitate" (Theodoret of Cyrrhus, *Comm. 2 Cor.* 332). Best suggests that Paul is setting them off against each other and is more concerned with the ends than the means.[239] Shaw also sees Paul as playing off "one congregation against another to encourage their generosity"[240] in a way that shows deviousness and manipulation.[241]

In contrast to this, Hughes sees this not as playing off one against the other, but rather encouraging them to fulfill their commitment. He notes

235. BDAG, 408–9.
236. Ibid.
237. Furnish, *Corinthians*, 411.
238. Matera, *Corinthians*, 5.
239. Best, *Second Corinthians*, 84.
240. Shaw, *Cost*, 116.
241. Ibid., 117.

that the past year had involved changes, which meant they had failed to complete the collection.²⁴² The Corinthians had begun their involvement well before the Macedonians.²⁴³ At the point that Paul speaks to the Macedonians about the collection, he could speak of the Corinthians' zeal and expect them to be well on their way with collecting.²⁴⁴ After this, it is likely that the conflict and misunderstandings "between him and the Corinthian community severely impeded the progress of the collection."²⁴⁵ Thus, when Paul discovers this and writes to the Corinthians, he is concerned to draw the Corinthians back into involvement in the collection and as part of that to preserve their reputation.²⁴⁶ Hughes argues that Paul's concern here is not their willingness but their organizational ability.²⁴⁷

While we follow Hughes' reconstruction of the timeline of the Corinthians' involvement in the collection, we would question the Corinthians' willingness to contribute at the point Paul writes 2 Corinthians. For although Paul appears confident that the Corinthians were willing in the past, the amount of time Paul spends exhorting them with reasons to be involved in the collection, suggests that they may also have lost some of their willingness.

The second question is what Paul means by using ὁμολογία, which can mean an "expression of allegiance as an action, *professing, confessing*" or a "statement of allegiance, as content of an action, *confession, acknowledgement that one makes.*"²⁴⁸

Betz argues that it indicates "sign of submission" to the church in Jerusalem and "means that the donors have entered into a contractual agreement,"²⁴⁹ which is why the giving is useful to the Corinthians.²⁵⁰ Betz acknowledges that Paul would disagree with such a submission and agreement and so suggests he is quoting from a homologia document.²⁵¹ These documents codified the legal process of donation and were to "establish personal relations."²⁵² Such documents include "legal and political

---

242. Hughes, *Second Corinthians*, 324.
243. Barrett, *Second Corinthians*, 224–25.
244. Ibid., 233–34.
245. Matera, *Corinthians*, 202.
246. Harris, *Second Corinthians*, 626; Barnett, *Second Corinthians*, 435.
247. Hughes, *Second Corinthians*, 325.
248. BDAG, 709.
249. Betz, *Corinthians*, 122.
250. Ibid., 124.
251. Ibid.
252. Ibid., 123.

terminology"²⁵³ and an explanation of why the donation would be useful to its recipients.²⁵⁴ However, there are other ways this phrase can be interpreted which would seem to fit better with the context. Harris suggests various possible meanings: "the obedience consisting of your confession," "the obedience prompted by your confession," "obedience to your confession," and "your professed obedience."²⁵⁵ Barnett sees Paul as referring to the gift as proof of their obedience.²⁵⁶ Héring argues that their participation in the collection proves their faith and generosity,²⁵⁷ and Hughes that it will give proof of the faith of the Gentile Christians.²⁵⁸ Their participation will also show the "reality of (their) love" and that they are one body.²⁵⁹ "The service of the Gentile churches to the poor saints is a part, or aspect of their confession of faith in the Gospel and shows this confession to be not a matter of words only but genuine obedience to God who is the author of the Gospel."²⁶⁰ Spencer notes that giving itself is confession because giving requires trust.²⁶¹ On each of these views, Paul links the reception of the gift with recognition of their faith and confession of the gospel.

Having considered Paul's account of the collection in 2 Cor 8 and 9 we turn to other passages where the collection may be referenced to see whether there is further evidence to augment our picture of the theology and practice provided by the example in 2 Cor 8 and 9.

OTHER TEXTS

1 Corinthians 16:1–4

In 1 Cor 16:1–4 Paul gives the Corinthians instructions about the collection. His use of περὶ δέ indicates that the subject is one that was known to him and the Corinthians²⁶² and probably that the Corinthians had asked

---

253. Ibid.
254. Ibid., 124.
255. Harris, *Second Corinthians*, 653–54.
256. Barnett, *Second Corinthians*, 445.
257. Héring, *Second Corinthians*, 68.
258. Hughes, *Second Corinthians*, 338.
259. Furnish, *Corinthians*, 417. "The test of obedience (2.8) and the test of love/loyalty, (8.8) is now a test of their being Christian at all" (McCant, *Corinthians*, 98).
260. Barrett, *Second Corinthians*, 240–41. Also Lim, "Generosity," 29.
261. Spencer, *Corinthians*, 163.
262. See pp. 115–20.

him about it.²⁶³ Murphy O'Connor asserts this would indicate that there had been a request or invitation for their involvement prior to 1 Corinthians²⁶⁴ and Downs suggests that Paul may have written to them about it in the letter referred to in 1 Cor 5:9.²⁶⁵ However, while it is clear the Corinthians knew about the collection, this may not have been from Paul.

Paul refers to the fact that it is not just the Corinthians that he has given directions to, but also the churches of Galatia which may indicate the Corinthians had heard about the collection by some means from Galatia,²⁶⁶ but it would also remind the Corinthians that the collection was "keine Augenblicksüberlegung"²⁶⁷ (no momentary consideration/flash in the pan).

Paul uses λογεία to describe the collection, which Fee notes is a "technical term for the actual activity of 'taking up' the contributions."²⁶⁸ Λογεία is used only here in the NT and was also used of religious collections.²⁶⁹

Paul's instructions are for each person to set something aside each week and Georgi argues that Paul focuses the Corinthians on taking personal initiative, and that the set aside money would have been pooled just before it was transported.²⁷⁰ Downs similarly argues that this instruction suggests that the congregation was not regularly administering funds.²⁷¹ The ἑαυτῷ would at the least imply personal initiative and possibly implies storing the money individually, although Downs argues it is not stored at home because of the references to Sunday and to not needing collections on his arrival.²⁷² The believers are to set aside ὅ τι ἐὰν εὐοδῶται (1 Cor 16:2) indicating their giving is to be related to their financial situation:²⁷³ "in accordance with how you may fare."²⁷⁴ Paul is concerned that the collecting should happen before his arrival and as Schrage points out this provides the opportunity to collect

---

263. Bruce, *Corinthians*, 157. Schrage asserts that Paul had not instructed the Corinthians about the collection during his stay (Schrage, *Brief*, 4:425). Fee argues Paul is possibly responding to their letter and that the Corinthians already know for whom the collection is intended because the opening verse lacks detailed information (Fee, *First Corinthians*, 809, 811).

264. Murphy-O'Connor, *Theology*, 79.

265. Downs, *Offering*, 40.

266. Schrage, *Brief*, 4:427.

267. Ibid., 4:427.

268. Fee, *First Corinthians*, 812.

269. BDAG, 597. See also MM, 377; P. Oxy. 11.239.

270. Georgi, *Remembering*, 54; Fee, *First Corinthians*, 813.

271. Downs, *Offering*, 101; Schrage, *Brief*, 4:429.

272. Downs, *Offering*, 128–29.

273. Schrage, *Brief*, 4:429.

274. Thiselton, *Epistle*, 1323.

more over time.²⁷⁵ Schrage also suggests other possible reasons: that Paul may not want to be involved in the actual collections; that Paul wants to encourage the Corinthians' partnership and involvement; or, which he sees as less likely, that there is some situation of mistrust.²⁷⁶ Thiselton suggests that Paul wishes to avoid a last minute appeal to the wealthy.²⁷⁷ While Paul does not specifically say this, it seems plausible as it would be the wealthy who could more easily give without saving up and Paul does emphasize the involvement of ἕκαστος ὑμῶν (1 Cor 16:2).

Paul also indicates that the Corinthians will choose delegates to accompany the gift to Jerusalem (1 Cor 16:3).²⁷⁸ Paul is uncertain about whether he will make the journey to Jerusalem and will only do so ἐὰν δὲ ἄξιον (1 Cor 16:4). There is some question about what the decision is contingent upon. Suggestions include: the attitude of the community, the value of the collection, and Paul's evaluation of his mission plans and the situation in Jerusalem.²⁷⁹ While Fee argues that it cannot refer to the gift as "[t]he adjective is impersonal and followed by an articular infinitive of purpose"²⁸⁰ and that therefore Paul's decision is dependent on how he thinks the gift will be received,²⁸¹ there is insufficient evidence to be certain.

Thrall notes that in 1 Corinthians Paul uses imperatives, while in 2 Cor 8 and 9 he makes requests of them.²⁸² This would fit with the way that Paul has less certainty about the Corinthians' response because of the various issues of contention between them, but also is indicative of the different questions Paul is addressing: in 1 Corinthians how to give, in 2 Corinthians motivation and rationale for giving.

Acts

In Acts there is the challenge of discerning which parts of the narrative may refer to the collection. Barrett notes that given that the collection was "one of [Paul's] major activities in the middle fifties," there is little in Acts unless 11:27-30 is misplaced.²⁸³ Furnish argues that, while Acts 21:17 does not

275. Schrage, *Brief*, 4:429-30.
276. Ibid.
277. Thiselton, *Epistle*, 1324.
278. Bruce, *Corinthians*, 158.
279. Schrage, *Brief*, 431-32.
280. Fee, *First Corinthians*, 816.
281. Ibid., 816; also Thiselton, *Epistle*, 1326.
282. Thrall, *Corinthians*, 2:519.
283. Barrett, *Second Corinthians*, 217.

mention the fund, it shows its glad receipt.[284] Nickle similarly argues that the fund is alluded to and well received and that the opposition that is faced is Jewish not Jewish Christian.[285]

While most scholars agree there is a paucity of evidence and suggest a range of reasons for this, Downs argues that Acts fails to mention the collection at all.[286] He considers the two places that are sometimes considered possible references and argues that neither of them are. He argues that Acts 11:27–30 is an authentic tradition responding to the prophecy of famine and suggests that it may be linked to Gal 2 but not to the collection referred to in 2 Cor 8 and 9.[287] Downs then turns to Acts 24:17 and argues that in this visit to Jerusalem there are a number of things that point to the visit not being the visit where Paul brings the collection.

First, Luke presents the reason for Paul's visit as one of divine necessity,[288] whereas Paul in his writing indicates that the purpose of the journey is to transport the collection. Second, Luke recounts Paul presenting his reason for coming to Jerusalem as coming to worship (Acts 24:11)[289] and in his speech Paul presents himself as a faithful Jew.[290] Therefore Downs argues that "Acts 24:17 far from being a reference to the collection, identifies Paul before his accusers as a faithful Jew whose individual piety is demonstrated by almsgiving and worship."[291]

Downs asserts that Acts does not refer to the collection and therefore cannot be used as evidence about it. Downs raises important questions about the limitations of Acts as evidence about the collection, however it is not clear that his arguments about Paul's visit in Acts 24:17 preclude the visit being multi-faceted and including the collection even if Luke does not present information about it. For example, the guidance of the Holy Spirit (Acts 19:21), Paul's assertions of divine necessity (Acts 21:13), Paul's explanation of his purpose as worship (Acts 24:11), and Paul's explanation of his actions as offering alms and sacrifices (Acts 24:17), do not necessarily mean that he could not also see part of the divine necessity or the worship as encompassing the collection, nor that the alms were necessarily for the temple rather than the believers (particularly if Paul saw the church as the inheritors of

---

284. Furnish, *Corinthians*, 453.
285. Nickle, *Collection*, 70.
286. Downs, "Collection," 52.
287. Ibid., 53–54.
288. Ibid., 64.
289. Ibid., 65.
290. Ibid., 66.
291. Downs, *Offering*, 63.

the role of God's chosen people, given that ἔθνος (Acts 24:17) can refer to a group of people as well as a nation).[292]

If Paul's visit in Acts 24:17 is one that included bringing the collection, it is notable that there is no mention of a representative from Corinth among those who are described as accompanying him (Acts 20:4).[293] The length of this list and the areas from which it draws people hints that this visit may have involved the collection. However, the lack of information raises the question about why Luke does not give more details or at least explicitly mention the collection. Nickle and Downs suggest a variety of possible reasons: maybe Luke did not have access to the epistles[294] or did not know about the collection, or if he did know about the collection, maybe he was unaware of its significance, knew that it might be considered illegal, or that it was rejected.[295] Nickle notes that if Luke is trying to present a positive picture for the Romans, then, if the collection raised tensions with the Jews, Luke may have omitted it.[296] Nickle also suggests that if the Christians had broken from Judaism then the collection could be seen as illegal,[297] however this seems unlikely as the final break was later. Additionally Thrall suggests that it is not clear that such a collection would be illegal,[298] but she does argue that, if the collection did not achieve Paul's aims, and if Luke wanted to present a positive picture of Christianity for Jews and Romans, he may have omitted the collection.[299] While we see Paul's visit in Acts 24:17 as including the collection, we agree that Acts provides insufficient evidence to add to the picture of the collection that Paul presents in 2 Cor 8 and 9. Acts does however raise the question of how well known the collection was, who in the end contributed, and what the outcome of its delivery was.

Galatians 2:10

Galatians 2:1–10 is often seen as an account of the agreement between Paul and the Jerusalem leaders which expected Gentile Christians to give to the Jerusalem believers almost in return for the blessing they had received in

---

292. BDAG, 276.
293. Tasker, *Corinthians*, 131.
294. Nickle, *Collection*, 149.
295. Downs, "Collection," 69; Downs, *Offering*, 69; Nickle, *Collection*, 149.
296. Nickle, *Collection*, 149.
297. Ibid., 150.
298. Thrall, *Corinthians*, 2:518.
299. Ibid., 2:517–18.

the gospel. Lim thus reminds us that the poor of verse 10 have often been seen as the poor in Jerusalem.[300]

Georgi sees the passage as an account of the agreement between Paul and the Jerusalem leaders which occurred at a convention in Jerusalem in which the Gentile believers were granted independence and recognition of their faith,[301] and the special position of believers in Jerusalem was acknowledged,[302] which included their role as watchmen and of making known the coming return of the king.[303] Gentile Christians were to grant "recognition to the exemplary performance on the part of their fellow believers in Jerusalem."[304] Thus, Georgi sees the agreement as one that was about "unity" between Jewish and Gentile leaders but not about authority of one group over the other.[305] Georgi then sees this agreement as breaking down[306] in Gal 2:11–21. Therefore when Paul returns to the collection, he does not talk about the agreement, but rather pursues it as a "purely Pauline initiative within the apostle's own congregations only."[307]

However, as Horrell points out, Gal 2:1–10 does not specifically mention the collection and could be more generally about help for the poor.[308] Key to this is whether "the poor" was a specific term to designate believers in Jerusalem. Longenecker argues that the association is a late one. By the late fourth century the association did exist, but before that the term tended to be seen more generally[309] and so Longenecker argues that the early fathers do not use "poor" to designate Jerusalem Jesus followers.[310] For example Tertullian in *Marc.* 5.3 sees Gal 2:10 as referring more generally to care for the poor. Longenecker argues that late fourth and early fifth century writers started to use the term through identifying later Ebionites with the early Jerusalem believers and points out "The linking of the Ebionite name to Jerusalem Jesus-followers has no precedent in the extant discussion of the early Jesus movement prior to Epiphanius" (d. 403).[311] Therefore it seems

---

300. Lim, "Generosity," 23.
301. Georgi, *Remembering*, 29, 31.
302. Ibid., 33.
303. Ibid., 37–38.
304. Ibid., 38.
305. Ibid., 42.
306. Ibid., 46.
307. Ibid., 49.
308. Horrell, *Solidarity*, 232.
309. Longenecker, *Remembering*, 158–82.
310. Ibid., 172.
311. Ibid., 171. Epiphanius *Pan.* 30.17.

likely that Gal 2:10 "demarcates caring for the poor without geographical restriction or specificity."[312]

This raises the question of why such an injunction was given. Longenecker argues that the Jerusalem leaders were not worried that Paul would be unconcerned about the poor, but rather that they were "worried about the credentials of his target audience."[313] Pagans were not well known for their care for the poor and it is possible that the Jewish Christians of Jerusalem were trying to ensure that this part of what it meant to be a believer was not lost. Longenecker suggests that the decision being made in the discussions was "about the moral matrix that was to mark out all communities of Jesus-followers, and at the heart of that matrix lies care for the vulnerable."[314]

Nickle takes a slightly different tack and sees Gal 2:1–10 and Acts 15 as describing the same meeting and agreement. He argues that "The 'Decrees' were formulated not as the fundamental requirement which a Gentile had to fulfill in order to become a Christian but as those basic regulations necessary to make full fellowship between Gentile and Jewish Christians within the same Christian community possible."[315] Longenecker sees this including care for the poor but excluding circumcision.[316]

As argued in chapter 4 we see the visit in Gal 2 referring to the visit in Acts 11. Therefore it seems likely that Gal 2 is more generally about the poor given that the identification of οἱ πτωχοί with the Jerusalem believers did not happen until significantly after Galatians was written. While Gal 2 indicates Paul's desire for care for the poor, and reminds us that this was an ongoing concern for Paul and therefore a motivation for the collection, it does not refer to an agreement for Gentile Christians to make a collection for the believers in Jerusalem.

Romans 15:25–32

In Rom 15:25–32 Paul writes to the Romans, probably just before he leaves Corinth,[317] and reports that he is on his way to Jerusalem (Rom 15:25). Macedonia and Achaia have contributed to the collection, which presumably means that Corinth gave[318] and Paul specifies that the collection is for

312. Ibid., 182.
313. Ibid., 203 (italics original).
314. Ibid., 211.
315. Nickle, *Collection*, 55.
316. Longenecker, *Remembering*, 203.
317. Furnish, *Corinthians*, 410.
318. Watson, *Second Corinthians*, 12; Horrell, *Solidarity*, 233; Furnish, *Corinthians*,

the poor among the Lord's people in Jerusalem (Rom 15:26), which suggests "a socio-economic group within the Jerusalem community."[319]

Paul's double use of εὐδόκησαν (Rom 15:26,27) points to the contributions being given with goodwill[320] and voluntarily/willingly.[321] However, Paul also argues that those who have contributed owe the contribution[322] in some way and describes it as material blessing in return for spiritual blessing (Rom 15:27). For some scholars the reception of the gift of the gospel with its Jewish Jerusalem based heritage causes a debt.[323] Fitzmyer suggests that the obligation was felt by the contributors.[324] As Joubert points out this could have been because of their Gentile background and suggests that for those of Jewish background reciprocity would not necessarily have been seen as important.[325] Therefore it could be that the debt Paul describes is the believer's sense of debt rather than his description of the obligation that they should feel. Similarly Watson points out that Paul "chooses to refer first to the attitude of those obliged, rather than to their state of obligation."[326] Dunn argues the obligation referred to partly relates to the obligation to care for the poor more generally.[327] While Paul includes the idea of reciprocity and obligation, he also emphasizes the fact that the collection was willing and freely given.[328]

Downs helpfully notes cultic metaphors in Rom 15:16 and in Rom 15:25–32 and therefore argues that, for Paul, an overarching metaphor for the collection is worship.[329]

Paul also requests the readers to pray for him, both that he will be kept safe from unbelievers in Judaea, but also that the collection may be favorably received (Rom 15:31). This request would suggest that either the collection may not be fulfilling a particular agreement[330] or that some breaking of the agreement has happened that makes it less likely to be accepted.

453.

319. Murphy-O'Connor, *Theology*, 75.
320. Sanday and Headlam, *Romans*, 412.
321. Morris, *Romans*, 520; Fitzmyer, *Romans*, 722.
322. Downs, *Offering*, 11.
323. Sanday and Headlam, *Romans*, 412; Morris, *Romans*, 521
324. Fitzmyer, *Romans*, 723.
325. Joubert, *Paul*, 129.
326. Watson, "Collection," 161.
327. Dunn, *Romans*, 2:874.
328. Ibid.
329. Downs, *Offering*, 154–56.
330. Ibid., 36. *Contra* Jewett, *Romans*, 927.

We noted in our analysis of Gal 2:10 that Paul seems to be expressing a duty for believers to be concerned for the poor more generally, not simply for the Jerusalem poor. This is seen more widely in his letters. Longenecker examines Paul's letters and highlights that in four of the seven undisputed letters, Paul includes care for the poor (Gal 6:9-10; 2 Cor 8-9; 1 Thess 4:9-12, 5:14-15; Rom 12:8-10, 13).[331] Similarly in 1 Cor 16:1-4 and 2 Cor 8-9 contributing to the collection is presented not as a requirement of the Gentiles, but as "voluntary expressions of grace for other Jesus-followers."[332] Even in Rom 15 where Paul speaks of debtors, he also implies an element of choice and the voluntary nature of the contributions in his use of εὐδόκησαν (Rom 15:26,27).[333] It is thus likely that Paul saw concern for the poor as key to the character of Christians,[334] but one that was characterized by voluntary (albeit expected) giving, and was part of a wider giving to and receiving from one another.

QUESTIONS ABOUT THE COLLECTION

This section considers questions about the intended recipients and aim of the collection which arise from the NT texts about the collection. The answers to these questions inform our conclusion about the example of sharing the collection in 2 Cor 8 and 9 provides.

For the Poor in Jerusalem or for All Believers in Jerusalem?

We have noted that Paul sees concern for the poor as a key part of the Christian life. In Galatians Paul argues that οἱ πτωχοί should be remembered, yet as we have seen this is unlikely to be specifically about the collection. In the passages specifically about the collection, Paul refers to the recipients as οἱ ἅγιοι, except for Rom 15:26 where he designates the recipients as the οἱ πτωχοί τῶν ἁγίων.[335] Therefore there is the question of whether Paul aim is for the collection to be for the poor in Jerusalem or for all in Jerusalem.

---

331. Longenecker, *Remembering*, 140-46; Watson, "Collection," 157-58. Hughes notes that Paul's visits to Jerusalem all have some connection to those in need in Jerusalem (Hughes, *Second Corinthians*, 284-85).

332. Longenecker, *Remembering*, 186.

333. Jewett notes that goodwill and obligation were not seen as mutually exclusive and argues for the collection to be part of "mutual indebtedness that binds the ethnic branches of the church together" (Jewett, *Romans*, 930-31).

334. Longenecker, *Remembering*, 298.

335. Thrall, *Corinthians*, 2:506.

Georgi sees οἱ πτωχοί as titular and referring to all in Jerusalem.³³⁶ We have argued earlier³³⁷ that the link between the title and the community is late and would not be applicable at the time when Paul is writing. Similarly Horrell and Thrall argue that Paul does not use it as a title, but rather that the collection is aimed for those in need in Jerusalem.³³⁸ However, Thrall does note that it is possible (given the evidence within Acts) that the whole Jerusalem community took care of those in need within the community and that the collection may have been handed over to the leaders within the community for them to distribute to those in need.³³⁹

Why Jerusalem?

However, if Paul's aim in the collection is the relief of need, why is the gift for those in need in Jerusalem and not elsewhere? Hughes argues that it is because Paul sees the Gentiles as having a spiritual debt to the believers in Jerusalem (Rom 15:27; 1 Cor 9:11).³⁴⁰ Others argue that it is because of the specific situation in Jerusalem.³⁴¹ We saw in the chapter on Acts some of the particular needs in Jerusalem.³⁴² Strachan argues in addition that the congregation was made up of the poorer classes and that the number of pilgrims led to an increase in demand for goods and thus an increase in prices.³⁴³ Martin and Best both see the common fund as playing a role.³⁴⁴ However, the common fund may be seen as an attempt to mitigate the situation, rather than the cause of the situation: "surely it is far more reasonable to understand it as an effect of the want of the majority, a measure spontaneously designed to counteract as far as possible the prevailing indigence and successfully so, for the time being at least, as the context shows (v. 34)."³⁴⁵

While Héring acknowledges that we do not know of the existence of other collections not to Jerusalem, he sees Paul in 2 Cor 9:14 as stressing "that generosity could be practiced in other similar urgent cases."³⁴⁶ There-

---

336. Georgi, *Remembering*, 33–34.
337. See pp. 171–73.
338. Horrell, *Solidarity*, 235; Thrall, *Corinthians*, 2:509.
339. Thrall, *Corinthians*, 2:509.
340. Hughes, *Second Corinthians*, 286.
341. Spencer, *Corinthians*, 138.
342. See pp. 66–71.
343. Strachan, *Second Corinthians*, 131–32.
344. Best, *Second Corinthians*, 76; Martin, *Corinthians*, 256.
345. Hughes, *Second Corinthians*, 284.
346. Héring, *Second Corinthians*, 68.

fore it is likely that the gift is for Jerusalem because of the specific needs that existed there.

Paul's Aim in the Collection.

Nickle argues that Paul has three aims with the collection: the relief of need, unity of believers, and an eschatological role.[347] We have already argued that the collection was for the poor in Jerusalem rather than the whole community in Jerusalem and that it was sent to Jerusalem because of specific needs. While there are other possible factors in Jerusalem as the destination of the collection (as we saw in Rom 15:27), Paul makes it clear that such contributions may be expected between other congregations and indeed from Jerusalem as and when their situation changed (8:14). We have also argued that Paul saw such practical concern as part and parcel of Christian life and Kreitzer argues such action was in continuity with Jewish practice.[348]

However, several scholars argue that Paul dreams of the collection accomplishing more than relief of need and see Paul hoping for unity between believers with Jews and Gentile being brought together.[349] Nickle argues that the collection provides proof of the Gentiles' faith[350] and that the number of representatives of the Gentile Christian communities accompanying it is indicative of Paul's desire for it to result in greater unity.[351] As the faith of the Gentile Christians is recognized,[352] Best argues that Paul hopes it will lead to their acceptance on an equal basis.[353] Georgi argues that this aim explains Paul's change of plan in Acts 20:4 (which he argues is an incomplete account) and that the threat from the Jews led to the believers in Jerusalem being in a difficult situation. If they accepted the collection, it would lead to risk for them and if they refused it would lead to greater tension with the church.[354]

While it seems likely that Paul was desirous of greater unity between Jewish and Gentile Christians,[355] and that such unity may be part of what he

---

347. Nickle, *Collection*, 100.

348. Kreitzer, *Corinthians*, 85.

349. Harris, *Second Corinthians*, 553; Martin, *Corinthians*, 251; Matera, *Corinthians*, 209; Nickle, *Collection*, 9.

350. Nickle, *Collection*, 114, 119.

351. Ibid., 130.

352. Betz, *Corinthians*, 126.

353. Best, *Second Corinthians*, 87.

354. Georgi, *Remembering*, 122–27.

355. Paul elsewhere writes of this unity being effected through Jesus (Gal 3:26–29).

hopes the collection will accomplish, it seems unlikely that it is his primary objective. The Gentile church was not monochrome and the Corinthian congregation was mixed and included both Gentiles and Jews.[356] Therefore it is not simply a gift from Gentile believers to Jewish believers. Also Paul asserts that such gifts may be expected to happen in reverse and between other groups. However, Paul does see increased affection between the Corinthian and Jerusalem believers (9:14)[357] as one of the outcomes of the collection and this is natural given the way gift-exchange was key to relationship formation in the Greco-Roman world.[358] Also as Hughes points out, it is likely that the collection would have increased unity more widely than simply with Jerusalem: it may well have increased unity between those who contributed to the collection.[359]

Nickle, Furnish and Martin all argue that there is also an eschatological role to the collection.[360] Furnish argues that the Gentile delegation and the collection are meant to show the success of the gospel amongst the Gentiles, prompting jealousy amongst the Jews and leading to Jews accepting the gospel. Nickle sees this happening through a reversal of the order of OT prophecies[361] in Isa 55:10 and Hos 10:12, whereby the Gentile believers "were coming as the true Israel" rather than as "the seekers and petitioners of Israel."[362] However, as Horrell and Thrall point out, for the collection to fit with Paul's argument in Rom 9–11, full evangelization would need to have happened (Rom 11:11–12, 25–27)[363] and we would expect Paul to be on his final journey, rather than to be going onto Rome after his visit to Jerusalem.[364] Downs also points out that Rom 15:14–32 "reveals no mention of the pilgrimage tradition in the one place within the Pauline correspondence in which the apostle reflects on the actual delivery of the collection to Jerusalem."[365] Barnett argues there is no evidence in 2 Corinthians that Paul intends the collection to prompt an eschatological ingathering of Jews.[366]

---

356. See pp. 108–15.
357. Héring, *Second Corinthians*, 68; Lambrecht, *Second Corinthians*, 152.
358. Joubert, *Paul*, 150, 153.
359. Hughes, *Second Corinthians*, 340.
360. Nickle, *Collection*, 100; Furnish, *Corinthians*, 412; Martin, *Corinthians*, 251.
361. Nickle, *Collection*, 133.
362. Ibid., 139.
363. Thrall, *Corinthians*, 2:513–14.
364. Horrell, *Solidarity*, 234.
365. Downs, *Offering*, 9.
366. Barnett, *Second Corinthians*, 449–50.

This suggests that Paul does not see the collection eschatologically, as does the fact he anticipates future possible collections (8:14).

Plummer and Spencer suggest a fourth possible motive and outcome of the collection. Plummer argues that the collection might well have increased Paul's authority in Jerusalem, because it would have confirmed the success of Paul's work; at the same time it could have increased Paul's authority in Corinth as it pointed out Paul's link with the mother church.[367] In a similar vein, Spencer suggests that the collection is a test of the loyalty of the Corinthians to Paul.[368]

It is likely that Paul had a range of motives in mind. The evidence points to: the alleviating of need; increased unity, concern and care; and as an expression of thankfulness to God (9:12–15) being primary. It seems unlikely that Paul foresees the collection having a specifically eschatological role given that he foresees possible future collections and as it seems unlikely, given his travel plans, that he saw the full evangelization of the Gentiles as having taken place.

THE EXAMPLE OF SHARING IN 2 CORINTHIANS 8 AND 9

Having considered 2 Cor 8 and 9 and other texts which may illuminate the collection, we now describe the example of the sharing in 2 Cor 8 and 9.

1. The example of sharing in 2 Cor 8 and 9 is one that is rooted in grace: it is God's grace that provides for those who give and motivates them (8:1; 9:8, 14), and it is with grace that giving takes place (8:4, 6).

2. It is an example where giving/sharing is core to being a Christian (9:13).[369] Paul persists in encouraging the Corinthians to give and addresses the topic of the collection even when there are issues between Paul and the Corinthians. Giving to other believers in need is part of the believers' faith, for example, the Macedonians give themselves to God, to Paul and to the collection (8:3–5). The giving to the collection is also seen as part of their confession of faith (9:13), as part of serving God and worshipping him (8:4–5; 9:12–13). Thus, the Corinthians' participation in the collection will mean that their faith is recognized (9:13–14).

---

367. Plummer, *Second Corinthians*, 230.
368. Spencer, *Corinthians*, 130.
369. Murphy-O'Connor, *Theology*, 76; check Hanson, *Second Corinthians*, 69.

3. The example is one that is rooted in Jesus and his example (8:9).[370]
4. The example is one which provides for those in need (8:13–14).[371]
5. The giving is voluntary. Paul encourages rather than asks and focuses on the Corinthians taking their own decision to give (8:7, 8; 9:5, 7). The Macedonians and Titus give themselves voluntarily[372] and the Corinthians themselves have already shown their willingness (8:11).[373] However, the fact that it is voluntary, does not preclude sacrificial giving (8:3, 9).[374] Participation in such giving is also a privilege (8:4).
6. The example is one where the giving is generous, it is based in God's grace and provision (8:1, 9; 9:8). Paul notes the generosity of the Macedonians (8:1–3). Such giving and generosity also result in blessing and reward (9:5–6, 10–11), particularly in God provision to continue giving (9:8, 10).
7. The example is one that is active and practical (8:11). While desire and decision to give are important it is not just enough to want to give or share, action should be involved: the giving needs to happen.[375]
8. The example is one where all are involved. In 1 Cor 16:2, Paul gives instructions for each person to set aside money for the collection and in 2 Corinthians, Paul encourages them to give cheerfully (8:12; 9:7).
9. Each person is to give in relation to what they have. The Macedonians gave beyond what they had (8:3) and Paul encourages the Corinthians to give according to what they have (8:12). It is not simply a matter of a set amount being given, but of individuals/communities making decisions in light of God's generosity and what they themselves have.
10. It is an example that is relational and has relational effects. The giving and sharing will lead to greater affection and prayer (9:14). Strengthened relationships will ensue, not simply between the Jerusalem and Corinthian believers but also probably between those who contribute to the collection.[376]
11. It is an example where there is potential reciprocity (8:13–14). Paul's aim is not one way giving, but provision for need in an ongoing

---

370. Lim, "Generosity," 21, 24.
371. Thrall, *Corinthians*, 2:511.
372. Harris, *Second Corinthians*, 599.
373. Lim, "Generosity," 28.
374. Hughes, *Second Corinthians*, 288.
375. Keener, *Corinthians*, 204.
376. Downs, *Offering*, 72.

relationship, which may change over time. It is based in relationship and responsibility, with the aim not of one group gaining at the expense of the other, but of equality and provision.

12. It is an example of giving where probity is important. Paul goes to great lengths to make sure that the collection is not just handled well, but that it is also seen to be handled with integrity (8:20–21).

13. In the whole example God is central. It is God who is the ultimate benefactor[377] who provides so that the Corinthians may give (and probably who provides not only the resources but also the desire)[378] and who will continue to provide (9:8, 10). It is thus that the thanksgiving and praise go to God, not the Corinthians, because it is he who is the ultimate provider (9:11–12, 15).

COMPARISONS

Acts 11

Having considered the example of sharing at a distance provided by 2 Cor 8 and 9, we now turn to look for suitable contemporary comparisons. We have already considered one "at a distance" example in the response to the prophecy of famine recounted in Acts 11.[379] In Acts 11:19–30, we see an example of sharing which is from one group of believers to another group of believers, which is based on and confirms committed relationships, where individuals contribute according to their ability, and yet there is corporate responsibility. It is also an example which shows such sharing/giving as key to being a disciple of Jesus and where the money sent is subject to careful stewardship.

When we compare this example to that in 2 Cor 8 and 9 we see a number of similarities: the giving occurs between two groups of believers, individuals take decisions to give, Paul exhorts the whole community about their responsibility, giving/sharing is key to being a believer, and the money which is given is subject to careful stewardship.

However, there are also differences. In the 2 Cor 8 and 9 example, there does not seem to be as developed or as ongoing a relationship with the church where the collection will go. The collection in 2 Cor 8 and 9 is also

---

377. Briones, *Policy*, 190.
378. Harris, *Second Corinthians*, 638.
379. Chapter 4.

from a group of churches over a wide area to the believers in Jerusalem as opposed to from one church to another.

The account in 2 Cor 8 and 9 also has a slightly different focus from that in Acts. In Acts 11, we read a narrative of sharing/giving, while in 2 Cor 8 and 9 we see Paul's exhortation of the Corinthians and therefore it includes more of the theological reasoning behind the exhortation to give. However, there are sufficient similarities and the differences do not preclude us from using the Acts 11 comparators for the 2 Cor 8 and 9 example.

Helena and Izates

When we looked at Acts 11, we compared it to the example of Helena and Izates, and to that of the *curator annonae*.[380] We will compare the collection in 2 Cor 8 and 9 to these two examples, before moving to two more detailed comparisons: that of the temple tax and that of patronage, benefaction and benefit-exchange.

As we saw in chapter 3 Helena goes to Jerusalem. When she discovers the need for food, she sends for and buys grain to distribute. When her son Izates hears about the need, he sends relief to the leaders in Jerusalem. Like the Corinthians Helena and Izates have a connection with Jerusalem. Helena and Izates are connected to Jerusalem, because of their conversion to Judaism; the Corinthians are connected to Jerusalem because of their conversion to following Christ and the fact that the first believers are based in Jerusalem.

However, there are a number of differences: Helena and Izates exhibit giving from individuals to a group rather than from (a) group(s) to a group and are wealthy people giving in a context of need, rather than all involved in giving. They are also an example of giving that the Corinthians are unlikely to be aware of and even if Paul is aware of them, he shows no evidence of being influenced by them or using them in his exhortation to the Corinthians.

Curator Annonae

In chapter 3 we examined the example of the *curator annonae*, where in the context of a famine, a powerful individual subsidized grain, or provided grain in return for honor. This example is similar to that in 2 Corinthians as it is in response to need, although it is not clear that it is the same kind of need. The Jerusalem believers may well have been affected by food

---

380. See pp. 93–96.

shortages, but there are numerous other reasons which are likely to have contributed to their need.[381]

There are also differences between the example in 2 Corinthians and the *curator annonae* example. These are similar to the differences between the *curator annonae* example and the Acts 11 example. The *curator annonae* example is by an individual or small group rather than the whole of a community participating, and that which is given does not necessarily go to the poorest or neediest.[382] The motives for giving are also somewhat different: in the *curator annonae* example, some of the motivation is probably due to the honor that those giving will gain,[383] while in 2 Corinthians Paul's teaching is that the motivation should be unity and relief of need (8:14) and thankfulness to God (9:12-15). Honor and thanks in the 2 Corinthians example is due to go to God (8:16; 9:11) rather than those who give.

Temple Tax

We turn now to two examples that may be more fruitful for comparison: the temple tax and patronage.

Kreitzer and Nickle both see the temple tax as a possible example and model for the collection.[384] The temple tax is first referred to in Neh 10:32 and was initially one third of a shekel but later increased. It is also referred to in Matt 17:24-27. It was an annual contribution from every male from 20 years of age (Josephus *Ant.* 3.194-6).[385] Those within or close to Jerusalem brought the tax themselves, but those who lived further away contributed to chests, which were then transported to Jerusalem three times a year (*m. Shek.* 1.3).[386]

There are some similarities between the temple tax and the collection in that the temple tax goes to Jerusalem, has men appointed to travel with it (Josephus *Ant.* 18.311-3), is collected in particular central places before

---

381. See pp. 84-88.
382. Longenecker, *Remembering*, 91.
383. Ibid., 91, 93.
384. Kreitzer, *Corinthians*, 83; Nickle, *Collection*, 99.
385. Women, slaves, and minors could contribute, but not Gentiles or Samaritans (*m. Shek.* 1.4).
386. Nickle, *Collection*, 74.

transportation, and care is taken about the probity of the collection and its transportation.[387] Regular set aside is encouraged.[388]

Nickle also suggests that Pentecost is a parallel, as Pentecost was one of the times that temple tax was delivered to Jerusalem and Acts reports that Paul is keen to arrive in Jerusalem by Pentecost (Acts 20:16).[389] However, it is not clear that Pentecost is key in the Acts passage in the same way, nor that it necessarily is specifically about the collection. Nickle posits that Silas and Judas's appointment in Acts 15:22 is to make sure that the collection is not seen as competing with the Jewish Temple tax.[390] However, this is based on a number of assumptions: that Acts 15 includes an agreement that the Gentile churches will send a gift to Jerusalem: that the appointment of Silas and Judas is to secure the probity of the collection rather than to communicate the result of the meeting and encourage believers (Acts 15:27); and that they return to accompany the collection having been sent back to Jerusalem in peace (Acts 15:33).

In contrast Downs argues that the only link between the two is "Paul's metaphorical language for the collection."[391] Additionally there are a number of differences between the temple tax and the collection. As Georgi notes, Paul avoids talking about the collection as tax and does not mention the temple.[392] While Paul includes language (as Downs above) that is rich in metaphors about service and worship, and presents the collection as worship, the collection is also about relieving need, which is less clearly the case with the temple tax.[393] The collection is also not regulated or an obligation in the way the temple tax was,[394] nor is there a specific amount required of individuals (Philo *Heir* 186, 189), rather individuals contribute voluntarily as they are able.[395] While Paul allows for similar collections taking place, the collection is primarily a one off event in response to need at a specific time, rather than an annual requirement like the temple tax.[396] Additionally, Paul makes it clear that such a collection could happen in the future in reverse

---

387. Ibid., 87–89. *m. Shek.* 2.1 indicates that Shekels could be changed into Darics to make transportation easier.

388. Ibid., 87–89.

389. Ibid., 87.

390. Ibid., 62.

391. Downs, *Offering*, 10.

392. Georgi, *Remembering*, 148.

393. Nickle, *Collection*, 90; Thrall, *Corinthians*, 2:511.

394. Barrett, *Second Corinthians*, 240.

395. Nickle, *Collection*, 91–92.

396. Thrall, *Corinthians*, 2:512.

(or we suspect between other communities of believers) and there is no provision for any such reversal or change within the temple tax.

Patronage, Benefaction, and Gift-Exchange

We considered patronage in the Greco-Roman world in chapter 5[397] and noted the way that it is characterized by unequal but reciprocal relationships where both patrons and clients gained in different ways from the relationships. We also noted that the emperor was central in the web of patronage ties.[398] In addition Downs notes the overlap of the Roman concept of patronage and the Greek concept of benefaction.[399]

The issues between Paul and the Corinthians with regard to Paul's refusal of their support tend to be seen as around patronage with Paul wanting to avoid being beholden to the Corinthians as a client by receiving money from them. Keener argues that the Corinthians want to be Paul's patron, but that Paul is their patron and thus only allows them to provide patronage to Jerusalem.[400] Witherington suggests that the Corinthians saw themselves as patrons, so the possibility to contribute may have helped the reconciliation between them and Paul.[401]

Briones argues against the consensus view, but for a patronage background,[402] arguing that Paul would not be seen as the Corinthians' client by receiving money, but that rather by Greco-Roman norms he would be the patron, because he is in the superior position and had the knowledge that the Corinthians would want to gain.[403] Briones further argues that at the point of refusing, Paul has already given the Corinthians the knowledge of the gospel and that they want to respond as clients by providing him with money[404] and his refusal upsets their patron-client expectations.[405] This argument seems to rest on Paul's status as a teacher giving him a superior status.[406] While pupils could be expected to show loyalty to teachers and

---

397. See pp. 106–8.
398. Chow, "Patronage in Corinth," 106; Wallace-Hadrill, "Patronage," 81.
399. Downs, *Offering*, 88.
400. Keener, *Corinthians*, 202.
401. Witherington, *Conflict*, 413.
402. Briones, *Policy*, 17–18.
403. Ibid.
404. Ibid., 160–218.
405. Ibid., 190–92.
406. Ibid., 190.

critique other teachers,[407] philosophers/teachers usually taught children which would suggest they had a rather different relationship with the parents of the children they were teaching, who would have been those paying them (Petronius *Satyricon* 46). Seneca allows for owing gratitude to a physician or teachers (*Ben.* 6.16.1—18.1), but this does not necessarily point to the physician or teacher being a patron. Rather Seneca is making a comparison with interaction with a trader (*Ben.* 6.14.4—15.4) and speaking of instances where what is exchanged is less tangible or goes beyond what might be expected—indeed he notes that masters and servants can owe gratitude to one another (*Ben.* 3.194—22.3). Clarke sees Paul criticizing exclusive loyalty to particular leaders,[408] however this would not necessarily mean that Paul and the other leaders were seen as patrons given that orators/philosophers would compete for acceptance (Aristides *Or.* 51.29) and in most situations those teaching/philosophizing became clients rather than patrons (Dio Chrysostom *Or.* 77/78.34; Tacitus *Ann.* 16.32).

While discerning the exact expectations of the Corinthians of their patron-client relationship to Paul may be difficult, it seems probable that they did have patron-client expectations (and we surmise that they [or at least some of them] hoped that they would be Paul's patrons). Therefore patronage may provide a helpful comparison, particularly as McCant notes that Paul uses the language of benefaction in his description of the collection.[409]

Danker's study of benefaction language in inscriptions notes the words that are typical in such examples and highlights where these words, phrases or ideas are used in the NT.[410] Second Corinthians 8 and 9 uses a number of words which were frequently used in benefaction contexts, for example σπουδή and cognates (8:16, 17, 22),[411] προθυμία (8:11, 12, 19; 9:2),[412] ἑαυτοὺς ἔδωκαν (8.5),[413] λειτοργ- family (9:12),[414] πρόνοια (8:21),[415] γνώμην (8:10),[416]

---

407. Winter, *Paul*, 39.

408. Clarke, *Leadership*, 112.

409. McCant, *Corinthians*, 99.

410. Danker, *Benefactor*. Aune and Smith question how Danker picks the inscriptions that he studies and how evenly he uses them in his analysis, but both note the value of his study as a starting point for examining benefaction language (Aune, "Search," 423; Smith, "Review," 151).

411. Danker, *Benefactor*, 320-21.

412. Ibid., 321.

413. Ibid., 321-22.

414. Ibid., 330.

415. Ibid., 360.

416. Ibid., 362.

and ἐπιτελέω (8:11).⁴¹⁷ In addition to these words and ideas, Aune notes that Danker misses χάρις from his analysis⁴¹⁸ which is used frequently in chapters 8 and 9,⁴¹⁹ and was used of benefaction.⁴²⁰

We have shown that there is evidence in 2 Corinthians of possible issues around patronage and that 2 Cor 8 and 9 contain benefaction language. Therefore we will now compare Paul's language and ideas with those found in patronage, benefaction, and benefit-exchange. As the main similarity or point of connection is language and descriptions of reasons, our comparison will be based in the arguments that Paul provides.

In chapter 5 we noted the key elements of patronage relationships and in this chapter we noted that patronage (from a Roman background) and benefaction (from a Greek background) have similarities and overlap. Patronage and benefaction are both forms of benefit-exchange. Benefit-exchange can take place in a friendship of equals.⁴²¹ In instances where there is not parity, benefit-exchange is part of a patronage relationship.⁴²² Benefit-exchange in both friendship and patronage/benefaction forms was key for relationships and access to resources⁴²³ and the relationships could be "flexible and dynamic."⁴²⁴

In order to examine more thoroughly some of the expectations in benefit-exchange (both in friendship and patronage relationships), we will look briefly at Seneca's *De Beneficiis* where Seneca is criticizing forms of giving and receiving benefits in the society around him (*Ben.* 1.1.1–8). He writes specific instructions for giving and receiving gifts and also about the rationale behind the giving and receiving of gifts to correct what he sees as the issues around him (*Ben.* 1.4.3). While Seneca writes from an ideal philosophical perspective, Griffin notes similar descriptions by non-philosophers

---

417. Ibid., 362.
418. Aune, "Search," 424.
419. See pp. 162–65.
420. Griffin, "*Beneficiis*," 92.
421. Peterman, *Paul*, 66, 72.
422. Clarke, *Leadership*, 32.
423. Wallace-Hadrill, "Patronage," 74.

424. Ibid., 78. Joubert argues for evidence of gift-exchange in the OT (Joubert, *Paul*, 93–96), including the examples of Jacob and Esau in Gen 33, Moses and Reuel's daughters (Exod 2:15–22), and David and Nabal in 1 Sam 25. Whether these limited examples indicate a widespread expectation of the kind of reciprocity seen in gift-exchange in the Greco-Roman world is less than certain, however Joubert also notes that giving frequently is related to divine reward in the OT (Joubert, *Paul*, 96), which can also be seen in the way that Paul reworks patronage and benefaction language in 2 Cor 8 and 9.

(although with a greater concern for glory than Seneca),[425] and that Seneca's descriptions fit the changing political context.[426]

For Seneca it is important to choose the right recipients:[427] those who will show gratitude (*Ben.* 1.1.2; 1.10.4) and those who are worthy (*Ben.* 4.35.2—36.2). It is also important to give in the right way. Giving should make the recipient know that they are preferred (*Ben.* 1.14.3-4). One should not hesitate in giving (*Ben.* 1.1.8, 2.1.1-2), so that the gift is not forced out of the giver or dropped upon the receiver (*Ben.* 1.7.2-3).[428] The way one gives can elicit thanks,[429] it should not be in a hardhearted way (*Ben.* 2.7.1). That which is given should be necessary, useful or pleasurable, and should endure (*Ben.* 1.11.1). For Seneca giving in and of itself is "a virtuous act" (*Ben.* 1.5.3) and therefore there is value in bestowing.[430] The one giving should aim to give "in the manner that will bring most advantage to the recipient" (*Ben.* 2.10.2, also 4.2.4).

When a benefit is given it consists of two things the "beneficent act" and the "object" (*Ben.* 2.35.1) and two things should be given in return: "Goodwill we have repaid with goodwill; for the object we still owe an object" (*Ben.* 2.35.1). While the one giving should not demand a return (*Ben.* 2.17.7) or even expect a return (Ben. 2.31.3-4), the one receiving a benefit should return gratitude (*Ben.* 2.35.1)[431] as well as in due course returning an object (Ben. 2.21.5—24.4).[432] Therefore, although "the one straightway forget that it was given the other should never forget that it was received" (*Ben.* 2.10.4).

In addition Seneca mentions the idea of being stewards of wealth (Ben. 6.3.2), although he does not significantly develop it. He also asserts that what is given is secure as it cannot be stolen (*Ben.* 6.3.1-4).

It is important to recognize that Seneca's *De Beneficiis* encompasses benefit-exchange as patronage as well as benefit-exchange as friendship (*Ben.* 2.28.1-29.1, as well as slave-master relationships *Ben.* 3.19.2—22.3, and father-son relationships *Ben.* 3.30.1—33.1).[433] Seneca also seems to be writing to a particular stratum of society, for example in *Ben.* 1.9.1-4

---

425. Griffin, "*Beneficiis*," 102–5.
426. Ibid., 106.
427. Peterman, *Paul*, 67.
428. Ibid., 68.
429. Joubert, *Paul*, 46.
430. Ibid., 45.
431. Peterman, 69.
432. Return of the object should not be straightaway (*Ben.* 4.40.4).
433. Joubert, 37–48.

he talks about the expectation of taking mistresses and suggests that the alternative is the accusation of affairs with maidservants. This fits Seneca's position as a senator and *amicus principis*.[434] While benefit-exchange could occur between equals (friendship), it more often occurred in unequal relationships (patronage/benefaction).[435] However, because Seneca critiques the practice of benefit-exchange he sees around him, *De Beneficiis* is helpful in giving a picture of what ideal benefit-exchange might look like and we can therefore use it as we compare Paul's use of benefaction language with the practice and ideas about patronage, benefaction and benefit-exchange in Greco-Roman society.

We have already noted similarities in language between that used by Paul in 2 Cor 8 and 9 and that used in benefaction inscriptions.

There are also some similarities between 2 Cor 8 and 9 and Seneca's teaching on benefits. Seneca makes it clear that one should not give in order to receive (even though on receiving one should give). Paul similarly exhorts the Corinthians to give following the example of the Macedonians and Jesus, who give generously and without return, and yet Paul also provides for the possibility of return and includes elements of reciprocity.

For Seneca benefit giving was not meant to place the giver in need and Paul notes his desire that the Corinthians should not be in need. However, Paul does also provide the examples of the Macedonians and Jesus who give beyond this point.

Seneca asserts that benefits (and returns) should be fitting to what is needed by the one receiving and Paul argues that the collection will supply what is needed in Jerusalem. However, we have noted that the level of need Seneca and Paul are talking about is probably different. Seneca encourages his readers to give to someone what they need or want, while Paul encourages the Corinthians to give to those in need.

While there are similarities in language and in some of the provisions of giving, Paul also subverts ideas of patronage. McCant argues that Paul subverts the benefaction/patron-client expectations, by bringing God into the equation as the supreme benefactor,[436] so that God is thanked rather than the Corinthians for their gift,[437] making it a three-way relationship.[438] As Downs points out

---

434. Griffin, "*Beneficiis*," 93.
435. Joubert 21.
436. Griffith, "Abounding," 72.
437. McCant, *Corinthians*, 96–99; Griffith, "Abounding," 242.
438. Joubert, *Paul*, 201.

> This rhetorical strategy subtly subverts the dominant ideology of pagan benefaction by highlighting the honor, praise, and thanksgiving due God, the one from whom all benefactions ultimately originate, thus also minimizing any competition for honor, praise, and thanksgiving among the Corinthians.[439]

In addition, Griffith argues that the reciprocity envisaged by Paul would not necessarily return to the original giver but could be given to another person.[440] While Paul does not specifically say this, it is plausible given his concern for responding to need and the number of congregations involved in the collection. Paul's exhortation to the Corinthians is based upon the centrality of God and his provision: for them, for them to give, and probably also the desire to give. It is part of the believer's wider receiving of χάρις and giving out of that. In contrast Seneca asserts benefits should be given in order to be virtuous, leading Griffith to conclude that the benefits were given to be righteous rather than out of the righteousness provided by God.[441]

The collection is also different from patron-client relationships in that its aim is equality and relief of need. While we have noted Seneca's teaching that those giving benefits should look for what the recipient needs or wants, it is not a targeted giving to those in need. In contrast Welborn argues that Paul presents an argument for equality through redistribution which includes "the equalization of resources between persons of *different* social classes through voluntary redistribution."[442] The collection is not free from benefits for the givers, indeed Paul enumerates some of them, however these benefits are rather different from those usually associated with giving and Lim argues that the collection is not about self-benefit, but rather about other-benefit.[443]

Downs also suggests that associations may provide another possible comparison and suggests that associations could have trans-local links where help was provided. He notes examples of help to a home city, the supply of Egyptian priests to the cults of Isis and Sarapis, accommodation while traveling and mutual assistance.[444] However, Downs acknowledges the

---

439. Downs, *Offering*, 143–44. It is possible that Paul's description of the brothers as the "glory of Christ" encourages the Corinthians to focus on the glory of Christ rather than their own glory (or that of an earthly patron/benefactor) (Harrison, "Brothers," 185).

440. Griffith, "Abounding," 242.

441. Ibid., 249.

442. Welborn, "Equality," 89.

443. Lim, "Generosity," 27.

444. Downs, *Offering*, 112–15.

paucity of evidence.[445] The example he does give is *CIG* 5853 where an association provides assistance in paying fees, so while it is from one related group to another it is not for those in need and is annual.[446] While there may be examples of similar "sharing at a distance" with associations, we do not currently have sufficient evidence of such examples to make a comparison. Longenecker notes that there could be care for those who were poor within associations.[447] However, these examples tend to be in one location rather than over a distance.

CONCLUSION

The example of sharing "at a distance" seen in the collection in 2 Cor 8 and 9 is one where giving/sharing: is core to being a Christian; is rooted in grace, in Jesus and his example; provides for need; is voluntary, generous and practical; involves all; is in relation to what one has; is relational; and has potential reciprocity. It is also an example where probity is important and God is central as the ultimate benefactor.

It is an example that is similar to the sharing at a distance in Acts 11:19–30, but involves multiple locations and communities contributing to the giving and less evidence of a deep ongoing relationship. Acts and 2 Corinthians are also different forms of writing and therefore focus on different aspects of the examples.

As the collection is relatively similar to Acts 11:19–30, its similarities to and differences from the *curator annonae* example and the account of Helena and Izates are much the same. However, the collection is also distinct from the examples of Helena and Izates and the *curator annonae* as it is from multiple locations and communities to one community.

The collection is similar to the temple tax in that it is directed to Jerusalem, is transported carefully with concern about the probity of the collection and is part of worship. However, the collection is different from the temple tax in that it is voluntary, not regulated, involves giving as one is able rather than a specified amount, is one off rather than an annual due, could happen in other directions, and is a response to need rather than for the temple.

When Paul writes about the collection, he uses language and ideas that relate to patronage and benefaction in his argument and patronage appears to be behind some of the issues for the Corinthian congregation. There are

445. Ibid., 113.
446. Ibid., 114–15.
447. Longenecker, *Remembering*, 69.

some similarities in ideas: not giving in order to receive, yet an expectation of receiving; not becoming in need through giving; and giving what is needed. However, there are differences. Paul subverts patronage. He shows God, rather than the giver, being thanked and honored. He provides the examples of Jesus and the Macedonians giving sacrificially. Paul also argues that the aim is equality where none are in need—communities give in times of plenty and receive in times of need. The benefits Paul lists of giving and sharing are also quite different from those usually associated with giving.

7

Limits on Sharing

1 and 2 Thessalonians

INTRODUCTION

In 1 Cor 11, Paul exhorts the Corinthians to share food together—an example of sharing within a community. In 2 Cor 8 and 9, Paul encourages the Corinthians to contribute to the collection for those in need in Jerusalem and Judaea—an example of sharing between communities. We now turn to look at 1 and 2 Thessalonians where Paul places boundaries on the sharing within a community, while at the same time praising them for their love for one another.[1] This example provides a situation where limitations are placed on sharing, but where sharing is still encouraged.

This chapter first considers the background of Thessalonica and the situation of the church to which Paul writes. It then looks at 1 Thessalonians, particularly 1 Thess 4:9–12 and 5:14–15, which talk about love and work, and the need to admonish the ἄτακτοι, before considering more briefly other passages which may contribute to understanding the situation that Paul is addressing. The chapter then examines 2 Thessalonians. After discussing whether the epistle is Pauline and the occasion of the letter, it considers 2 Thess 3:6–15, which addresses the issue of the ἄτακτοι and work in greater depth.

---

1. The authorship of 2 Thessalonians will be considered later in the chapter.

Having considered 1 and 2 Thessalonians, the chapter looks at the possible backgrounds to the issues behind the ἀτάκτοι. It provides an overview of the example of sharing (and its limits) that Paul provides in 1 and 2 Thessalonians before comparing it to Epicurean practice, family life, voluntary associations (VAs), and patronage practices to ascertain how these compare to the example Paul promotes.

THESSALONICA

The City

Thessalonica was founded by Alexander's general in 316/315 BCE,[2] had Roman influence from 197 BCE,[3] was made capital of Macedonia in 148 BCE, and became a free city in 42 BCE.[4] Thessalonica was on the *Via Egnatia*[5] and was a port city.[6] It was militarily important.[7]

The city had a temple of Caesar (*IG*[X] II/I 31)[8] and a statue of Augustus.[9] There is evidence of coins with images of Augustus instead of Zeus and that Roma/Roman benefactors were seen as gods.[10] Pillar also notes close connections between emperors and deities, the way that emperors were involved in promoting particular gods, and the identification of individual emperors with deities; for example Caligula claimed divinity in his lifetime.[11] This may have been an easy transition for the Thessalonians as the Macedonian king had been seen as divine.[12]

The imperial cult was not the sole religious presence. Rulmu points to the worship of Egyptian gods[13] and Donfried to the presence of the Cabirus

---

2. Malherbe, *Letters*, 14; Jewett, *Correspondence*, 123.
3. Pillar, *Resurrection*, 2.
4. Fee, *Thessalonians*, 5.
5. Morris, *1 and 2 Thessalonians*, 17.
6. Witherington, *Thessalonians*, 2.
7. Ibid., 2; Míguez, *Practice*, 51.
8. Harrison, "Paul," 81.
9. Witherington, *Thessalonians*, 5.
10. Donfried, "Cults," 218.
11. Pillar, *Resurrection*, 83–103.
12. Jewett, *Correspondence*, 126.
13. Rulmu, "Ambition," 405.

cult.[14] However, the cult varied from place to place and therefore comparisons are difficult.[15]

Religious activity and honor were also part of voluntary associations (VAs). VAs could be focused round a particular god[16] or person and were used by patrons looking for honor,[17] as those financing and serving in leadership roles in a VA were honored (*IG* II2 1343). VAs were viewed with suspicion as potential sources of political unrest and subversion and a number of decrees were passed to limit them.[18] While these decrees generally focused on Rome, Rulmu suggests that the Roman administrators probably took a level of suspicion with them.[19] This can been seen in the letter exchange between Pliny and Trajan where the emperor argues against forming a guild of firemen because "men who are banded together for a common end will all the same be a political association before long" (*Ep. Tra.* 33, 34).

The Church

Acts 17:1–15 recounts the beginnings of the church in Thessalonica. As well as more general questions about the historicity of Acts, which we have addressed earlier,[20] there are two particular questions about this account: first the short time that Paul appears to stay in the city and secondly the situation with Jason—why is it Jason and not Paul taken before the city officials (17:6) and what are the decrees of Caesar (17:7) that they are meant to have defied?

Acts 17:1–2 indicates that Paul and his companions went to a Jewish synagogue and spent three Sabbaths reasoning with those there. While there is no evidence of a Greek synagogue or Jewish inscriptions[21] it seems likely, due to the dispersal of the Jews and the evidence of a Samaritan synagogue in Thessalonica from the third century BCE,[22] that there were Jews with a synagogue when Paul visited.

---

14. Donfried, *Paul*, 25–26.
15. Jewett, *Correspondence*, 127. It was absorbed into the imperial cult during the reign of Augustus (Jewett, *Correspondence*, 131)
16. Ascough, "Thessalonian Mission," 67.
17. Rulmu, "Ambition," 398.
18. Ibid., 399–400.
19. Ibid., 401.
20. See pp. 43–45.
21. Jewett, *Correspondence*, 119.
22. Ibid., 120.

While three Sabbaths is a short time for Paul to spend in a town, this might just be the initial period.[23] Paul may have followed his habit elsewhere of going first to the synagogue and then have spoken in Gentile contexts and Luke may have compressed the account.[24]

There are a number of options for the decrees that they are accused of contravening (Acts 17:7). First, the accusation could have been around Paul "proclaiming another king"[25] which would have been seen as being treasonous. However, as Hardin points out, if this were the case we might expect a more severe response from the authorities.[26] Second, the problem could be around ruler changes and oaths of loyalty[27] as there were decrees against predicting a change of ruler. However, these were really focused against politicians trying to raise themselves to positions of power and were generally restricted to Italy.[28] Third, it is possible that the decrees could involve the oaths of allegiance,[29] but again defying these would usually have fallen under the treason law and elicited a stronger response.[30] Hardin proposes a fourth possibility: that the decrees involved are around the regulation of VAs.[31] From the mid first century BCE there were increasing restrictions on VAs and Augustus banned all political clubs.[32] While these regulations were generally focused in Rome there is evidence that they were spreading.[33] This can be seen in the *Lex Iritania* (Spain) which "stated that all gatherings, groups and voluntary associations (*collegia*) were forbidden to meet, with the penalty for doing so being a monetary fine to the municipal authorities."[34] Hardin suggests that the issue at hand is an unauthorized gathering and that the politarchs are concerned to avoid any report reaching the proconsul and from there Rome.[35] Therefore the politarchs act to deal with the situation and take money from Jason (and potentially the group) as bond money.

---

23. Walton, *Leadership*, 146.
24. Malherbe, *Letters*, 59–60.
25. Hardin, "Decrees," 31.
26. Ibid., 33.
27. Donfried, "Cults," 215; Hardin, "Decrees," 33.
28. Hardin, "Decrees," 35.
29. Donfried, "Cults," 216; Hardin, "Decrees," 33.
30. Hardin, "Decrees," 36.
31. Ibid., 39–40.
32. Ibid., 40.
33. Ibid.
34. Ibid., 46.
35. Ibid., 43–45.

Hardin's proposal might explain why Paul is not the primary focus as it was Jason's house that the group are meeting in. Jewett adds the possibility that Paul may have left before this point.[36]

While 1 Thessalonians portrays the Thessalonians as suffering persecution and hardship (see below), it says little about their social standing. Acts 17:4 indicates that the initial believers were potentially a mixed group including some prominent women.[37] In contrast Ascough argues that the congregation were predominantly male due to the lack of reference to women or children and the way that 1 Thess 4:4–6 is addressed only to men,[38] however Galatians does not refer to women or children within the congregation either. In 2 Cor 8:2 Paul talks about the churches in Macedonia as experiencing extreme poverty. Míguez argues that the presence of the plural indicates the inclusion of the Thessalonians in this group,[39] and that the fact that 1 Thess 5:27 indicates that the letter is to be *read πᾶσιν τοῖς ἀδελφοῖς* supports this.[40] However, while reading and writing were specialized skills and few people would have been able to read or write fluently,[41] literacy did not always equate to affluence, as slaves could be literate for reading and writing on behalf of their masters. In addition this public reading of the letter may simply indicate the communal nature of the way the early church met.

It seems likely that, as with the Corinthians,[42] the Thessalonian church did include some people of higher social class,[43] but 1 Thessalonians and 2 Cor 8:2 suggest that the church as a whole was not affluent and may have had fewer people of higher social status than some of the other churches. Indeed Ascough goes as far as to argue that there was no patron as Paul chose to work,[44] but this does not necessarily follow, given that there are those in Corinth who are keen to be Paul's patron and Paul is still concerned not to be a burden and to work (1 Cor 9:6, 13; 2 Cor 11:7–9; 12:14–16). Ascough additionally argues that Paul's reference to manual work (2:7–9; 4:1, 11) would

---

36. Jewett, *Correspondence*, 117.

37. Winter points to Aristarchus who is mentioned in Acts 19:29 and 20:4 who could be the Aristarchus son of Aristarchus "who heads up a list of politarchs in that city" (Winter, *Welfare*, 46).

38. Ascough, "Community as Association," 325–26.

39. Míguez, *Practice*, 61.

40. Ibid., 70.

41. Keith, "Hand," 46.

42. See pp. 108–15.

43. Morris, *1 and 2 Thessalonians*, 18.

44. Ascough, *Paul's Macedonian Associations*, 166.

dishonor the Thessalonians if they were not laborers.⁴⁵ However, Paul may have been affirming those who were manual workers as well encouraging others who thought manual work beneath them to take it up. Even if there were some people with a bit more money or status, persecution may have affected their position. As Schnabel points out, work-related metaphors do not prove that the Thessalonians were all manual laborers.⁴⁶ Thus, Russell argues that the Thessalonian church had some higher status people and the others were clients, freedmen and slaves.⁴⁷ Given the evidence here and the evidence discussed in chapter 5,⁴⁸ this seems a reasonable assumption.

The accounts in Acts (17:5–9) and 1 Thessalonians (1:6; 2:14; 3:1–5) both indicate that the Thessalonians endured persecution and suffering. Ascough argues that this opposition may have arisen because of the way the Thessalonians declared the honor of their new-found faith,⁴⁹ undermining the focus on the imperial cult. Pillar analyzes 1 Thess 1:9b–10 and identifies a number of ways that Paul's use of language would have had anti-imperial resonances, including his appropriating of imperial cult language, for example his use of ἀναμένειν (1:10).⁵⁰ Pillar sees the Thessalonians turning from idols as a "decisive rejection of things imperial."⁵¹ He may be overstating the case, but he does show evidence of the ways in which the Thessalonians' following of Jesus could have been seen as anti-imperial. Persecution could be related to the focus on eschatology⁵² and Paul's responses do use words that would have been used politically about the empire (1 Thess 2:12, 18; 5:3).⁵³ Persecution could also have led to the questions about those who died before Jesus' return (1 Thess 4:13–18).⁵⁴ While Barclay argues that it is unlikely that the deaths were directly related to the persecution that they endured,⁵⁵ he does suggest that outsiders may have linked the deaths to their abandonment of traditional Greco-Roman religion.⁵⁶

---

45. Ascough, "Community as Association," 315.
46. Schnabel, "Review," 336. Also Oakes notes that Ascough does not investigate counter arguments to his assertion (Oakes, "Review," 378).
47. Russell, "Idle," 110–11.
48. See pp. 108–15.
49. Ascough, "Thessalonian Mission," 81.
50. Pillar, *Resurrection*, 185–92.
51. Ibid., 256.
52. Barclay, "Thessalonica and Corinth."
53. Donfried, "Cults," 216, 219.
54. Barclay, "Conflict," 512–14.
55. Ibid., 514.
56. Ibid., 516.

FIRST THESSALONIANS[57]

Introduction

Paul writes 1 Thessalonians just after Timothy has returned (3:7-8) with good news from the visit to the Thessalonians that Paul sent him on to encourage and strengthen them (3:1-2). It is probable that Paul writes from Corinth (Acts 18:5).[58] Paul's affection for the Thessalonians is clear in the letter (for example 2:7b-8, 17; 3:12). This affection can be seen in the long thanksgiving section,[59] and in the range of affective images that Paul uses as he speaks of being gentle (2:7), orphaned (2:17) and a caring father (2:11-12).[60] While Richards raises questions about the unity of 1 Thessalonians,[61] the strong consensus is for a unified letter written by Paul.[62] For, while there are some differences in tone (between 2:13-14, where Richards sees Paul expressing relief after anxiety and 1:2-3; 4:3-4, where he is confident in his preaching and addresses issues), these are natural if Paul is writing after both anxiety and reassurance.[63] Also, while Paul does note that reports about the Thessalonians' faith have reached other areas, these note how they received Paul and his message initially (1:6-10). Therefore it is not necessary to presume a later date.[64]

Paul writes to encourage and teach the Thessalonians in the midst of θλίψις (1:6). Barclay argues that the parallels with Jesus and Paul (1:6) suggest not simply a mental distress but more substantial persecution.[65] DeSilva argues that part of Paul's aim is to encourage the Thessalonians to find their "honor and security before God and the supra-local Christian community,"[66] particularly where persecution was aimed at correcting the Thessalonians' behavior.[67]

---

57. Scripture references in this section will be to 1 Thessalonians unless noted otherwise.

58. Blomberg, *Poverty*, 179.

59. While different scholars see this section ending in different places it is long in each of the options (Jewett, *Correspondence*, 63, 69).

60. Malherbe, "Ethics," 206.

61. Richards, *Thessalonians*, 11.

62. Malherbe provides a helpful summary of the various theories, noting the most common alternative to unity is 2:13-16 being an interpolation (Malherbe, *Letters*, 79-81). Also Wanamaker, *Thessalonians*, 29-37.

63. deSilva, "Worthy," 76.

64. Ibid., 77.

65. Barclay, "Thessalonica and Corinth," 53.

66. deSilva, "Worthy," 50.

67. Ibid., 55.

Paul addresses questions that presumably have been sent in some form by the Thessalonians or situations that Timothy has highlighted from his visit. These include questions about eschatology and those believers who die before Jesus' return (4:13-18). Paul reinforces his previous eschatological teaching (5:1-2),[68] preparing the Thessalonians for the parousia, while speaking against an over-realized eschatology.[69]

First Thessalonians 4:9-12

These verses are part of a section on living to please God, with 4:1-8 focusing on purity and holiness and 4:9-12 on brotherly love and work. Paul introduces the section with περὶ δέ (4:9). Frame argues this means that Paul is responding to a letter sent by the Thessalonians,[70] while others see it as introducing a new topic.[71] Walton acknowledges that περὶ δέ could indicate a reply to a letter. The places where Paul uses it in 1 Thessalonians are abrupt transitions which might indicate Paul is responding to a letter (4:9, 13; 5:1) and it would fit with epistolary convention.[72] However, Walton notes that περὶ δέ does not necessarily indicate that Paul is responding to a letter.[73] Also, as Malherbe points out, Paul does not refer to a letter.[74] Paul could be replying to a verbal report,[75] which Wanamaker suggests is from Timothy.[76] While there may be parallels with epistolary convention, this does not imply that Paul always followed such conventions.[77]

Paul starts the section by praising the Thessalonians for their love before responding to the issues.[78] Paul speaks of their love as φιλαδελφία (4:9) which is used elsewhere of blood siblings (Plutarch *Mor.* 478a—492D, 4 Macc 13:21,23, 26).[79] Wanamaker asserts that the only example of it referring to love outside the family in Greek and Jewish literature is 2 Macc

---

68. Barclay, "Thessalonica and Corinth," 51.

69. Jewett, *Correspondence*, 97-98.

70. Frame, *Thessalonians*, 157.

71. Agrell, *Work*, 95; Koester, "Ideology," 161; Best, *Thessalonians*, 171.

72. Walton, *Leadership*, 148.

73. Ibid., 149.

74. Malherbe, *Letters*, 77. Malherbe therefore allows for the source to be a verbal report or a letter (252).

75. Walton, *Leadership*, 149.

76. Wanamaker, *Thessalonians*, 159. Also Malherbe, *Letters*, 77-78.

77. Walton, *Leadership*, 149.

78. Fee, *Thessalonians*, 157; Rigaux, *Paul*, 516.

79. BDAG, 1055.

15:14.⁸⁰ However, Harland points to a figurative use in *IG* XIV 902a in Latium.⁸¹ Even if we accept this example, Paul uses a word which prompts his readers to think in terms of family rather than friendship,⁸² which may be particularly important if their new-found faith had caused issues within their blood family relationships.⁸³ Horrell also notes from his survey of Pauline letters that Paul often uses ἀδελφοί to encourage believers to show "solidarity and mutual care."⁸⁴

They are θεοδίδακτοί (4:9). While this has possible links to Isa 54:13 and Jer 31:33–34,⁸⁵ Gaventa points out that the LXX of Isa 54:13 uses a different word⁸⁶ and Wanamaker argues that the word is not known prior to Paul.⁸⁷ It may be that Paul uses the word in contrast to the Epicurean idea of being "self-taught"/ἀδιδάκτως (Sextus Empiricus *Math.* 11.96). Paddison sees the teaching as being by the indwelling Holy Spirit⁸⁸ with Turner arguing that it is part of ongoing sanctification.⁸⁹

The Thessalonians have shown this love throughout Macedonia (4:10). Wanamaker and Neil suggest that they have done so through their hospitality.⁹⁰ Witherington adds that they may have sent aid to other cities.⁹¹ While there is no clear evidence for this, the churches of Macedonia are those who are quick to contribute to the gift to Jerusalem (2 Cor 8:1–6), which may indicate that they were already in the practice of sending aid elsewhere. It is possible that such hospitality and help was more necessary in a situation of persecution.⁹²

Paul links their love for one another to work using καί (4:10). Agrell acknowledges that there is some connection to the previous verses but argues that the καί indicates that Paul sees this as a new topic.⁹³ However,

---

80. Wanamaker, *Thessalonians*, 160.
81. Harland, *Dynamics*, 70.
82. Witherington, *Thessalonians*, 119. Burke notes that Paul uses a range of "kinship terminology" (Burke, "New Family," 270).
83. Richards, *Thessalonians*, 214.
84. Horrell, "ἀδελφοί," 309, also 302.
85. Williams, *Thessalonians*, 76.
86. Gaventa, *Thessalonians*, 57.
87. Wanamaker, *Thessalonians*, 160.
88. Paddison, *Hermeneutics*, 172.
89. Turner, *Holy Spirit*, 104.
90. Neil, *Thessalonians*, 86; Wanamaker, *Thessalonians*, 160.
91. Witherington, *Thessalonians*, 120.
92. Barclay, "Thessalonica and Corinth," 54.
93. Agrell, *Work*, 96.

earlier in his book Agrell sees these verses as showing love as a motive for work.[94] Malherbe argues that the καί is explicative.[95] Bruce and Milligan see it as adverbial, translating it "indeed."[96] Either of these later options seems more likely than reading it as "and" as it introduces four infinitives that are dependent on παρακαλοῦμεν (4:10) from the previous verse.[97] Paul has already made a link between love and work in his own life in 1 Thess 2:8–9. Therefore Best's conclusion that work is a specific application of φιλαδελφία seems sensible.[98] Thus, the aspiring to live quietly, minding their own things, and working with their own hands are all part of their love for one another.

Paul exhorts the Thessalonians φιλοτιμεῖσθαι ἡσυχάζειν (4:11). Φιλοτιμέομαι is generally used of political ambition (Philo *Rewards* 11)[99] and seeking honor.[100] BDAG translates it "consider it an honor, aspire."[101] Winter notes that it is used of benefactors.[102] Ἡσυχάζειν is used elsewhere in the NT of resting on the Sabbath (Luke 23:56), being silent (Luke 14:4, Acts 11:18), and having an undisturbed/quiet life (1 Tim 2:2).[103] Thus, the phrase is somewhat of an oxymoron,[104] with Williams suggesting "to seek restlessly to be quiet."[105]

Barclay helpfully points out that this cannot simply refer to an issue that is just about working because if individuals were not working, they would be quiet.[106] There are possible parallels with philosophical teaching about withdrawal from political life.[107] There are various suggestions about the background to this exhortation which include: Paul discouraging particularly aggressive evangelism,[108] Paul arguing the Thessalonians should not be noisy on behalf of their patrons and dependent on them,[109] the Thes-

94. Ibid., 3.
95. Malherbe, *Letters*, 246.
96. Bruce, *Thessalonians*, 90; Milligan, *Thessalonians*, 53.
97. Wanamaker, *Thessalonians*, 162. Also Jones, *Thessalonians*, 57 (though he argues for five infinitives).
98. Best, *Thessalonians*, 171.
99. Malherbe, *Letters*, 246.
100. Rigaux, *Paul*, 520.
101. BDAG, 1059.
102. Winter, *Welfare*, 48.
103. Agrell, *Work*, 98; Moore, *Thessalonians*, 66.
104. Malherbe, *Letters*, 247.
105. Williams, *Thessalonians*, 77.
106. Barclay, "Conflict," 521.
107. Gaventa, *Thessalonians*, 58; Rigaux, *Paul*, 521.
108. Barclay, "Conflict," 524.
109. Witherington, *Thessalonians*, 112.

salonians thinking that the new age meant they had freedom to do what they wanted,[110] and Miguez's suggestion, which seems less plausible, that Paul is addressing the hardworking about how to use their time off.[111] The first three of these possibilities will be explored further later.[112]

Paul then says they should πράσσειν τὰ ἴδια. This may be linked to the Stoic ideal of independence.[113] This could simply be a call to concern themselves with their private life or own affairs,[114] but the phrase is also used to contrast with being a busybody (Plato *Resp.* 433AB), could include the idea of oversight of others if it is their proper concern (Arrian *Epict. diss.* 3.22.97), and was used in the sense of own affairs appropriate to a person's function (Plato *Resp.* 4.441DE). Winter and Walton argue that Paul's exhortation to the Thessalonians is that they should not be running around after their patron's affairs.[115] Thus, πράσσειν τὰ ἴδια is then "the opposite to being concerned about the public activities of one's patron."[116] This fits with the idea that being a client was an inappropriate role for a Christian.

Agrell asserts that Paul's use of ἐργάζεσθαι ταῖς χερσὶν ὑμῶν (4:11) refers to manual work and notes that Paul uses it elsewhere only of his own work (1 Cor 4:12; 1 Thess 2:9). Therefore Agrell argues this indicates that the Thessalonians were mainly lower class.[117] However, the phrase τὰ ἔργα τῶν χειρῶν is common in the OT (Deut 2:7, Job 1:10; Ps 90:17) and therefore the phrase does not need to be limited to just manual labor.[118]

Paul's concern that they live quietly and work is not simply about love, it is also about right relationships with those outside the community (4:12), which is probably about how they appear and their consequent witness.[119] This would be particularly important in a situation where they have been perceived as being trouble makers (Acts 17:1–9),[120] have faced hostility, and may have a lack of opportunities to socialize if many of the opportunities involve worship of other gods.[121] Thus, how they lived and worked could

---

110. Gaventa, *Thessalonians*, 59.
111. Míguez, *Practice*, 69.
112. See pp. 213–20.
113. Best, *Thessalonians*, 178; Winter, *Welfare*, 50.
114. Agrell, *Work*, 98.
115. Winter, *Welfare*, 48–49; Walton, *Leadership*, 170.
116. Winter, *Welfare*, 49.
117. Agrell, *Work*, 99.
118. Richards, *Thessalonians*, 220.
119. Agrell, *Work*, 99; Neil, *Thessalonians*, 88.
120. Whiteley, *Thessalonians*, 66.
121. Witherington, *Thessalonians*, 124.

counter accusations and rumors.¹²² Those outsiders who may have been former patrons of Christians may have been struck by the believers' newfound focus on work.¹²³

This right relationship with those outside involves μηδενὸς χρείαν ἔχητε (4:12). This could either mean to lack nothing or to depend on no one.¹²⁴ However, χρεία usually takes a thing rather than a person as its object¹²⁵ which would point to the sense being lacking nothing, rather than independence from any other person. This would also fit with Paul's example of himself sharing his soul with the Thessalonians. Jewett provides the interesting possibility that this lacking nothing need not be an individual attribute but could be a collective one.¹²⁶ Aasgaard similarly argues the plural verb indicates group self-sufficiency.¹²⁷

First Thessalonians 5:14–15

The other passage in 1 Thessalonians that relates to the issue is 1 Thess 5:14–15. It comes after two verses where Paul encourages them in good treatment of their leaders (vv. 12–13). Paul then gives three-fold directions encouraging them to admonish the ἀτάκτοι, to encourage the faint-hearted, and to help the weak. Some of these issues might be seen as the responsibility of the leaders,¹²⁸ and Burke argues that Paul is referring to leading brothers.¹²⁹ However, while Burke provides helpful background information about family relationships, it is not clear that Paul has only some brothers in mind. Paul makes it clear that it is the responsibility of all of them, addressing the whole body of believers as ἀδελφοί (5:14).¹³⁰

Ἀτάκτοι is often translated as "idle" (NIV/ ESV) or "idlers" (NRSV) and there are papyri that exist with this meaning (P. Oxy. 275 (66 CE), P. Oxy. 725 (183 CE)).¹³¹ However, this is unlikely to be its only meaning otherwise Paul might be expected to use ἀργοί or ἄπρακτοι.¹³² BDAG gives the

---

122. Winter, "Honouring," 94.
123. Winter, *Welfare*, 51.
124. Richards, *Thessalonians*, 212.
125. Williams, *Thessalonians*, 78.
126. Jewett, "Tenement," 42.
127. Aasgaard, *Brothers*, 165.
128. Fee, *Thessalonians*, 209.
129. Burke, "New Family," 285.
130. Fee, *Thessalonians*, 209; Jones, *Thessalonians*, 70; Moore, *Thessalonians*, 81.
131. Milligan, *Thessalonians*, 153–54.
132. Malherbe, *Letters*, 317.

main background as a military one where someone is not in order.[133] Williams notes that it was used particularly in battle:[134] thus "out of line"[135] and "not in battle-order."[136]

Jewett thinks this "standing against the order"[137] may have included using the idea of privilege to get support.[138] If the ἄτακτοι thought they were being good leaders or being good community by reliance on others, Paul's use of ἄτακτοι corrects them in no uncertain terms.

In addition, and possibly in contrast, Paul wants them to avoid repaying evil with evil and to pursue good to each other and to all (5:15). This reminds the Thessalonians that, while some may need admonishing, this should not include repaying with evil. The wording of pursuing good (ἀγαθός) has benefaction connotations[139] and is to be done not simply to those within the congregation but also to those beyond. This reiterates Paul's point in 4:12 about proper relationships with outsiders and takes it further to doing good to outsiders.

Other Texts

There are a number of other texts in 1 Thessalonians which may help us understand the situation Paul is addressing and what he is saying. As Paul begins the letter he refers to τοῦ ἔργου τῆς πίστεως καὶ τοῦ κόπου τῆς ἀγάπης (1:3), possibly anticipating the issues he addresses later,[140] but also linking work and love.

In 1 Thess 2:1–6 Paul writes about his first visit to Thessalonica in a way that contrasts with how philosophers entered and acted,[141] particularly the way they boasted and promoted themselves (Dio Chrysostom *Or.* 77/78.27).[142]

Then in 2:8 Paul reminds the Thessalonians of the way that he and his companions shared their own souls with them. This deep sharing of

---

133. BDAG, 148.
134. Williams, *Thessalonians*, 96.
135. Fee, *Thessalonians*, 210.
136. Moore, *Thessalonians*, 81.
137. Jewett, *Correspondence*, 104.
138. Ibid., 105.
139. Winter, *Welfare*, 42.
140. Fee, *Thessalonians*, 26.
141. Winter, "Entries."
142. Ibid., 60–61.

themselves and commitment can also be seen in 2:17—3.6 and 3:9–12.[143] Paul then links this sharing of himself with hard work (2:9): "sharing life is also about sharing work."[144] Paul's work may again be in contrast to the way many orators entered a city and supported themselves. As we saw in chapter 5[145] orators and philosophers might charge fees, become a client, beg, or work[146] and Russell suggests that Paul works in order to distance himself from Cynic philosophers.[147] As Walton points out this could suggest that Paul is contrasting himself with orators rather than opponents in the church.[148] Fee and Moore suggest a Jewish background referencing *m. 'Abot* 2.2 and 4.5[149] While these are later, it is plausible that the expectation that rabbis would have a trade preceded the Mishnah.

Paul works so as not to be a burden. In his entry and his working Paul models what he then teaches in 1 Thess 4:9–12 and 5:14–15. This could mean that the issue was already present when Paul was first with the Thessalonians;[150] however, this is hard to discern as Paul also works when he first proclaims the gospel in Corinth (1 Cor 9:9–18; Acts 18:1–3). Still it does give us an example of Paul teaching through his actions as well as his words,[151] living out the virtues that he teaches,[152] and showing that it was possible to do so.[153]

SECOND THESSALONIANS[154]

Introduction

Second Thessalonians is more specific about the issues surrounding the ἄτακτοι. There are questions about whether it is a Pauline letter or not.[155]

---

143. Fee, *Thessalonians*, 73–74; Malherbe, *Letters*, 147.
144. Míguez, *Practice*, 66.
145. See pp. 108–15.
146. Hock, *Context*, 52.
147. Russell, "Idle," 109.
148. Walton, *Leadership*, 155–56.
149. Fee, *Thessalonians*, 78; Moore, *Thessalonians*, 39.
150. Marshall, *Thessalonians*, 72.
151. Skeen, "Enemies," 292.
152. Winter, "Entries," 63.
153. Malherbe, "Ethics," 203.
154. In this section scripture references will be to 2 Thessalonians unless otherwise indicated.
155. This section will conclude on balance that 2 Thessalonians is Pauline and will

Agrell and Donfried both see the letter as non-Pauline[156] and similarly Menken sees the letter as an "authentic reinterpretation" of 1 Thessalonians.[157]

There are a number of issues that raise questions about the letter's authenticity, particularly when compared to 1 Thessalonians. First, the tone of the letter—Jewett notes that 2 Thessalonians is seen as more authoritative[158] and lacking in personal references.[159] However, while not as affectionate as 1 Thessalonians, the tone of 2 Thessalonians is still warm.[160] This can be seen in 1:3-4 where Paul is still positive about the Thessalonians and in 1.11 speaks of praying continually for them. Malherbe notes that some of the change of tone can be attributed to the change in situation between the two letters,[161] and Foster notes that the Corinthian correspondence exhibits "greater variation of tone" and its authenticity is not questioned.[162] Also if the letter is Pauline, the Thessalonians would have recently received 1 Thessalonians and therefore have had Paul's affection clear in their minds.[163]

Second, the eschatology between the two letters is seen as different. Jewett notes the differences in eschatology between 2 Thess 2:1-12 and 1 Thess 5:1-11 and Menken argues that 1 Thess 4:15-18 indicates an imminent parousia while 2 Thess 2:1-12 does not.[164] However, as Menken himself acknowledges 2 Thessalonians does not deny the parousia; it just indicates that it will happen after some events (1:7; 2:3).[165] While 2 Thess 2:2 speaks against the idea that the parousia is already here, 1 Thess 5:1-10 urges its readers to be prepared for the coming of the parousia and so the two passages are not necessarily contradictory. Foster notes that Paul's eschatology

---

thus refer to the author of 2 Thessalonians as Paul.

156. Agrell, *Work*, 116; Donfried, *Paul*, 53.

157. Menken, *Thessalonians*, 43.

158. Jewett, *Correspondence*, 81.

159. Ibid., 7.

160. Malherbe, *Letters*, 351.

161. Ibid., 367.

162. Foster, "Thessalonians," 157.

163. Wanamaker argues that 2 Thessalonians (persecution present) precedes 1 Thessalonians (persecution past) (Wanamaker, *Thessalonians*, 38, 42) and that 3:17 makes more sense if 2 Thessalonians is the first letter (Wanamaker, *Thessalonians*, 38). However, the Thessalonians could have experienced more than one time of persecution and while the reference in 2:15 could point to a previous non-extant letter, 1 Thessalonians seems a good fit (Foster, "Thessalonians," 162). In addition 2 Thessalonians is narrower in focus, which would make sense if Paul were writing to clarify areas of the first letter that had not been fully understood (Foster, "Thessalonians," 162).

164. Menken, *Thessalonians*, 28.

165. Ibid., 29-30.

could have developed and that Paul may have adapted his teaching to the Thessalonians' response.[166]

In addition Barclay notes that apocalyptic writings are not necessarily consistent in their eschatology.[167] He also suggests a possible situation where the Thessalonians had misinterpreted Paul and thought that the Day of the Lord was a separate event from the parousia, which may explain some of the nuances in Paul's argument.[168]

Third, Menken argues that the literary correlations between the two letters are too close unless someone was copying 1 Thessalonians,[169] but as Malherbe and Morris point out, while there are similarities between the letters they are not so similar.[170] Morris notes that apart from the framework, similarities account for no more than a third of the letters and that sometimes they are used in different places and for different purposes.[171] For example, Paul talks about working with his hands in 1 Thess 2:9 as he points out his love for the Thessalonians and then in 2 Thess 3:7–9 in order to exhort them to follow his example.[172]

If 2 Thessalonians is not Pauline, we might expect it to have been produced at a later date, otherwise there would be a greater danger of it being discovered as non-Pauline. If 2 Thessalonians is non-Pauline and written later, the author would probably have known other Pauline letters and might well have included aspects from them. However, Fee notes that 2 Thessalonians shows similarities to 1 Thessalonians but less so to later Pauline letters.[173]

Fourth, 2:2 is sometimes seen as referring to 1 Thessalonians as a "forged" letter,[174] and the reference in 3:17 to his own writing and signature is then seen as authenticating 2 Thessalonians in contrast to 1 Thessalonians.[175] However, 2:15 speaks positively about the previous letter.[176] Additionally, as Foster points out, if 2 Thessalonians was non-Pauline, the person writing it would need a substantial knowledge of Paul's letters to know that

---

166. Foster, "Thessalonians," 169.
167. Barclay, "Conflict," 525.
168. Ibid., 527.
169. Menken, *Thessalonians*, 39.
170. Morris, *1 and 2 Thessalonians*, 29; Malherbe, *Letters*, 357.
171. Morris, *1 and 2 Thessalonians*, 29.
172. Ibid., 29–30.
173. Fee, *Thessalonians*, 240.
174. Jewett, *Correspondence*, 7.
175. Ibid., 7.
176. Ibid., 17.

the signature was authenticating, making it difficult for it to be an early non-Pauline letter, but later copies of it would not have included the signature making it difficult to envisage a late setting.[177] Also while a handwritten signature could be used to show authenticity,[178] it could also show ability and status.[179]

None of these arguments for 2 Thessalonians being non-Pauline are conclusive. In addition, the letter is attested by Polycarp, Ignatius and Justin;[180] indeed Morris notes that 2 Thessalonians has better attestation than 1 Thessalonians.[181] It is therefore likely that 2 Thessalonians was written by Paul shortly after Timothy brought a report from his visit to Thessalonica.

Second Thessalonians 3:6-15

In 3:6-15 Paul takes up the issue of ἄτακτοι, this time at greater length. Again the letter includes issues around eschatology, but discussion of the eschatology is separated from discussion of the ἄτακτοι by the request for prayer, and blessing (3:1-5).[182] As has already been noted the letter has a sharper tone, probably due to the need for correction,[183] and this can be seen in Paul's use of ἐν ὀνόματι τοῦ κυρίου ἡμῶν Ἰησοῦ Χριστοῦ (3:6).[184]

This time Paul commands the believers to keep away from ἀτάκτως περιπατοῦντος (3:6) and later contrasts these people's actions with his actions using the verbal form: οὐκ ἠτακτήσαμεν ἐν ὑμῖν (3:7). Ἄτακτοι was examined in the 1 Thess 5:14-15 section and both the words in 2 Thess 3:6-7 are related. BDAG defines ἀτάκτως περιπατεῖν as "*behave irresponsibly*" and ἀτάκτως on its own as "in defiance of good order, *disorderly.*"[185]

Paul teaches that this behavior is against the tradition that the Thessalonians received from him.[186] He explains this tradition by using the

---

177. Foster, "Thessalonians," 166.
178. Keith, "Hand," 45.
179. Ibid., 54, 56.
180. Morris, *1 and 2 Thessalonians*, 26.
181. Ibid., 26.
182. Witherington, *Thessalonians*, 245.
183. Jones, *Thessalonians*, 115.
184. Menken, *Thessalonians*, 130.
185. BDAG, 148.
186. Witherington, *Thessalonians*, 251. Richards argues that Paul is focusing on disorder not lack of work, but the passage's later focus on work seems to belie this point (and Richards' assertion that the ἄτακτοι and eating one's own bread refer to different situations) (Richards, *Thessalonians*, 282, 382).

example of himself and his companions (3:7–9). As in 1 Thess 2:9, Paul's intention is not to be a burden (3:8). He is careful not to deny his right to support (3:9), but notes that he wanted to be a model for the Thessalonians (3:9).[187] Agrell observes that being an example is much more important as a reason in 2 Thess 3 than it is in 1 Cor 9.[188]

It is not simply Paul's and his companions' actions which show the tradition, but also the particular rule εἴ τις οὐ θέλει ἐργάζεσθαι μηδὲ ἐσθιέτω (3:10), which they taught while they were there. Skeen suggests that this tradition goes back to Jesus,[189] although there is not really sufficient evidence to discern whether this may be the case.

However, there is some evidence of possible backgrounds. Menken argues that the Jewish tradition saw an obligation to work based on Gen 3:17–19,[190] and Gaventa points to Ps 128:2. Agrell highlights that eating one's bread is a Hebraism.[191] There are a number of suggested Jewish parallels. These include Prov 10:4 and *Gen. Rab.* 2; however these tend to be about the consequences of not working rather than about being unwilling to work.[192]

Jewett argues that the rule is casuistic and therefore implies that an issue arose within the Christian community that was sufficiently important for regulation.[193] He notes that there are similar situations where exclusion from food is used for punishment in Qumran (1 QS 6.24—7.24)[194] and in other situations where communities ate together regularly.[195] One of the examples he gives is Lucian *Bis acc.* 13, which notes the withholding of food by parents as punishment for not studying well. While Jewett's highlighting of such parallels is helpful, it is unclear that all his examples are of situations where meals were regularly taken together, for example guild meals.[196] However, his conclusion that Paul's reference is to eating in general (because of the absolute nature of the verb), not simply to "exclusion from occasional sacramental celebrations,"[197] seems likely.

187. Fee, *Thessalonians*, 331.
188. Agrell, *Work*, 119.
189. Skeen, "Enemies," 293.
190. Menken, *Thessalonians*, 132.
191. Gaventa, *Thessalonians*; Agrell, *Work*, 119.
192. Best, *Thessalonians*, 338–39.
193. Jewett, "Tenement," 34, 38.
194. Ibid., 35.
195. Ibid., 36–37.
196. Ibid., 36.
197. Ibid., 37.

Paul's expectation that the Thessalonians would be able to prevent some of their members eating (3:10) suggests that they were eating together often enough so that they could implement the teaching. Paul's own description of his time with the Thessalonians points to a deep sharing of himself and those with him (1 Thess 2:8). This seems to indicate quite a deep and intimate sharing which may well have included regular meals and even other possessions.

The rule in 3:10 is sharp because the actions of those refusing to work affects the others (indeed Agrell goes as far as to say that they endanger others).[198] The use of the continuous tense (οὐ θέλει ἐργάζεσθαι) implies that the attitude of refusal to work is habitual,[199] and the use of the imperative (μηδὲ ἐσθιέτω) implies that the community had the capacity to withhold food.[200]

Paul's criticism is of those who are περιπατοῦντας ἐν ὑμῖν ἀτάκτως, μηδὲν ἐργαζομένους ἀλλὰ περιεργαζομένους (3:11), which includes a play on words with ἐργαζομένους and περιεργαζομένους.[201] BDAG defines περιεργαζομέναι as intrusive meddling[202] and it is used in a number of contexts by Greek writers. Plutarch uses it of a man correcting others, but not correcting his own behavior (*Mor.* 516A). Polybius uses περιεργαζομέναι of someone concerning themselves with affairs that are not their own (Polybius *His.* 18.51.2), and Plato uses it in contrast to justice and doing one's own business (*Resp.* 433AB).

Agrell suggests that those who were not working may have been stopping others working.[203] Alternatively Frame suggests they may have been meddling in church management.[204] This could have been through trying to get support from the church,[205] which might explain why Paul is keen to emphasize that he was not a burden while he was with them. Irrespective of the details of how they were meddling, they were "disturbing the shalom of the community as a whole."[206]

Having spoken about how those who are not the ἄτακτοι should respond to them, Paul then speaks to the ἄτακτοι/περιπατοῦντας ἀτάκτως.

---

198. Agrell, *Work*, 121.
199. Morris, *Epistles*, 254.
200. Jewett, "Tenement"; Morris, *Epistles*, 255.
201. Malherbe, *Letters*, 453.
202. BDAG, 800.
203. Agrell, *Work*, 123.
204. Frame, *Thessalonians*, 162.
205. Ibid., 162.
206. Fee, *Thessalonians*, 333.

Here he speaks less directly and adds παρακαλοῦμεν to παραγγέλλομεν, leading Williams to comment that his "pastoral concern for them is evident."[207] He also does not use ἐν ὀνόματι τοῦ κυρίου ἡμῶν Ἰησοῦ Χριστοῦ, as in verse 6 but rather ἐν κυρίῳ Ἰησοῦ Χριστῷ (3:12). Thus, Morris argues that Paul gives it more of a "brotherly ring, and at the same time it has the effect of drawing attention to the obligations consequent on the fact they were in Christ."[208] Paul's instruction to the ἄτακτοι is that they are to work quietly and eat their own bread. "Although this is usually interpreted in terms of each person providing for his or her own sustenance, the choice of a plural possessive pronoun ἑαυτῶν more naturally fits the context of communal self-sufficiency."[209]

Russell notes that there is a tradition of living quietly in Hellenistic thought used of a philosopher retiring "from public life to pursue his studies";[210] for example P. Oxy. 128 uses ἡσυχία in the context of giving up "honorary public duties."[211] Similarly Plato uses ἡσυχία of a philosopher minding his own affairs (*Resp.* 6.496D). This is unlikely to be Paul's intention here as Paul goes on to exhort the congregation as a whole: μὴ ἐγκακήσητε καλοποιοῦντες (3:13). The Thessalonians are not to be weary because some sponge or are dependent, nor because of opposition in the city.[212] Rather they are to do good. Καλοποιέω has a range of meanings including to do right and to confer benefits. BDAG notes "*do what is right, good.*"[213] Wanamaker points out this is a call not to be like the ἄτακτοι.[214] It is not just a call to keep out of trouble, but rather an expectation of "doing of good which benefitted the lives of others."[215] Thus, work is not simply to provide for oneself (or the group), but as a means of serving.[216]

Paul then gives instructions about what to do if his instructions are not followed—the Thessalonians are to mark such people and not associate with them (3:14–15). As Oakes notes in Roman society there would have been an obligation not to associate with a troublemaker.[217] However, the aim of

207. Williams, *Thessalonians*, 147.
208. Morris, *Epistles*, 256.
209. Jewett, "Tenement," 42.
210. Russell, "Idle," 109.
211. Winter, *Welfare*, 49.
212. Whiteley, *Thessalonians*, 110; Winter, "Man," 314–15.
213. BDAG, 504.
214. Wanamaker, *Thessalonians*, 288.
215. Winter, *Welfare*, 57.
216. Best, *Thessalonians*, 337.
217. Oakes, *Philippians*, 101.

Paul's instruction is not exclusion, but change[218]—those who are affected are brothers, not outsiders. Also avoidance may have been the "only way of relieving the Christian patron of his obligation."[219]

POSSIBLE BACKGROUNDS

So what exactly is going on? What causes some to stop working and be disruptive? There are various possibilities.

Eschatology

Both 1 and 2 Thessalonians include sections on eschatological questions and use apocalyptic imagery or language. Therefore some scholars have seen the eschatological expectations of the Thessalonians as linked to the ἄτακτοι. Agrell sees the problems being a result of a "combination of near-expectation and the delay of the parousia."[220] A belief in an arrived or imminent parousia may have relativized other actions. For example it may have meant that the spiritual was seen as more important than the physical or practical.[221] Thiselton argues that Paul's eschatology, in both Thessalonians and Corinthians, relativizes everyday activities; however Paul "does not say that they are hardly worth doing, only that they take second place."[222] It may be that some Thessalonians heard the relativization but not the form of the relativization. Jewett suggests that the belief in the presence of a new age may have led to a belief that traditional mores about the social order, work, and sex were superseded.[223] Alternatively if the Day of the Lord was believed to have arrived, some Thessalonians may have thought they had entered into the Sabbath rest.[224] Frame suggests that the ἄτακτοι were so excited that they were unfit to work and therefore were idle and meddling.[225]

A related possibility is that the imminence of the parousia may have led some Thessalonians to see evangelism as a priority.[226] If they saw themselves

218. Fee, *Thessalonians*, 337–38.
219. Winter, "Man," 313.
220. Agrell, *Work*, 103.
221. Russell, "Idle," 106.
222. Thiselton, *Epistle*, 581.
223. Jewett, *Correspondence*, 172–73; also Donfried, *Paul*, 230.
224. Whiteley, *Thessalonians*, 108.
225. Frame, *Thessalonians*, 160.
226. 1 Thess 1:8 is sometimes seen as referring to the missionary preaching activity

as doing apostolic work,[227] it may have led to an expectation or request for food to be provided for them. Giving up work to evangelize may have led others to see these Thessalonians in a similar light to Cynics who gave up work and begged.[228] In addition Paul may have been concerned about the way such Thessalonians were evangelizing. Barclay suggests that Paul's exhortation to the Thessalonians to live quietly may have been to counter "the dangers of aggressive evangelism which ridicules 'idols' and calls attention repeatedly to the sudden destruction about to fall on all who do not believe in Jesus."[229]

Eschatological issues and concerns around work/the ἄτακτοι are present in both letters, so both are at the least "focal issues."[230] However, Paul does not make a link between the two.[231] Paul tells the Thessalonians that he has already instructed them about the issue around the ἄτακτοι when he was with them (2 Thess 3:6) and Fee argues that there is not evidence of eschatological fervor at that point.[232] Fee also argues that while Paul does address eschatological issues in the letters, there does not seem to be "a heightened or intense eschatological expectation."[233] If eschatology was the issue at hand we might expect Paul to have said "all must work right up to the Parousia" or "all must work because the Parousia might not come as soon as you suppose."[234] In addition the eschatological explanation does not explain why Paul links work with brotherly love.[235] Ascough helpfully notes the shift in 1 Thess 5:12–22 to talking about "internal community relationships" and argues that therefore the ἄτακτοι reference within this section is not necessarily linked to the eschatology section.[236]

---

of the Thessalonians (Malherbe, *Letters*, 117), however, as it refers to reports of how the Thessalonians received Paul, his companions, and the gospel, this seems unlikely. It probably refers to reports traveling with individuals or, as Ascough argues, it could refer to honors that the Thessalonians ascribed to God and the missionaries (Ascough, "Thessalonian Mission," 61).

227. Skeen, "Enemies," 291.
228. Malherbe, *Letters*, 254.
229. Barclay, "Thessalonica and Corinth," 53.
230. Skeen, "Enemies," 289.
231. Agrell, *Work*; Shaw, *Cost*, 39; Blomberg, *Poverty*, 180; Fee, *Thessalonians*, 324; Malherbe, *Letters*, 254.
232. Fee, *Thessalonians*, 324.
233. Ibid., 324.
234. Moore, *Thessalonians*, 118.
235. Wanamaker, *Thessalonians*, 162.
236. Ascough, "Community as Association," 319.

Paul's use of eschatological language and imagery could have wider reasons than simply questions that the Thessalonians or Timothy had reported. Paul's language and imagery does include Jewish eschatological imagery (for example end-time signs 1 Thess 4:16; heavenly ascent and theophanic clouds 4:17; and the day of the Lord 5:2).[237] Paul may have taught Gentile believers about Jewish eschatology;[238] however parallels in language can also be seen in the imperial cult.

We have already highlighted the presence of the imperial cult in Thessalonica and some of the risks for believers.[239] Paul's eschatology could be in response to imperial eschatology.[240] There are a number of key linguistic links.[241] Koester notes that παρουσία is not used in a technical sense in pre-Christian apocalyptic literature for the coming of the Lord,[242] and Rulmu notes the Latin equivalent is found on coins commemorating Nero's visit to Patras and Corinth.[243] It is often used "for the arrival of a king or emperor."[244] Ἐπιφανής is often used of the Julio-Claudians.[245] Imperial inscriptions often use words that overlap with the terminology of 1 Thessalonians, for example εἰρήνη, ἐπιφάνεια, ἐλπίς, εὐαγγέλιον, σωτηρία, and χάρα.[246] Εἰρήνη καὶ ἀσφάλεια (1 Thess 5:3) also has a Roman background connected with the security brought about by empire.[247] Ἀπάντησις which is used in 1 Thess 4:17 of meeting with Jesus is also used by Cicero of the welcome Julius Caesar received in towns (*Att.* 8.16—ἀπαντήσεις).[248] Thus, Paul's focus on eschatological questions and use of eschatological language may be, at least in part, to emphasize that "There is only one epiphany and parousia worth waiting for—Christ's."[249]

---

237. Harrison, "Paul," 77.

238. Although Harrison notes that Paul's letters have less apocalyptic imagery as time progresses (ibid., 78).

239. See pp. 194–98.

240. Horsley, *Paul*, 6.

241. Ibid., 140.

242. Koester, "Ideology," 158.

243. Mendel, *Fouilles*; Rulmu, "Ambition," 407–8.

244. Koester, "Ideology," 158; also Horsley, *Paul*, 142.

245. Harrison, "Paul," 83.

246. Ibid., 91; Horsley, *Paul*, 142.

247. Koester, "Ideology," 162; Harrison, "Paul," 86.

248. Rulmu, "Ambition," 408.

249. Harrison, "Paul," 84.

Suffering and Persecution

Acts 17 notes the uproar in Thessalonica. If Christians continued to be associated with the disturbance, they may well have been seen as disorderly and thus have been condemned.[250] In addition becoming followers of Jesus could lead to a variety of challenges for believers. They may have found it difficult to find work or to find a patron outside the faith community, as their exclusive worship would have "weakened connection with Roma-related benefactors."[251] Therefore they may have been tempted not to look for work. Paul's exhortation in 1 Thess 4:11 φιλοτιμεῖσθαι ἡσυχάζειν may have been to encourage them to "remain incognito"[252] and "avoid further trouble for themselves."[253]

Barclay also notes the reinforcing nature of apocalyptic symbols in situations of persecution and conflict.[254] Therefore Paul's focus on eschatological themes may have been to encourage the Thessalonians in the face of persecution.[255]

Patronage

Another possible background to the issue of the ἄτακτοι is patronage. Paul is concerned in 1 and 2 Thessalonians as well as in other letters to emphasize that he has not been a burden (1 Thess 2:9; 2 Thess 3:7–8; 2 Cor 11:8–9)—i.e., that he has not acted in a manner seeking patronage. Paul exhorts the Thessalonians to do good (1 Thess 5:15; 2 Thess 3:13). Both καλός and ἀγαθός were used in connection with praising benefactors.[256] *SIG* §174, §167 and §1105 all link doing good with being a benefactor.[257] In addition it is suggested the words used to praise a benefactor referred to by Dio Chrysostom in *Or.* 75.7–8 may be ἀνὴρ ἀγαθός ἐστι.[258] Winter argues that καλοποιέω is a synonym for ἀγαθοποιέω with both being benefaction terms.[259] Similarly deSilva sees 1 Thess 3:12 and 5:15 as directing Christians to be

---

250. Oakes, *Philippians*, 101.
251. Rulmu, "Ambition," 409.
252. Ibid., 416.
253. Wanamaker, *Thessalonians*, 163.
254. Barclay, "Thessalonica and Corinth," 49–56.
255. See pp. 194–98.
256. Winter, *Welfare*, 31–32. Rigaux sees them as synonymous (Rigaux, *Paul*, 714).
257. Winter, *Welfare*, 35.
258. Ibid., 31.
259. Ibid., 58.

benefactors.[260] Paul also encourages them to be quiet which may be against "political rabble-rousing behavior by clients on behalf of their patrons."[261]

Russell argues that there is likely to be a patronage background to the issue and that those Christian who were poorer may have looked to the new community to find patrons rather than to their old patrons.[262] This may in part have been because continuing with their old patrons could have led to potentially difficult compromises.[263] Even if someone had been previously working and not particularly dependent on a patron, when they became a Christian, they may have found greater difficulties in finding or continuing their work, because of how they were perceived as Christians.[264] This may have led them to expect richer Christians to support them.[265]

Paul was concerned that the lifestyle of the believers should be a good witness to the gospel and as "clients were not generally admired"[266] (for example see Juvenal *Sat.* 5.1–5) this may have also lent weight to his concern that the Thessalonians should not be clients. However, with his focus on doing good, Paul goes further than simply self-sufficiency. Winter argues that for Paul "[t]he secular client must now become a private Christian benefactor."[267] While it is not clear that Paul is necessarily encouraging private as opposed to collective benefaction, he certainly encourages the Thessalonians to actions that would have been seen as acting as patrons.

Famine

Winter suggests that the patronage issue is exacerbated by famine. He argues that idleness is an issue in 2 Thessalonians but not in 1 Thessalonians[268] and that after Paul writes 1 Thessalonians there is a year of some form of hardship, possibly famine (Tacitus *Ann.* 12.43).[269] Therefore those who

260. deSilva, *Honor*, 147.
261. Winter, *Welfare*, 48.
262. Russell, "Idle," 112–13.
263. Witherington, *Thessalonians*, 249.
264. Oakes, *Philippians*, 90–92: writing in the Philippian context.
265. Blomberg, *Poverty*, 180. Issues around political representation may have exacerbated issues for the early believers. Rulmu reports that Rome was increasing privileges to artisans, but that this could lead to difficulties in relationship with elites (Rulmu, "Ambition," 410–15).
266. Walton, *Leadership*, 170.
267. Winter, *Welfare*, 42.
268. Winter, "Man," 331.
269. Winter, *Welfare*, 56.

were less well off sought out patrons in order to survive and then after the famine abated continued to depend on them.[270] Thus, Paul's concern in 2 Thessalonians is to encourage these people back to work. While there is evidence of food shortages in this era[271] and there is more detailed instruction about work and the ἄτακτοι in 2 Thessalonians compared to 1 Thessalonians, there is already an issue at the time that 1 Thessalonians was written (4:11–12; 5:14). While a food shortage may have exacerbated the situation, it seems unlikely that it was the sole cause or that it can be narrowed to have affected Thessalonica simply between the writing of the two letters.

Gnosticism

Schmithals sees similar issues of idleness in 1 Timothy (e.g. 1 Tim 5:13, 15)[272] where he also sees Gnosticism. This together with the evidence of religious zeal and mission in 1 and 2 Thessalonians leads him to argue there is a Gnostic background to the problems in Thessalonica which involves a focus on religious experience and neglect of manual labor.[273] However, 1 Tim 5:13 does not use ἄτακτοι to describe the idle, but rather ἀργαί. In addition the absence of Gnostic language in the Thessalonian letters[274] and the lack of evidence of the presence of Gnostic missionaries[275] make it very unlikely that Gnosticism is a factor in the issue of the ἄτακτοι.

Cynics and Philosophers

Hock suggests that the ἄτακτοι may have modeled themselves on the Cynics, who tended to beg (Diogenes Laertius *LEP* 6.6, 49).[276] Those laborers who stopped work on taking up philosophy were criticized (Lucian *Fug.* 12–16),[277] and being a Cynic was generally seen as shameful (ps Diogenes *Ep.* 34, also Diogenes Laertius *LEP* 10.119–20). Thus, Jewett argues that Paul may have used ἡσυχάζειν as an encouragement to the Thessalonians to

---

270. Ibid., 56–57.
271. See pp. 79–84.
272. Schmithals, *Paul*, 159.
273. Ibid., 160
274. Russell, "Idle," 110; Jewett, *Correspondence*, 149.
275. Jewett, *Correspondence*, 148.
276. Hock, *Context*, 30, 55.
277. Malherbe, "Ethics," 216.

distance themselves from the Cynics.²⁷⁸ However, the Cynic practice is not clear-cut, as there are examples of them teaching in workshops, particularly Simon the shoemaker (Ps Soc *Ep.* 13, 18).²⁷⁹ Therefore the ἄτακτοι cannot be following all Cynic practice, as there are examples of working and of begging. It is possible some of the ἄτακτοι may have partly been following the practice of those who gave up working (Lucian *Fug.* 17), although this seems unlikely given Paul's clear example of working while he was with them.

Views on Work

The issue of the ἄτακτοι is often seen as being influenced by the Hellenistic view of work, in comparison with Paul's more Jewish approach to work. Agrell notes that the rabbis were generally positive about work and cites *m. 'Abot* 1.10 (this could be late);²⁸⁰ however Malherbe notes that Sir 38:24—39.11 has a less high view of work.²⁸¹

Agrell argues that the Greek view of manual work was very low.²⁸² Best notes that this included the belief that only intellectual work was appropriate for free men.²⁸³ Cicero sees different work as appropriate for different people and says of manual work "the very wage they receive is a pledge of their slavery" (Cicero *Off.* 1.42), seeing it as "appropriate for slaves, but not free men."²⁸⁴ Artisans were also despised (Plutarch *Per.* 1.4—2.2). Thus, Gaventa suggests that the ἄτακτοι issue may have been caused by the believers seeing their freedom in Christ meaning that they were not slaves and therefore that they were not subject to work in the same way as they had been.²⁸⁵ Morris suggests they may have asked themselves "why should they work like slaves?"²⁸⁶

However, Greek thought was not monochrome in its approach to work.²⁸⁷ For example Dio Chrysostom was more positive about it, although he also talks about the appropriateness of different types of work and speaks against those that might cause the person harm or be too sedentary (*Or.*

278. Jewett, "Tenement," 41.
279. Hock, *Context*, 38–39; Malherbe, *Letters*, 161.
280. Agrell, *Work*, 47.
281. Malherbe, *Letters*, 160–61.
282. Agrell, *Work*, 101.
283. Best, *Thessalonians*, 338.
284. Walton, "Paul," 222; also Hock, *Context*, 45.
285. Gaventa, *Thessalonians*, 59.
286. Morris, *1 and 2 Thessalonians*, 147.
287. Richards, *Thessalonians*, 211–12.

7.103-27). Hock notes that Paul's approach, which saw "idleness as inappropriate for believers,"[288] was similar to Dio's.[289] In addition Russell notes that there are examples of aristocrats who took up work when they needed to.[290]

This range of views within Greek and Jewish thought means that there were potentially various views of manual labor in Thessalonica and within the Thessalonian church. While the view that saw manual work as incompatible with being free may have contributed to the issue, it does not explain the whole situation.

Living Quarters: Tenements or Households?

Jewett argues that the Thessalonian church may well have been based in tenements rather than households and that this may have contributed to the issues around the ἄτακτοι. He argues that if there were a richer householder providing support as a patron there would have been less of a problem with those who refused to work.[291] He notes that οἶκος can be used of a range of building types[292] and that the majority of buildings in a city did not have an atrium or peristyle but rather were tenement buildings.[293] Such buildings sometimes had flimsy partitions that could be moved for residents to meet together[294] and some remains suggest that there were communal common rooms in some buildings.[295] However, Gehring notes that Jewett does not provide evidence that the partitions were moveable and the archeological evidence does not support it.[296]

Frier also argues that some lodging houses had a common kitchen and so residents may have eaten together,[297] and cites Petronius' *Satyricon* as evidence. While Petronius provides evidence of lodging houses having a cook, being able to arrange with the cook what they were going to eat (*Satyricon* 90, 92), and a pot which was empty "all the guests having drunk from it" (95), guests appear to be eating in different places, because of the references to entering and exiting (95, 96). Therefore it is not clear that it

---

288. Walton, "Paul," 225.
289. Hock, *Context*, 45.
290. Russell, "Idle," 112.
291. Jewett, "Tenement," 38.
292. Ibid., 24.
293. Ibid., 32.
294. Frier, *Landlords*, 4.
295. Ibid., 28. For example Insula Orientalis II.4-19 in Herculaneum (Balch, "Houses," 34).
296. Gehring, *Church*, 149; also Adams, *Places*, 8.
297. Frier, *Landlords*, 28.

provides evidence of the whole lodging house eating together. While Adams acknowledges inns as a possible place for Christians to meet, he notes that they would only be suitable for limited numbers and therefore posits that they might be used by small groups of Christians traveling together.[298]

Jewett suggests that Rom 16:14–15 with its lists of a number of leaders for particular churches without the use of κατ' οἶκον αὐτῶν may indicate believers meeting together with a joint collective leadership in a tenement situation.[299] He argues that if similar groups existed in Thessalonica, none of the believers within the group would have been rich enough to provide for the rest of the group and therefore all would have needed to contribute when they ate together.[300] It is probable that there were groups of Christians meeting together who may not have had a patron; however it seems less likely that Jewett's tenement proposal would work as he suggests it. Nevertheless there are a number of possible meeting places, including workshops, for such a group.[301]

THE EXAMPLE OF SHARING IN 1 AND 2 THESSALONIANS

The example of sharing in the Thessalonian letters is rooted in familial love. Paul links love for brothers and sisters with work (1 Thess 4:9–12) as well as love with provision for brothers and sisters (1 Thess 4:9–10). Weaver notes Paul's focus on the Thessalonians being brothers[302] and Donfried concludes that "family structures lie at the heart of this new family in Christ."[303] As noted earlier, Burke argues that in 1 Thessalonians Paul focuses on church as family in his use of "kinship terminology."[304] This love involves deep sharing, which is seen both in Paul's and his companions' example (1 Thess 2:8) and in his praise for the Thessalonians (1 Thess 4:9–10). In 1 Thess 2:8 Paul speaks of them sharing their very selves with the Thessalonians. This does seem to indicate quite a deep intimate sharing which may well have included possessions. This sharing and love is present within the Thessalonian community as well as from them to believers further afield (1 Thess 4:10).

---

298. Adams, *Places*, 165.
299. Jewett, "Tenement," 29–31.
300. Ibid., 32.
301. For further evidence of other possibilities see Adams, *Places*.
302. Weaver, "Thessalonians," 427–28.
303. Donfried, *Paul*, 155.
304. Burke, "New Family," 270.

However, there are issues within the Thessalonian community with a group who seem to choose to be dependent on others and disruptive (1 Thess 5:14; 2 Thess 3:11). There are a number of possible causes for this and it seems likely that there is a mix of reasons behind this group's actions. While it is probable that patronage norms are a key part of the reason that the ἄτακτοι are not working, this does not preclude issues around eschatology, particularly of individuals involved in evangelism presuming to depend on the congregation for support, also contributing to the situation. It is likely from Paul's use of ἄτακτοι that it is not simply that this group are choosing not to work, but that they are also being disruptive. Admittedly this disruption may be as a result of them not working, either through then having time to occupy themselves in other ways, or through difficulties within the community as a result of a group of people not pulling their weight.

While Paul makes it clear that the Thessalonians' love and sharing is commendable, he uses the same focus on love to place boundaries on the ways that the sharing takes place. He links love and work and places responsibility on individuals not to exploit others (1 Thess 4:11–12; 2 Thess 3:7–8).[305] Rather all are to work (1 Thess 4:11; 1 Thess 3:12) and to play their part.[306] This is not a question of those who are unable to find work being penalized, but rather of those who refuse to work (2 Thess 3:10), and Winter notes that Paul presumes that the believers should respond to "real needs."[307] Paul is concerned that the believers should not be burdens. He has indicated this on an individual basis with his actions to avoid burdening the believers, but Jewett indicates this could also be a communal sufficiency.[308] This focus on individual working and on not being a burden could also indicate Paul espousing parity between individuals within the community rather than dependency,[309] and Paul's intention that social differentiation should not be "determinative of the structure of Christian community life."[310]

However, the example Paul provides is not simply of love and sharing within the community at Thessalonica, it is also one of sharing with believers elsewhere (1 Thess 4:10), presumably through hospitality and possibly through contributing to need (2 Cor 8:1–2).

The example is also one where sharing, relationships, and work are key to right relationships with those outside the community. Paul is concerned

---

305. Wanamaker, *Thessalonians*, 163.
306. Moore, *Thessalonians*, 118.
307. Winter, *Welfare*, 59.
308. Jewett, "Tenement," 42.
309. Witherington, *Thessalonians*, 118.
310. Jones, *Thessalonians*, 117.

that the Thessalonians should behave properly towards outsiders and be dependent on no one (1 Thess 4:12), which would support Jewett's suggestion that the sufficiency is communal. The example includes doing good beyond the Christian community using words that are used of benefaction[311] and thus Winter concludes that Paul is calling the Thessalonians to be benefactors.[312]

The example is one that includes individual and community responsibility. Paul has been clear that individuals are to work and concern themselves with their own affairs (1 Thess 4:11). However, it seems plausible that the call not to be a burden is both individual and communal, and the call to benefaction also encompasses the whole community.

The example is one where there is a relationship between teaching and actions and where the teacher's actions are to be imitated (2 Thess 3:7).[313]

COMPARISONS

Having considered the example of sharing evidenced in 1 and 2 Thessalonians, we now turn to compare this example with other first century examples: the Epicureans, who focused on quiet living and were known for being dependent on others; family life, because of Paul's use of fictive kinship language; Macedonian Associations, which Ascough argues provide a number of parallels to the Thessalonian church; and patronage, which we have previously noted pervaded Greco-Roman relationships and could lead to an expectation of being dependent on a patron.

Epicureans

Epicureans (followers of the philosophical school founded by Epicurus 341–270 BCE)[314] were known for their focus on a quiet and private life (Diogenes Laertius *LEP* 10.119)[315] and withdrawal from society (Plutarch *Mor.* 1098DE).[316] They believed it was preferable to "live off others' manual labour."[317] Epicurus advises those who would be wise only to earn by wis-

---

311. See pp. 216–18.
312. Winter, "Man," 318.
313. Weaver, "Thessalonians," 428.
314. Tomlin, "Christians," 53.
315. Malherbe, *Letters*, 259.
316. Hock, *Context*, 46.
317. Malherbe, *Aspects*, 25. Malherbe references Philodemus *Peri Oikonomias* 23.

dom, and if they find themselves poor to court the king (Diogenes Laertius, *LEP* 10.119–20).

The Epicureans formed communities. Within them they would exhort and encourage one another with frank criticism.[318] They saw one another as friends and in each community there were ranks based on friendship,[319] where more mature members guided less mature members. There is some evidence of them providing limited help and sharing to one another as friends, although it should not be all the time (Vatican Collection 39).[320]

As Malherbe notes they were "severely criticized in antiquity, partly for their withdrawal from and disregard for society."[321]

While the focus on quiet is similar to Paul's exhortation to the Thessalonians and while the idea of living off others' manual work has parallels with the actions of the ἄτακτοι, there are a number of differences.

First, it is not clear that the dependency on others is the same. For the Thessalonians the dependency seems to be mainly within the congregation, for Paul is able to presume that the congregation has the capacity to refuse food to ἄτακτοι (2 Thess 3:10). Where the Epicureans were dependent, it was generally on those outside the community.

Second, the quiet espoused by Paul is different from the quiet that characterized the Epicureans' lives. For Paul not only advocates quiet, he also advocates work and encourages the Thessalonians to have a right relationship with outsiders and do good to them (1 Thess 4:12; 5:15; 2 Thess 3:13). This focus on quiet and work is also about not living off others.

Third, Malherbe also notes the difference between Paul's claim to be God-taught (1 Thess 4:9) and the Epicurean claim to be self-taught (Cicero *Fin.* 1.71; *Nat. d.* 1.72).[322]

Fourth, Downing highlights the way the Epicureans focused on one another as friends while Paul does not use the language of friends but of brothers (1 Thess 4:10; 5:12, 14; 2 Thess 3:6).[323]

Fifth, while there is some help/sharing as friends within the Epicurean communities, and there is an expected limit to such help, there are differences in the help/sharing and in the limit. The Epicurean community presumes a particular social level in order to avoid manual work and it does not appear to include eating together regularly, while the Thessalonians are

---

318. Malherbe, *Paul*, 40, 42.
319. Ibid., 85, 87.
320. Ibid., 43, 103; Malherbe, *Aspects*, 27.
321. Malherbe, *Aspects*, 25.
322. Malherbe, *Paul*, 104–5.
323. Downing, *Cynics and Pauline Churches*, 283.

eating together regularly. The limit also seems to be more about friendship expectations rather than the limit Paul puts in for those who refuse to participate in work and thus contribute.

Family Life

The way that ἀδελφοί is an important metaphor both for Paul[324] and for Jesus[325] suggests that family life and relationships may be a helpful comparator for the example of sharing in the Thessalonian church.[326] However, there are a number of issues with attempting such a comparison. First, which society to consider as a possible comparator: Greek, as Thessalonica was founded by Alexander's general; Roman, because of Roman influence in Thessalonica from 197 BCE;[327] or Second Temple Judaism, because it is Paul writing?

Second, even if it were possible to choose one of the cultural backgrounds, it is important to recognize that they are not homogeneous entities and there is variety depending on location, date, and influence from other cultures.[328]

Third, literary and judicial sources tend to give an upper class perspective and while epitaphs include a greater social range, they still do not include those who would have been unable to commission one.[329] Therefore it is important to recognize the limitations of the comparison.

Family relationships included an expectation of fulfilling roles and partnership. In all three cultures, there is evidence about marriage relationships, including the norms of property ownership and the expected roles and work of husband and wife to contribute to the family.[330] In some instances sharing is seen as the ideal in marriage and family (Cicero *Off.* 1.54),[331] although if the Roman marriage was not a *manus* marriage, that is

324. Horrell, "ἀδελφοί," 299.

325. Köstenberger, "Marriage," 245–47.

326. While sibling language is used metaphorically in philosophical groups, mystery cults, and occasionally in religious associations (Aasgaard, *Brothers*, 108–11, also Günter, "Brother," 255), it is rarely central in the way that it is in the early church (Aasgaard, *Brothers*, 116). Also φιλαδελφία is not used in the same way (von Soden, "ἀδελφος," 146).

327. See pp. 194–95.

328. Burke, *Adopted*, 47; Baugh, "Marriage and Family"; Treggiari, "Marriage"; Chapman, "Marriage."

329. Treggiari, "Marriage," 141.

330. Burke, *Adopted*, 47; Baugh, "Marriage and Family," 103; Treggiari, "Marriage," 133–4; Chapman, "Marriage," 183.

331. Treggiari also notes that Musonius Rufus also sees sharing as part of married

the wife remained part of her birth family, gifts between husband and wife were discouraged.[332]

However, Paul's language in Thessalonians points to sibling relationships rather than marriage relationships and therefore while the expectations of participation and partnership in work and roles in the marriage are a helpful background, our focus for this comparator will be sibling relationships. These are less formally defined.[333] Aasgaard points out that in the Twelve Tables (Table 5) brothers were "financially and legally responsible for each other's family," however it is unclear how important the Twelve Tables were in the imperial era.[334] Aasgaard points to Plutarch's *On Brotherly Love* as a possible source of information about sibling relationships during the first century. While Plutarch writes from an aristocratic male background, Aasgaard argues he is generally seen as reflecting wider sibling relationships.[335]

Plutarch stresses the importance of sibling relationships (*Mor.* 478BC) and of love between siblings (*Mor.* 480A–C). He notes the importance of siblings supporting one another through "mutual preservation and assistance" (*Mor.* 478DE). Siblings should not compete with one another (*Mor.* 484A, 485F—486B). Rather they should strive for equality (*Mor.* 484B–D). They should bear with one another's faults (*Mor.* 482A) and forgive one another (*Mor.* 489CD). Older brothers should care for younger brothers (*Mor.* 486F—487B). If a brother incurs the anger of the father, the brother should seek to restore him to favor (*Mor.* 482EF). Brothers are to serve each other (*Mor.* 486BC) and have a responsibility to help the sons of brothers (*Mor.* 492A–D). While brothers are to love and share, Plutarch does not provide that much information on the practical responsibilities, and speaks of brothers sharing "with each other their studies and recreations and games" (*Mor.* 480BC).

This has been a very brief overview of some aspects of family life; however it is possible to suggest a number of possible similarities and differences. First, there is a similarity in affection and Paul uses kinship language. Second, there is evidence of mutual commitment and expectation of participation/work. Third, there is evidence of sharing and helping being expected in family life and the possibility of food being used as a sanction

---

life (Treggiari, "Marriage," 147).

332. Ibid., 163.
333. Aasgaard, *Brothers*, 63.
334. Ibid., 67.
335. Ibid., 93.

was noted earlier.[336] Fourth, the evidence around property suggests some mix of individual and communal responsibility/ownership within families which may correlate to the individual and communal responsibility seen in the Thessalonian example as well as the individual and communal approach to possessions seen in the two Acts examples.[337] Fifth, Plutarch's injunction for brothers to bear with and forgive one another shows similarities to the depth of relationship Paul expects in Thessalonians and elsewhere. Sixth, Plutarch's concern for equality may bear some similarity to Paul's concern for all to play a part.

There do appear to be differences. The evidence we have found for families does not include an expectation or call to be benefactors, or to sharing further afield, although there is some evidence of sharing further afield within families. In addition while love and sharing are advocated between siblings, there is little on the practical outworking of this.

There are significant limitations in attempting to do a comparison to family life and expectations, including the fact that much of the economic evidence is from marriage documents, while Paul more frequently uses ἀδελφοί, where we have more limited economic evidence. Therefore these similarities and particularly differences are tentative. However, Paul's language and some of the evidence gathered do suggest some points of similarity.

Macedonian Associations

There are a number of reasons to consider associations as a possible comparator for the Thessalonian church. There is lots of evidence of a variety of associations in Macedonia despite the restrictions brought in by the Roman authorities.[338] While Acts 17 points to Paul preaching in the synagogue, 1 Thess 1:9 would imply that the majority of the Thessalonian church were Gentiles. In addition there is limited evidence of Jews in Macedonia.[339] Ascough argues that the references to κόπος (2:9; 3:5 and the verbal form in 5:12) together with the references to manual labor (2:7–9; 4:1, 11) would make sense in the setting of a community of manual workers or trades people, which would fit with the expectation of individuals working.[340] He also argues that Paul's use of these words and phrases would dishonor any

336. See pp. 209–13.
337. See pp. 66–71, 96.
338. Ascough, *Paul's Macedonian Associations*, 17, 42.
339. Ascough, "Community as Association," 311–13.
340. Ibid., 318.

who were not manual workers,[341] but Paul could be using the words to reorientate the Thessalonians' approach to work. Ascough suggests that associations are a plausible context for 1 Thess 5:14.[342]

There were various kinds of associations with different characteristics.[343] They were generally religious or based round particular trades.[344] Associations provided an opportunity for social belonging and those who were part of associations were normally lower rank,[345] although associations could include patrons.[346] Therefore Ascough argues that the associations in Macedonia were either lower rank or mixed.[347]

Membership of an association could be used to gain honor, if one were a founder or patron.[348] Also associations provided for burial and funerary rites.[349] While there was a hierarchy between members and founders/officials, there was equality between members.[350] Harland notes that there is some evidence of the use of ἀδελφοί in association epitaphs, for example IKilikiaBM II 201 which speaks of the co-owners of a tomb (Cilicia, first century CE),[351] and a third century CE inscription on a tomb in Thessalonica (*IG* X.2.1 824).[352] However, the context of this second example indicates that the term is not used in a way that expresses love or affection between the brothers. Harland acknowledges that associations do not necessarily use ἀδελφοί with the same meaning as the Christian community, but that it does indicate a sense of belonging.[353]

Belonging to an association involved paying regular dues[354] and there were fines for disorderly behavior (*IG* II2 1368; *P. Lond.* VII 2193). Some could provide assistance if a person was wronged (*IG* II2 1275).

There is also some limited translocal evidence. *CIG* 5853 has already been mentioned where the Tyrian senate agreed that the Roman association

---

341. Ibid., 315.
342. Ascough, *Paul's Macedonian Associations*, 177–78.
343. Ibid., 14.
344. Ascough, "Community as Association," 316.
345. Ascough, *Paul's Macedonian Associations*, 47.
346. Ibid., 51.
347. Ibid., 53.
348. Ibid., 28–29, 79.
349. Ibid., 24–25.
350. Ibid., 59.
351. Harland, *Dynamics*, 68–69.
352. Ibid., 71.
353. Ibid., 80.
354. Ascough, *Paul's Macedonian Associations*, 63–64.

of Tyrian merchants should pay rent for the Puteolian group.[355] For some religious associations, there was provision for the priests to be brought from the country of origin, for example Egypt.[356] However, as Oakes points out, Ascough's work does not examine the extent to which such links are present in VAs in comparison with churches.[357]

There are a number of similarities between associations and the Thessalonian community. Both ate together. Both included manual workers. There is some overlap of language, for example Paul's use of φιλοτιμέομαι[358] and the use of ἀδελφοί.

However, there are also differences. First, there is no evidence that associations were eating together as frequently[359] as is suggested by Paul's injunction about preventing people from eating. Second, associations are also not shown as focusing on love and sharing, that is they have a different community ethos.[360] Third, there are also some differences in how the groups correct and deal with idleness and disruptive behavior. Paul encourages the Thessalonians to admonish the ἄτακτοι and reminds them that those who are unwilling to work should not eat. In contrast the associations usually imposed fines. Fourth, there is not the same evidence of an external focus for associations, while Paul is clear that he wants the Thessalonians to do good outside their group.

Patronage

Patronage has already been described and discussed in chapter 5 and chapter 6,[361] including its ubiquity in the ancient world. In this chapter evidence has been provided of some of the probable issues connected to patronage in Thessalonica.

The similarities with patronage are mainly around the ἄτακτοι rather than the example that Paul presents or that which is evidenced in the actions of the wider Thessalonian congregation. The ἄτακτοι issue seems to have a patronage background with some Thessalonians having an expectation of being able to be dependent on others in return for concerning themselves with the patron's affairs. More widely it is possible that Greek ideas of what

---

355. See pp. 185–91. Ascough, *Paul's Macedonian Associations*, 95.
356. Ibid., 95–96.
357. Oakes, "Review," 377.
358. Ascough, "Community as Association," 321.
359. Schnabel, "Review," 336.
360. Ascough, "Community as Association," 322.
361. See pp. 106–8, 185–91.

work was appropriate to free men may have also influenced the ἄτακτοι. The other similarity is Paul's use of τὸ ἀγαθὸν διώκετε εἰς ἀλλήλους καὶ εἰς πάντας (1 Thess 5:14) and μὴ ἐγκακήσητε καλοποιοῦντες (2 Thess 3:13) where Paul uses phrases that would often be used of benefaction.[362]

However, there are a number of differences. First, the focus on love and sharing in the example of Thessalonian community contrasts with the absence of love and sharing language in patronage writing. Second, the focus on work and not being a burden—having a sufficiency—is different from patronage, where there was an expectation of being able to receive food and/or money from a patron. Third, who the benefactors are is different. While Paul uses benefaction language, he urges all the Thessalonians to acts of benefaction rather than simply those who are better off. Thus, fourthly, the example of the Thessalonians does not provide the same kind of stratification that was part and parcel of patronage relationships. This can be seen in the way the key relationships are within the community and then to outsiders in blessing rather than hierarchical triangles.

CONCLUSION

The Thessalonian community is one which showed familial love and provision and deep sharing relationships. However, there were some—the ἄτακτοι—who were dependent and disruptive, probably for a mix of reasons. Paul commends the Thessalonians for their love. He uses love as the rationale and motivation for working, so that they do not exploit one another and are not burdens. Paul's expectation that those who are able to work should work (and thus the boundaries he puts in place) suggests an egalitarian approach to community. The Thessalonians not only shared with one another, but also showed love to believers elsewhere. Paul reminds them that their work and relationships are key for their relationships with those outside. Paul does not just want them to not be dependent, he wants them to be doing good to those outside. There is both an individual responsibility to work and a collective responsibility to do good.

The comparators provide possible backgrounds to some of the actions of the ἄτακτοι and to some of Paul's language. There are also some similarities between the comparators, particularly family life, and Paul's exhortation to the Thessalonians, but there are also clear distinctives, particularly in comparison with the Epicureans, Voluntary Associations (VAs) and patronage.

---

362. See pp. 216–18.

LIMITS ON SHARING 231

First, there is a focus on love and sharing in the Thessalonian community, which is not seen in the same way in the Epicureans, VAs, and patronage. For example, Paul addresses the Thessalonians as brothers, the Epicureans saw one another as friends.

Second, there is a greater focus on doing good to those outside the community, which is not seen in the VA, family and Epicurean comparators. While this element is present in patronage, Paul reorientates their patronage expectations and calls all to benefaction rather than simply a few.

Third, the focus on love and sharing, the call to all to benefaction, and the exhortation to work suggest that Paul wanted to encourage a community without the social stratification that was seen in patronage relationships.

Fourth, the Thessalonian example of sharing involves more frequent eating together than is seen in the Epicurean, patronage or VA comparators.

8

Sharing Possessions in Community in the NT

Christian Distinctives

WE HAVE EXAMINED THE sharing of possessions in community in the NT with particular reference to Jesus and his disciples, the earliest Christians, and Paul. This chapter summarizes the rationale for the approach of this book in examining NT examples of sharing of possessions. It then draws out the common characteristics in the NT examples of sharing possessions in community. Having reviewed the comparisons with the surrounding culture, and similarities to and differences from the cultural context that individual NT examples show, it then compares across the comparisons. This identifies the ways in which the NT examples examined show similarities to their cultural context as well as ways they are consistently different to their contemporary surroundings. It then highlights the common motivations for sharing evidenced in the NT texts before concluding and suggesting future research possibilities.

SUMMARY

The introduction highlighted the importance of sharing possessions in the NT, the key questions this book address (how the early church held and shared possessions together and how Christians were distinctive when compared to the surrounding cultures), how it addresses the questions (by considering specific examples of sharing and then comparing them with similar examples in the surrounding culture) and why this method is used (to hold the diversity in the NT in tension rather than privileging one model over another and to show when these comparisons are compared the ways Christians were consistently distinctive in how they shared possessions).

We have considered the common purse in John's gospel, an example which shows sharing in the small group of Jesus and itinerant disciples with support from non-itinerant disciples. The γλωσσόκομον was one form of sharing which was used to buy food, give to the poor, and for wider needs.

We then looked at the early chapters of Acts (2–6) and the example of selling, sharing, and holding in common in the context of the earliest days of the church. Here the sharing is linked to God's grace and the presence of the Holy Spirit. It is voluntary, yet with assumptions about how the giving takes place. While private property in name continues, possessions are seen as common and are sold and used as needs arise within the community.

Later in Acts we considered the example of the church in Antioch sharing with believers in Judaea with whom they had an ongoing relationship (11:19–30). It is an example where individuals contribute according to their ability, but where there is also corporate responsibility for sharing. Sharing is presented as key to being disciples of Jesus. The example evidences practical and careful stewardship.

In 1 Cor 11 we considered the example of sharing of food at the Lord's Supper in Corinth, where Paul instructs the Corinthians that their sharing of food should show equality and care for one another as members of one united body made up of people from diverse backgrounds, for whom Christ died.

In 2 Cor 8 and 9 we considered another example of sharing at a distance, but one with a less established relationship between those giving and those receiving. It is an example where sharing/giving: is core to being a Christian; is rooted in grace, in Jesus, and his example; provides for need; is voluntary, generous, and practical; involves all; is in relation to what one has; is relational; and has potential reciprocity. It is also an example where probity is important and God is central as the ultimate benefactor.

In 1 and 2 Thessalonians we considered the presence of limits or boundaries to sharing in the context of regular shared meals in a community which showed familial love and provision, and deep sharing relationships. Paul instructs the Thessalonians to work as part of the way they love each other and he exhorts them to do good not only to those within the group, but also to those outside.

COMMON CHARACTERISTICS OF THE NT EXAMPLES

The specifics of each NT situation and example are such that we would not necessarily expect to find identical approaches to sharing possessions in each of the examples, as different situations create different needs and therefore different responses. For example, we would not expect the same approaches to sharing for a group of itinerant disciples in Galilee and Judaea as for a settled community in Corinth. However, when we look across the six NT examples of sharing that we have examined there are commonalities. Some exist across several examples, some across just a couple of examples.

The following characteristics exist across four or more examples and are not contradicted by the characteristics of the examples in which they do not appear. All of the examples exhibit more than one of the common characteristics. None of the examples exhibits all of them.

First, the examples are *practical and responsive* (John, Acts 2–6, Acts 11, 2 Cor 8–9, Thessalonians). This indicates that sharing was not simply an ideal but something that was part of the practical life of the communities. In John the γλωσσόκομον provides for the practical needs of the disciples and others. In the early chapters of Acts, selling happens in response to need, and when issues arise in the distribution of food, steps are taken to address them. In Acts 11 the giving is in response to a prophecy and care is taken over the transportation and delivery of the gift. In 2 Cor 8 and 9 Paul shows care for the practical details of the delivery of the collection and in 1 Cor 16:2 gives guidance for how to collect the gift. The practical nature of the examples is also seen in the responsiveness to changing circumstances (for example the move in Acts 4 to proceeds being brought to the apostles' feet) and in the responses to conflicting ideas of what is appropriate sharing. This is probably partly as a result of the communities being relatively new and therefore in a formational stage, where the practicalities of expectations are still being established. For example, Paul puts a boundary in place in 2 Thess 3:10 which limits those who share food.

Second, the examples are *based in a sense of communal identity, unity or relationships between individuals or communities* (John, Acts 2–6, 1 Cor 11, 2 Cor 8–9, Thessalonians). In John, the disciples travel together and Jesus teaches about their relationship with one another, with him and the

Father. In Acts 2–6 the community is one in heart and mind. In 1 Corinthians Paul emphasizes that the Corinthians are brought into communion with God and one another through Jesus' death, and are one body. Therefore they should not be divided, and their actions should be in character with the reality of the covenant meal they are eating. In 2 Cor 8 and 9 Paul focuses on the way the giving of the Macedonians is part of their giving to the Lord and Paul. Paul reminds the Corinthians that giving will lead to prayer, thanksgiving, and to the Jerusalem believers longing for the Corinthians. In Thessalonians Paul uses sibling language and speaks of the deep sharing between the Thessalonians and between him and the Thessalonians.

Third, the groups sharing often show *a mix of backgrounds, either of different cultural backgrounds and/or of different social classes* (John, Acts 11, 1 Cor 11, 2 Cor 8–9). In the γλωσσόκομον example there are disciples who leave their jobs and homes and the women who have resources not only to support themselves but also to contribute to the γλωσσόκομον. In Acts 11 the community includes those who are not from Jewish backgrounds. In 1 Corinthians there is evidence of a mix of social backgrounds and of the presence of both Gentile and Jewish background believers. In 2 Corinthians Paul exhorts the Corinthian community, who include people from a range of religious and social backgrounds to give to a community, which is probably a predominantly Jewish Christian community.

Fourth, the examples often *do not have only one way of an individual contributing to the sharing, but multiple ways* (John, Acts 2–6, Acts 11, 2 Cor 8–9). For example, some disciples leave behind possessions and follow Jesus; some travel with and contribute to the common purse; and others do not travel with, but provide hospitality to the traveling group. In Acts 2–6 it seems unlikely that each member was in a position to sell land or property to contribute to the common fund, but those who were able to do so did when the need arose and the community held what they had in common. In Acts 11 each person gave according to their ability, i.e. they did not all give the same amount. In 2 Cor 8 and 9 Paul exhorts the Corinthians to give according to what they have and to alleviate need rather than to put themselves in need, while the Macedonians have given beyond their means. Frequently these different ways of contributing go alongside the importance of the individual making a choice to contribute with a tension between the voluntary nature of contributing and the existence of assumptions about contributing. This can be seen in the way Ananias and Sapphira are free to decide and yet there are assumptions about how contributions take place.

Fifth, while it is often individuals that make the decision to contribute, there is *a tension between the individual and the community in terms of responsibility or ownership of sharing* (John, Acts 2–6, Acts 11, Thessalonians).

In John individuals give to the γλωσσόκομον, and Judas holds it for the group. Yet it is used for the needs of the group and for the poor. In Acts 2–6 individuals decide to sell and give, but all see what they have as common. In Acts 11:27–30 each of the believers contributes according to what they have and yet they decide. In Thessalonians food is shared together and there are close relationships, yet each person has a responsibility to work. Individually and collectively they are called to do good.

Sixth, the examples nearly all *involve responding to need* (except Thessalonians) as opposed to gaining honor or security. In John the γλωσσόκομον seems to be used to give to the poor. In Acts 2–6 the community responds to need by individuals selling property and possessions for the common fund, and also by dealing with the issue of the widows left out in the distribution of food. In Acts 11 the Antiochene church responds to the need created by the famine/food shortages. In 1 Corinthians Paul is clear that the actions of the Corinthians should be such that there are none who are remaining hungry or without when they eat together. In 2 Cor 8 and 9 the collection is to alleviate need in the Jerusalem community.

Seventh, four of the examples include *eating together* (John, Acts 2–6, 1 Cor 11, Thessalonians). Jesus and the disciples eat together and the disciples are also shown going to buy food for the group. In Acts 2–6 the believers eat together in the temple courts and homes. In 1 Cor 11 and Thessalonians the church communities eat together.

COMPARISONS WITH THE SURROUNDING CULTURE

Each example was also compared with similar situations or examples in the Jewish and/or Greco-Roman worlds to discover the ways in which the early church behaved in ways similar to and different from the surrounding culture.

The example of the γλωσσόκομον in John was compared with the practice of the Rabbis and their disciples, the Qumran/Essene communities, and the Cynics. The sharing in the early chapter of Acts was compared with Jewish relief for the poor, the Qumran/Essene communities, and the Pythagorean community. The gift from the church in Antioch to believers in Judaea was compared with the practice of appointing a *curator annonae*, and the gifts of Helena and Izates during a time of need in Jerusalem. The sharing of food in 1 Corinthians was compared to Greco-Roman meal practices. The gift to the believers in Jerusalem was compared to: the example in Acts 11; the practice of appointing a *curator annonae*; the example of Helena and Izates; the practice of gathering Temple Tax in the Diaspora; and expectations in patronage, benefaction, and gift exchange. The sharing in 1 and 2 Thessalonians and issues around the ἄτακτοι were compared to the Epicureans, expectations in family life, associations, and patronage practice.

SIMILARITIES TO THE CULTURAL CONTEXT

Detailed examinations of the similarities and differences are found in each chapter.[1] We now turn to consider whether there are common similarities or differences across our comparisons.

With seventeen different comparisons it is less easy to identify areas where there are similarities across all the comparisons (although we should not expect to find the same similarities due to the diversity of both the examples and the comparators). However, the presence of seventeen, and arguably more, possible comparators, shows something of the variety of examples of ways of sharing possessions/food and reminds us of the key role that sharing food and possessions played in society.

Response to need, one of the characteristics that was found across five of the six examples that we examined, is also present in the Jewish comparators and in the example of the *curator annonae*. However, it should be noted that in the *curator annonae* example, there is not necessarily a concern for those most in need and there is a deeper concern to avoid civil disruption, a rather different kind of need.

There are a number of comparators where there are similarities to the example being presented within the NT text, or to the example being argued against in the NT text, and where there may be possible influences. For example the Epicureans and the ἄτακτοι in Thessalonica show similarities in avoidance of manual work and it is possible that some of the behavior of the ἄτακτοι may have been influenced by knowledge of Epicurean practice or expectations of philosophical teaching and practice. In contrast, while the example of the temple tax has been mooted as a possible comparator to the gift to Jerusalem, we saw that this was less likely to have influenced the conception or practice of the gift to Jerusalem. We also noted possible connections between the practice of Jesus and his disciples and the early church in Acts with the Essene/Qumran communities. In addition specific similarities in practice can be seen. In both John and the Essenes/Qumran there is holding in common of possessions, a treasurer, eating together and provision for those in need. In Acts 2–6 and in Jewish almsgiving there is concern for those in need. In Acts 2–6 and the Essenes/Qumran there is handing over of property and provision for the group. In 1 Cor 11 association meals also

1. See pp. 25–27, 33–35, 37–39, 71–77, 93–96, 138–40, 185–91, 223–30.

show concern for good order and the formation of the community. In Thessalonians Voluntary Associations also eat together and included manual workers. However, there were also differences.

DIFFERENCES FROM THE CULTURAL CONTEXT

When we turn to look at differences, there are some striking individual differences for specific examples.

For example, the way Jesus and his disciples eat with others outside the group is different to the firm boundaries of the Essene/Qumran communities. In the early chapters of Acts individuals remain in possession of their property even when it is held in common, until the point at which it is sold to provide for need, while in the Essene/Qumran communities property is handed over and held centrally.

In Acts 11 the participation of each person in the gift to the believers in Judea is very different from the practice of *curator annonae* or of Helena and Izates, where a wealthy individual or a few wealthy people provide.

In 1 Cor 11, Paul's desire for those of different social backgrounds to eat together as equals contrasts with general Greco-Roman meal practice, where social differentiation is a key part of how people ate together.

In 2 Cor 8 and 9 Paul's presentation of God as supreme benefactor and introduction of a three way relationship between giver, receiver, and God changes the strong expectation of reciprocity in the relationship between giver and receiver in patronage and benefaction.

In 1 and 2 Thessalonians the focus on manual work is different from the Epicureans, who avoided it. The call to benefaction is different from the Epicureans, the associations, and family life, where there is not the same call to do good outside the group. The call to all to benefaction is different from the expectations of who a benefactor is in patronage practice.

CONSISTENT DISTINCTIVES

When we look across the examples and comparators, we find a number of characteristic differences that are seen in four or more examples compared to their contemporary surroundings.

First, we see *patronage expectations subverted* in some way in all the examples apart from the one in John's gospel. In Acts 4 what is sold is brought to the feet of the disciples, thus preventing individuals acting as patrons. In Acts 11 it is not just the relatively affluent who give. In 1 Cor 11, Paul expects a socially diverse group to eat together as equals rather than to have different amounts of food and different quality food to eat. In 2 Cor 8 and 9 God is the ultimate benefactor and receiver of thanks. In 1 and 2 Thessalonians, Paul urges all Thessalonians to be involved in benefaction as opposed to expecting some of them to be clients.

Second, there is evidence of *greater diversity* in the early Christian groups compared to the comparator groups. With the γλωσσόκομον there are men and women in the group. Some have left whatever they have behind. Others seem more affluent and have retained their possessions and use them to contribute to the common purse. In Acts 11 the Antiochene church includes Jewish and Gentile believers. In 1 and 2 Corinthians the church includes those from different social backgrounds (Roman, Greek and Jewish; slave and free; richer and poorer).

Third, the NT examples present *a more flexible, fluid or less structured example of sharing* than the surrounding practices. This may be in part due to the fact that the early church examples are of communities at an early stage of formation. In John this can be seen in the different ways of contributing and participating as disciples of Jesus, including: leaving and following, contributing to the γλωσσόκομον, and hosting Jesus and his disciples. In Acts 2-6 individuals sell in response to need as opposed to at a particular point of entry into the community. Thus, there are those within the community who have given in this way, others who have yet to give in this way and still others who may not have the ability to give in this way. In Acts 11 each person gives according to their ability rather than a set amount. In 2 Cor 8 and 9 Paul exhorts the Corinthians to give according to what they have, so that they are not in need, yet praises the Macedonians for giving beyond their means.

Fourth, there is *an emphasis on the free choice of individuals to contribute or participate in sharing* in the examples in John, Acts 2-6, Acts 11, and 2 Cor 8-9, compared to the more defined expectations in some of the comparators. With the γλωσσόκομον this is seen in the choice of the women to contribute. In Acts 2-6 it is seen in Peter's question to Ananias and Sapphira where he is clear that the property and money was at their disposal. In Acts 11 each person makes a choice to give according to what they have. In 2 Cor 8 and 9 Paul emphasizes the voluntary nature of the giving. However, there is also the clear expectation in 1 and 2 Thessalonians that refusal to work and thus participate in contributing to the community, precludes an individual from participating in sharing food in the community.

Fifth, in a number of NT examples there is an emphasis on *each person being involved in the sharing and on participation in the sharing being a key part of the life of faith*. In Acts 11 sharing possessions is presented as being part of what it means to follow/be discipled to Jesus. In 1 Cor 11 each person is to be included and the way they eat together is to reflect their relationships with one another because of Jesus. In 2 Cor 8 and 9 Paul points to the example of Jesus' giving. In Thessalonians, Paul's exhortation to work underlines the importance of each person contributing and participating.

Sixth, in those NT examples where there is evidence of eating together, there is sometimes evidence *of a greater focus on eating together and on the eating together being more frequent*. It is likely that the disciples who traveled with Jesus ate together frequently. In Acts 2-6 the community is shown eating regular meals together in Acts 2:46 and then responding to issues around eating together in Acts 6. In Corinth and Thessalonica the communities are eating together more frequently than Voluntary Associations or clubs would have.

Seventh, there is also evidence of *stronger relational bonds between the early believers or a greater focus on relational bonds* compared to the comparator examples. This could in part be a result of the greater fluidity of the NT examples, which may necessitate stronger relational bonds in the absence of the more defined rules of some of the comparator examples, for example the Essenes/Qumran community. In John, Jesus' call to come and see and then his teaching on the relationship of the disciples with him and the Father point to the importance of relationships rather than the entry rules of Qumran. In Acts 2-6 the believers are of one heart and mind. In Acts 11 and 2 Cor 8 and 9 the giving shows relationship and commitment over a distance, even when some of those giving have not met those to whom they are giving. This focus on strong relationships can be seen in the use of sibling language in the letters to the Thessalonians.

MOTIVATION

The NT examples also exhibit some common motivations for sharing. These include God's grace, action and provision (Acts 2-6, 2 Cor 8-9, Thessalonians);[2] the relationship and unity between believers (Acts 2-6, Acts 11, 1 Cor 11, 2 Cor 8-9, Thessalonians);[3] and the example and actions

---

2. The role of the Holy Spirit (Acts 2:1-4; 4:31; see pp. 46-66); God's grace (Acts 4:33; 2 Cor 8:1-6; see pp. 50-56, 162-65); God's provision (2 Cor 9:8; see pp. 156-62); God as Father (1 Thess 1:3; 3:11, 13; 2 Thess 2:16); God has loved and chosen believers (1 Thess 1:4; 4:9; 2 Thess 2:13, 16-17).

3. Unity (Acts 2:44; 4:32; 1 Cor 11:18; see pp. 46-66); relationship between the churches (Acts 11:22, 25, 27; see pp. 79-84); body of Christ (1 Cor 12:12-31; see pp. 127-32); fellowship with God and other believers (2 Cor 9:12-15; see pp. 156-62); brothers/sisters (1 Cor 11:33; 2 Cor 8:1; 1 Thess 4:1, 13; 2 Thess 3:6, 13; see pp. 221-23).

of Jesus, particularly his death (Acts 2-6, 1 Cor 11, 2 Cor 8-9).[4] It is more difficult to compare these characteristics with the surrounding culture, as not all the comparator examples include specific motivation for the sharing which takes place. However, as we have already noted above, the NT examples do consistently show stronger relational bonds or a greater focus on relationships than the comparator examples. In addition, apart from some possible evidence in the Jewish comparators (e.g., Jewish almsgiving), we have not found evidence of God's provision and grace as motivation for sharing.

While there is some evidence of individuals being models for action (for example older siblings in the family life comparator), the example of Jesus and his death operates in a somewhat different way. It is not Jesus' death that the believers are to imitate directly, but rather the character of self-giving evidenced in it. Also believers are to live in the reality of the new relationships with God and one another that Jesus' death has established.

Therefore, we tentatively offer these three motivations for sharing as Christian distinctives: God's grace, action and provision; the relationship and unity between believers; and the example and actions of Jesus, particularly his death.

CONCLUSION

This study has examined six examples of sharing in NT texts and highlighted similarities across the examples. The NT examples show sharing which: is practical and responsive; is based in a sense of communal identity, unity or relationships between individuals or communities; is in groups with a mix of backgrounds, either of different cultural backgrounds and/or of different social classes; does not have only one way of an individual contributing to the sharing, but multiple ways; has a tension between the individual and the community in terms of responsibility or ownership of the sharing; involves responding to need; and includes eating together. It has also compared each example to the contemporary sharing practices and examined similarities and differences. It has then identified the similarities and differences across these comparisons and analyzed areas where the early church shows similarities to surrounding communities and/or may have been influenced by other communities, and also where there seems to be a pattern of particular distinctive characteristics in how the early church approached sharing possessions compared to the surrounding culture. In comparison with the

---

4. Response to the gospel (Acts 2:14-47; see pp. 46-50); Jesus' death (1 Cor 11:23-29; 2 Cor 8:9; see pp. 125-27, 148-54).

surrounding cultures, the NT examples show groups with greater social diversity; sharing where everyone is involved in contributing; sharing which is voluntary and yet with expectations; more flexible approaches to sharing; and sharing which is based on relationship with God and other believers. The NT examples also often undermine patronage expectations and present sharing as a key part of the life of faith.

FUTURE RESEARCH POSSIBILITIES

There are a number of possible future research opportunities that are highlighted by this study. First, the method of comparison with comparators could be used in other areas where the NT presents a diversity of examples of practice. Second, the example of sharing in 1 and 2 Thessalonians was compared with family life and we noted the limitations of doing this, given the range of possible family life practices to use for comparison and the limited evidence about the expected financial/sharing relationships between siblings. A possible area of further research would be to examine the evidence of such relationships in greater detail to provide a more suitable body of evidence for comparison. Third, across the examples we noted the ways that patronage is subverted and another area for possible research would be to compare a range of examples to patronage and benefaction practice alone.

Bibliography

All primary sources are from the Loeb Classical Library unless listed below:

Aasgaard, Reidar. *"My Beloved Brothers and Sisters!" Christian Siblingship in Paul*. JSNTSup. London: T. & T. Clark, 2004.
Adams, Edward. *The Earliest Christian Meeting Places: Almost Exclusively Houses?* LNTS. London: Bloomsbury, 2013.
Agrell, Göran. *Work, Toil and Sustenance*. Verbum: Häkan Ohlssons, 1976.
Alexander, Loveday. *Acts: The People's Commentary*. Oxford: BRF, 2006.
Ambrose. *Selected Works and Letters*. Vol. 10. NPNF. Oxford: James Parker, n.d.
Anderson, Digby, ed. *The Kindness that Kills*. London: SPCK, 1984.
Ascough, Richard S. *Paul's Macedonian Associations*. Tübingen: Mohr Siebeck, 2003.
———. "Redescribing the Thessalonian 'Mission' in the Light of Graeco-Roman Associations." *NTS* 60 (2014) 61–82.
———. "The Thessalonian Christian Community as a Professional Voluntary Association." *JBL* 119 (2000) 311–28.
Ascough, Richard S., Philip A. Harland, and John S. Kloppenborg, eds. *Associations in the Greco-Roman World: A Sourcebook*. Waco: Baylor University Press, 2012. Online: http://philipharland.com/greco-roman-associations/ for inscriptions.
Atkinson, Kenneth, and Jodi Magness. "Josephus's Essenes and the Qumran Community." *JBL* 129 (2010) 317–42.
Augustine. *Tractates on the Gospel of John 28–54*. Translated by John W. Rettig. The Fathers of the Church 88. Washington, DC: CUA Press, 1993.
———. *Tractates on the Gospel of John 55–111*. Translated by John W. Rettig. The Fathers of the Church Volume 90. Washington, DC: CUA Press, 1994.
Aune, David E. "In Search of a Profile of the 'Benefactor' (review of Frederick W. Danker, *Benefactor: Epigraphic Study of a Graeco-Roman and New Testament Semantic Field*)." *Int* 38 (1984) 421–5.
Bach, Alice, and Jennifer Glancy. "The Morning After in Corinth: Bread and Butter Notes, Part 1." *Biblical Interpretation* 11 (2003) 449–67.
Balch, David. "Rich Pompeiian Houses, Shops for Rent, and the Huge Apartment Building in Herculaneum as Typical Spaces for Pauline House Churches." *JSNT* 27 (2004) 27–46.
Barclay, John M. G. "Because He was Rich He became Poor." Unpublished paper.

———. "Conflict in Thessalonica." *CBQ* 55 (1993) 512-30.
———. "Manna and the Circulation of Grace: A Study of 2 Corinthians 8:1-15." In *The Word Leaps the Gap: Essays on Scripture and Theology in Honor of Richard B. Hays*, edited by J. Ross Wagner et al., 409-26. Grand Rapids: Eerdmans, 2008.
———. "Thessalonica and Corinth: Social Contrasts in Pauline Christianity." *JSNT* 47 (1992) 49-74.
Barnett, Paul. *The Second Epistle to the Corinthians*. NICNT. Grand Rapids: Eerdmans, 1997.
Barrett, C. K. *Acts*. ICC. Edinburgh: T. & T. Clark, 1994
———. *A Commentary on the First Epistle to the Corinthians*. London: Adam and Charles Black, 1968.
———. *A Commentary on the Second Epistle to the Corinthians*. London: Blacks, 1973.
———. *The Gospel According to St. John*. 2nd ed. London: SPCK, 1978.
———, ed. *The New Testament Background: Selected Documents*. London: SPCK, 1956.
Bassler, Jouette M. *God and Mammon: Asking for Money in the New Testament*. Nashville: Abingdon, 1991.
Bauckham, R. *Gospel Women: Studies of Named Women in the Gospels*. Grand Rapids: Eerdmans, 2002.
Bauernfeind, Otto. *Kommentar und Studien zur Apostelgeschichte*. Tübingen: Mohr Siebeck, 1980.
Baugh, S. M. "Marriage and Family in Ancient Greek Society." In *Marriage and Family in the Biblical World*, edited by Ken M. Campbell, 103-31. Downers Grove, IL: IVP Academic, 2003.
Baumgarten, Albert. "Who Cares and Why Does It Matter? Qumran and the Essenes, Once Again!" *DSD* 11 (2004) 174-90.
Beall, Todd. *Josephus' Description of the Essenes*. Cambridge: CUP, 1988.
Beasley-Murray, George R. *John*. Nashville: Thomas Nelson, 1999.
Becker, Joseph Peter. *Paul's Usage of Χάρις in 2 Corinthians 8-9: An Ontology of Grace*. Lewiston: Edwin Mellen, 2011.
Best, Ernest. *The First and Second Letter to the Thessalonians*. BNTC. London: Blacks, n.d.
———. *Second Corinthians*. Interpretation. Louisville: John Knox, 1987.
Betz, Hans Dieter. *2 Corinthians 8 and 9*. Hermeneia. Philadelphia: Fortress, 1985.
Blomberg, Craig L. *Neither Poverty nor Riches*. NSBT. Leicester: Apollos, 1999.
Blue, Bradley B. "The House Church at Corinth and the Lord's Supper: Famine, Food Supply, and the Present Distress." *CTR* 5 (1991) 221-39.
Bock, Darrell L. *Acts*. BECNT. Grand Rapids: Baker Academic, 2007.
Bornkamm, Günter. *Early Christian Experience*. London: SCM, 1969.
Braund, David. "Function and Dysfunction: Personal Patronage in Roman Imperialism." In *Patronage in Ancient Society*, edited by Andrew Wallace-Hadrill, 137-52. London: Routledge, 1989.
Bray, Gerald, ed. *1-2 Corinthians*. ACC NT. Downers Grove, IL: IVP, 1999.
Briones, David E. *Paul's Financial Policy: A Social-Theological Approach*. LNTS. London: T. & T. Clark, 2013.
Broshi, Magen. "Essenes at Qumran? A Rejoinder to Albert Baumgarten." *Dead Sea Discoveries* 14 (2007) 25-33.
Brown, Colin, ed. *The New International Dictionary of New Testament Theology*. 3 vols. Exeter: Paternoster, 1975.

Brown, Raymond. *The Gospel according to John I-XII*. AB, Garden City: Doubleday, 1966.

———. *The Gospel according to John XIII-XXI*. AB. London: Geoffrey Chapman, 1966.

Browne, Gerald M. *Documentary Papyri from the Michigan Collection*. American Studies in Papyrology. Toronto: Hakkert, 1970.

Bruce, F. F. *The Book of Acts*. Grand Rapids: Eerdmans, 1988.

———. *1 and 2 Corinthians*. NCB. London: Oliphants, 1971.

———. *1 and 2 Thessalonians*. WBC. Waco: Word, 1982.

Bulletin de Correspondance Hellénique. Vol. 25. Paris: Librairie Fontemoing, 1901.

Burke, Trevor J. *Adopted into God's Family. Exploring a Pauline Metaphor*. NSBT. Nottingham: Apollos, 2006.

———. "Paul's New Family in Thessalonica." *NovT* 54 (2012) 269–87.

Burridge, Richard A. *Imitating Jesus*. Grand Rapids: Eerdmans, 2007.

Cagnat, R., ed. *Inscriptiones Graecae ad res Romanas Pertinentes*. Tomus Tertius. Paris: Leroux, 1906.

Calvin, John. *Acts*. The Crossway Classic Commentaries, Wheaton: Crossway, 1995.

———. *Calvin's Commentaries St. John 11-21 and First John*. Edinburgh: Oliver and Boyd, 1961.

———. *The Second Epistle of Paul the Apostle to the Corinthians and the Epistles to Timothy, Titus and Philemon*. Calvin's Commentaries. Edinburgh: Oliver and Boyd, 1964.

Capper, Brian J. "Holy Community of Life and Property amongst the Poor: A Response to Steve Walton." *EQ* 80.2 (2008) 113–27.

———. "Jesus, Virtuoso Religion, and the Community of Goods." In *Engaging Economics*, edited by Bruce W. Longenecker and Kelly D. Liebengood, 60–80. Grand Rapids: Eerdmans, 2009.

———. "The Palestinian Cultural Context of the Earliest Christian Community of Goods." In *The Book of Acts in its Palestinian Setting*, edited by Richard Bauckham, 323–56. The Book of Acts in its First Century Setting. Grand Rapids: Eerdmans, 1995.

———. "Reciprocity and the Ethic of Acts." Online: http://www.canterbury.ac.uk/arts-humanities/theology-and-religious-studies/docs/bjc2/acts.doc.

———. "Review Article: Two Types of Discipleship in Early Christianity." *JTS* 52 (2001) 105–23.

———. "'With the Oldest Monks . . .' Light from Essene History on the Career of the Beloved Disciple." *JTS* 49 (1998) 1–55.

Carson, D. A. *The Gospel According to John*. Leicester: IVP, 1991.

Cary, M., et al., eds. *The Oxford Classical Dictionary*. Oxford: Claredon, 1949.

Cassidy, Richard J. *Society and Politics in the Acts of the Apostles*. Maryknoll, NY: Orbis, 1987.

Chapman, David W. "Marriage and Family in Second Temple Judaism." In *Marriage and Family in the Biblical World*, edited by Ken M. Campbell, 183–239. Downers Grove, IL: IVP Academic, 2003.

Charlesworth, James H. "The Dead Sea Scrolls: Their Discovery and Challenge to Biblical Studies." In *Scripture and Scrolls*, edited by James H. Charlesworth, 1–24. Waco: Baylor University Press, 2006.

Cheung, Alex T. *Idol Food in Corinth: Jewish Background and Pauline Legacy*. Sheffield: Sheffield Academic Press, 1999.

Chow, John K. *Patronage and Power: A Study of Social Networks in Corinth*. Sheffield: Sheffield Academic Press, 1992.
———. "Patronage in Roman Corinth." In *Paul and Empire*, edited by Richard A. Horsley, 104–25. Harrisburg: Trinity, 1997.
Ciampa, Roy E., and Brian S. Rosner. *The First Letter to the Corinthians*. Nottingham: Apollos, 2010.
Clark, Gillian. *Iamblichus: On the Pythagorean Life*. Liverpool: Liverpool University Press, 1989.
Clarke, Andrew D. *Secular and Christian Leadership in Corinth: A Socio-Historical and Exegetical Study of 1 Corinthians 1–6*. Leiden: Brill, 1993.
Cloud, Duncan. "The Client-Patron Relationship: Emblem and Reality in Juvenal's First Book." In *Patronage in Ancient Society*, edited by Andrew Wallace-Hadrill, 205–18. London: Routledge, 1989.
Conzelmann, Hans. *1 Corinthians*. Philadelphia: Fortress, 1975.
———. *Acts of the Apostles*. Hermeneia. Philadelphia: Fortress, 1987.
Coutsoumpos, Panayotis. *Paul and the Lord's Supper: A Socio-Historical Investigation*. New York: Peter Lang, 2005.
Cross, Frank Moore. "The Early History of the Qumran Community." In *New Directions in Biblical Archeology*, edited by David Noel Freedman and Jonas C. Greenfield, 63–79. Garden City, NY: Doubleday, 1969.
Crossan, John Dominic. *The Historical Jesus*. Edinburgh: T. & T. Clark, 1991.
Crossan, John Dominic, and Jonathan L. Reed. *In Search of Paul: How Jesus's Apostle Opposed Rome's Empire with God's Kingdom*. London: SPCK, 2005.
d'Arms, John. "The Roman *Convivium* and the Idea of Equality." In *Sympotica: A Symposium on the Symposion*, edited by Oswyn Murray, 308–19. Oxford: Claredon, 1990.
Danker, Frederick W. *Benefactor: Epigraphic Study of a Graeco-Roman and New Testament Semantic Field*. St. Louis: Clayton, 1982.
———, ed. *A Greek-English Lexicon of the New Testament and Other Early Christian Literature*. 3rd ed. Chicago: University of Chicago Press, 2000.
Daube, David. *The New Testament and Rabbinic Judaism*. London: Athlone, 1956.
deSilva, David A. *Honor, Patronage, Kinship and Purity: Unlocking New Testament Culture*. Downers Grove, IL: IVP, 2000.
———. "'Worthy of His Kingdom': Honor Discourse and Social Engineering in 1 Thessalonians." *JSNT* 64 (1996) 49–79.
Deutsche Akademie der Wissenschaft, and C. Edson. *Inscriptiones Graecae Volumen 10: Epiri, Macedoniae, Thraciae, Scythiae*. Berolini: de Gruyter, 1972.
Dibelius, Martin. *Studies in the Acts of the Apostles*. London: SCM, 1956.
Dittenberger, William, ed. *Inscriptiones Megaridis et Boeotiae*, Berolini apud Georgium Reimerum. 1892.
———. *Orientis Graeci. Inscriptiones Selectae*. Hildesheim: Georg Olms, 1960.
———. *Sylloge Inscriptionum Graecarum, Volumen Tertium*. Leipzig: Hirzel, 1920.
Donfried, Karl Paul. "The Imperial Cults of Thessalonica and Political Conflict in 1 Thessalonians." In *Paul and Empire: Religion and Power in Roman Imperial Society*, edited by Richard A. Horsley, 215–23. Valley Forge, PA: Trinity International, 1997.
———. *Paul, Thessalonica and Early Christianity*. London: T. & T. Clark, 2002.
Downing, F. Gerald. *Christ and the Cynics*. Sheffield: Sheffield Academic Press, 1988.

———. *Cynics and Christian Origins*. Edinburgh: T. & T. Clark, 1992.
———. *Cynics, Paul and the Pauline Churches*. London: Routledge, 1998.
Downs, David J. *The Offering of the Gentiles*. WUNT. Tübingen: Mohr Siebeck, 2008.
———. "Paul's Collection and the Book of Acts Revisited." *NTS* 52 (2006) 50–70.
Dunn, James D. G. *The Acts of the Apostles*. Epworth Commentaries. Peterborough: Epworth, 1996.
———. *Jesus Remembered*. Christianity in the Making 1. Grand Rapids: Eerdmans, 2003.
———. *Romans*. 2 vols. WBC. Dallas: Word, 1988.
Dupont, Jacques. *Études sur les Actes des Apôtres*. Paris: Les Éditions du Cerf, 1967.
———. *The Salvation of the Gentiles*. New York: Paulist, 1979.
Edwards, Ruth. *Discovering John*. London: SPCK, 2003.
Ehrhardt, Arnold. *The Acts of the Apostles*. Manchester: Manchester University Press, 1969.
Epstein, I., ed. *The Babylonian Talmud*. 34 vols. London: Socino, 1935–48.
Euripides. *The Bacchae and Other Plays*. Translated by Philip Vellacott. London: Penguin, 1972.
Fee, Gordon D. *The First Epistle to the Corinthians*. NICNT. Grand Rapids: Eerdmans, 1987.
———. *The First and Second Letters to the Thessalonians*. Grand Rapids: Eerdmans, 2009.
Fiensy, D. A. "The Composition of the Jerusalem Church." In *The Book of Acts in its Palestinian Setting*, edited by Richard Bauckham, 213–36. Grand Rapids: Eerdmans, 1995.
Finger, Reta Halteman. *Of Widows and Meals*. Grand Rapids: Eerdmans, 2007.
Fitzmyer, Joseph A. *The Acts of the Apostles*. New York: Doubleday, 1998.
———. *Romans: a New Translation with Introduction and Commentary*. London: Geoffrey Chapman, 1993.
Foster, Paul. "Who Wrote 2 Thessalonians? A Fresh Look at an Old Problem." *JSNT* 35 (2012) 150–75.
Fotopoulos, John. "Greco-Roman Dining, the Lord's Supper, and Communion in the Body of Christ." In *Paul et l'Unité des Chrétiens*, edited by Jacques Schlosser, 141–60. Leuven: Peeters, 2010.
Frame, James Everett. *The Epistles of St. Paul to the Thessalonians*. ICC. Edinburgh: T. & T. Clark, 1912.
Freedman, D., ed. *The Anchor Bible Dictionary*. 6 vols. New York: Doubleday, 1992.
Freedman, H. *Midrash Rabbah*. London: Soncino, 1939.
Frier, Bruce W. *Landlords and Tenants in Imperial Rome*. Princeton: Princeton University Press, 1980.
Furnish, Victor Paul. *2 Corinthians*. AB. Garden City, NY: Doubleday, 1984.
Gapp, Kenneth Sperber. "The Universal Famine under Claudius." *HTR* 28 (1935) 258–65.
Garland, David E. *1 Corinthians*. BECNT. Grand Rapids: Baker Academic, 2003.
Garnsey, Peter. *Famine and Food Supply in the Greco-Roman World: Responses to Risk and Crisis*. Cambridge: CUP, 1988.
Garnsey, Peter, and Richard Saller. *The Roman Empire: Economy, Society and Culture*. London: Duckworth, 1987.
Gaventa, Beverly Roberts. *Acts*. ANTC. Nashville: Abingdon, 2003.

———. *First and Second Thessalonians*. Interpretation. Louisville: John Knox, 1998.
Gehring, Roger W. *House Church and Mission: The Importance of Household Structures in Early Christianity*. Peabody, MA: Hendrickson, 2004.
Georgi, Dieter. *Remembering the Poor: The History of Paul's Collection for Jerusalem*. Nashville: Abingdon, 1992.
Gonzalez, Justo L. *Faith and Wealth: A History of Early Christian Ideas on the Origin, Significance and Use of Money*. San Francisco: Harper and Row, 1990.
Goodman, Martin D., and Geza Vermes, eds. *The Essenes According to the Classical Sources*. Sheffield: JSOT, 1989.
Grant, Robert M. *Early Christianity and Society*. London: Collins, 1978.
Gregson, Fiona J. R. "Everything in Common? The Theology and Practice of the Sharing of Possessions in Community in the New Testament with Particular Reference to Jesus and his Disciples, the Earliest Christians, and Paul." PhD diss., Middlesex University, 2014.
Griffin, Miriam. "*De Beneficiis* and Roman Society." *JRS* 93 (2003) 92–113.
Griffith, Gary W. "Abounding in Generosity: A Study of Charis in 2 Corinthians 8–9." PhD diss., Durham University, 2005.
Grosheide, F. W. *Commentary on the First Epistle to the Corinthians*. Grand Rapids: Eerdmans, 1953.
Guijarro, S. "The Family in First-Century Galilee." In *Constructing Early Christian Families*, edited by Halvor Moxnes, 42–65. London: Routledge, 1997.
Günter, W. "Brother." In *NIDNTT* 1:254–8.
Haenchen, Ernst. *The Acts of the Apostles*. Oxford: Basil Blackwell, 1971.
———. *John*. 2 vols. Philadelphia: Fortress, 1984.
Han, Paul. "Swimming in the Sea of Scripture: Paul's Use of the Old Testament in 2 Corinthians 4:7—13:13." PhD diss., Middlesex University, 2011.
Hands, Arthur Robinson. *Charities and Social Aid in Greece and Rome*. London: Thames and Hudson, 1968.
Hanson, R. P. C. *The Second Epistle to the Corinthians*. Torch Bible Commentaries. London: SCM, 1954.
Hardin, Justin K. "Decrees and Drachmas at Thessalonica: An Illegal Assembly in Jason's House (Acts 17.1–10a)." *NTS* 52 (2006) 29–49.
Hargreaves, John. *A Guide to Acts*. London: SPCK, 1990.
Harland, Philip A. *Dynamics of Identity in the World of the Early Christians: Associations, Judeans, and Cultural Minorities*. London: T. & T. Clark, 2009.
Harries, Richard. *Is There a Gospel for the Rich?* London: Mowbray, 1992.
Harrill, J. Albert. "Divine Judgment against Ananias and Sapphira (Acts 5:1–11): A Stock Scene of Perjury and Death." *JBL* 130 (2011) 351–69.
Harris, Murray J. *The Second Epistle to the Cornthians*. NIGTC. Grand Rapids: Eerdmans, 2005.
Harrison, James R. "The Brothers as the 'Glory of Christ' (2 Cor 8:23)." *NovT* 52 (2010) 156–88.
———. "Paul and the Imperial Gospel at Thessaloniki." *JSNT* 25 (2002) 71–96.
Hays, Richard B. *The Moral Vision of the New Testament*. London: Continuum, 1997.
Hellerman, Joseph H. *The Ancient Church as Family*. Minneapolis: Fortress, 2001.
Hemer, Colin. *The Book of Acts in the Setting of Hellenistic History*. Tübingen: Mohr Siebeck, 1989.
Hengel, Martin. *Acts and the History of Earliest Christianity*. London: SCM, 1979.

―――. *The Charismatic Leader and His Followers*. Edinburgh: T. & T. Clark, 1981.
―――. *Property and Riches in the Early Church*. London: SCM, 1974.
Héring, Jean. *The Second Epistle of Saint Paul to the Corinthians*. London: Epworth, 1967.
Hock, Ronald F. "Cynics." In *ABD* 1:1221–6.
―――. *The Social Context of Paul's Ministry: Tentmaking and Apostleship*. Philadelphia: Fortress, 2007.
Holmberg, Bengt. "Methods of Historical Reconstruction." In *Christianity at Corinth: The Quest for the Pauline Church*, edited by Edward Adams and David G. Horrell, 255–71. London: Westminster John Knox, 2004.
Hoppe, Leslie J. *There Shall Be No Poor among You*. Nashville: Abingdon, 2004.
Horrell, David G. "Domestic Space and Christian Meetings at Corinth: Imagining New Contexts and the Buildings East of the Theatre." *NTS* 50 (2004) 349–69.
―――. "From ἀδελφοί to οἶκος θεοῦ: Social Transformation in Pauline Christianity." *JBL* 120 (2001) 293–311.
―――. *The Social Ethos of the Corinthian Correspondence*. Edinburgh: T. & T. Clark, 1996.
―――. *Solidarity and Difference. A Contemporary Reading of Paul's Ethics*. London: T. & T. Clark, 2005.
Horsley, Richard A., ed. *Paul and Empire: Religion and Power in Roman Imperial Society*. Harrisburg: Trinity International, 1997.
Howard-Brook, Wes. *Becoming Children of God*. Maryknoll, NY: Orbis, 1994.
Hughes, Philip E. *Paul's Second Epistle to the Corinthians*. London: Marshall, Morgan & Scott, 1962.
Hume, Douglas A. *The Early Christian Community*. Tübingen: Mohr Siebeck, 2011.
Hurd, John Coolidge. *The Origins of 1 Corinthians*. London: SPCK, 1965.
Inscriptiones Graecae. 14 vols. Berolini: de Gruyter, 1828.
IG II2 1343. Online: http://philipharland.com/greco-roman-associations/honors-by-the-soteriasts-for-their-founder-37-35-bce/.
IG II2 1368. Online: http:philipharland.com/Greco-roman-associations/regulations-of-a bacchic-association-the-iobacchoi/.
IG V, 1 209. Online: http://philipharland.com/greco-roman-associations/29-membership-list-of-an-association-of-banqueters/.
IG X, 2.1 259. Online: http://philipharland.com/greco-roman-associations/50-bequest-to-an-association-of-initiates-of-zeus-dionysos-gongylos/.
IG XIV 902a. Online: http://epigraphy.packhum.org/inscriptions/main?url=bib.
Inscriptiones Graecae ad res Romanas Pertinentes. 4 vols. Paris: E. Leroux, 1911–1927.
IGRP I 1151. Online: http://philipharland.com/greco-roman-associations/meeting-place-of-an-association-of-stonemasons/.
Instone-Brewer, David. *Feasts and Sabbaths: Passover and Atonement*. TRENT. Grand Rapids: Eerdmans, 2011.
―――. *Prayer and Agriculture*. TRENT. Grand Rapids: Eerdmans, 2004.
―――. "Review Article: The Use of Rabbinic Sources in Gospel Studies." *TynBul* 50.2 (1999) 281–98.
Jamir, Lanu. "Exclusion and Judgment in Fellowship Meals." PhD diss., Middlesex University, 2012.
Jeremias, Joachim. "Die Salbungsgeschichte Mc 14 3–9." *ZNW* 35 (1936) 75–82.
―――. *The Eucharistic Words of Jesus*. London: SCM, 1966.

———. *The Eucharistic Words of Jesus*. Oxford: Basil Blackwell, 1955.
———. *Jerusalem in the Time of Jesus*. London: SCM, 1969.
———. "Sabbathjahr und neutestamentliche Chronologie." *ZNW* 27 (1928) 98–103.
Jervell, Jacob. *Die Apostelgeschichte*. Göttingen: Vandenhoeck & Ruprecht, 1998.
Jewett, Robert. *Romans*. Hermeneia. Minneapolis: Fortress, 2007.
———. "Tenement Churches and Communal Meals in the Early Church: the Implications of a Form-Critical Analysis of 2 Thessalonians 3.10." *BR* 38 (1993) 23–43.
———. *The Thessalonian Correspondence: Pauline Rhetoric and Millenarian Piety*. Philadelphia: Fortress, 1986.
Johnson, Alan F. *1 Corinthians*. Leicester: IVP, 2004.
Johnson, Luke Timothy. *The Acts of the Apostles*. Sacra Pagina. Collegeville, MN: Liturgical, 1995.
———. *The Gospel of Luke*. Sacra Pagina. Collegeville, MN: Liturgical, 1991.
———. *The Literary Function of Possessions in Luke-Acts*. SBLDS. Missoula: Scholars, 1977.
———. *Prophetic Jesus, Prophetic Church. The Challenge of Luke-Acts to Contemporary Christians*. Grand Rapids: Eerdmans, 2011.
———. *Sharing Possessions*. London: SCM, 1981.
Johnson, Sherman E. "The Dead Sea Manual of Discipline and the Jerusalem Church of Acts." In *The Scrolls and the New Testament*, edited by Krister Stendahl, 129–42. London: SCM, 1958.
Jones, Ivor H. *The Epistles to the Thessalonians*. Epworth Commentaries, Peterborough: Epworth, 2005.
"Joseph and Aseneth." Taken from H. F. D. Sparks, ed. *The Apocryphal Old Testament*. Translated by David Cook. Oxford: Oxford University Press, 1984. Online: http://www.markgoodacre.org/aseneth/translat.htm.
Joubert, Stephan. *Paul as Benefactor*. WUNT. Tübingen: Mohr Siebeck, 2000.
Käsemann, Ernst. "Guests of the Crucified." *WW* 33 (2013) 62–73.
Keener, Craig S. *1–2 Corinthians*. NCBC. Cambridge: CUP, 2005.
———. *The Gospel of John*. 2 vols. Peabody: Hendrickson, 2003.
Keith, Chris. "'In My Own Hand': Grapho-Literacy and the Apostle Paul." *Biblica* 89 (2008) 39–58.
Kent, John Harvey. *Corinth: The Inscriptions, 1926–1950. Results of Excavations conducted by the American School of Classical Studies at Athens*, vol. 8, part 3. Princeton, NJ: The American School of Classical Studies at Athens, 1966.
Kim, Kyoung-Jin. *Stewardship and Almsgiving in Luke's Theology*. Sheffield: Sheffield Academic Press, 1998.
Kirchner, Johannes, ed. *Inscriptiones Atticae Euclidis anno Posteriores*, Berolini apud Georgium Reimerum. 1916.
Kittel, Gerhard, ed. *Theological Dictionary of the New Testament*. 10 vols. Grand Rapids: Eerdmans, 1985.
Klauck, Hans-Josef. "Gütergemeinschaft in der Klassischen Antike, in Qumran und im Neuen Testament." *Revue de Qumran* 11 (1982) 47–79.
———. *Herrenmahl und hellenistischer Kult: eine religionsgeschichtliche Untersuchung zum ersten Korintherbrief*. Münster: Aschendorff, 1982.

Koester, Helmut. "Imperial Ideology and Paul's Eschatology in 1 Thessalonians." In *Paul and Empire: Religion and Power in Roman Imperial Society*, edited by Richard A. Horsley, 158–66. Harrisburg: Trinity International, 1997.
Köstenberger, Andreas. "Marriage and Family in the New Testament." In *Marriage and Family in the Biblical World*, edited by Ken M. Campbell, 240–84. Downers Grove, IL: IVP Academic, 2003.
Kreitzer, Larry. *2 Corinthians*. Sheffield: Sheffield Academic Press, 1996.
Krodel, Gerhard A. *Acts*. Augsburg Commentary. Minneapolis: Augsburg, 1986.
Lake, Kirsopp, and Henry J. Cadbury. *The Acts of the Apostles*. London: Macmillan, 1933.
Lambrecht, Jan. *Second Corinthians*. Sacra Pagina. Collegeville, MN: Liturgical, 1999.
Lampe, Peter. "The Eucharistic Dinner Party: Exegesis of a Cultural Context (1 Cor. 11:17–34)." *Affirmation* 4 (1991) 1–16.
Le Bas, Philippe, and William Henry Waddington. *Inscriptions Grecques et Latines recueillies en Asie Mineure*. Hildesheim: Georg Olms Verlag, 1972.
Lewis, Naphtali, and Meyer Reinhold, eds. *Roman Civilization Selected Readings*. Vol. 2, *The Empire*. New York: Columbia University Press, 1990.
———. *Roman Civilization*. Vol. 1, *The Republic*. New York: Columbia University Press, 1951.
Lillie, William. *Studies in New Testament Ethics*. Edinburgh: Oliver and Boyd, 1961.
Lim, Kar Yong. "Generosity from Pauline Perspective: Insights from Paul's Letter to the Corinthians." *ERT* 37 (2013) 20–33.
Lincoln, Andrew T. *The Gospel According to St. John*. BNTC. London: Continuum, 2005.
Longenecker, Bruce W. *Remembering the Poor: Paul, Poverty and the Greco-Roman World*. Grand Rapids: Eerdmans, 2010.
Longenecker, Richard N. *Galatians*. WBC. Dallas: Word, 1990.
Maddox, Robert. *The Purpose of Luke-Acts*. Edinburgh: T. & T. Clark, 1982.
Malherbe, Abraham J. *The Cynic Epistles: A Study Edition*. Missoula: Scholars, 1977.
———. "Ethics in Their Context: The Thessalonians and Their Neighbors." *ResQ* 54 (2012) 201–18.
———. *The Letters to the Thessalonians*. Anchor Bible. New York: Doubleday, 2000.
———. *Paul and the Thessalonians: The Philosophic Tradition of Pastoral Care*. Philadelphia: Fortress, 1987.
———. *Social Aspects of Early Christianity*. Baton Rouge: Louisiana State University Press, 1977.
Malina, Bruce J., and John J. Pilch. *Social-Science Commentary on the Book of Acts*. Minneapolis: Fortress, 2008.
Manson, T. W. *The Teaching of Jesus*. Cambridge: CUP, 1931.
Marshall, I. Howard. *1 and 2 Thessalonians*. NCB. Grand Rapids: Eerdmans, 1983.
———. *Acts*. TNTC. Leicester: IVP, 1980.
———. *The Gospel of Luke*. NIGTC. Grand Rapids: Eerdmans, 1978.
———. *Last Supper and Lord's Supper*. Exeter: Paternoster, 1980.
Martin, Ralph P. *2 Corinthians*. WBC. Waco: Word, 1986.
Matera, Frank J. *II Corinthians: A Commentary*. NTL. Louisville: Westminster John Knox, 2003.
McCant, Jerry W. *2 Corinthians*. NBC. Sheffield: Sheffield Academic Press, 1999.
McRae, Rachel M. "Eating with Honor: The Corinthian Lord's Supper in Light of Voluntary Association Meal Practices." *JBL* 130 (2011) 165–81.

Meeks, Wayne A. *The First Urban Christians*. 2nd ed. New Haven: Yale University Press, 2003.
———. *The Moral World of the First Christians*. Philadelphia: Westminister, 1986.
Meggitt, Justin J. "Meat Consumption and Social Conflict in Corinth." *JTS* 45 (1994) 137–41.
———. *Paul, Poverty and Survival*. SNTW. Edinburgh: T. & T. Clark, 1998.
———. "Sources: Use, Abuse, Neglect. The Importance of Ancient Popular Culture." In *Christianity at Corinth: The Quest for the Pauline Church*, edited by Edward Adams and David G. Horrell, 241–54. London: Westminster John Knox, 2004.
Meier, John P. *A Marginal Jew*. Vol. 3, *Rethinking the Historical Jesus*. New York: Doubleday, 2001.
Mendel, Gustave. *Fouilles de Tégée: rapport sommaire sur la campagne de 1900–1901*. Bulletin de correspondance hellénique, 1901.
Menken, Maarten J. J. *2 Thessalonians*. New Testament Readings. London: Routledge, 1994.
Metzger, Bruce M. *A Textual Commentary on the Greek New Testament*. 2nd ed. Stuttgart: Deutsche Bibelgesellschaft, 1994.
Míguez, Néstor O. *The Practice of Hope. Ideology and Intention in 1 Thessalonians*. Minneapolis: Fortress, 2012.
Milligan, G. *St. Paul's Epistles to the Thessalonians*. London: MacMillan, 1908.
Miranda, Jose P. *Communism in the Bible*. London: SCM, 1982.
Mitchell, Alan C. "The Social Function of Friendship in Acts 2:44–47 and 4:32–37." *JBL* 111 (1992) 255–72.
Mitchell, Margaret M. "Concerning Περὶ δέ in 1 Corinthians." *NovT* 31 (1989) 229–56.
———. *Paul and the Rhetoric of Reconciliation*. Tübingen: Mohr, 1991.
Mitchell, Nathan D. "The Amen Corner: Paul's Eucharistic Theology." *Worship* 83 (2009) 250–62.
Moore, Arthur L. *1 and 2 Thessalonians*. NCB. London: Nelson, 1969.
Moore, George Foot. *Judaism in the First Centuries of the Christian Era: The Age of the Tannaim*. 3 vols. Cambridge: Harvard University Press, 1944.
Moreland, Milton. "The Jerusalem Community in Acts: Mythmaking and the Sociorhetorical Functions of a Lukan Setting." In *Contextualizing Acts*, edited by Todd Penner and Caroline Van der Stichele, 285–310. Atlanta: SBL, 2003.
Morris, Leon. *1 and 2 Thessalonians*. TNTC. Leicester: IVP, 1984.
———. *The Epistle to the Romans*. Grand Rapids: Eerdmans, 1988.
———. *The First and Second Epistles to the Thessalonians*. NICNT. Grand Rapids: Eerdmans, 1984.
Moulton, J. H., and G. Milligan. *Vocabulary of the Greek New Testament*. London: Hodder and Stoughton, 1930.
Moulton, James, et al. *A Grammar of New Testament Greek : Based on W. F. Moulton's Ed. of G. B. Winer's Grammar*. 3rd ed. Edinburgh: T. & T. Clark, 1930–63.
Munck, Johannes. *The Acts of the Apostles*. AB. Garden City, NY: Doubleday, 1967.
Murphy, Catherine. *Wealth in the Dead Sea Scrolls and in the Qumran Community*. Leiden: Brill, 2002.
Murphy-O'Connor, Jerome. *St. Paul's Corinth: Texts and Archaeology*. Good News Studies. Wilmington: Michael Glazier, 1983.
———. *St. Paul's Corinth: Texts and Archaelogy*. 3rd ed. Collegeville: Liturgical, 2002.
———. *The Theology of the Second Letter to the Corinthians*. Cambridge: CUP, 1991.

Neil, William. *Thessalonians*. MNTC. London: Hodder and Stoughton, 1950.
Nestle, E. et al. *Novum Testamentum Graece, Nestle-Aland*. 27th rev. ed. Stuttgart: Deutsche Bibelgesellschaft, 2001.
Neusner, J., *The Mishnah: A New Translation*. New Haven: Yale University Press, 1988.
Newman, Barclay M., and Eugene A. Nida. *A Handbook on the Acts of the Apostles*. UBS Handbook Series. New York: UBS, 1972.
Newton, Derek. *Deity and Diet: The Dilemma of Sacrificial Food at Corinth*. JSNTSSup. Sheffield: Sheffield Academic Press, 1998.
Nickle, Keith F. *The Collection: A Study in Paul's Strategy*. SBT. London: SCM, 1966.
O'Mahony, Kieran J. *Pauline Persuasion: A Sounding in 2 Corinthians 8–9*. JSNTSup. Sheffield: Sheffield Academic Press, 2000.
Oakes, Peter. *Philippians from People to Letter*. SNTS Monograph Series. Cambridge: CUP, 2001.
———. "Review of *Paul's Macedonian Associations: The Social Context of Philippians and 1 Thessalonians*." *JSNT* 28 (2006) 376–8.
Oddie, W. "Christian Socialism: An Old Heresy?" In *The Kindness that Kills*, edited by Digby Anderson, 123–33. London: SPCK, 1984.
Ogereau, Julien M. "The Jerusalem Collection as Κοινωνία: Paul's Global Politics of Socio-Economic Equality and Solidarity." *NTS* 58 (2012) 360–78.
Orosius, Paulus. *Seven Books of History against the Pagans: The Apology of Paulus Orosius*. Online: http://hdl.handle.net/2027/heb.06032.0001.001.
Osterley, W. O. E., trans. *The Mishnah*. London: SPCK, 1919.
The Oxyrhychus Papyri. 79 vols. London: Egypt Exploration Fund, 1898–.
P. Lond. VII 2193. Online: http://philipharland.com/greco-roman-associations/295-regulations-of-an-association-of-zeus-hypsistos/.
Paddison, Angus. *Theological Hermeneutics and 1 Thessalonians*. SNTS. Cambridge: CUP, 2005.
Panikulam, George. *Koinōnia in the New Testament: A Dynamic Expression of Christian Life*. Rome: Biblical Institute Press, 1979.
Pao, David W. "Waiters or Preachers: Acts 6:1–7 and the Lukan Table Fellowship Motif." *JBL* 130 (2011) 127–44.
Pervo, Richard I. *Acts*. Hermeneia. Minneapolis: Fortress, 2009.
———. "PANTA KOINA: The Feeding Stories in the Light of Economic Data and Social Practice." In *Religious Propaganda and Missionary Competition in the New Testament World: Essays Honoring Dieter Georgi*, edited by L. Bormann et al., NovTSup 74, 164–94. Leiden: Brill, 1994.
Peterman, G. W. *Paul's Gift from Philippi: Conventions of Gift Exchange and Christian Giving*. SNTS. Cambridge: CUP, 1997.
Peterson, David. *The Acts of the Apostles*. Grand Rapids: Eerdmans, 2009.
Pillar, Edward. *Resurrection as Anti-Imperial Gospel: 1 Thessalonians 1:9b–10 in Context*. Minneapolis: Fortress, 2013.
Plummer, Alfred. *A Critical and Exegetical Commentary on the Second Epistle of St. Paul to the Corinthians*. ICC. Edinburgh: T. & T. Clark, 1915.
Porphyry. *Life of Pythagoras*. Translated by Kenneth Sylvan Gurthrie, 1920. Online: http://www.tertullian.org/fathers/porphyry_life_ofpythagoras_02_text.htm.
Rabens, Volker. *The Holy Spirit and Ethics in Paul: Transformation and Empowering for Religious-Ethical Life*. WUNT. Tübingen: Mohr Siebeck, 2010.

Rahlfs, Alfred, ed. *Septuaginta*. 2 vols. Stuttgart: Deutsche Bibelgesellschaft, 1982. Online: http://ccat.sas.upenn.edu/nets/).

Ramelli, Ilaria L. E. "Spiritual Weakness, Illness, and Death in 1 Corinthians 11:30." *JBL* 130 (2011) 145–63.

Richards, Earl J. *First and Second Thessalonians*. Sacra Pagina. Collegeville, MN: Liturgical, 2007.

Riesner, Rainer. "Jesus, the Primitive Community, and the Essene Quarter of Jerusalem." In *Jesus and the Dead Sea Scrolls*, edited by James H. Charlesworth, 198–234. New York: Doubleday, 1992.

Rigaux, B. *Saint Paul: Les Épitres aux Thessaloniciens*. Paris: Lecoffre, 1956.

Robinson, Anthony B., and Robert W. Wall. *Called to Be Church*. Grand Rapids: Eerdmans, 2006.

Rostovtzeff, M. *The Social and Economic History of the Hellenistic World*. Oxford: Claredon, 1941.

Rowland, R. J. "The 'Very Poor' and the Grain Dole at Rome and Oxyrhynchus." *ZPE* 21 (1976) 69–72.

Rulmu, Callia. "Between Ambition and Quietism: The Socio-Political Background of 1 Thessalonians 4.9–12." *Biblica* 91 (2010) 393–417.

Russell, Ronald. "The Idle in 2 Thess 3.6–12: Eschatological or a Social Problem?" *NTS* 34 (1988) 105–19.

Saller, Richard P. "Patronage and Friendship in Early Imperial Rome: Drawing the Distinction." In *Patronage in Ancient Society*, edited by Andrew Wallace-Hadrill, 49–62. London: Routledge, 1989.

———. *Personal Patronage under the Early Empire*. Cambridge: CUP, 1982.

Sanday, William, and Arthur C. Headlam. *A Critical and Exegetical Commentary on the Epistle to the Romans*. ICC, Edinburgh: T. & T. Clark, 1902.

Sanders, E. P. *The Historical Figure of Jesus*. London: Penguin, 1993.

———. *Judaism: Practice and Belief 63 BCE–66 CE*. London: SCM, 1992.

Saxby, Trevor J. *Pilgrims of a Common Life: Christian Community of Goods through the Centuries*. Scottdale: Herald, 1987.

Schiffman, Lawrence H. *Reclaiming the Dead Sea Scrolls*. Philedelphia: The Jewish Publication Society, 1994.

Schmithals, Walter. *Gnosticism in Corinth*. Nashville: Abingdon, 1971.

———. *Paul and the Gnostics*. Nashville: Abingdon, 1972.

Schnabel, Eckhard. "Review of *Paul's Macedonian Associations: The Social Context of Philippians and 1 Thessalonians*." *TJ* 26 (2005) 334–7.

Schneider, John. *Godly Materialism: Rethinking Money and Possessions*. Downers Grove, IL: IVP, 1994.

Schottroff, Luise. "Holiness and Justice: Exegetical Comments on 1 Corinthians 11.17–34." *JSNT* 79 (2000) 51–60.

Schrage, Wolfgang. *Der Erste Brief an die Korinther*. 4 vols. Zurich: Benziger, 1991–2001.

Schürer, E., G. Vermes, F. Millar, and M. Black. *The History of the Jewish People in the Age of Jesus Christ*. 3 vols. Edinburgh: T. & T. Clark, 1979.

Seccombe, David. "Was There Organized Charity in Jerusalem before the Christians?" *JTS* 29 (1978) 140–3.

Shaw, Graham. *The Cost of Authority: Manipulation and Freedom in the New Testament*. Philadelphia: Fortress, 1983.

Sider, Ronald J. *Rich Christians in an Age of Hunger*. London: Hodder and Stoughton, 1977.
Sim, Margaret. "Recognising Irony in the Corinthian Correspondence," Paper presented at London School of Theology Research Conference, 2012.
Skeen, Judy. "Not as Enemies, But Kin: Discipline in the Family of God—2 Thessalonians 3:6–10." *RevExp* 96 (1999) 287–94.
Smith, Barry D. "The Problem with the Observance of the Lord's Supper in the Corinthian Church." *BBR* 20 (2010) 517–44.
Smith, Dennis E. "Review of Frederick W. Danker, *Benefactor: Epigraphic Study of a Graeco-Roman and New Testament Semantic Field*." *CBQ* 46 (1984) 150–52.
———. *From Symposium to Eucharist*. Minneapolis: Fortress, 2003.
Society at Lanuvium *CIL* XIV 2112 from Naphtali Lewis and Meyer Reinhold, eds. *Roman Civilization Selected Readings*. Vol. 2, *The Empire*. New York: Columbia University Press, 1990.
Spencer, Aída Besançon. *2 Corinthians*. The People's Bible Commentary. Oxford: BRF, 2001.
Spencer, F. Scott. *Journeying through Acts. A Literary-Cultural Reading*. Peabody: Hendrickson, 2004.
Stambaugh, John. "The Functions of Roman Temples." In *ANRW* 2.16.1, 554–608. Berlin: deGruyter, 1978.
Stambaugh, John, and David Balch. *The Social World of the First Christians*. London: SPCK, 1986.
Stirewalt, M. Luther. *Paul, the Letter Writer*. Grand Rapids: Eerdmans, 2003.
Strachan, R. H. *The Second Epistle to the Corinthians*. MNTC. London: Hodder and Stoughton, 1935.
Surburg, Mark P. "The Situation at the Corinthian Lord's Supper in Light of 1 Corinthians 11:21: A Reconsideration." *Concordia* (2006) 17–37.
Talbert, Charles H. *Reading Acts*. New York: Crossroad, 1997.
Tannehill, Robert C. "Do the Ethics of Acts include the Ethical Teaching in Luke?" In *Acts and Ethics*, edited by Thomas E. Phillips, 109–22. Sheffield: Sheffield Phoenix, 2005.
Tanner, Kathryn. *Economy of Grace*. Minneapolis: Fortress, 2005.
Tasker, R. V. G. *2 Corinthians*. TNTC. London: Tyndale, 1958.
Temporini, Hildegard, and Wolfgang Haase. *Aufstieg und Niedergang der Römischen Welt*. Berlin: de Gruyter, 1978.
Tertullian, *Adversus Marcionem Books 4 and 5*. Oxford: Clarendon, 1972.
Theissen, Gerd. *The First Followers of Jesus*. London: SCM, 1978.
———. *Social Reality and the Early Christians*. Edinburgh: T. & T. Clark, 1992.
———. *The Social Setting of Pauline Christianity*. Edinburgh: T. & T. Clark, 1982.
Thiselton, Anthony C. *1 Corinthians: A Shorter Exegetical and Pastoral Commentary*. Grand Rapids: Eerdmans, 2006.
———. *The First Epistle to the Corinthians*. NIGTC. Grand Rapids: Eerdmans, 2000.
———. "Realized Eschatology at Corinth." *NTS* 24 (1978) 510–26.
Thomas, Norman E. "The Church at Antioch: Crossing Racial, Cultural, and Class Barriers Acts 11.19–30; 13.1–3." In *Mission in Acts: Ancient Narrative in Contemporary Context*, edited by Robert L. Gallagher and Paul Hertig, 144–56. Maryknoll, NY: Orbis, 2004.
Thrall, Margaret E. *2 Corinthians*. 2 vols. ICC. Edinburgh: T. & T. Clark, 2000.

Tomlin, Graham. "Christians and Epicureans in 1 Corinthians." *JSNT* 68 (1997) 51–72.
Treggiari, Susan. "Marriage and Family in Roman Society." In *Marriage and Family in the Biblical World*, edited by Ken M. Campbell, 132–82. Downers Grove, IL: IVP Academic, 2003.
Turner, Max. *The Holy Spirit and Spiritual Gifts Then and Now*. Carlisle: Paternoster, 1996.
Twelftree, Graham H. *People of the Spirit*. London: SPCK, 2009.
Vanderkam, James C. "The People of the Dead Sea Scrolls: Essenes or Sadducees?" In *Understanding the Dead Sea Scrolls*, edited by Hershel Shanks, 50–62. London: SPCK, 1993.
Vermes, Geza, *The Complete Dead Sea Scrolls in English*. London: Penguin, 1997.
von Soden, Hans Freiherr. "ἀδελφος." In TDNT 1:144–6.
Wallace, Daniel B. *Greek Grammar Beyond the Basics*. Grand Rapids: Zondervan, 1996.
Wallace-Hadrill, Andrew. "Patronage in Roman Society: From Republic to Empire." In *Patronage in Ancient Society*, edited by Andrew Wallace-Hadrill, 63–87. London: Routledge, 1989.
Wallis, J. *The Call to Conversion*. Tring: Lion, 1981.
Walters, James C. "Paul and the Politics of Meals in Roman Corinth." In *Corinth in Context: Comparative Studies on Religion and Society*, edited by Steven J. Friesen, et al., 343–64. Leiden: Brill, 2010.
Walton, Steve. "How Mighty a Minority were the Hellenists?" In *Earliest Christian History*, edited by Michael F. Bird and Jason Maston, 305–28. Tübingen: Mohr Siebeck, 2012.
———. *Leadership and Lifestyle: The Portrait of Paul in the Miletus Speech and 1 Thessalonians*. Cambridge: CUP, 2000.
———. "Paul, Patronage and Pay: What Do We Know about the Apostle's Financial Support?" In *Paul as Missionary: Identity, Activity, Theology, and Practice*, edited by Trevor J. Burke and Brian S. Rosner, 220–33. London: T. & T. Clark, 2011.
———. "Primitive Communism in Acts? Does Acts Present the Community of Goods (2:44–45; 4:32–35) as Mistaken?" *EQ* 80 (2008) 99–111.
Wanamaker, Charles A. *The Epistles to the Thessalonians*. Grand Rapids: Eerdmans, 1990.
Watson, Deborah Elaine. "Paul's Collection in Light of Motivations and Mechanisms for Aid to the Poor in the First-Century World." PhD diss., Durham University, 2006.
Watson, Nigel. *The Second Epistle to the Corinthians*. Epworth Commentaries. London: Epworth, 1993.
Weaver, D. J. "2 Thessalonians 3:6–15." *Int* 61 (2007) 426–8.
Welborn, L. L. "'That There May be Equality': The Contexts and Consequences of a Pauline Ideal." *NTS* 59 (2013) 73–90.
Wendel, U. *Gemeinde in Kraft: Das Gemeindeverständnis in den Summarien der Apostelgeschichte*. NTDH. Neukirchener: Neukirchen-Vluyn, 1998.
Wheeler, Sondra Ely. *Wealth as Peril and Obligation: The New Testament on Possessions*. Grand Rapids: Eerdmans, 1995.
Whiteley, Denys Edward Hugh. *Thessalonians*. New Clarendon Bible. Oxford: OUP, 1969.
Williams, David J. *1 and 2 Thessalonians*. NIBC. Peabody: Hendrickson, 1992.

Winter, Bruce W. "Acts and Food Shortages." In *The Book of Acts in its Graeco-Roman Setting*, edited by David W. J. Gill and Conrad Gempf, 59–78. The Book of Acts in its First Century Setting. Grand Rapids: Eerdmans, 1994.

———. *After Paul Left Corinth*. Grand Rapids: Eerdmans, 2001.

———. "The Entries and Ethics of Orators and Paul (1 Thessalonians 2:1–12)." *TynBul* 44 (1993) 55–74.

———. "'If a Man Does not Wish to Work . . .' A Cultural and Historical Setting for 2 Thessalonians 3:6–16." *TynBul* 40 (1989) 303–15.

———. "The Public Honouring of Christian Benefactors Romans 13.3–4 and 1 Peter 2.14–15." *JSNT* 34 (1988) 87–103.

———. *Seek the Welfare of the City: Christians as Benefactors and Citizens*. Grand Rapids: Eerdmans, 1994.

Witherington, Ben. *1 and 2 Thessalonians: A Socio-Rhetorical Commentary*. Grand Rapids: Eerdmans, 2006.

———. *The Acts of the Apostles*. Grand Rapids: Eerdmans, 1998.

———. *Conflict and Community in Corinth*. Grand Rapids: Eerdmans, 1995.

———. *Jesus and Money*. London: SPCK, 2010.

———. *Jesus the Sage*. Edinburgh: T. & T. Clark, 1994.

Wright, Tom. *Paul for Everyone: 1 Corinthians*. London: SPCK, 2003.

Zerwick, Max, and Mary Grosvenor. *A Grammatical Analysis of the Greek New Testament*. 2 vols. Rome: Biblical Institute Press, 1974.

Zias, Joseph E. "The Cemeteries of Qumran and Celibacy: Confusion Laid to Rest?" *DSD* 7 (2000) 220–53.

Modern Authors Index

Aasgaard, Reidar, 204, 225-26
Adams, Edward, 116, 119-21
Agrell, Göran, , 200-203, 207, 210-11, 213-14, 219
Alexander, Loveday, 48, 56, 60
Ascough, Richard S., 5, 195, 197-98, 214, 223, 227-29
Atkinson, Kenneth, and Jodi Magness, 27, 31
Aune, David E., 186-87

Bach, Alice, and Jennifer Glancy, 102, 128, 130
Balch, David, 220
Barclay, John M. G. , 146, 150-51, 154, 163, 198-202, 208, 214, 216
Barnett, Paul, 142, 145-50, 152-53, 155, 158, 160, 162, 166-67, 178
Barrett, C. K., 9, 11, 47, 49, 60, 64, 85, 88, 109-10, 113, 115, 118-19, 124-30, 134, 139, 142, 148-49, 158-59, 161, 166-67, 169, 184
Bassler, Jouette M., 2
Bauckham, R., 17
Bauernfeind, Otto, 47
Baugh, S. M., 225
Baumgarten, Albert, 31
Beall, Todd, 27-28, 31
Beasley-Murray, George R., 8
Becker, Joseph, 155, 159, 163
Best, Ernest, 145-46, 148, 150, 152-53, 155, 161, 165, 176-77, 200, 202-3, 210, 212, 219
Betz, Hans Dieter, 143-44, 146-47, 153, 155, 157, 160, 163, 166, 177

Blomberg, Craig, 2, 44-45, 48, 87, 199, 214, 217
Blue, Bradley B., 104-5, 116-17, 121, 123-24, 129
Bock, Darrell L., 44-47, 49, 53, 56-57, 60, 65-66
Bornkamm, Günter, 116, 120, 125, 127-28, 130, 134, 138
Braund, David, 106
Bray, Gerald, 162
Briones, David E., 148, 164, 181, 185
Broshi, Magen, 28, 31
Brown, Raymond, 9-10, 12, 82
Bruce, F. F., 51, 60-61, 66-67, 88, 92, 118, 124, 130, 143, 145, 168-69, 202
Burke, Trevor J., 201, 204, 221, 225
Burridge, Richard A., 2

Calvin, John, 9-10, 12, 85-86, 93, 142-43
Capper, Brian J., 5, 12, 17, 30, 32-33, 43-44, 58-59, 61-62, 64, 66, 68, 71, 73-75
Carson, D. A., 9-10, 12
Cassidy, Richard J., 42, 86
Chapman, David W., 225
Charlesworth, James H., 33
Cheung, Alex T., 103
Chow, John K., 106-8, 110-13, 118, 128, 133-34, 185
Ciampa, Roy E. and Brian S. Rosner, 126, 129-31, 134
Clark, Gillian, 75-76
Clarke, Andrew D., 109, 111, 186-87

Cloud, Duncan, 106, 133
Conzelmann, Hans, 47, 57, 66–67, 82, 85, 87, 109–10, 120, 130
Coutsoumpos, Panayotis, 100–103, 105, 113, 115, 120, 123–25, 129, 138
Cross, Frank Moore, 32
Crossan John Dominic, 35
Crossan, John Dominic, and Jonathan L. Reed, 105–7, 109–11, 116, 118–19, 121–22, 129

D'Arms, John, 102
Danker, Frederick, W., 149, 186–87
Daube, David, 22
deSilva, David, 199, 216–17
Dibelius, Martin, 89
Donfried, Karl Paul, 194–96, 198, 207, 213, 221
Downing, F. Gerald, 37–39, 224
Downs, David J., 143, 148–49, 155, 160, 163, 168, 170–71, 174, 178, 180, 184–85, 189–90
Dunn, James D. G., 22, 25, 37, 45, 84, 174
Dupont, Jacques, 47, 53–57, 67, 70, 83

Edwards, Ruth, 10–11
Ehrhardt, Arnold, 50

Fee, Gordon D., 168–69, 194, 200, 204–6, 208, 210–11, 213–14
Fiensy, D. A., 36, 61, 86
Finger, Reta Halteman, 43, 57, 60–64, 67
Fitzmyer, Joseph A., 47–48, 53, 60, 74, 82, 174
Foster, Paul, 207–9
Fotopoulos, John, 119
Frame, James Everett, 200, 211, 213
Frier, Bruce W., 220
Furnish, Victor Paul, 142–46, 148–49, 151–52, 158–59, 161–63, 165, 167, 169–70, 173, 178

Gapp, Kenneth Sperber, 81, 83, 87
Garland, David E., 117, 124, 127
Garnsey, Peter, 81, 93–94
Garnsey, Peter, and Richard Saller, 107–8
Gaventa, Beverly Roberts, 53, 58, 82, 201, 210, 219
Gehring, Roger W., 119–20
Georgi, Dieter, 143–44, 150, 152, 155, 158, 161, 168, 172, 176–77, 184
Gonzalez, Justo L., 2
Grant, Robert M., 2, 75
Gregson, Fiona J. R., 2, 31
Griffin, Miriam, 187
Griffith, Gary W., 147, 159, 160, 163, 189–90
Grosheide, F. W., 110, 122, 130
Guijarro, S., 86–87
Günter, W., 225

Haenchen, Ernst, 13, 45, 47–49, 56–57, 63, 67, 82, 84, 87, 90
Han, Paul, 160
Hands, Arthur Robinson, 94
Hanson, R. P. C., 143, 163, 179
Hardin, Justin K., 196, 197
Hargreaves, John, 46, 74
Harland, Philip A., 201, 228
Harries, Richard, 1
Harrill, J. Albert, 59
Harris, Murray J., 142–43, 145, 148–50, 158–59, 161–63, 167
Harrison, James R., 154, 190, 215
Hays, Richard B., 2
Hellerman, Joseph H., 26
Hemer, Colin, 83, 90
Hengel, Martin, 2, 17–18, 86, 89
Héring, Jean, 149
Hock, Ronald F., 35, 218–20
Holmberg, Bengt, 111
Hoppe, Leslie J., 2
Horrell, David G., 110, 112, 115, 119–20, 172–73, 178, 201
Horsley, Richard A., 106, 215
Howard-Brook, Wes, 13
Hughes, Philip E., 144, 153, 159, 162, 165–67, 175–76, 178
Hume, Douglas A., 46, 51, 55, 67
Hurd, John Coolidge, 115

Instone-Brewer, David, 22, 72

Jamir, Lanu, 100–104, 106, 109, 111, 114–15, 117, 120–21, 123–24, 126, 128–31
Jeremias, Joachim, 9, 22, 47, 71–72, 87–88
Jervell, Jacob, 57, 60, 62, 82, 91
Jewett, Robert, 174–75, 194–95, 197, 199–220, 204–5, 207–8, 210–13, 218–23
Johnson, Alan F., 117, 128
Johnson, Luke Timothy, 2, 42, 49, 51, 54, 71, 80, 85, 88, 90–91
Johnson, Sherman E., 86
Jones, Ivor H., 202, 204, 209, 222
Joubert, Stephan, 174, 178, 187–89

Käsemann, Ernst, 120
Keener, Craig S., 10–11, 144, 158, 164, 180, 185
Keith, Chris, 197, 209
Kim, Kyoung-Jin, 42–43, 46, 53, 66–69, 74–75
Klauck, Hans-Josef, 48, 52, 54, 58, 70, 74, 99–100, 125
Koester, Helmut, 200, 215
Köstenberger, Andreas, 225
Kreitzer, Larry, 154, 177, 183
Krodel, Gerhard A., 48–49, 52, 56, 60, 82, 85

Lake, Kirsopp, and Henry J. Cadbury, 58, 81
Lambrecht, Jan, 143–45, 150, 152, 156–57, 159, 178
Lampe, Peter, 102
Lillie, William, 4
Lim, Kar Yong, 153, 167, 172, 180, 190
Lincoln, Andrew T., 13–14
Longenecker, Bruce W., 101, 112, 125, 172–73, 175, 183, 191
Longenecker, Richard N., 89

Maddox, Robert, 45
Malherbe, Abraham J., , 194, 196, 199–200, 202, 204, 206–8, 211, 214, 218–19, 223–24

Malina, Bruce J., and John J. Pilch, 45–47, 51, 56, 61,
Manson, T. W., 26
Marshall, I. Howard, 17, 48–49, 56, 58, 87, 89–90, 130, 206
Martin, Ralph P., 149, 153, 157–58, 161, 164, 176–78
Matera, Frank J., 142, 143, 145–46, 149–51, 153, 155, 157–60, 162, 165–66, 177
McCant, Jerry W., 145–46, 149, 155, 157–58, 167, 186, 189
McRae, Rachel M., 106, 120
Meeks, Wayne A., 2, 107, 109, 111–12, 116–18, 134, 139
Meggitt, Justin J., 101, 111–12, 114, 117
Meier, John P., 16, 23, 35
Mendel, Gustave, 215
Menken, Maarten J. J., 207–9, 210
Metzger, Bruce M., 18, 90
Míguez, Néstor O., 194, 197, 203, 206
Milligan, G., 202
Miranda, Jose P., 2
Mitchell, Alan C., 54–56
Mitchell, Margaret M., 115, 128, 131
Mitchell, Nathan D., 102, 107, 124, 129
Moore, Arthur L., 202, 204–6, 214, 222
Moore, George Foot, 23
Moreland, Milton , 43–44
Morris, Leon, 174, 194, 197, 208–9, 211–12, 219
Moulton, J. H., and G. Milligan, 8
Moulton, James, et al., 87
Munck, Johannes, 57
Murphy, Catherine, 27–30
Murphy-O'Connor, 109, 119, 159, 168, 174, 179

Neil, William, , 201, 203
Newman, Barclay M., and Eugene A. Nida, 50
Newton, Derek, 132–33
Nickle, Keith F., 143, 170–71, 173, 177–78, 183–84

O'Mahony, Kieran J.
Oakes, Peter, 198, 212, 216–17, 229
Oddie, W., 4
Ogereau, Julien M., 164

Paddison, Angus, 201
Panikulam, George, 2
Pao, David W., 60–61
Pervo, Richard I., 45, 67, 84, 90, 100, 106, 124, 131
Peterman, G. W., 160, 187–88
Peterson, David, 46
Pillar, Edward, , 194, 198
Plummer, Alfred, 144, 147–50, 153, 158, 179

Rabens, Volker, 159
Ramelli, Ilaria L. E., 126
Richards, Earl J., 199, 201, 203–4, 209, 219
Riesner, Rainer, 32, 73
Rigaux, B., 200, 202, 216
Robinson, Anthony B., and Robert W. Wall, 51–52, 56
Rulmu, Callia, 194–95, 215–17
Russell, Ronald, 198, 206, 212–13, 217–18, 220

Saller, Richard P., 107–8
Sanday, William, and Arthur C. Headlam, 174
Sanders, E. P, 12, 15–17, 67, 71
Saxby, Trevor, , 2
Schiffman, Lawrence H., 31
Schmithals, Walter, 114, 218
Schnabel, Eckhard, 198, 229
Schneider, John, 2
Schottroff, Luise, 118, 124–25, 130–31
Schrage, Wolfgang, 117, 120, 124–25, 168–69
Schürer, E., G. Vermes, F. Millar, and M. Black, 23, 49, 72
Seccombe, David, 72–73
Shaw, Graham, 165, 214
Sider, Ronald J., 2
Sim, Margaret, 131
Skeen, Judy, 206, 210, 214
Smith, Barry D., 186

Smith, Dennis E., 99–104, 106, 113, 115, 118–19, 123, 125, 131, 133, 137,
Spencer, Aída Besançon, 150–51, 154, 167, 176, 179
Spencer, F. Scott, 47, 63–64
Stambaugh, John, 100, 103, 139
Stambaugh, John, and David Balch, 100, 104, 107
Stirewalt, M. Luther, 144
Strachan, R. H., 151, 156, 162–63, 176
Surburg, Mark P., 117, 120, 128–29

Talbert, Charles H., 91
Tannehill, Robert C., , 42, 52, 92
Tanner, Kathryn, 150
Tasker, R. V. G., 144, 146–47, 150, 156–58, 171
Theissen, Gerd, 67, 86, 113–14, 117–18, 122–24, 130–31, 133
Thiselton, Anthony C., 109–15, 119, 124–26, 128, 130, 168, 213
Thomas, Norman E., 91,
Thrall, Margaret E., 143, 145, 147–48, 153, 155–56, 159, 161, 169, 171, 175–76, 178, 180, 184
Tomlin, Graham, 114, 223
Treggiari, Susan, 225–26
Turner, Max, 201
Twelftree, Graham H., 42

Vanderkam, James C., 31
von Soden, Hans Freiherr, 225

Wallace, Daniel B., 118
Wallace-Hadrill, Andrew, 106–8, 185, 187
Wallis, J., 1–2
Walters, James C., 120
Walton, Steve, , 48, 67, 84–85, 109, 196, 200, 203, 206, 217, 219–20
Wanamaker, Charles A., 199–201, 207, 212, 214, 216, 222
Watson, Deborah Elaine, 155, 174–75
Watson, Nigel, 146, 158, 163, 173
Weaver, D. J., 221, 223
Welborn, L. L., 190
Wendel, U., 49, 62, 67

Wheeler, Sondra Ely, 2
Whiteley, Denys Edward Hugh, 203, 212–13
Williams, David J., 201–2, 204–5, 212
Winter, Bruce W., 5, 80–81, 94–95, 109, 114–15, 117, 122–23, 126, 128, 180, 197, 202–6, 212–13, 216–17, 22–23
Witherington, Ben, 1–2, 36–39, 45, 56, 81–83, 89–90, 104, 110, 114, 116–17, 119, 124, 133, 138, 153, 158–60, 185, 194, 201–3, 209, 217, 222
Wright, Tom, 156, 161

Zerwick, Max, and Mary Grosvenor, 52
Zias, Joseph E., 31

Subject Index

12 / 72 , the, 14, 16–19, 25, 32–34, 39–41, 87

Achaia, 109, 144–45, 147, 173
Ananias and Sapphira, 42, 48, 51, 57–59, 68, 70–71, 235, 239
Antinous — see Society of Diana and Antinous
Antioch / Antiochene church, ix, 5, 43, 46, 66, 79–80, 84–87, 89–93, 95–97, 123, 141, 233, 236, 239
ἄτακτοι, 4, 193–94, 204–6, 209, 211–14, 216, 218–20, 222, 224, 229–30, 237

Barnabas, 43, 48, 51, 56–58, 61, 68, 80, 83–93, 96
benefaction — see patronage, benefaction, and gift exchange
burial , 9, 37, 71, 99, 136, 228

χάρις, 52, 145, 148, 158–59, 162–64, 187, 190
charity, 9, 71–72, 106, 164
collection, 43, 66, 74, 79–96, 141–93, 234, 236
collegia, 100–101, 105, 140, 196
Community at Croton — see Pythagoras
common characteristics of NT examples, 234–36
Corinth and the Corinthian church , 109–15
Cynics, (and philosophers), 35–41, 206, 214, 218–19, 236

curator annonae, 79, 93–96, 107, 142, 182–83, 191, 236–38

Dead Sea Scrolls — see Qumran Community and Essenes
Diana — see Society of Diana and Antinous
disciples (Jesus'), 3–5, 7–21, 25–26, 31–35, 37–41, 44–45, 62, 67–68, 73, 86, 92, 96, 232–40
disciples (rabbis') — see rabbis and their disciples, 7, 21–26, 41
distinctives (consistent) , 238–40
diversity (in social status etc), 92, 111–13, 123, 140, 239, 242

Ebionite, 172
Epicureans, 114, 194, 201, 223–25, 230–31, 237–38
equality, 30, 55, 104–6, 116, 122, 124, 127, 130, 132, 135, 139–40, 151–54, 161, 181, 190, 192, 226–28, 233
eschatology, 114, 198, 200, 207–9, 213–15, 222
Essenes — see Qumran Community

family life, 194, 223, 225–27, 237–38, 241–42
famine, , 66–67, 79–84, 86, 88–90, 93–96, 117, 121, 170, 181–82, 217–18, 236
fictive kinship , 223
food shortage —see famine

SUBJECT INDEX

generosity, 47, 68, 122, 141, 146–48, 150–51, 153, 156–57, 161–63, 165, 167, 176, 180
γλωσσόκομον, 7–16, 20–21, 40–41, 233–36, 239
Gnosticism, 114, 218
Greco-Roman meals, 98–106
Greco-Roman responses to famine — see *curator annonae*

Helena and Izates, 82–83, 94–96, 142, 182, 191, 236, 238
Hellenists, 60–64, 74, 84–85, 92
historical questions
  Acts, 43–45
  Acts 11, Acts 15, Galatians 2, , 88–90
Holy Spirit, 46, 50, 58, 65, 70, 77–78, 170, 201, 233, 240
honor, , 10, 14, 24, 26, 55, 63, 94–95, 100, 103, 105, 107–8, 113, 120, 124, 129, 133, 136–37, 148, 157, 161, 182–83, 190, 192, 195, 198–99, 202, 214, 227–28, 236
hospitality, 7, 16, 20, 65–66, 68, 201, 222, 235,
household, 32–33, 77, 107, 110, 112–13, 116, 118, 220

idol meat, 113, 115, 121, 123, 132–35
idolatry / idols, 1, 112, 134, 198, 214
imitation, 116
incarnation, 150, 163
Iobacchoi — see Society of the Iobacchoi
Izates — see Helena and Izates

Jerusalem, 5, 31–32, 36, 46–48, 52, 61–63, 66–67, 70, 72–75, 80, 82–96, 115, 141–42, 146, 151–53, 155, 160–61, 163–64, 166, 169–80, 182–85, 189, 191, 193, 201, 235–37
Jesus, example of, 136, 148–51, 157, 180, 189, 192, 240–241
Jewish almsgiving practice, 9, 43, 47, 65, 71–73, 77–78, 170, 237, 241
Joseph and Aseneth, 101

Judas, 8–15, 20–21, 33–35, 40–42, 55, 58, 236
Judea, 26, 56, 79, 82–88, 90–93, 148, 224, 238

Khirbet Qumran — see Qumran Community and Essenes
κοινωνία, 47–48, 148, 164

Macedonian associations, 227–29 see also Voluntary Associations
Macedonians, example of, 144–51, 159, 163, 165, 179–80, 189, 192, 235, 239
Martha, Mary, and Lazarus, 7, 16, 20
manna, 152–54
meals
  funeral / memorial, 100, 133, 138
  Jewish, 100–101
  public, 100
  sacrificial, 100, 133,
motivation , 4, 8, 19–20, 23, 38–39, 56, 74, 169, 173, 179, 183, 230, 232, 240–41

non-itinerant associates, 16, 69, 233

patronage, benefaction, and gift exchange, 21, 74, 98–99, 106–8, 113, 117, 129, 134–36, 142, 182–83, 185–92, 194, , 216–17, 222–23, 229–30, 237–38, 242
parousia, 45, 200, 207–8, 213–15
persecution — see suffering and persecution
Pharisees, 21, 24–26, 31
poor / those in need, 7–10, 12–13, 15–17, 21, 30, 33, 38, 40, 42, 43, 45–46, 53, 62, 71–73, 75, 77–78, 81, 83, 89–90, 100, 103–4, 106, 113–14, 117–18, 123, 133, 150–51, 159, 161, 167, 172–77, 183, 191, 217, 224, 233, 236, 239
possessions, 1–5, 7, 16–17, 20–21, 26–30, 33–36, 38–44, 46–55, 60, 64–65, 67–70, 74–78, 91–92, 96, 98, 151, 158, 211, 221, 227, 232–37, 239, 241

poverty, 1-2, 48, 147-48, 150, 197,
prayer, 4, 22, 47, 49-50, 64-65, 125,
    161-62, 180, 209, 235
Pythagoras, 43, 75-78

Qumran Community / Essenes, 5,
    7-8, 24, 26-35, 40-41, 43, 59, 66,
    68, 70, 73-75, 77-78, 100-101,
    210, 236-38

rabbis and their disciples — see disciples (rabbis')
reciprocity, 78, 91, 152-53, 174, 180,
    187, 189-91, 233, 238

sacred, 101, 103, 149
Sapphira — see Ananias and Sapphira
Sarapis, 190
schools, 23
scribes — see rabbis and their disciples
shared meals / eating together, 33,
    50-52, 62, 70, 73-74, 77-78,
    97-98, 105, 115-16, 119, 122,
    129, 131, 134-36, 137-38, 140,
    211, 221, 224-25, 229, 231, 233,
    236-37, 240-41
social status, 108, 197
Society of Diana and Antinous, 98,
    103, 136-38

Society of the Iobacchoi, 98, 137-38
suffering and persecution, 60, 62,
    64-65, 67, 77, 80, 86, 91-92, 148,
    164, 197-99, 201, 207, 216

taberna, 119
temple tax, 67, 142, 182-85, 191,
    236-37
tenements, 220-21
Therapeutae, 5
Thessalonica, 194-95
Thessalonican church, 118, 195-98
Titus and the brothers, 143-45,
    154-56, 180

villa, 27, 102, 110, 117, 119-20
virtuoso religion, 68
voluntary, 70, 77, 94, 146, 149, 154,
    157, 163, 175, 180, 190-91, 233,
    235, 239, 242
Voluntary Associations, 99-100, 106,
    140, 194-96, 227-31, 238, 240

widows, 60-64, 67, 69, 85, 92, 236
women disciples, 7, 12, 17-18, 20,
    21, 41
work, 9, 26, 29, 62, 65-66, 92, 95, 113,
    119, 193, 197-98, 200, 208-14,
    219-21, 226-31, 234, 236-40
workshop, 119, 219, 221

Ancient Documents Index

OLD TESTAMENT

Genesis
3:17–19	210
33	187

Exodus
2:15–22	187
16	154
16:18	152, 153
37:19	163

Numbers
8:22	163
18:20	56

Deuteronomy
2:7	203
6:5	53
10:9	56
10:12	53
12:12	56
14:27–29	71
15:4	53, 71
15:7–11	71

Joshua
7:1	58
10:24	51
14:3–4	56
14:4	56
15:19	65

Ruth
2:14	10
4:7	51

1 Samuel
21–30	26
25	187
25:24	51

1 Chronicles
12:38	53

2 Chron
24:8	8
24:10	8

Neh
10:32	183

Job
1:10	203

Psalms
90:17	203
111	159
111:9	159
128:2	210

Proverbs
10:4	210
22:8–9	157

Proverbs (continued)

22:8	156, 157
30:8	158

Isaiah

55:10	160, 178
54:13	201

Jeremiah

31:33–34	201
32:39	53

Hosea

10:12	178

Micah

6:8	9

APOCRYPHA

1 Maccabees

1:14	36

2 Maccabees

4:9	36
4:32	58
15:4	200–201

3 Maccabees

4:6	47
5:26	128

4 Maccabees

13:21	200
13:23	200
13:26	200

Sirach

6:34–36	23
6:35	23–24
38:24—39:11	219
51.23	23

Tobit

1:6–8	9
1:16	71
1:17	71
2:2–3	71, 73
2:4	71
4:7–11	71
4:16	71
12:8–9	71
14:8–9	71

PSEUDEPIGRAPHA

Joseph and Aseneth

8:5	101
8:11	101

Psalms of Solomon

5:16	158

NEW TESTAMENT

Matthew

2:1	24
4:18–22	15, 38
6:25–34	39
6	38
8:20	16
9:10	34
10	18
10:8	18
10:10	18, 37
10:37	25, 26
12:11	33
14:13–21	97
15:29–39	97
17:24–27	183
26:6	17
26:25	21
26:26	126
26:49	21
26:69–75	19
28	19
28:16	19

Mark

1:17–20	15, 38
2:8	21
2:13–17	97
3:31–35	38
3:35	38
6:8	18
9:5	21
10:17–22	38
10:17	38
10:21	16
10:28	15
10:32–46	38
11:19	38
11:27	38
14:22	126

Luke

1:5–25	85
2:1	80
4:5	80
5:1	38
5:11	15
5:28	15, 38
6:34–35A	55
7:37–39	51
8	7, 12, 18, 20–21, 45
8:1–3	20, 41
8:2–3	12
8:3	7
8:22–26	16
8:35	51
8:41	51
9:3	18, 37
9:16	50
9:51	85
9:57–62	25
10	7, 18, 37
10:4	8, 18, 37
10:5–8	18
10:7–8	18
10:7	18
10:38–42	16, 97
12:33	8, 16
14:4	202
14:12–14	55
14:26	26
16:21	61
17:22	85
18:18–25	38
18:22	16, 52
18:28	15, 55
19:1–10	17
19:23	61
22:3	58
22:19	50
22:19	126
22:21–30	61
22:21	61
22:35–36	8
22:54–62	19
23:56	202
24:30	50
24:30–32	97
24:35	50
24:50–53	80

John

1:37	15, 23, 38
1:39	15, 21
1:46	15, 38
1:47–48	13
1:49	21
2:24	13
3:15–16	14
4	11, 16
4:8	10, 13, 33
4:29	15, 38
6	12
6:5	11, 13
6:9	12
6:70–71	13
11	17
11:5	17
12	7, 8, 13, 17
12:2	33
12:3	12
12:4–8	8
12:5	10, 13, 33
12:6	7, 8
12:8	13
13:1–5	97
13:2	13, 33
13:27	9, 13
13:28–29	9, 10

John *(continued)*

13:29	7, 12, 33
13:38	14
14:20	14
15	14
16:32	14
17:3	14
17:20–26	14
17:21	14
18:3–5	13
18:7	14
18:25	14
18:27	14
19:26–27	19
19:27	19
20:31	14
21	19
21:2	19
21:15–23	19
21:15–22	14
21:7–14	97

Acts

1–7	85
1:18	42, 55
1:25	55
2–6	4, 43, 233–37, 239–41
2	43, 45, 50, 67, 74, 78, 86
2:1–4	46, 70, 240
2:14–47	241
4:23–26	50
2:37–39	59
2:41–47	46
2:42–47	46–50
2:42	47, 50, 61, 70, 77
2:43–47	47
2:43	47
2:44	47–48, 241
2:45	47, 49, 52, 62, 64, 69, 70
2:46	47, 49, 50, 61–63, 77, 97, 240
2:47	47
3	49, 55
3:1	49–50
3:6	48
3:7–8	50
3:36	56
4	43, 67, 74, 78, 234, 238
4:4	50
4:23	50
4:31	50, 70, 240
4:32–35	50–56
4:32	52–53, 58–59, 240
4:33	52, 70, 240
4:34–35	64
4:34	42, 49, 52–53, 71, 77, 86
4:35	51, 62, 69
4:36—5:11	56–60
4:36–37	43
4:37	56
5	43
5:1–11	42, 45, 57
5:1	59
5:2–3	58
5:2	58
5:3	58
5:4	58, 70
5:14	59
5:18	63
5:40—6:1	64
6	43, 63, 71, 74, 92, 97, 240
6:1–6	60–65, 70, 87
6:1	60–61, 85, 92
6:2	61
6:3	65, 70, 73
6:7	60
7	64
8:5	64
8:18–24	42
8:18–23	65
8:20	65
8:24–40	64
8:36–39	59
9:26–29	88
9:29	85
9:36	43, 65
10	79
10:1	43, 65
11	4–5, 83, 88–90, 92–93, 95, 173, 181–83, 234–36, 238–39, 240
11:1–18	45, 79
11:18	202
11:19–30	66, 84, 142, 181, 191, 233
11:19–26	80
11:19–21	80

11:19–20	92
11:19	92, 96
11:20	84–85, 96
11:21	92
11:22	85, 96, 240
11:25	240
11:26	84, 89, 91
11:27–30	79–88, 90–91, 96, 141, 169–70, 236
11:27	84–85, 89, 96, 240
11:28	80, 84
11:29	87
11:30	93
12	92
12:1–24	84
12:1–3	83
12:1	84
12:2	89
12:12	49, 52, 90
12:2–3	83
12:25	79, 90–92, 96
13:2	90
15	79, 88–89, 114–15, 173, 184
15:1–21	85, 133
15:2	89
15:4–5	89
15:7	89
15:12	89
15:13	89
15:22	184
15:27	184
15:33	184
15:36–41	45
16:11—17:15	148
16:15	65
17	228
17:1–15	195
17:1–9	203
17:1–2	195–96
17:4	197
17:6	195
17:7	195
17:5–9	198
18	110
18:1–21	142
18:1–18	110
18:1–3	206
18:2	110, 112
18:5	112, 199
18:8	112
18:12	110
18:18	122
19:19	197
19:21	169
20:4	171, 177, 197
20:7–11	61
20:7	50
20:11	50
20:16	184
20:33–35	65
20:35	55, 65, 92
21:1—23:22	85
21:13	170
21:17–26	141
21:17	169
24:11	170
24:17	66, 170–71
27:35	50
28:23	66
28:30	65

Romans

9–11	178
11:11–12	178
11:25–27	178
12:8–10	175
12:8	146
12:13	175
15	175
14	134
15:7	128
15:14–32	178
15:16	174
15:24–32	141
15:25–32	174
15:25	88, 174
15:26–27	174
15:26	161, 174, 175
15:27	153, 174, 176–77
15:31	174
16	88
16:2	111
16:14–15	221
16:18	165
16:23	111

1 Corinthians

1	122
1:7	128
1:10–12	122, 135
1:11	110, 116
1:12	112, 122
1:14	110
1:16	112, 116
1:26–27	133
1:26	111
1:27–31	135
3:1–4	135
3:3	112
3:4	112
3:5–9	135
3:9	112
4	114
4:7	157
4:8	114
4:10–13	114
4:10	111
4:12	203
5:7	125, 135
5:9	115, 142, 146, 168
5:11	134
6	111
7	111
7:1	110
7:21	111
7:22	111
8	136
8:1	114
8:8	132
8:9–13	136
8:10	132
8:12	134
9	3, 210
9:1–27	145
9:6	197
9:9–18	206
9:11	176
9:13	197
9:19–23	136
10	136
10:2	133
10:5	133
10:14–22	133
10:14	134
10:16–17	135
10:16	165
10:17	135
10:20	132
10:21	132, 134–35
10:23	114
10:27	132
10:28	134
11	4, 97–140, 193, 233–41
11:17–34	61, 98, 115–32, 140
11:17	116
11:18	115, 122–23, 135, 138, 240
11:20–21	124
11:20	123, 125
11:21	111, 116–17, 123, 135, 138
11:22	116, 123, 127, 129, 136, 139
11:23–29	241
11:23–26	125
11:23	125
11:24	126
11:25	117, 120
11:26	125–26, 136
11:27–29	135
11:27	129, 135
11:28	129
11:29	127, 129, 135, 138
11:32	127
11:33	128, 131, 138, 240
11:34	123, 130
12:2	112
12:4–7	135
12:12–31	240
12:12–14	135
12:12	129, 131
12:13	127
12:17	135
12:21–26	135
12:23	129, 136
12:27	127, 129, 135
14:1–5	136
14:23	116
14:26–33	138
14:26	136
14:30	119
15:3	135
15:10	159
16:1–4	141, 167–69, 175
16:1	161, 167–69

16:2	113, 116, 143, 168–69, 180, 234	8:5	147, 159, 186
16:3	146, 169	8:6	162–63, 179
16:4	169	8:7	144, 148–50, 162–64, 180
16:11	128	8:8	144, 149, 167, 180
16:12	112	8:9	149, 151, 157, 163, 180, 241
16:17	111	8:10–12	155
16:19	116	8:10–11	149
		8:10	149, 186
		8:11	148–49, 180, 186–87

2 Corinthians

1–9	143	8:12	151, 180, 186
1:12—2:4	143	8:13–14	151, 180
2:1	142	8:13	150, 152
2:2–4	142	8:14	152, 160–61, 177, 179, 183
2:5–11	142	8:15	144, 153
2:8	167	8:16–24	145
2:14—7:4	143	8:19–20	164
2:17	155	8:16	144, 162, 183, 186
3:3	164	8:17	144, 154, 186
3:7	164	8:18	154
3:9	164	8:19	162, 186
4:1—5:10	143	8:20–21	155, 181
4:1	164	8:20	144
5:11–21	143	8:21–22	155
5:18	164	8:21	186
6:3	164	8:22	144, 154, 186
6:14—7:1	143	8:23	154
7	145	9	159, 144
7:2	155	9:1–5	145
7:5–16	143	9:1	143–44
7:8–9	142	9:2	143–45, 149, 165, 186
7:11–12	145	9:3–5	144
7:13–15	145	9:3	145
8–9	4, 88, 141–93, 233–36, 238–41	9:5–6	180
8	144–45, 158	9:5	155–56, 165, 180
8:1–6	201, 140	9:5A	165
8:1–5	144–45, 165	9:5B	165
8:1–3	180	9:6–15	158
8:1–2	222	9:6	165, 157, 165
8:1	146, 158, 162–63, 179–80, 240	9:7	157, 180
8:2	150–51, 197	9:8	156–62, 179–81, 240
8:3–5	179	9:9	159–60
8:3–4	146	9:10–11	160, 180
8:3	87, 148, 159, 180	9:10	180–81
8:4–5	179	9:11–12	160, 181
8:4	148, 151, 162–63, 179	9:11B–13	163
		9:11	146, 157, 160–61, 183
		9:12–15	145, 179, 183, 240
		9:12–13	164, 179

2 Corinthians *(continued)*

9:12	160, 163–64, 186
9:13–14	179
9:13	146, 157, 160–61, 164, 179
9:14–15	156
9:14	161–62, 176, 178–80
9:15	162–63, 181
9:23	154
10–13	142–43
11:5	143
11:7–9	197
11:8–9	216
11:8	164
12:11–18	143
12:14–18	155
12:14–16	197
12:14	142
13:1–3	142

Galatians

1:9	88
1:18	88
2	79, 88, 89, 90, 170, 173
2:1–10	89, 172
2:2	89, 90
2:7	89
2:9	89
2:10	89, 90, 141, 171–73, 175
2:11–21	172
3:14	165
3:26–29	177
6:9–10	175

Philippians

1:3	160
1:5	147
1:29–30	148
2:13	159
4:10–20	160
4:11	158
4:14–15	164
4:15–16	147

1 Thessalonians

1:2–3	199
1:3	215, 240
1:4	240
1:6–10	199
1:6	148, 198–99
1:8	213
1:9	227
1:9B–10	198
1:10	198
2:1–6	205
2:7–9	197, 227
2:7	199
2:7B–8	199
2:8–9	202
2:8	205, 211, 221
2:9	203, 206, 208, 210, 216, 227
2:11–12	199
2:12	198
2:13–16	199
2:13–14	199
2:14	148, 198
2:17—3.6	206
2:17	199
2:18	198
3:1–5	198
3:1–2	199
3:3–5	148
3:5	227
3:7–8	199
3:9–12	206
3:11	240
3:12	199, 216, 222
3:13	240
4:1–8	200
4:1	197, 227, 240
4:3–4	199
4:4–6	197
4:9–12	175, 193, 200, 206, 221
4:9–10	221
4:9	200–201, 224, 240
4:10	201, 221–22
4:11–12	218, 222
4:11	197, 216, 202–3, 222–23, 227
4:12–13	204
4:12	203–5, 223–24
4:13–18	198, 200
4:13	200, 240
4:15–18	207
4:16	215

4:17	215	5:15	218
5	206	6:6	158
5:1–11	207		
5:1–10	207	## Titus	
5:1–2	200		
5:1	200	2:10	58
5:2	215		
5:3	198	## James	
5:12–22	214		
5:12	224, 227	2	3
5:14–15	175, 193, 204, 206, 209		
5:14	204, 218, 222, 224	## Jude	
5:15	205, 216, 224, 228, 230	12	61
5:27	193		

2 Thessalonians

DEAD SEA SCROLLS

1 QS

1:3–4	207	3.13–15	34
1:7	207	6.1–4	28
1:11	207	6.13–24	34
2:2	208	6.14	28
2:1–12	207	6.16–17	28
2:2	207–8	6.17	34
2:3	207	6.19–20	28
2:13	240	6.20–21	34
2:15	207–8	6.23–24	28
2:16–17	240	6.24—7.24	210
2:16	240	6.25	28
3	210	7.6–8	28, 34
3:1–5	209		
3:6–15	193	## CD	
3:6–7	209		
3:6	209, 214, 224, 240	B2.2–5	29
3:7–9	208–9	6.15–20	29
3:7–8	216, 222	7.1–5	29
3:7	209, 223	7.6–9	29
3:8	209	9.10–13	29
3:10	209–10, 222, 224, 234	9.20–25	29
3:11	222	9.20–24	34
3:12	212	10.20	29
3:13	212, 216, 224, 230, 240	11.13–14	33
3:14–15	212	13.13–16	29
3:17	207–8	14:13–18	29

1 Timothy

4Q345

2:2	202
5	3
5:13	218

	30

GRECO-ROMAN WRITINGS

Aristides

Orations

51.29	186

Aristotle

Nichomachean Ethics

5.5.8–10	152
9.2	54
1130A	55
1131A	55
1158B—1159A	55
1158B	55
1159A	55
1159B	55
1163B	55

Politics

1261B	54
1263A	54

Arrian

Epicteti dissertationes

3.22.97	203

Cicero

Epistulae ad Atticum

8.16	215

De Amiticia

25.92	53

Epistulae ad familiares

7.9.3	108

De finibus

1.71	224

De natura deorum

1.72	224

De Officiis

1.42	219
1.54	225

Dio Chrysostom

Orations

1.50	39
7.103–27	219–20
75.7–8	216
77/78.27	205
77/78.34	186

Diodorus of Sicily

1.21.7	163

ps. Diogenes

Epistles

38.4	37
38.5	35, 38

Diogenes Laertius

Lives of Eminent Philosophers

2.48	36, 38
2.50	36
4.53	54
4.87	36
5.19–20	53
6.6	218
6.34	37
6.37	37
10.11	54
10.119–20	218, 224
10.119	223
11.18	100

Dionysius of Halicarnassus

Antiquitates romanae

12.1.1	93
12.1.2–3	93

Epictetus

Diatribai / Dissertationes

3.22.9–11	38
3.22.47	36
3.22.50	36
3.22.81–82	36, 38

Homer

Odyssey

1.226–27	102
3.309–11	100
3.330–47	103
7.135–40	103
7.162–67	103
7.170–79	102

Iamblichus

On the Pythagorean Life (VP)

5.20	76
6.30	76
8.44	77
9.47	76
17.71	76
17.72–73	76
17.72	76
18.81	76
18.88	76
21.98	77
22.102	76

Josephus

The Life

2.7–12	23
2.9–10	24
2.10	30
2.11	24, 26
2.12	25, 26
15	56
76	56

Jewish Antiquities

3.194–96	183
3.320–21	82
4.240	71
6.10	8
8.332	147
14.65	49
14.259–61	123
15.299–316	10
15.371	5, 75, 77
18.12	25
18.20–21	73
18.20	30
18.311–13	183
20.1	82
20.17	82
20.38	82
20.51–53	10
20.51	82, 95
20.53	95

Jewish War (J.W.)

1.26	163
2.12–15	73
2.120	30
2.122	30
2.124–25	30
2.160–61	30

Juvenal

Satirae

5.1–5	217
5.12–18	104
5.80–85	104
5.150–55	104

Livy

4.13	93
45.30C	148

Lucian

Bis accusatus

13	210

Fugitavi

12–16	218
17	219

Saturnalia

15	104
16	104
17	104

Symposium

13	106

Pausanias

Graeciae description

2.6	109

Petronius

Satyricon

46	186
90	220
92	220
95	220
96	220

Plato

Respublica

416D	54
416E	54
433AB	203, 211
441DE	203
449C	54
496D	212

Symposium

175B	139
175CD	103
176A	103

Philo

Legatio ad Gaium

281–82	109

Who Is the Heir?

144	152
145	152

186	184
189	184
191	153

Good Person

75	30, 73
80–85	30

De congressueru ditionis gratia

127	23

Hypothetica

10.10–11	74
10.10	74
11.1	30, 73
11.10	31
11.13	74

Pliny the Elder

Naturalis historica

5.58	82
18.168	82

Pliny the Younger

Epistulae

2.6	105, 139
2.13.2	108
9.5	106

Epistulae ad Trajanum

33	195
34	195

Plutarch

Moralia

478A—492D	200
478BC	226
478DE	226
480A–C	226
480BC	226
482A	226
482EF	226
484A	226

484B–D	226	1.1.8	188
485F—486B	226	1.7.2–3	188
486BC	226	1.9.1–4	188
486F—487B	226	1.10.4	188
489CD	226	1.11.1	188
492A–D	226	1.14.3–4	188
516A	211	1.4.3	187
767E	53	2.2.1–2	188
1098DE	223	2.7.1	188
		2.10.2	188

Quaestionum convivialum libri IX

		2.10.4	188
		2.17.7	188
		2.21.5—24.4	188
615–16B	105	2.31.3–4	188
615—616B	139	2.35.1	188
615	105	3.19.2—22.3	188
615D	105	3.194—22.3	186
616C	131	3.30.1—33.1	188
625	139	4.2.4	188
643C	105	4.35.2—36.2	188
643E—644D	105, 139	4.40.4	188
643E	105	6.3.1–4	188
646C	102	6.3.2	188
703	102–3	6.14.4—15.4	186
703DE	106	6.16.1—18.1	186

Pericles

ps Socrates

Ep.

1.4—2.2	219	13	219
		18	219

Polybius

Historiae

Suetonius

Divus Claudius

18.51.2	211	18.2-19	93
		18.2	82, 93

Porphyry

Vit. Pyth.

Domitianus

18–19	76		
19	76		
20	76	7	107
33	76		

Seneca

Vespasianus

		19	107

De Beneficiis

1.1.1–8	187
1.1.2	188

Tacitus

Annales

2.87	93
12.43	82–83, 93, 217
16.32	186

Twelve Tables

5	226

Xenophon

Memorabilia

3.14.1	102

MISHNAH AND TALMUD

m. 'Abot

1.10	219
2.2	26, 206
4.5	206
6.3	24
6.4	24

m. Pe'ah

8.7	72

m. Pesaḥim

2.6	10
9.11	9
10.1	9, 72

m. Kerithot

6.9	24

m. Shekalim

1.3	183
1.4	183
2.1	184
5.6	10, 72

b. Berakot

24A	23
38B	23
61A	23

b. Giṭṭin

7B	9–10, 71

b. Ketubbot

66B	72
96A	24

b. Sukkah

49B	9

b. Yoma

35B	23, 26

Midrash Rabbah

Num. Rab.

14.2	23

INSCRIPTIONS AND PAPYRI

CIG

5853	191, 228

CIL

14.2112	136, 139
LINE 24	138

IG

II2

1343	195
1368	228
32–41	137
42–44	137
46–47	137
65	138
73–83	137
84–90	137

118–26	137	11.9	118
151–55	137	11.16	118
157–59	137		
1275	228	**Vatican Collection**	
X		39	224
2.1 31	194		
2.1 259	95	**EARLY CHRISTIAN**	
2.1 824	228	**WRITINGS**	
XIV		*Didache*	
902A	201	11:6	18
IGRP		*Ambrose*	
I		*De officiiministorum*	
1151	139	1.16.64	14
III			
493	94	*Augustine*	
IKilikia BM II		*Epistulae*	
201	228	268	161
P. Lond.		*In Evangelium Johannis tractatus*	
VII		40	12
2193	228	50	14
P. Mich.		62.5	12
594	82	*Chrysostom*	
P. Oxy.		*Homiliae*	
11.239	168	10.4	161
128	212	*Homiliae in epistulam ii ad Corinthios*	
275	204		
725	204	15.2–3	142
SIG		16.3	147
174	216	18.1	155
167	216	20.2	162
1105	216	*Homiliae in Joannem*	
1170		72	12, 18
11.7	118		

Eusebius

Ecclesiatical History

2.8–12	83

Orosius

Hist.

7.6	82–83

Tertullian

Adversus Marcionem

5.3	172

Theodoret of Cyrrhus

Comm. 2 Cor.

332	165
336	161

www.ingramcontent.com/pod-product-compliance
Lightning Source LLC
Chambersburg PA
CBHW061432300426
44114CB00014B/1654